The Property of Shaker Pointe
of Carondelet's Library

NEW
YORK
POLITICS

For updates, links, and articles related to
New York Politics: A Tale of Two States,
visit <u>NewYorkStatePolitics.com</u>.

NEW YORK POLITICS

POLITICS

A Tale of Two States

SECOND EDITION

Edward V. Schneier
John Brian Murtaugh
Antoinette Pole

M.E.Sharpe
Armonk, New York
London, England

Library of Congress Cataloging-in-Publication Data

Schneier, Edward V.
  New York politics : a tale of two states / by Edward V. Schneier, John Brian Murtaugh,
and Antoinette Pole. — 2nd ed.
    p. cm.
  Includes bibliographical references and index.
  ISBN 978-0-7656-2204-4 (cloth : alk. paper)
  1. New York (State)—Politics and government. I. Murtaugh, Brian, 1937–
II. Pole, Antoinette. III. Title.

JK3416.S25 2009
320.9747—dc22   2009006534

Printed in the United States of America

The paper used in this publication meets the minimum requirements of
American National Standard for Information Sciences
Permanence of Paper for Printed Library Materials,
ANSI Z 39.48-1984.

MV (c)   10   9   8   7   6   5   4   3   2   1

Contents

List of Tables, Figure, Boxes, and Maps

Tables

Figure

Boxes

Maps

Preface

A Tale of Two States

The famous opening lines of Charles Dickens's *Tale of Two Cities* describe the people of France as living, on the eve of revolution, in both the "best of times" and the "worst of times." Much the same could be said, in the first decade of the twenty-first century, about the people of New York. While it ranks second among the fifty states in per capita personal income, New York ranks tenth in the proportion of its residents below the poverty line. More than 1.5 million of its citizens have advanced degrees, but even more have never finished high school. It has 225 four-year colleges, far more than any other state, but also ranks second in prisons and spends more state money on prisoners than on college students. It is number one in health spending per family, but ranks eleventh in the percentage of its population described as "medically underserviced." While it is often depicted as a state low on traditional family values, it has one of the *lowest* divorce rates in the nation.

"New York," as Sinclair Lewis once said, "is not America," to which the residents of many other states would add a fervent "Amen." Yet there is a simultaneous sense in which the Empire State is widely perceived as the quintessence, if not of the United States as it is, then of what it is about to become. From the Metropolitan Opera to *Saturday Night Live*; from Saratoga Race Track to Madison Square Garden; from the Broadway stage to Chautauqua; and from the art galleries of SoHo to the publishing houses of midtown Manhattan, it has endured—for better or worse—as the cultural capital of the New World. Kodak, General Electric, Xerox, and IBM made New York the early leader in the development of high-technology industries. Wall Street remains the financial capital of the nation and its global economy. At the same time, upstate cities remained virtually detached from the economic boom of the 1990s, farms are disappearing at an increasing rate, and the state's accumulated debt is among the nation's highest.

New York's political history is studded with innovations: Al Smith's initiatives in passing minimum-wage and worker-safety laws anticipated the New Deal by twenty years; Robert Moses created an empire of parks and highways, and a governing structure to go with them, that became prototypes for all fifty states; and the state was a pioneer in creating the nation's first equal opportunity commissions. It has received its share of dubious achievement awards as well. The financial collapse of New York City in the 1970s and the subsequent bailout of the city by the federal government continue to serve as a symbol of urban decline. Although its state taxes are comparatively low, its combined state and local tax burden is among the nation's highest. The New York congressional delegation has distinguished itself neither by providing its share of national leaders nor for bringing barrels of federal dollars into the state. And for all of their putative sophistication, New Yorkers probably know less about their own state's government than do the residents of any other state. Voter turnout is shockingly low, and the state's election laws are Byzantine at best. The state's progressive policies are increasingly regarded less as prototypes of what ought to be than as cautions against the paving stones of good intentions.

This book, then, is a tale of two states: a state that is at once the richest and the poorest, sophisticated yet politically detached, liberal in intents yet slow to deliver. Our purpose in this book is to explain the politics of this dualism, giving particular attention to the changes in recent years that have challenged if not overthrown the Empire State's tradition of political liberalism. Is New York governed as badly as many of its citizens believe? How does the political system work? From our perspectives in the worlds of academic political science on one hand and of practical politics on the other, what we have tried to write is a citizen's textbook, a book that tries to make sense of what is arguably the nation's most complicated and secretive political system.

Were New York a corporation, the state's finances would rank it in the top twenty-fourth of *Fortune* magazine's ranking of the 500 largest corporations. Were it a country, it would be among the world's twenty-five largest. Because it is part of the federal union of the United States of America, it neither can nor should be treated as a significant sovereign nation, but it is an important place, far more important politically and economically than many national governments that have received considerable attention both from the media and from academics. In part because New Yorkers tend to focus on a national and global scale, and in part— more parochially—because the state does not require its high school or college students to take a course in New York government, there are few scholarly books available on the system. Schneier and Murtaugh wrote the first edition of this book in 2001 in an attempt to fill that gap.

Few governments have ever satisfied all their citizens or done all that they could to satisfy their citizens' needs. Because of its enormous wealth and proud history, there is an expectation that New York is better positioned than most states to deliver the goods effectively and efficiently. The first half of this book is devoted to an analysis of that issue. What we hope to show is that despite its economic and cultural advantages, New York is an extraordinarily difficult state to govern. The bond of a common political culture, of the kind of basic underlying consensus on fundamental values that makes political discourse productive, is at best minimally evident in New York. The cleavages that divide the state ethnically, regionally, and economically are, as we argue in Chapter 1, sharper than in other states, less susceptible to compromise, and—in the final analysis—inimical to good government.

Although the dynamic of partisanship remains much as it was, one of the arguments in this book is that both the substance and the style of politics in New York have changed significantly in the last twenty years. What we have seen in the past decade is the flowering of a new political paradigm that has its roots in the twelve years that Mario Cuomo (1983–1994) served as governor. It may or may not be permanent, but it has significantly altered the political landscape. New York, in ways that both parody and reflect national changes, has drifted toward a conservative political agenda. This shift away from liberal democracy is a shift not simply in the substance of politics, but of process as well. The substantive shift is perhaps best symbolized through a crude assessment of the legacies of the state's most prominent governors: George Clinton made the state the commercial center of the New World by building the Erie Canal; Al Smith virtually invented the welfare state; Franklin Roosevelt, Herbert Lehman, and Thomas Dewey created the parkway and thruway systems; Nelson Rockefeller built the state university. Mario Cuomo's and George Pataki's legacies might be in the form of prisons.

Until the Democrats won a fragile majority in the state senate in 2008, divided government had become the norm. Not since 1974 had the executive branch and both houses of the legislature been in the hands of the same political party. The divided legislature, frozen in place with the assembly almost unassailably Democratic and the senate firmly Republican, was locked in symbolic rituals of division without substance. In almost no other state do incumbent legislators need to worry less about defeat than in New York, yet with their feet locked in the permafrost of permanent division, the two houses of the legislature for more than three decades engaged in a ritualistic show of partisan posturing so often devoid of real meaning that the state government was frequently described as "dysfunctional." A system of tight party discipline that in theory could produce a responsible party government that simplifies complicated electoral divisions and reaches out to the electorate by offering competitive visions of better public policy seldom did either.

For the first time in perhaps a century New York stands upon the fault lines of real change. Eliot Spitzer will, unfortunately, be remembered more for the sexual capers that forced his resignation than for his reforms in the budgetary process and the state's formula for funding its schools. But when we started on this second edition of New York Politics, the winds of change seemed to be blowing strong. And change things did: Spitzer got caught with his pants down and resigned; the economy went into its deepest dive in decades; the Democrats won control of the senate, but found it almost impossible to put together a governing team. As soon as we finished revising one chapter of the book, it seemed as if we had to go back and rewrite another. We could, it seems, hardly have picked a worse year than 2008 to write a text on New York politics.

Two States, Two Systems, Three Authors

Social and economic cleavages in New York reinforce and confound each other. There are two New Yorks, both socially and politically, and the political system has become increasingly unwilling and unable to bridge the gap. These patterns of cleavage and division in New York—regional, partisan, economic, and political—are so extraordinarily dualistic as to put traditional theories of government in the United States to a severe test. The diminished quality of political dialogue, the rise of posturing over substance, and the decline in common civility that others have found invading the halls of the U.S. Congress have gained a strong foothold in New York as well. Whether New York politics represents the triumph of politics over social adversity or the failure of the system, we leave it to the reader to decide.

This book was Brian Murtaugh's idea. As a member of the state assembly asked to teach a course on state politics at City College, he was frustrated to find that there were no current textbooks in print. As chair of the political science department, Edward Schneier—whose primary field of research was focused on the U.S. Congress—agreed to co-author a book on New York that would combine his own academic insights and experiences as a lobbyist with Murtaugh's understanding of the inside world of New York politics. For this second edition we brought in Toni Pole whose research on the Internet and the New York State legislature and interest groups brings her senior co-authors kicking and screaming into the new world of cyberspace.

The outline of this book was a cooperative endeavor. Schneier and Pole did the bulk of the academic research. Between the three of us, together and sometimes separately, we interviewed more than eighty present and former members of the legislature (including six party leaders) and numerous department heads, budget aides, and lobbyists. With each of us taking separate sections, Schneier wrote the final copy. In the often closed world of New York politics, there is no doubt that Murtaugh's status in the legislature gave us access to people who would not otherwise have spoken candidly to academics or journalists. Even with this advantage, tight party discipline in the state makes it unusually difficult to get participants to speak on or off the record in such a way that they may somehow be identified. One state senator we interviewed in 1997 begged us not to include him in our list of interviewees when he admitted that party discipline was sometimes a very potent force. For this reason we have followed the convention of quoting members and staff assistants in ways that hide their identities. In general, however, the willingness of people like the late senate majority leader Ralph Marino and former assembly speaker Mel Miller to be open, candid, and highly cooperative is what made this collaboration workable. A few people deserve special mention: Christina Katsanos, previously employed by the New York City Council's Finance Division, assisted with budget figures for New York City, and Frank Mauro of the Fiscal Policy Institute was always available for questions about state finances. And the staff members of the assembly information office went out of their way to be helpful.

To the citizens of New York we dedicate this book as an effort to facilitate their understanding of their government, what's right about it, what's wrong, and what the individual citizen can do.

To our families and friends, we owe debts of forbearance and fortitude. Carolyn and Sean Murtaugh let their husband and father cancel out on more than one vacation activity. Margrit Schneier put up with Ned's many rants and read the whole manuscript to let us know where we were getting too cute, too biased, or too arcane for a nonacademic reader. Toni Pole owes a debt of gratitude to her future husband, Scott Simock, who bore the burden of not one but two books simultaneously. We were lucky to have Patricia Kolb of M.E. Sharpe as our editor. Her patience was extraordinary. Our thanks go to the many colleagues and friends who at various points commented on specific chapters or offered research advice and information.

NEW
YORK
POLITICS

1

The States of New York

In 1524, a Florentine explorer, Giovanni da Verrazano, sailed through the narrows that now bear his name and "discovered" New York harbor. Despite his glowing reports, some eighty-five years went by without further significant exploration. As Mark Twain wrote of a comparable period in the history of the Mississippi, the Hudson and its magnificent harbor were "left unvisited by whites during a term of years which seems incredible in our energetic days."[1] Between Verrazano's first sighting and Henry Hudson's more fruitful venture in 1609, Copernicus revolutionized the view of the solar system, Shakespeare wrote most of his plays, Henry VIII divorced or executed four of his six wives, and the Reformation began in Europe. In those same years, Ivan the Terrible began and ended his bloody rule as czar of Russia, Tokyo became the capital of Japan, Rubens and Rembrandt painted their greatest masterpieces, and Machiavelli's *The Prince* was posthumously published. By 1609, the Spanish and Portuguese conquests of South America were nearly complete and Magellan's feat of circumnavigating the globe had become almost commonplace. Only then did a small group of Dutch settlers arrive at the southern tip of Manhattan Island.

Growth and Development: The People of New York

Given the riches of North America, it is difficult retrospectively to understand why the Europeans took so long to appreciate them. Distracted by the more obvious wealth of the Incas and Aztecs, diverted by the lure of spices and other exotic products from climates radically different from their own, and encumbered by religious upheavals and wars, Europeans came to North America almost as an afterthought to their age of exploration. The Dutch, in particular, seem never to have paid much attention to their outpost in the New Netherlands and indeed left its affairs largely in the hands of the privately held Dutch West India Company, which viewed its outposts in the Hudson Valley essentially as points of contact for a lucrative fur trade with the Indians.

The Dutch were not settling on virgin lands: human beings had lived in what

Box 1.1
The Purchase of Manhattan Island

The origins of most great cities are wrapped in stories and myths of heroic sacrifice and divine guidance. The enduring story of New York City is that of a mercantile transaction in which the wily Dutch supposedly "bought" Manhattan Island for twenty-four dollars. The amount and nature of this transaction have been questioned in a variety of ways. Since the Native Americans who allegedly made the deal had no tradition of land ownership and were not even residents of the island they supposedly sold, it is not at all clear that the Dutch actually got the best of the deal.

Sometimes, however, the real meaning of myths and rituals is best discerned not by focusing on the stories and events themselves but on those who observe and recount them. The story of New York's purchase, as it contrasts the cunning of the white settler with the primitive lust of the natives for beads and trinkets, resonates enduringly with tales of the shrewd city slicker conning the rural rube. It also serves nicely to at least partially absolve subsequent New Yorkers from potential feelings of guilt: unlike other colonies, the tale implies, New York was founded in a commercial deal rather than by violent conquest.

"Finally, however," as Burrows and Wallace point out, "as is usually the case with myths and legends, the notion that New York is rooted in a commercial transaction gets at a deeper kind of truth." Unlike many of the world's great cities, New York was to become neither the military base of an empire nor the seat of religion or government. "Its civic chieftains would be merchants, bankers, landlords, lawyers; its mightiest buildings, office towers. . . . As the twenty-four dollar saga suggests, New York would become a city of deal-makers, a city of commerce, a City of Capital."[1]

1. Edwin G. Burrows and Mike Wallace, *Gotham: A History of New York City to 1898* (New York: Oxford University Press, 1999), p. xvi.

is now New York for more than 5,000 years. It is tempting, like Thoreau in his eulogy to Walden Pond, to contrast the ravages of European settlement with a golden age of unsullied wilderness: "The choice is not between two landscapes, one with and one without a human influence; it is between two human ways of living, two ways of belonging to the ecosystem."[2] The Indians first contacted by the European settlers—the ones from whom Peter Minuet allegedly "bought" Manhattan Island—were members of various tribes of the Algonquians, one of the most peaceable groups on the eastern seaboard. As they pushed up past Albany, the settlers encountered the feistier Five Nations of the Iroquois—the Senecas, Cayugas, Onondagas, Oneidas, and Mohawks—then approaching the height of their population and influence. Contacts between the Dutch and the indigenous peoples were seldom confrontational, but as the European lust for furs increased, conflicts intensified. European diseases, against which the Native Americans had no immunity, proved particularly devastating, and the more aggressive settlement patterns of the English and French eventually pushed the Iroquois and Algonquian nations into a long period of numerical and economic decline.

Patterns of Settlement and Their Legacies

If the Dutch were slow to colonize and reproduce in the New World, their largely British neighbors to the north and east were not. By 1664, when the English captured New Amsterdam, the population of the city had reached barely 1,500, but there were close to 50,000 settlers in New England, 9,000 in Boston alone. And while the Dutch confined their settlements largely to the 150-mile section of the Hudson River Valley between Albany and New Amsterdam, the New England colonists were encroaching rapidly from Long Island, Connecticut, and Massachusetts, pushing the frontier farther west. When the British fleet in 1664 demanded and received Governor Peter Stuyvesant's surrender of the New Netherlands, it was as much a reflection of demographics as of military might.

The Early Settlements

Despite their minority status and rather swift assimilation into the dominant Anglo culture, the Dutch left a legacy that continues to give a distinctive twist to both the city and the state.

> New York City had a unique sequence of development among American colonial cities which cannot be understood without recognizing the enduring impact of the Dutch society and culture. . . . [T]he Dutch introduced institutions, laws, and customary practices, altered the landscape, set the pattern for interaction with native peoples and imported Africans, and selectively transplanted their culture.[3]

The Dutch culture of New York was itself an amalgam in which as early as 1644 eighteen distinct languages were spoken.[4] Indeed, the fledgling city called New Amsterdam was a true melting pot, less distinctively Dutch or British than prototypically "American." Unlike their fellow settlers in New England, the Dutch did not arrive or settle as religious communities and tended to be more tolerant of diversity and to separate religion from citizenship. This spirit of tolerance became very much a part of the British colony, remaining a defining characteristic of New York City for generations to come. It was, moreover, a self-reinforcing tendency in which "the pluralistic nature of New York's social structure virtually assured a similarly heterogeneous immigrant population."[5]

No other English colony in America faced the challenge of absorbing and including an already established European culture. In further contrast with the New England colonies and neighboring Pennsylvania and New Jersey, the governors of New York inherited a system in which slavery was nearly as firmly established as in the South, but with the added quirk of including more freedmen of African descent than any other colony. New York was also, in its vast northern regions, very much a frontier state, constantly encroaching upon its Native American population, forging westward for nearly two centuries, creating new towns and settlements. In developing his famous frontier theory of American democracy, Frederick Jackson Turner placed particular emphasis on its roots in the middle region of the Atlantic coast, with New York, more than any other state, providing the multicultural, commercial, and industrial base from which the new society would emerge.

New York's combination of a magnificent natural harbor and historic tradition of commerce soon made it a world trade center on a par with the great commercial cities of the world, but the primacy of trade also helped put New Yorkers at odds with their fellow colonists (even, at times, distancing the city from the rest of the state). Beyond commerce, the city attracted the cultural amenities that come with it, from opera and ballet to whorehouses and burlesque. It also became the port of entry for millions of immigrants. Many immigrants arrived in the United States without passing through Ellis Island, but the incredible fact is that for almost a century, between 1800 and 1921, a majority of the permanent settlers coming into the United States entered through the port of New York.

From the Revolution to the Civil War

On the eve of the American Revolution, New York had already begun both to differentiate itself from the emerging new nation and to embody what that nation was becoming. Because it was a center of commerce, most of it with Britain, many of New York's leading citizens were appalled by the very idea of rebellion. Once the War of Independence had begun, the British sent their main force to New York and used the city, throughout the conflict, as its headquarters. With the city the seat of British power and hub of Loyalist sentiment, and the Iroquois Indians allied through most of the war with the British,

> No other state suffered more for the cause of independence than did New York. . . . Nearly one-third of the engagements of the war were fought on New York soil. New York City, which controlled most of the commerce of the state, was continuously in enemy hands from 1776 to 1783. Two major fires destroyed many buildings in the great seaport. After British evacuation the population of the city fell to ten thousand, half of what it had been on the eve of revolution.[6]

Both the city and the state were quick to recover. Large tracts of land, confiscated from Loyalists, were widely distributed. The tribes of the Iroquois nation, loosed from British protection, surrendered, or had taken from them, virtually all their territory. But independence did not dramatically affect the distribution of political power. A constitution, adopted at the outset of the Revolution, created an elected legislature and eliminated the veto power of the royal governor. It also secured the legal rights of citizens in conformity with the basic patterns of English law. It was, however, silent on the issue of slavery, conferred no rights on Native

Map 1.1 **New York State Towns by Population**

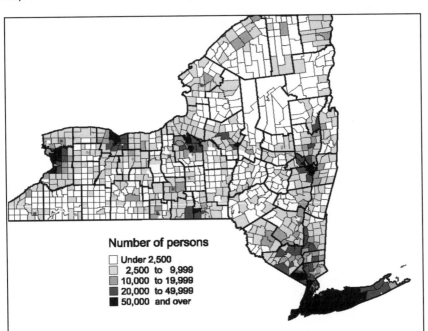

Number of persons

☐ Under 2,500
☐ 2,500 to 9,999
▦ 10,000 to 19,999
▪ 20,000 to 49,999
■ 50,000 and over

Americans, and restricted the right to vote to a handful of male property owners. Nor did it modify the increasingly resented system of aristocratic land distribution rooted in the Dutch patroon system of the Hudson Valley. While homesteaders were setting up small farms across confiscated Indian lands in western New York and other yeoman farmers staked claims to the estates of fleeing Loyalists, one New York farmer in six was a tenant leaseholder. The huge estates of the Livingstons, Van Rensselaers, and Clarks remained intact until the 1840s despite frequent rent strikes and occasional violence.

The death of the leasehold system came less from political agitation than from the move west that superseded it. The trickle of New Englanders who began settling on Long Island and in Westchester County in the 1640s became a torrent in the early nineteenth century. The amount of improved farmland increased from about 1 million acres in 1784 to 5.5 million in 1821, almost all of it on newly cleared, owner-occupied homesteads.[7] Meanwhile, urban areas were growing as well, exploding in size with the completion of the Erie Canal in 1825. Rochester quadrupled its population in a single decade and became the nation's first boomtown. Buffalo and Syracuse grew almost as rapidly after the canal linked the riches of the Great Lakes basin with the Atlantic Ocean, and New York City soon became the nation's largest metropolis.

The canal route connecting the Hudson and Mohawk rivers with the Great Lakes has had a continuing impact. As the state's commerce developed along this corridor, it became the logical route, in the railroad boom of the 1840s, for major rail beds and—a century later—for the New York State Thruway. Excluding Long Island, more than 80 percent of the state's citizens still reside in counties that lie along this inverted L-shaped route (see Map 1.1). Once it became the first state to burst through the Appalachian mountain barrier that divided coastal cities from the farms and mineral resources of the Midwest, New York's ascension to commercial and industrial preeminence was swift. By the eve of the Civil War, New York City was the banking capital of the nation, and "whether one considers value of output, number of workers employed in manufacturing, or the diversity of industrial production, New York scored first."[8] Access to capital was a factor in this rise, as was transportation, but nothing fed the industrial boom more than the flow of cheap labor through Ellis Island.

As a commercial center for the nation, New York was as ambivalent about the Civil War as it had been about the Revolution. Slavery had not been abolished until 1827, and the state's black population declined by 1860 to less than 2 percent of the population, most of it centered in Brooklyn and Manhattan, where blacks competed with immigrants for low-level jobs. Three times, between 1846 and 1867, the state's voters refused to approve a constitutional amendment giving blacks the right to vote.[9] Small wonder that the draft riots of 1863, which began as a protest against the ability of the rich to buy exemptions from the military, quickly turned into a lynch party. New York had its share of abolitionists and contributed more men and materials to the Union cause than any other state, but the race tensions manifested in the draft riots remain part of the state heritage.

The Gilded Age

Early in the nineteenth century, the state's largely Dutch and English population was supplemented by a steady flow of Germans escaping a series of upheavals in Europe. The Irish potato blight of 1845–1854, which sent more than 3 million residents across the ocean, brought an even greater wave of change, adding a largely Catholic group to New York's religious mix. By the census of 1880, the Irish constituted nearly one-third of the city's residents and had become "the first of New York's ethnic groups to arrive in large enough numbers to establish themselves as a coherent political force."[10] In 1880, self-made millionaire William Grace became New York City's first mayor of Irish ancestry, one of a growing number of immigrants and their offspring who enjoyed success in New York. Few of his compatriots did so well. While the Irish and other immigrant groups were able to penetrate the city's political and economic elites, the gap between rich and poor loomed large. The difference between the wealth of the Rockefellers, Vanderbilts, and Morgans—most of it newly acquired—on the one hand, and the miseries of the urban poor on the other, was probably as great in the late nineteenth century in New York City as it has been in almost any society. At the same time, upstate New York—and to some extent New York City—was the scene of the growth of a middle class that was perhaps equally unprecedented, particularly among farmers: "In 1870 New York led all other states in the number of farms and the value of farm property . . . and its farm population of over one million constituted the largest single occupational group and nearly one-fourth of the total population of the state."[11] Even in the cities, there was a rising middle class of skilled artisans, merchants, and, toward the end of the century, clerks and junior executives. But it was manufacturing—labor-intensive, highly profitable industrial enterprise—that symbolized the future of the nation and increasingly characterized New York. In the census of 1880, New York became the first state to manifest an urban majority; the United States did not officially become an urban nation until 1920. For more than 150 years, New York, with its access to capital, public transportation, and cheap labor, was the nation's leading industrial state, sometimes accounting for as much as one-sixth of the nation's total output.[12] Those immigrants who lacked the resources to travel beyond their port of entry constituted an enormous reserve labor supply that further fueled an industrial revolution of incredible proportions. By the turn of the century, when the United States passed Great Britain and Germany to become the world's leading economic power, New York, truly now the Empire State, was the engine that pulled the train.

The influx of industrial wage earners experienced throughout the nineteenth century was accompanied by a dramatic withering of the farm population. By 1860, although New York was still the nation's leading farm state, "more than 800,000 New Yorkers (one-fourth of those born in the state as of that date) had resettled in the West."[13] A century later, New York had fallen from first to twenty-fifth in farm income, focused on such specialty crops as apples and grapes along with dairy products and fresh produce for local markets. The movement of farmers to the flatter, more fertile lands of the Midwest was the logical by-product of improved transportation networks and storage systems; the decline in manufacturing that New York began to experience has more complex roots.

The Twentieth Century

In the 1920s, Congress virtually shut off the flow of new immigration to the United States and, of course, to New York. Many of the immigrants who had arrived in the 1890s and early 1900s, meanwhile, came out of the socialist and trade union movements of Central Europe. As the supply of new labor diminished and the militancy of the existing workforce increased, the state became both a cradle of an emerging American union movement and an incubator of legislation protecting working people. In the 1920s, even as the Harding and Coolidge administrations were taking the national government in a strongly pro-business direction, Al Smith, as governor of New York, put through a bill reducing the workweek to forty-eight hours, a child labor law, and a workers' compensation law described by Smith—with considerable justification—as "perhaps the most liberal statute of its kind in the world."[14] The Smith administration also dramatically increased expenditures on education, public works, and parks, with higher taxes an inevitable result. Although the growth of government slowed in the early years of the Great Depression under the cautious governorship of Franklin D. Roosevelt, it took off again when Roosevelt became president and Herbert Lehman, his successor as governor, brought the "Little New Deal" to Albany. Laws establishing a welfare system, strengthening unions, mandating public education until age sixteen, establishing a minimum wage, and regulating public utilities both complemented and extended similar programs adopted during the early years of Roosevelt's New Deal in Washington. The election of Thomas E. Dewey in 1943—the state's first Republican governor since World War I—did not significantly derail this progressive tradition. Extending the system of parkways developed during the Smith, Roosevelt, and Lehman years, Dewey developed a turnpike system (including the state thruway that now bears his name) that became a model for other states and eventually the nation. A decade later, another progressive Republican governor, Nelson Rockefeller, brought New York up to the standards of many other state systems of higher education by making the State University of New York (SUNY) a major institution of higher learning. Ironically, it was the Republican Rockefeller who put through the big tax increases that brought New York into the ranks of the nation's most highly burdened states.

The election of Hugh Carey in 1975 began a period of twenty years in which the Democrats controlled the executive mansion (see Table 1.1). The Carey-Cuomo years were not marked by the kinds of policy initiatives that marked the tenures of Smith or Rockefeller, but they essentially continued, at gradually decreasing levels, the state's support for public works, social welfare, and education. The Carey-Cuomo years also were marked by a series of fiscal crises unmatched since the Great Depression. New York City's near bankruptcy in 1975 was the first shock wave of what has become an almost steady series of economic tremors at both state and local levels. George Pataki was elected governor in 1994 and reelected twice on platforms promising tax cuts to stimulate economic development, but his policies did little to stem the loss of well-paying jobs that have increasingly afflicted the upstate economy in particular. Riding a tide of resentment against these failures and a national tilt toward the Democrats, Eliot Spitzer in 2006 won 71 percent of the statewide major party vote and carried all but two counties. Like Governors Cuomo and Pataki before him, however, Governor Spitzer had to work with a legislature divided between the Republicans, who controlled the state senate, and the Democrats, who controlled the assembly. Thus, despite his impressive election victory, his short term as governor (ended by scandal in 2008) was short on major achievements. And despite the landslide victory of his fellow Democrats in 2008, Governor David Paterson has his problems with the legislature as well.

Table 1.1

Democratic Percentage of the Major Party Gubernatorial Vote, 1974–2006

Election year and winner	New York City	Suburbs	Upstate cities	Upstate rural	Total
1974 Carey (Democrat)	72	53	58	49	58
1978 Carey (Democrat)	70	49	53	44	52
1982 Cuomo (Democrat)	70	50	51	39	52
1986 Cuomo (Democrat)	80	64	72	59	66
1990 Cuomo (Democrat)	73	50	48	43	53
1994 Pataki (Republican)	71	42	38	27	48
1998 Pataki (Republican)	67	35	31	19	41
2002 Pataki (Republican)	58	31	41	28	41
2006 Spitzer (Democrat)	86	67	69	62	71

Source: Mark D. Brewer and Jeffrey M. Stonecash, "Political Parties and Elections," in *Governing New York State*, 4th ed., ed. Jeffrey M. Stonecash (Albany: State University of New York Press, 2001); state Board of Elections.

Notes: Following Brewer and Stonecash, p. 51, the suburbs are defined as comprising the counties of Dutchess, Nassau, Orange, Rockland, Suffolk, and Westchester. Upstate cities are defined as Albany, Broome, Erie, Monroe, and Onondaga counties.

New York in the Twenty-First Century

If the Industrial Revolution in the United States began in New York, its industrial decline started there as well. Just as New York was among the first states to have a majority of its workforce in manufacturing, it was among the first to lose it and to record the rise of a service sector majority. The massive, continuing shift away from the production and shipment of goods to the provision of services and the accompanying shift from blue-collar to white-collar employment characteristic of what has been called "postindustrial society" hit New York first, and it hit hard. Its aging industrial plants and rigid union-management relations were ripe for the shift of manufacturing south, west, and overseas that helped create the high-unemployment area of the northeast and mid-central regions known colloquially as the "rust belt." The total number of production workers in manufacturing in-dustries in New York State fell from roughly 2 million in the 1960s to fewer than 1 million in 1990 and just 596,000 in 2004. Buffalo, perhaps the symbol of urban decline, fell from its position as one of the ten largest cities in the census of 1900 to fifty-eighth in 2000.

Nowhere was the change to a postindustrial mode more rapid or dramatic than in New York City, once the heart of industrial America. By the end of the twentieth century, less than 10 percent of the city's workforce was employed in manufac-turing. "Uses and places associated with the industrial city and the poor declined heavily, while investment surged into office construction, the institutional expan-sion of hospitals and universities, the conversion of former loft-manufacturing areas, the gentrification of late-nineteenth-century upper class neighborhoods, and the growth of new immigrant neighborhoods."[15] The demography of the city also changed rapidly as a series of economic revolutions produced both new traumas and new opportunities.

New York has the dubious distinction of leading the nation in its industrial decline. In one frequently cited study, its "manufacturing climate" ranked twenty-third among the twenty-nine industrial states examined. "New York's negative rating," some have argued, "results from a combination of its high average hourly wages, high percent-age of union workers, high unemployment and workers' compensation benefits, high state taxes, and poor education systems."[16] Without underestimating the roles played by each of these factors, reality is considerably more complex in the vortex of a worldwide economic transformation in work, populations, and societies. Many of these changes hit New York first. We will deal at greater length with the nature of this economic transformation in later chapters. We introduce the topic here because of its connection with demographic changes that are at least equally dramatic.

Race, Class, Geography, and Ethnicity

"Every important aspect of the U.S. demographic situation is linked to every other."[17] Immigrants came to New York because there were jobs; their presence as a pool of cheap labor created more jobs; their fertility rates, economic successes and failures, marriages, divorces, and death rates changed the roles of governments and further altered the opportunities available for new immigrants. At the national level, the policy consequences of such transformations—most notably in the connections between the aging of the population and the financing of Social Security and Medicare—are receiving increasing attention. As the federal government in Washington increasingly shifts the financial burden and policy responsibility for such programs to the states, regional variations loom larger. The composition of a state's population—from the distribution of age groups to its overall educational levels—strongly affects its government's willingness, need, and ability to deal with policy problems. As the population ages, for example, and people retire, the income-tax-paying workforce shrinks at the same time as costs for programs for senior citizens grow. New York's native population continues to age. In rural Hamilton County, for example, one person in five is over sixty-five. In contrast with most other states, however, the aging of New York has been increasingly offset by waves of relatively young immigrants. Fewer than 6 percent of the state's Hispanics and Asians counted in the 2000 Census were over sixty-five years of age, compared with nearly 16 percent of white non-Hispanics. The youth of the Hispanic and Asian cohorts, of course, raises other policy problems in areas like education.

Politically and economically, these demographics make for a volatile mix. The young, largely foreign-born newcomers live mainly in the poor sections of large urban areas while the elderly, older immigrant groups are scattered throughout urban, rural, and suburban areas. Only 11.5 percent of New York City residents are over sixty-five, as compared with 13.8 percent in the rest of the state. The competition for government resources thus takes on geographic and ethnic as well as political dimensions.

Old Newcomers and New Immigrants

The major ancestral groups succeeding the early Dutch and British settlers in New York were largely German and Irish in the mid-nineteenth century; Italian and Eastern European around the turn of the century; and African-American and Puerto Rican in the years surrounding World War II. Liberalization of the immigration laws in 1965 brought a new wave dominated by Asians, Caribbean blacks, and a highly diverse group of Latinos. None of these groups has been randomly distributed by either occupation or place of residence. Of the millions of immigrants who came to the New World through New York, large numbers stayed within shouting distance of the Statue of Liberty. As recently as 1950, more than half of the city's residents were foreign-born or of foreign or mixed parentage. But although the city was the home of more than 70 percent of the state's foreign-born white inhabitants, upstate cities like Rochester (45 percent first and second generation) and Buffalo (44 percent) also housed large percentages of first- and second-generation immigrants. These figures have changed dramatically. New York City is still 36 percent foreign-born, and some of its older suburbs—such as Port Chester (41.4 percent), Rye (32.5 percent), and Brentwood (34.7 percent)—are equally high, but the foreign-born percentages in Syracuse and Rochester have fallen below 7 percent, and Buffalo is down to 4.4. No single census can render a full picture of the state's ethnic profile, and many citizens find it difficult to trace a distinctive foreign heritage; however, census questions asking nonimmigrants to report their perceived ancestries put Germany, Italy, and Ireland in a near tie for first, with England fifth, just behind those who identified themselves as African-American. If all of those identifying themselves as Puerto Rican, Dominican, and so on had identified themselves simply as Latino, they would constitute the single largest group, but the heterogeneity of this population serves only to further underscore the ethnic diversity of the state.

In the 1980s and 1990s, the state's population was deceptively stable, growing by a modest 4.1 percent from 17,558,072 in 1980 to 18,976,457 in 2000. This seeming stability masks two decades of enormous mobility. As the number of Asians nearly tripled and the percentage of Hispanics increased to 15.1 from 9.4, these two groups alone added nearly 1.5 million persons to the state's total, which means, by inference, that a similar number of non-Hispanics and non-Asians left. Within the state, too, there have been dramatic shifts. One study, cited by Glazer, estimated an overall out-migration of 15 percent of New York City's population in just the five-year period between 1975 and 1980. The most successful of these emigrants, whites and Asians, moved "up," it appears, to nearby suburbs in New York, New Jersey, and Connecticut, while a number of less successful blacks and Puerto Ricans moved back to their southern and Caribbean roots.[18] In both cases, their places were taken by new immigrants who have settled almost entirely in and around the city: fully 90 percent of the state's foreign-born counted in 2000 were in the metropolitan area. Between 2000 and 2006, the Census Bureau estimates that 1 million immigrants settled in the area; without them, the region would have lost nearly 600,000. As in the past,

> New York stands out as America's quintessential immigrant city. It served as the historic port of entry for European immigrants in the late nineteenth and early twentieth centuries and still attracts a significant share of the nation's new arrivals. . . . Since 1900, 10 percent or more of the nation's foreign-born population has lived in New York City. For much of the twentieth century, a fifth or more of New York City residents were foreign-born, the figure reaching 41 percent in 1910 and, by 1999, almost as high as 35 percent.[19]

They are, moreover, a very diverse group. The Dominican Republic (15 percent) is the largest single country of origin, with the former Soviet Union second at just under 10 percent. Between 1990 and 1998 there were, quite remarkably, forty different countries that generated more than 5,000 immigrants each to New York City.[20]

Wealth and Poverty

The period from 1980 to the present was hard on America's poor and good for the rich. While the incomes of the wealthiest Americans rose dramatically, those of the poorest 40 percent failed to keep pace with inflation. The same pattern appeared in New York State, but to an even greater degree. The income of New York's poorest 20 percent increased by a total of just $1,091 (about $40 a year) to an average of $16,076 in 2005. New York's wealthiest 20 percent, conversely, augmented their incomes by 64.6 percent, an average of $2,440 a year; and the richest 1 percent more than doubled their income to $206,061. The average income of the top fifth of New York families, as a result, grew to 8.1 times greater than that of the bottom fifth, second only to Louisiana in the gap between rich and poor.[21] These disparities, moreover, have important regional and ethnic correlatives. Long Island's suburban Nassau County, at one extreme, contains significant pockets of poverty, but its 2003 median household income of $71,226 was $27,000 above the state average and roughly two and a half times that of the Bronx ($27,550) and of rural Franklin County ($32,531). And the income differentials *within* counties are even more striking: in Suffolk County, household median income ranged from as high as $181,000 in Lloyd Harbor and $193,000 in Old Field to $33,000 in Greenport and only $15,000 on the Shinnecock Indian reservation.[22] Nathan Glazer, whose early studies of race and ethnicity virtually defined the field, once reflected on his own work and that of others as follows:

> In the 1950s and 1960s, it was reasonable to project that the newest entrants into New York's complex ethnic mix, blacks and Puerto Ricans, would in time rise in the city's economic structure and become only modestly differentiated, in economic position and political power, from those who had preceded them—just as the Jews and Italians before them rose, in the economic and political spheres, to the level of the Irish and Germans who had preceded them. This was the expectation voiced by Oscar Handlin in *The Newcomers*, and it was my expectation in *Beyond the Melting Pot*. But it hasn't happened.[23]

Just as civil rights laws were changing the job atmosphere for the better, as the last wave of black and Puerto Rican migrants hit New York, the nature of the job market shifted. Between 1950 and 1970, the net job increase was 275,000, with 575,000 new jobs in the service sector more than offsetting the loss of close to 300,000 jobs in those industries that had traditionally served as springboards to the success of less-educated immigrant groups.[24] African-Americans arriving from the South often lacked the educational background, and Puerto Ricans the linguistic ability, to compete for jobs in the growing service sector and, unlike some newer immigrants, did not have the capital resources to start their own businesses. Thus, while the median hourly wage of white workers was $16 in 2004, the comparable figures for blacks ($13) and Hispanics ($12) were considerably lower.

Box 1.2
Ah, Wilderness!

While New York is among the most urbanized states in the union, even its own residents often fail to realize how vast and thinly populated much of the state is. There are more than 50,000 people per square mile living in Manhattan. Not counting tourists and commuters, each of them has a little over 500 square feet, something like the space between the goal line and the fifteen-yard line at Giant Stadium.

At the other extreme, there are 3.1 persons per square mile in Hamilton County. Folks in this area—just an hour or so north of Albany—could each put a thousand football fields on their share of the land and still have room left for parking. These patterns are, of course, largely the product of economic and social choices having little to do with government. New York, however, was the first among the American states to choose to preserve its wilderness heritage. Article XIV, Section 1, of the 1894 constitution provides that more than 2 million acres in the Adirondacks and Catskills "shall be forever kept as wild forest lands." To this day, no other state has so sweeping and strong a land conservation provision inscribed in its constitution.

Not surprisingly, few other states—even those that are far more recently and thinly settled—have better preserved their wilderness areas. There are places within the Adirondack preserve where you can entirely escape the sights and sounds of human habitation. You can go so deep into the woods that you will neither see the glow of distant electric lights nor hear the faintest rumble of far-off trucks and trains. There is not another place east of the Mississippi River in which this solitude is possible.

Upstate, Downstate, and In Between

The north-south split in California is cultural and increasingly ethnic, but has few economic correlatives; Colorado, Illinois, Michigan, and Pennsylvania display significant conflicts between large urban centers with large minority populations and surrounding rural and suburban areas of very different ethnic, economic, and political hues. But New York City stands alone among American cities in its relationship to the state of which it is a part. Size alone distinguishes it: New York City's population exceeds that of the nation's next two cities, Los Angeles and Chicago, combined and has accounted for roughly half of the state's population for more than a century. In almost every way—in its wealth as in its poverty, in its culture and diversity—it is a force too large to ignore. More than one contemporary New Yorker would concur in the 1905 observation of city politician George Washington Plunkitt that: "The feeling between this city and the hayseeds that make a livin' by plunderin' it is every bit as bitter as the feelin' between the North and the South before the [Civil] War."[25]

Although there are persistent differences between the city and the rest of the state, the boundaries between what New Yorkers mean by "upstate" and "downstate" are elusive. The core of New York City, Manhattan Island, is relatively as small in population (about a fifth of the city's total) as it is large in image. Its surrounding boroughs are often as much at odds with Manhattan as in alliance, and the boundaries between eastern Queens and neighboring communities in Nassau County, or between the north Bronx and Westchester, are virtually indiscernible. The larger upstate cities, such as Rochester and Buffalo, moreover, have much, if not more, in common with the Big Apple than with the small towns immediately surrounding them, while New York City's smallest borough, Staten Island, identifies somewhat tenuously with the metropolis and has actually voted to secede. But if New Yorkers find it difficult to trace the precise geographic boundary between upstate and downstate, the chances are that most have a fairly precise cultural concept of the division. Citizens of Staten Island, whatever their feelings about secession, feel a far closer identity with Manhattan than with, say, Buffalo. And even the residents of Yonkers—though less than a mile from the New York City line—are likely to take a certain satisfaction in the fact that they live in Westchester and not the Bronx. Ninety percent of the newer immigrants live in or near the city. Almost all of the state's substantial Jewish population lives within fifty miles of Times Square. And the bulk of the state's openly gay community is in the city, more specifically, in Manhattan. Unlike the residents of any other American city, moreover, New Yorkers are really packed in together "where densities reach a staggering 66,835 persons per square mile."[26] New York City, unlike any other place in the state or in the United States, is a vertical city in which people live on top of and under each other instead of next door. In a nation sometimes said to be governed by the automobile, fewer than half of the city's adults have a driver's license.

A strong argument can be made that this is no longer, if it ever really was, a tale of *two* states. As a mental construct, the upstate/downstate distinction colors almost every aspect of New York politics, but the boundaries become increasingly elusive. Cornell University economist Rolf Pendall argues that the state is made up of essentially *three* broad regional economies. New York City's large, globally connected financial and service sectors swing widely in response to changing world trends. Its dynamic economy tends to both rise and decline sharply, steepening the entire state's cycles of boom and bust, absorbing most of the state's new residents and just as quickly sending others out. The rest of eastern New York (including Long Island, the northern suburbs, the Hudson Valley, and the Capital District) rather closely mirrors the trends of the nation as a whole, gaining in population and enjoying moderate overall job growth, but with a continuing switch from high-paying jobs in manufacturing to lower-wage service sector jobs. Pendall calls the rest of New York—its western and northern sectors—the "the third slowest growing state," noting that if it were a state in its own right it would rank forty-eighth of fifty on a number of indicators.[27] While the total real wages of the rest of the state rose by nearly 5 percent between 1995 and 2005, upstate wages rose by only 1.1.[28] Not surprisingly, the number of young adults ages twenty to thirty-four in the region dropped by 23 percent between 1990 and 2000. And although more than half of the state's poor people are in New

Table 1.2

New York by the Numbers: Where New York Ranks in Comparison With the Other Forty-Nine States

Population (2000)	18,976,821	(3rd)
Land area	47,251 sq. mi.	(30th)
Percentage African-American	15.8%	(10th)
Percentage Hispanic	15.1%	(8th)
Percentage Asian	5.5%	(4th)
Percentage of population under 5 years old	6.6%	(3rd)
Percentage of population over 65	13.1%	(21st)
Divorce rate	7.0%	(38th)
Crime rate	3.1%	(45th)
Prisoners in state corrections institutions	70,617	(4th)
Per capita personal income (2003)	$36,112	(5th)
Poverty rate	14.2%	(10th)
Enrollment in public colleges and universities	634,687	(4th)
Enrollment in private colleges and universities	458,785	(1st)
High school graduation rate (2006)	63.1%	(43rd)
Average ACT (college test) score (2006)		(4th)
Net farm income (total)	$527,123,000	(26th)

Sources: Kendra A. Hovey and Harold A. Hovey, *State Fact Finder 2007* (Washington, DC: CQ Press, 2007); Kathleen O'Leary Morgan and Scott Morgan, *State Rankings 2007*, 18th ed. (Lawrence, KA: Morgan Quitno Press, 2007); United States Census.

York City, the poverty rates of upstate cities like Buffalo (26 percent), Syracuse (31.3 percent), and Rochester (30 percent) are comparable (Table 1.2).

Whether we describe New York as embodying a tale of two states or three, the continuing diversity of the state is fundamental to its politics. New York was the first of the American states forged out of the colonial settlements of two European powers; it has continuously absorbed immigrants from all over the world; and it has, through most of its history, been a center simultaneously of both extraordinary wealth and poverty. To understand New York politics, it is first necessary to understand the state's diversity and indeed *fragmentation*. In a long tradition, dating back to Dutch New Amsterdam, New Yorkers have been noted for their tolerance of diversity: the streets and stores of Manhattan are probably more ethnically, culturally, and economically mixed than those of any other place in the world. But this surface of multicultural integration masks the blunt reality that "New York City is hypersegregated."[29] Urban sociologists have developed an "index of dissimilarity" to define the extent to which different ethnic groups are distributed among geographic areas. What it shows for New York City is that black neighborhoods are more purely black, white neighborhoods more purely white than in almost any city in the United States.[30] Five miles from neighborhoods in the city where 90 percent of the residents live on less than $25,000 a year are neighborhoods where a tiny studio apartment rents for $30,000 and it costs more per month to park a car than a minimum wage worker takes home. The suburbs are similarly stratified. Politicians, moreover, have compounded the fractures of demography by constructing political boundaries that reinforce rather than transcend ethnic, racial, and economic boundaries.

That many of the state's economic, ethnic, and cultural divisions have regional correlatives intensifies the potential for conflict, which is strikingly reflected in different relationships with and expectations from government:

> Given the social interdependence that defines their existence, cities need more activist government than do rural areas. The urban economy, for example, requires public transportation systems. While nearly 53 percent of New York City residents use mass transit to get to work, fewer than 7 percent of residents of other parts of the state do. . . . While nearly two-thirds of New York City households live in rental units, many of which are government price stabilized, fewer than 27 percent of households outside the city reside in rental units. Moreover, the nature and extent of urban social problems require roughly two-thirds of all state spending on welfare and health care programs. These diverse needs generate rural-urban conflicts over the size and scope of government generally as well as conflicts over the degree of autonomy that city government should have.[31]

Demography and Politics

While New Yorkers are different from, say, Texans, these sharp differences make it difficult to generalize about the state and its changing politics. Elazar's widely used categories of "political culture" work poorly for New York.[32] Its upstate regions, the Hudson Valley, and the downstate suburbs in their early years could generally fit his category of "moralistic." Derived from the Puritan settlements of New England and Long Island, it sees government as a positive force in the lives of its citizens and stresses the importance of rectitude, citizen participation, and issue-oriented politics. But these forces always have been threatened if not overwhelmed by the "individualistic" culture emanating from the city that Elazar attributes to the state as a whole. Individualistic states, with their roots in commerce and industry, tend to limit government intrusions into private activities, to downplay the importance of participation in politics, and to be more than usually tolerant of political corruption. The struggle between these competing views of politics has indeed served as a running theme in the politics of both the city and the state, where cycles of reform have periodically punctuated the state's political history with periods of major, though seldom enduring, realignment. "It cannot be denied that reform movements have been the motor of change in New York City's political system. The periodic challenges that defector insiders and outside reformers have intermittently mounted against the regular Democratic Party organization of 'the machine' constitute a central theme in the city's political development."[33] These oscillations are more muddied on a state-wide basis, where the political dynamics are more complex, but the enduring reality of New York politics is its foundation in change and diversity and the absence of a clearly defined statewide political culture in Elazar's terms.

Pluralism, Diversity, and Constitutional Politics

In the absence of a dominant political culture, a recurring problem has been finding sufficient unity in diversity to make the state governable. Throughout its history New York has embodied a quintessentially Madisonian political system in which "the greater number of citizens and extent of territory" assures a pluralistic politics. In 1788, James Madison wrote:

> Extend the sphere and you take in a greater variety of parties and interests; you make it less probable that a majority of the whole will have a common motive to invade the rights of other citizens; or if such a common motive exists, it will be more difficult for all who feel it to discover their own strength, and to act in unison with each other.[34]

The primary safeguard against one group depriving another of its basic rights, to put Madison's argument in more modern terms, is pluralism, a network of diverse groups—none of them strong enough to take over the government by themselves—who must bargain and compromise if they are to get anything done.

Madison and the other Founders were skeptical of the ability of the masses to govern responsibly, even in a pluralistic system. In his widely cited defense of the proposed Constitution, Madison argued in the tenth *Federalist* that the "regulation of these various and interfering interests forms the principal task of modern legislation."[35] Thus the Constitution was designed to divide the power of government into separate institutions and to distribute them between the national and state levels of government. Such a fragmentation and dispersion of power, the Founders believed, would make it difficult, even in a pluralistic society, for a single faction or temporary coalition to impose its will on minorities. Democracy, in Madisonian terms, was not majority rule, but rather decisions made through bargaining and institutional negotiation between shifting coalitions of minorities.

The government of New York State is structured along these same lines, under-scored—in New York's case—by an abiding, mutual mistrust between the residents of its largest city and the rest of the state. Two economic systems, two cultures—as different, really, as the South and North in eighteenth-century America—put together a government that was every bit as fragmented as that of the new nation of which it was a part. In parallel with the new national government of the United States, local and minority interests were protected from mass movements by a complicated set of institutional devices that would serve as "auxiliary precautions" (to use Madison's term) against unchecked majority rule.

Limited Government

The most obvious, though perhaps least formidable of these precautions was the state constitution itself. Unlike the Constitution of the United States, which, in its original form, had no Bill of Rights, the constitution of New York is—even today—one of

---

Box 1.3
The Federalist Papers

The reverential tones in which Americans discuss the work of the Founders gloss over one of the most bitter debates in the history of the nation's politics. Writing both in their own names and under such pseudonyms as Cato and Brutus, journalists, politicians, and most of those who attended the constitutional convention vigorously set forth the arguments for and against ratification. With nine of the thirteen former colonies needed to ratify the new constitution, the only thing all agreed upon was that the vote would be close. New York was a particularly important and uncertain battleground.

With some early help from the patrician John Jay, two of the convention's most active participants—thirty-one-year-old Alexander Hamilton of New York and thirty-seven-year-old James Madison of Virginia—entered the fray with a series of eighty-five articles under the pen name "Publius" published in the New York press and later as a book. Although *The Federalist*, as the book was titled, was intended as a campaign tract, and although "it is doubtful whether it had much influence in determining the issue of ratification of the Constitution," it is still cited in cases before the Supreme Court and assigned to thousands of students in political science. "It was," as Edward Mead Earle wrote in his introduction to the Modern Library edition, "and continues to be the most important discussion of federal government, for which the Constitution of the United States set a significant precedent. . . . It is also a work of first-rank importance in the history of political philosophy and, in particular, in the theory of representative government."

Source: Edward Mead Earle, "Introduction," *The Federalist* (New York: Modern Library, 1937), pp. 10–11.

---

the most rights-protective in the country. The constitution also protects individuals and minorities by placing limits not just on what the government can do but how it goes about doing it. When the state wants to borrow money, say, to rebuild its aging highways, the proposal must be approved by both the governor and the legislature and then placed before the people in a public referendum. Many relatively trivial policies, moreover, are embedded in the constitution where they can be changed only by a rather cumbersome process of amendment, again involving a public vote. Even so seemingly trivial an issue as whether a small town in the Adirondacks could improve its water system had to be approved by the state's voters in 2007 because of a provision in the state constitution governing Adirondack water.

The power of government in New York also is strongly constrained by that of the United States. Because the federal government has the exclusive power to coin money and to regulate interstate commerce, the most important economic policy decisions are made in Washington, not Albany. And despite sharing a long border with Canada, the state is precluded by the U.S. Constitution from making treaties or many other kinds of agreements with its neighbor to the north. While it is true that there are ways of circumventing some of these restrictions, the real power, in cases of conflict, almost invariably resides with the federal government. For many years, for example, New York resisted calls from neighboring states to raise the legal drinking age from eighteen to twenty-one. But when Congress passed a law cutting off federal highway funds to states that did not raise the drinking age, New York fell into line.

Representation and Elite Control

Although Madison was skeptical of the ability of constitutions to serve as an effective check on political power, referring to them rather scornfully as "mere parchment barriers," he was both acutely and astutely aware of the importance of the process of decision-making, and of the ways in which the outcomes of political conflicts could be shaped by the rules of the game. Among the most important checks on democratic excess was what he called the republican principle of representative as opposed to direct democracy. Public participation in government, Madison argued, was best filtered through elected representatives whose "wisdom . . . patriotism and love of justice" would "be more consonant to the public good than if pronounced by the people them-selves."[36] The prototype of Madison's ideal representative was perhaps his co-author John Jay, who resigned from his position as first Chief Justice of the Supreme Court of the United States to run for governor of New York in 1794. William Brouck, who was elected in 1842, was the first German-American and first working farmer to serve as governor: all his predecessors were, like Jay, gentleman "farmers" of English or Dutch descent from rural areas of what is now the city or the nearby Hudson Valley. As this agrarian aristocracy gradually yielded to the new captains of industry and those with legal training, the socioeconomic evolution of the governorship paralleled the shift in New Haven described by Robert Dahl, from the early period when "public office was almost the exclusive prerogative of the patrician families," through a nineteenth-century ascension of "the new self-made men of business, the entrepreneurs," to the twentieth-century sons of "working class or lower middle class families of immigrant origins."[37]

The pivotal figure in the modern governorship of New York State is Al Smith, who served from 1919 to 1920 and again from 1923 to 1928, when he ran, unsuccessfully, for president. Aside from the unfortunate William Sulzer—the only New York governor to be impeached—Smith was the first urban, working-class non-Protestant to reach the state's highest office. Since Smith, the road to higher office in New York has been widened to accommodate wealthy Protestant patricians (Franklin D. Roosevelt and Nelson Rockefeller); urban Catholics (Hugh Carey and Mario Cuomo); Jews from the city (Herbert Lehman and Eliot Spitzer); and a suburban white ethnic (George Pataki). But aside from the African-American Carl McCall, who ran unsuccessfully as the Democratic nominee in 2002, no woman, black, or Latino has won the nomination of a major party for governor. David Paterson became the first African-American governor upon Spitzer's resignation in 2008.

The legislature has gone through similar phases. Today, it strikingly underscores the tendency of geographic and ethnic differences to be mutually reinforcing. Of the twenty assembly members of African-American descent in 2008, nineteen were from the five largest cities, as were eleven of the twelve Hispanics and the lone Asian-American. All fourteen minority members of the senate were from New York City, Buffalo, Rochester, or Yonkers. Women have increased their presence in the legislature to nearly 25 percent of the overall membership, slightly above the national average of 23.4 percent. But what is perhaps most striking is the almost complete professionalization of politics in the state. As early as 1988, Benjamin and Nakamura, looking at the legislators' own self-descriptions, found "more than two-thirds of Assembly members and more than half of Senators were describing themselves not as lawyers, businessmen, or consultants but as legislators."[38] Today, virtually every member of the legislature is a full-time politician. Whether Madison would have favored the development of a political "class" is debatable, but he almost certainly would have applauded the tendency increasingly to entrust the making of public policy to those who know how laws are made.

In contrast with other states, New York has been slow to expand and sustain popular participation in elections. It was, as we have noted, very late in offering the right to vote to former slaves. And despite the fact that the women's suffrage movement was essentially born in Seneca Falls in 1848, it was not until 1917 that New York allowed women to vote. Even in the twenty-first century, as we shall see at greater length in Chapter 3, New York has comparatively low rates of voter participation, particularly among its less affluent and less educated citizens. Democracy in New York, in sum, is filtered through professional politicians who represent a relatively narrow stratum of affluent, educated citizens.

Checks and Balances

The third layer of Madison's checks on the mischief of faction was the creation of a complex structure of government in which it would be difficult to get anything done in the absence of a very strong consensus. The separation of powers between the legislative, executive, and judicial branches is designed, as in the Constitution of the United States, to ensure "that each department should have a will of its own; and consequently be so structured that the members of each should have as little agency as possible in the appointment of the others."[39] New York's constitution, like the Constitution of the United States, incorporates a separation and blending of the respective powers of the governor, the legislature, and the judiciary.

Unlike most of the other former colonies, New York's first constitution created a strong office of the governor. Both subsequent constitutions and political traditions have made the office even more powerful, particularly in its ability to check and balance the powers of the legislature. The political process has been rendered still more complex by an elaborate structure of public corporations and authorities that often operate quite independently of both the legislature and the governor. The

Metropolitan Transit Authority, for example, has its own independent budget of more than $9 billion (larger than the budgets of seventeen states).

Finally, New York has one of the most complex networks of local governments of any state. In addition to counties, cities, towns, and villages, there are 699 school districts with independent taxing power, 6,500 special-purpose units of local government such as fire districts and water authorities, and another 810 special-purpose units such as libraries and parking authorities. The office of the comptroller puts the total of the major classes of local government at 3,177, plus another 6,658 special districts.[40] The problem of coordinating the acts of these 10,000 or more governments in a single state is formidable, but despite the obvious gains in efficiency that might be achieved through consolidation, the forces of local control remain remarkably strong.

Making the System Work

Calling it "the graveyard of good intentions," one author has written that "New York's immense size, its multitude of racial and ethnic rivalries, its complex political structure, and its many-layered bureaucracies put it in a class by itself as a hard place to get anything done."[41] Many others have called it "ungovernable." Yet the state has often been both effective and innovative: it was among the first in the nation to set up a system of public schools, regulate working conditions, protect civil rights, and construct a system of parkways and turnpikes. Despite its fragmentation, New York historically has been a "liberal" state. Looking at survey data for the years 1976 through 1988, Erikson, Wright, and McIver found New Yorkers consistently among the most liberal Americans surveyed, with the state ranking third (behind Massachusetts and Rhode Island) on a broad range of issues. Even when the authors controlled for socioeconomic differences—statistically eliminating the effects of large minority populations and union members—the state's political climate remained, comparatively, among the most liberal in the nation.[42] As the country turned to the right in the 1980s and 1990s, the turn in New York was slower to arrive and less decisive than in most other states.

If its liberal inclination helps explain New York's record of liberal legislation, it does not tell us how generations of politicians have managed to overcome the impediments to action that seem to be woven into the fabric of the state's demography and politics. The answers are both institutional and political.

Strong Governors

Wary of their experiences in the colonial period, most of the American states gave their governors only limited powers and short terms in office. New York was the exception. The constitutional scope of the office, moreover, has historically tended to attract strong leaders. "Great men," as Nelson Rockefeller once immodestly observed, "are not drawn to small office."[43] Governors like Rockefeller used their manifest powers not just to promote their policy agendas and to expand the reach of the office, but to advance their own careers as well (four former governors have gone on to the presidency, six to the vice presidency, and at least ten others have tried). The twentieth-century institutionalization of the office of the governor made it a powerful force in the state, with or without a strong incumbent. Even the relatively disengaged George Pataki was able to leave a fairly substantial mark on public policy.

A defining figure in this process was former governor Al Smith. Traveling extensively, using the media, and riding a rising tide of reform, Smith was able both to enact a substantial program of social and economic policies and to dramatically strengthen the formal powers of his office. Preparing the budget, for the first time under Smith, became the governor's responsibility. By combining his control over its funding with reforms in the structure of the bureaucracy, moreover, Smith (and his successors) were able to set the policy agenda and ensure its implementation. Particularly when the governor and the legislature were of the same party, Smith's command of the resources of the executive combined with his access to the media enabled him to dominate the part-time, amateur legislature.

Gradually, the legislature began to reassert itself. Increasingly professionalized and no longer dependent on the declining party machines, the legislature in the 1960s developed the staff and physical resources to reassert itself in the budgetary and policy processes. For more than forty years, until the elections of 2008, Albany settled into a relatively stable three-way policy process of bargaining between the governor, the Republican-controlled state senate, and the Democratic state assembly. The governor's nearly absolute ability to control the bureaucracy combined with the highly disciplined parties in the legislature to keep the policy process highly centralized. The legislature's public prestige is low, and a scathing academic report characterizing it as "dysfunctional" has been frequently reported and repeated in the press. But as Eliot Spitzer discovered in his first year as governor, those who underestimate the legislature's potential powers will soon learn otherwise. When Spitzer attempted to dictate the legislature's choice of successor to Comptroller Alan Hevesi, threatening to "fucking steamroller" anyone who got in the way, it was the governor who was flattened by the choice of Assemblyman Tom DiNapoli. Later, Spitzer bragged that "after the Senate left town without acting on much that he thought lawmakers needed to do, . . . he could do much governing without the Legislature using state agencies and executive orders to work his will." Four months later, "as he finally acknowledged . . . when he retreated from his edict that illegal immigrants should be granted driver's licenses, having the technical power to do something doesn't always translate into the actual ability to do something if the politics doesn't work."[44] Spitzer was forced to resign in 2008 in the wake of a highly publicized encounter with an expensive call girl, but as one Democratic assemblyman put it, "he was toast before he got fried."

What makes the legislature particularly important—even when it is not in formal session—is a highly centralized, professional division of labor that gives it the institutional capacity to respond quickly and effectively to gubernatorial initiatives.

Few democratic legislatures are efficient, and New York's is not. What it does do and, in Madisonian terms, does quite effectively is to broker the conflicting interests of highly diverse constituencies and bring them to a central location (Albany) for resolution, using the mechanism of party government.

Strong Parties

James Madison's fear of factions and mistrust of political parties did not stop him, the practical politician, from working with his fellow Virginian to form what is now the Democratic Party as a vehicle for countering the economic policies of Secretary of the Treasury Alexander Hamilton.

> Neither Madison nor Jefferson abandoned their philosophical views that parties are divisive and dangerous. But, like anyone who acts as well as writes about politics, they were faced with a fact, not a theory. The fact was that Hamilton's designs could be defeated only by unifying the anti-Hamiltonians in Congress and by increasing their number in the elections of 1792 and after. . . . And so it was that James Madison, the distinguished antiparty theorist, became the cofounder of the world's first modern political party.[45]

The Jeffersonian Republicans—the ancestors of the modern Democratic Party—quickly became the dominant force in New York State. By striking an alliance with New York City's Tammany Hall, Kinderhook's Martin Van Buren consolidated what was arguably the first statewide political party organization (and paved Van Buren's own road to the White House in 1836). In the city, Mayor Fernando Wood took over Tammany and "led the way in using techniques that were to become virtual Tammany staples, such as catering to the urban lower-class voter and the immigrant, manipulating the police for partisan purposes, stealing elections, and artfully using bribes and financial skullduggery for political gain."[46] But he also made the party system an effective vehicle for governance, for overcoming the problems of deadlock that inhere in the Madisonian system.

Discipline, not democracy, marked the internal politics of the machine, and in this sense the rise of Tammany and its counterparts was a continuation of oligarchic political relationships that had dominated in pre-Revolutionary New York.

> While the revolution ushered in a new era of liberal democracy, it simultaneously welcomed the intermingling of new and old elites and their fusion into local, regional, and national establishments. And high on the agendas of many of these groups were the modulation of democratic demands and the exercise of control over the various processes of partisan politics, much in the way the old oligarchies had done.[47]

But the parties of the machine age could not develop a coherent statewide system. By the end of the nineteenth century, the state was divided into a crazy quilt of well-organized, one-party-dominant enclaves of machine-like fiefdoms. Organized around questions of patronage and payoffs rather than ideology, the machines in effect took New York politics out of the electoral arena and into the proverbial smoke-filled rooms where the deals were cut. If the state was no longer run by the patricians of the city and the Hudson Valley, it continued—and continues—to contain the process of political bargaining in a relatively small circle of professional politicians. Governors, if they were not beholden to a coalition of the machines that put them into office, had to negotiate their programs with the machines' representatives in the legislature who, by and large, were far more focused on local politics and patronage rather than state issues. Governor Smith's administrative and budgetary reforms, to give an example, were achieved in part through a deal that gave the party organizations new patronage positions.

The ability of strong governors to divide and conquer the legislative parties was nakedly revealed in 1964 when the Democrats, having won control of the state assembly, were unable to agree on a candidate for speaker because of a split in the county organizations. By throwing Republican support behind one of the candidates, Governor Rockefeller in effect chose his own assembly leader and effectively dominated the session. Over the next ten years, both parties worked hard to secure their independence by displacing the nominating and campaign finance roles of the county leaders with more centralized systems. By the early 1970s the modern system was in place: the remaining local machines—the Republicans in Nassau and Suffolk counties, the Democrats in Brooklyn, Queens, and Albany—had been pretty much marginalized on a statewide basis in favor of six professional, highly disciplined statewide parties—one for each party in each house of the legislature—plus the statewide organizations of the Republicans and Democrats focused on the office of governor.

Strong party states like New York are not without fractious divisions between interests. What they do succeed in doing is to channel the clashes of these factions through the filters of a central party apparatus. The bargaining process takes place in the party caucuses rather than the specialized arenas of committees and lower levels of the bureaucracy. Particularly when party control of the governorship and the two houses of the legislature is divided—as it was from 1967 through 2008—it requires conflicts that cannot be solved locally to come to the highest levels of the state system. Whether this almost uniquely centralized concentration of political power makes the system less susceptible to special interests ("factions," in Madison's term) is one of the open questions that make the study of New York politics of interest in other states as well.

"Three Men in a Room"

Most major issues in New York are negotiated at some point in face-to-face discussions among the governor, the majority leader of the state senate, and the speaker of the assembly. Thus the beginning of wisdom among political observers is that state politics essentially revolve around these three men. This is what we might call the journalists' theory of New York politics. But just as knowing that the earth revolves around the sun does not make you a physicist, you really do not know much about politics in New York if your understanding stops at "three men in a room." The three men (none of these offices has ever been occupied by a woman) are not nearly as autonomous or omniscient as the popular myth would hold.

In the first place, there is simply no human way in which three people—no matter how diligent and intelligent—could have more than a superficial understanding of a budget of more than $100 billion and be on top of the numerous other issues that come to them. Second, as important as are the roles the speaker and majority leader in New York politics, they do not come into the room with the same resources as the governor. Institutionally, as we shall show in Chapter 5, New York's already strong governors are becoming stronger with a major decision by the Court of Appeals giving them almost unfettered authority to use the budget as a comprehensive weapon of public policy. The budget has increasingly become the black hole of New York politics, drawing into its gubernocentric vortex virtually any kind of policy issue the governor chooses to remove from the normal process of legislation. Third, the "three men in a room" operate in a political and economic environment over which they have relatively little control. As much as the dynamics of New York politics serve Mr. Madison's objective of controlling the "mischief of faction," there are powerful private, political, and bureaucratic interests in New York that cannot be ignored. We will look at these in Chapter 4. Fourth, the supposedly ruling triumvirate is in fact institutionally constrained by federal rules and regulations, by the courts, and by the many powers they have delegated to local governments, to public agencies and authorities, and to private parties. Finally, at every stage of their negotiations, the "three men in a room" operate in a complex web of socioeconomic and political relations that are, in essence, the subject of this book. The constraints on the speaker and majority leader are most overt—every deal they cut must pass muster in their party caucuses—but governors must consider not just what they need to be reelected, but also how to keep their own administrative houses in order. How governors balance these pressures with and against the comparable pressures on the legislative leaders is the stuff of New York politics.

2

New York in the Federal System

The dichotomies and differences described in Chapter 1—between upstate and New York City, between rich and poor, between the cultures of moralism and individualism—continue to play key roles in New York politics, but they explain only a part of the context within which the government acts. Although New York is larger in area, population, and gross domestic product (GDP) than most countries, it is not a fully sovereign state. By design the Founders established a federal system dividing power between the national government and the states. The Constitution of the United States grants certain powers to the states, limits and proscribes others, and is silent on most. New York, for example, has significant latitude in crafting education policy, shares power with Washington in administering Medicare, and has almost no say about foreign affairs.

Subsumed under the states is local government, a complicated mélange of cities, towns, villages, counties, and special districts, which essentially adds a third layer of government. Legally, local governments do not have the same independence vis-à-vis the state as states have in the federal system. Localities are creatures of the state. With their powers derived from state charters, the governor and state legislature could abolish Syracuse, give Staten Island its independence, or break New York City into separate towns. The federal government cannot do this to the states without their consent.

The reality of intergovernmental relations in the United States bears only a passing resemblance to this legal ordering. Professor Morton Grodzins's famous analogy of a swirled marble cake aptly describes the federal system in practice: "The federal system is not accurately symbolized by a neat layer cake of three distinct and separate planes. A far more realistic symbol is that of the marble cake. Wherever you slice through it you reveal an inseparable mixture of differently colored ingredients."[1] To make this analogy even more accurate, it would need a dynamic quality in which the relationships between federal, state, and local authorities are in constant flux. This is pretty much what those who drafted the U.S. Constitution expected: "The proposed Constitution," as James Madison put it, "is, in strictness, neither a national nor a federal Constitution, but a composition of both." While the federal government may be stronger at times and the state governments at others, "the people, by throwing themselves into either scale, will infallibly make it preponderate. If their rights are invaded by either, they can make use of the other as the instrument of redress."[2]

The Constitution and the Changing Face of American Federalism

At the heart of the Constitution's definition of federalism are four key articles. The Tenth Amendment guarantees that "powers not delegated" to the federal government, nor "prohibited by it to the States, are reserved to the States." Since the Constitution enumerates relatively few federal powers and prohibits the exercise of few state powers, advocates of states' rights have historically argued that most government powers are, and should be, "reserved to the states."[3] Although this position still finds an occasional adherent and produces some powerful political rhetoric, it has little standing in the face of three more forceful constitutional provisions. The first of these, Article I, Section 8, is the so-called elastic clause. By giving the federal government the power to "make all laws which shall be necessary and proper for carrying into execution" its enumerated powers, the Constitution created a large loophole made even larger by the Supreme Court's willingness to broadly interpret these powers. Chief Justice John Marshall set the tone for subsequent decisions in the landmark case of *McCulloch v. Maryland* (1819) when he wrote, "Let the end be legitimate, let it be within the scope of the Constitution, and all means which are appropriate, which are plainly adapted to that end, which are not prohibited, but consist[ent] with the letter and spirit of the Constitution, are constitutional."[4]

The second source of federal power is the commerce clause, also found in Article I, Section 8. The commerce clause gives Congress the power "to regulate Commerce . . . among the several States." Justice Marshall's insistence that the definition of interstate commerce should be "comprehensive," extending to "every species of commercial intercourse,"[5] has been carried to the fullest possible degree by subsequent courts, particularly since the acceptance by the Court of the major programs of Roosevelt's New Deal in the 1930s.

Finally, the Fourteenth Amendment, ratified after the Civil War, guarantees all citizens—regardless of where they reside—the "equal protection of the laws." Seeking to avoid Southern retribution against freed slaves following the Civil War, this clause suggests that the national government would protect all citizens of the United States against state actions in violation of the federal Constitution. Thus, for example, the First Amendment, which says, "*Congress* shall make no law respecting an establishment of religion," might also be invoked to prohibit a *state* act that similarly favored one religion over another. Although this interpretation of the Fourteenth Amendment was not immediately accepted, and remains controversial, the courts have tended, until quite recently, to expand the kinds of state actions subject to federal review. Hence, state laws mandating school prayer or abridging other First Amendment rights like freedom of speech; criminal procedures not permitted under the U.S. Constitution; and protections against invasions of privacy have come under the umbrella of citizen rights protected from state law through the Fourteenth Amendment. More conservative courts in the twenty-first century have given states more latitude, but despite continuing controversies regarding the scope of protected rights, the amendment's essential limitation on state power remains in force. To put it another way, the ability of federal courts—and, with the courts' sanction—of Congress and the president to limit state powers in violation of civil rights has been very much enhanced by this modern reading of the Fourteenth Amendment.

Whether the Supreme Court's recent readings of the Fourteenth Amendment and the commerce clause were historically accurate continues to be a topic of academic and political debate. A strong argument can be made, nonetheless, that whatever the intent of the framers, the economic and social realities of the late twenty-first century make many state powers obsolete. A mobile population expects to take its rights with it as it travels, knowing that a religious practice tolerated in New York is not forbidden in Texas. A changing economy has made most commerce "interstate" in nature, regardless of what the courts might say. And the globalization of economic and social forces has served, almost automatically, to enhance the powers of the national government. So has its growing access to money: by granting or withholding funds the federal government virtually can force the states to act in ways that no constitutional doctrine supports. In the 1980s, for example, Congress managed effectively to raise the legal drinking age in every state to twenty-one, despite a general legal and scholarly consensus that the so-called police powers—laws governing crime and morality—are state and not national. What Congress did was simply to threaten to deny federal highway funds to any state that refused to raise its drinking age. Within a year, every state had complied. (New York, incidentally, was one of the last and most reluctant: "We are doing this," said one member of the state assembly, "with a gun to our heads.")

Fiscal Federalism

An old political adage suggests that to understand power you should "follow the money." One way, then, of tracing the locus of power between different levels of government is to follow the funding trail and ask who spends how much for what. Until the later years of Franklin Roosevelt's New Deal, the bulk of the money spent on domestic government programs was spent by the states and, within the states, by local governments. Compared to today, moreover, the amounts spent at all levels of government were—before World War II, the Cold War, and Iraq—relatively modest. Congress, along with presidents such as Harding, Coolidge, and Hoover, was reluctant to involve the federal government in major programs even in the face of a major crisis such as the Great Depression.

All this changed, however, with the New Deal under President Roosevelt. Some of the New Deal programs, such as Social Security, were administered almost entirely by the federal government; many others used federal resources to subsidize state and local projects. State activities also expanded in the 1930s, as state governments also sought to combat the Depression. In cumulative terms, total spending by all levels of government rose from less than 10 percent of the GDP in 1929 to as much as 30 percent in modern times, with the rise in federal spending particularly substantial. Even if we exclude military spending and national security—which accounted for roughly one out of every five federal dollars spent between World War II and today—the federal share of direct government spending has risen to as high as 19 percent of GDP. Direct state and local spending has totaled as much as 16.5 percent, but much of this was money that came to the states from the federal government. If we eliminate the duplications caused by these transfers, the overall numbers have been remarkably stable for a number of years: between 1965 and 2005, the total tax burden on the American people increased from 24.3 percent of GDP to 25.8. What this number obscures is a rather dramatic shift in the ways in which government funds are mixed together, largely through the device of what is known as grants-in-aid.

Grants-in-Aid

Grants-in-aid are monetary allocations from the federal government to state and local governments. These grants are designed to give states and localities financial assistance in meeting certain nationally set goals. They come in two broad categories: unrestricted funds, or block grants, which allow considerable state and local discretion in how the money will be spent, and categorical grants, which define quite precisely where each dollar should go. A classic early example of a grant-in-aid was the Morrill Land Grant Act of 1862, which granted each state 30,000 acres of public land for the express purpose of establishing agricultural and mechanical arts colleges. Under the Morrill Act, the states could obtain land only if they provided some of their own resources to meet federal standards.[6] The land was offered as an inducement designed to get the states to do something the federal government thought they should do but was reluctant to do itself. Indeed, a national system of federally funded colleges would almost certainly have been ruled unconstitutional, even if Congress had wanted to establish it. No such strictures applied to a transfer of land.

The number and scope of grants-in-aid increased markedly in the 1930s as the Roosevelt administration pushed the states to be more proactive in combating the Depression. During and after World War II, federal grants-in-aid accounted for roughly 10 percent of state and local expenditures. Unlike the Morrill grants, moreover, most of the New Deal programs were designed to continue over a number of years, thus inculcating enduring relationships between state, local, and national governments. The number and spending levels of federal grant programs rose slowly in the years following World War II and then rapidly in the 1960s. During President Lyndon Johnson's administration alone, over 200 new categorical grants were created. The three layers of government, which traditionally had remained relatively disconnected, increasingly came to resemble Professor Grodzins's marble cake. Before 1964, as Walker suggests, the pattern of intergovernmental relations was only moderately marbleized:

> A full 92 percent of the aid funds in 1960 went to states, and four programs dominated the grant picture fiscally (highways, aid to the aged, [welfare], and unemployment compensation). . . . Only four state agencies were heavily involved with federal grant programs. Moreover, while all the grants were categorical, their conditions by current standards were quite reasonable—again facilitating federal intergovernmental administration. Most state programs and agencies and nearly all of their local counterparts were unaffected by this expansion of the federal grant role.[7]

By 1980, more than 25 percent of state and local expenditures were of funds derived from federal grants-in-aid, leading one governor to complain that "four out of every ten state and local employees are actually federal employees in disguise, marching like a secret army to the guidelines and regulations of Washington."[8] Many state and local officials began to view federal funds less as gifts than in terms of the limitations that came with them. Categorical grants, particularly in such new areas of government action as air and water pollution control, forced the states to create whole new agencies shaped by federal rather than state standards. The experts staffing these new agencies, moreover, often worked more closely with their counterparts in Washington than with local elected officials, becoming increasingly proficient at devising new ways to spend and match federal funds. The Nixon administration came into office in 1972 determined to break the power of these administrative subgovernments and slow the upward spiral of spending it helped produce.

The centerpiece of Nixon's "New Federalism" was the introduction of general revenue sharing in which the federal government allocated funds to states and localities according to their population and income, with no conditions attached. Guidelines for revenue-sharing funds were left vague in a deliberate attempt to decentralize power. Some revenue-sharing funds went to the states, but the primary beneficiaries were municipalities, particularly the faster growing suburbs and small cities of the South, which were an important part of the Republican Party's developing political constituency.[9] The losers ("victims," they would probably call themselves) were those sophisticated bureaucrats in big-government states like New York who had become highly adept at maximizing their share of categorical grants.

It was also under President Nixon that the government began to move away from categorical grants toward more flexible block grants. By design, block grants encouraged states to meet national goals related to pollution control, education, and social services without specifying how each state could spend its share of the funds. One result of the Nixon reforms was to reverse the growth in the number of federal grant-in-aid programs, a trend that was to continue for almost twenty years. The number of specific programs—which had grown by nearly 500 percent in the 1960s—declined substantially in the 1970s and, by 1985, had virtually returned to 1965 numbers. This shift to block grants and revenue sharing that began in the Nixon years was seen by many liberals as a smokescreen for the wholesale destruction of the programs themselves. Whatever President Nixon's real agenda, however, the level of federal grant activity actually sustained in the Nixon-Ford years grew by substantial amounts. There were, in other words, more dollars of aid squeezed into a smaller number of programs. The conventional view of marble-cake federalists— that the federal government could give the states both money and power at the same time—still held, but the liberals' worst fears were soon proved real.

Devolution and Diminution

The ongoing debate in American politics about *who* should govern—whether power should be lodged primarily at the local, state, or national level—tilted, particularly in the 1930s and again in the 1960s, toward Washington. In the Nixon years it began to tilt back toward the states, and President Jimmy Carter, himself a former governor, continued the process. Midway through the Carter presidency, however, the often hidden subtext in the debate over *who* should govern—that is, the question of *how much* government in general is a good thing—reemerged. Nixon's New Federalism showed that it was possible to increase the federal government's fiscal role in funding domestic programs while simultaneously giving state and local governments greater autonomy in deciding just how the money should be spent. Ronald Reagan campaigned for the presidency with a commitment both to scale back the overall level of domestic spending in government and to decentralize what remained. He was not elected until 1980, but in fiscal terms, the Reagan years really began in 1978 when Jimmy Carter began trying to preempt the Reagan position. As seen in Figure 2.1, the Carter-Reagan years slowed the growth of grants-in-aid to a rate that barely matched inflation. Between 1978 and 1990, the story of federal grants-in-aid was, with one exception, a story of stability and even decline both in the number of programs funded and in the total dollar amounts transferred to the states. The exception, and it is a *big* exception, is health care, with Medicaid, "the 400 pound gorilla of federal aid to states and localities,"[10] now accounting for almost half of all federal grants to the states, more than double the comparable proportion in 1978; and the Office of Management and Budget predicts that the costs of grants for health care will exceed those of all other grants-in-aid by 2010.

As costs for state governments continue to rise far faster than federal funds,

Figure 2.1   **Federal Grants to the States, 1960–2010**

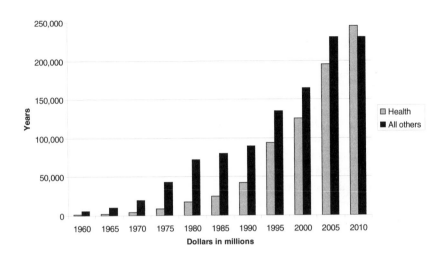

Source: Office of Management and Budget, *The Budget of the United States Government*, Fiscal Year 2006, Historical Tables (Washington, DC: Government Printing Office, 2005), pp. 211–212.

the nonhealth federal percentage of state and local outlays—which peaked at more than 20 percent in the mid-1970s—was down to less than 14 percent in 1993, the lowest level since 1961, and it has stayed at that lower level for most of the past fifteen years. Grant-in-aid funds have continued to grow, but not as rapidly as the state and local costs associated with sustaining the programs. The Reagan cuts have, in essence, proven permanent. As Reagan predicted, "It is far easier for people to come to Washington to get their special programs. It would be a hell of a lot tougher if we diffuse them and send them to the states."[11] Confronted by a Democratic House of Representatives throughout his eight years in office and by a Democratic Senate for four years, Reagan did not get all the cuts he wanted, but he was able to shift the terms of debate.

Neither of his immediate successors, Republican George Bush nor Democrat Bill Clinton, attempted in any significant way to restore the federal role in setting the direction of government spending. Indeed, the election of Republican majorities in both the Senate and House in 1994 set the stage for even more devolutions and diminutions of federal power. President Clinton also came to office with a commitment "to giving more responsibility to the states." As a former governor, he admitted, in a 1995 speech to the Florida legislature, that he "loved block grants." But Clinton went on to warn against too uncritical an embrace of the concept:

"The Congress," he warned, "gives block grants primarily to save money. And now we're talking about block grants in areas that could be really painful to the high-growth states."[12] What particularly concerned Clinton was the likely impact on politically weak groups in hard times. Although he refused to side with many Democrats in predicting an immediate "race to the bottom," a contest to see which state could be toughest on the poor in the absence of federal requirements for public assistance, he signed a welfare "reform" bill that both decentralized funding and added new federal restrictions on state benefits. After twice blocking more drastic measures, Clinton signed the Personal Responsibility and Work Opportunity Reconciliation Act in 1996, effectively converting most income support programs into block grants, excluding resident aliens from coverage, and prohibiting states from providing public assistance to any family for more than five years. New York, with one of the largest poverty populations in the country, literally lost billions of federal dollars in this reform.

President George W. Bush never articulated an explicit policy regarding federalism and the role of states and localities. Yet the events of 9/11 clearly shaped the Bush administration and the policies it decided to pursue. At the national level, wars in Afghanistan and Iraq and a general preoccupation with fighting terrorism were the focus of the administration, leaving diminishing funds available for grants-in-aid. In contrast with his Republican predecessors, George W. Bush frequently proposed policies that took away power from the states: his administration, for example, attempted to void state antipollution laws that exceed federal standards; overrode state statutes regarding cloning, abortion, gay marriage, and gun control; imposed new national standards on local schools; and developed federal standards on state driver's licenses and identity cards. In general, conservative Republicans have been particularly critical of Bush's abandonment of what they see as a party tradition of support for devolution. "Sadly," wrote the Cato Institute's Chris Edwards, "the Bush administration has buried federalism."[13] Not only was Bush willing to override the traditional state prerogatives in areas such as education, but also his administration increased the total number of grant-in-aid programs from 653 in 2000 to 814 in 2006,[14] the largest addition of new grant programs since the 1960s. Federal aid grew from an average of 18 to 19 percent of state and local revenues to a peak of 23 percent in 2004.[15] At the same time, the total amount of funding committed to existing programs was not large, amounting to about 5 percent a year in constant dollars, with most of that going to health care and a variety of new homeland security initiatives. Thus the percentage of the federal budget allocated to the states was virtually unchanged in the same period. In fact, the rapid growth in the number of grant programs combined with virtually no growth in nonhealth dollars allocated (see Figure 2.1), means that most grant programs were diminishing. In direct contrast with the Nixon years, when the states had more dollars to fund fewer programs, the states in more recent years had fewer dollars to fund more federally mandated programs. For the states this meant more programs to administer, more bureaucrats to administer them, and fewer net federal dollars to do it with. The stimulus package crafted by the Obama administration to confront the 2009 collapse of the economy, while it pumped more money into the system, was a mixed bag for the states and provides few real clues as to the future of fiscal federalism. While many of the stimulus dollars went to discretionary state accounts, others—such as those extending unemployment benefits—were rejected by conservative governors on the grounds that they came with too many federal mandates attached.

New York's Declining Share of Federal Funds

New York benefited as much as if not more than any state from the early growth of grant-in-aid programs. Because of its progressive heritage, many of the New Deal and Kennedy-Johnson programs were already in place; the new federal dollars were icing on the cake; and because of their experience and knowledge, New York bureaucrats proved remarkably adept at securing categorical grant funds. With the shift to block grants, New York not only lost this edge, but because many of the grant formulas were directed toward less affluent, lower-performing states, funds flowed elsewhere. Nonetheless, New York remains second only to California in federal aid revenues, and its state and local governments receive almost 10 percent of all federal grant funds. Programs such as Medicaid, which reward matching grants to states such as New York that both have large numbers of needy citizens and are generous in supporting them, have led many non-New Yorkers to conclude that the state's high-spending policies were costing the nation's taxpayers more than their fair share. In 2006–2007 just about one-third of New York's state budget was derived from federal funds, compared with an average of 29 percent for the other forty-nine states. This percentage has fluctuated only slightly since the peak grant-in-aid years of the 1970s; what has changed is the growing percentage of the total taken up by Medicaid, a health program for the poor, which is eight times as large as the number two federally supported program in New York.

In most other respects, however, New York does rather poorly in its fiscal relationships with the federal government. Its high poverty rate, to be sure, qualifies it for large grants in areas such as Medicaid, but its high levels of affluence, paradoxically, make it a highly taxed state as well. For each of his twenty-four years as a senator from New York, Daniel Patrick Moynihan worked with a group of Harvard University economists to conduct a study of the financial flows between the federal government and the states. The Moynihan studies looked beyond formal grants-in-aid to examine the full range of federal funds transferred to and from each state. In his final report, as he retired in 2001, Moynihan found that although New York had become number one in assistance programs for the poor, it was forty-eighth in defense spending. Overall, Moynihan found that New York was forty-first in its overall balance sheet with the federal government, with a net deficit of $16.2 billion, or $890 more paid in taxes per capita than the state received in return from Washington.[16]

There is little reason to believe that New York's relative position in this regard has changed significantly since 2000. To put it bluntly, New York is a "blue state" in national politics (network television maps of recent elections have shown majority Democratic states in blue and states voting Republican in red) and tends to suffer when Republicans control both Congress and the presidency, as they did from 2001 through 2006. Homeland security funds, for example, originally intended for the targets of the 9/11 attacks gradually were spread by political pressures to give states such as Montana per capita aid comparable to that given to New York. The formulas used to calculate how grant-in-aid funds should be allocated are arcane, not widely understood, controversial, perverse, and extraordinarily important. It probably makes sense, for example, for Washington to give more money per mile for interstate highways in a mountainous state such as West Virginia than in a flat state like Kansas. In the same way it makes sense for the federal government to provide a higher match for Medicare funds for low-income states. But how should this differential be calculated?

> In ordinary years, the federal share can be as high as 83 percent for a very low-income state and as low as 50 percent for a high-income state. This effectively changes the "price" a state pays to provide health care for its poor and medically needy: a state with an 80 percent match rate pays only twenty cents to purchase a dollar of care while a state with a 50 percent match rate pays fifty cents to purchase a dollar of care, or two and one-half times as much as the low-income state.[17]

While this formula can be considered "fair" in the sense that it takes account of a state's ability to pay for health services, it does not account for need, which in the New York case is also high.

Whatever the right answer to the question of what constitutes a fair formula, the issue is increasingly less abstract. Sophisticated computer programs have now enabled every member of Congress to know quite precisely how each iterative tweaking of the aid formula will affect his or her district or state. What Stanfield calls "politics by printout" has increasingly politicized the calculation of grant formulas.[18] In contrast with previous Republican presidents and Congresses, those in control from 2001 through 2006 actually favored more easily targeted categorical grants over the party's traditionally preferred block grants. While these allocation formulas rather generally hurt New York from 2000 until 2006, the turning of the political tide toward the Democrats, coming in a period of massive deficits, has not been as helpful as many New York politicians might have hoped. It could be that the Bush years were exceptional, but the better bet is that the issue of federalism no longer inspires the kinds of partisan wrangling that marked the Nixon and Reagan eras. "National elected officials," as Paul Posner puts it,

> have converted from being ambassadors of state and local party leaders to independent political entrepreneurs. . . . These trends toward congressional and

presidential policy activism span partisan boundaries, obscuring differences on federal role questions that used to define our party system. The relatively recent shift of business groups from allies of the states to advocates of national regulation further underscored the nationalization of the policy agenda in the American system, reflecting in good measure the policy implications of a more globalized economy.[19]

Federal Mandates: Funded, Unfunded, and Underfunded

Although there is a relatively extensive grants-in-aid system that allows the federal government to funnel funds to states and localities, on occasion the federal government requires state and local action but does not provide funding. In its boldest and most objectionable form, a mandate is an act of Congress that spells out a new direction in public policy without assuming any of its costs. In effect, the federal government gives orders to the states "as if they were administrative agents of the national government, while expecting state officials and electorates to bear whatever costs ensue."[20] Tension between the federal government and the states is arguably lowest when there are few mandates and lots of federal funding. In contrast, intergovernmental relations are most strained when the opposite is true.

The Advisory Commission on Intergovernmental Regulation (ACIR) classifies mandates in four basic forms.[21] The most expensive, from a state perspective, are direct orders, such as those found in the Marine Protection Amendments of 1977, which prohibit cities from dumping sewage into the ocean. Direct orders are legal decrees that are enforced with threat of civil or criminal sanctions. Implementing this particular amendment has been very costly for New York City, because it has been forced to ship tons of waste as far away as Texas rather than simply towing it out to sea. The second type, and the most common, is that which simply withhold federal dollars absent more substantial, often narrowly defined state policies. The third type, so-called crosscutting sanctions, seldom involve criminal penalties, but they use the threat of terminating funding to one kind of program if a state does not comply with the requirements of another. Eligibility for federal highway funds, for example, depends on whether states adopt 0.08 blood alcohol content laws. Finally, partial preemptions establish minimum national standards. The No Child Left Behind Act illustrates a partial preemption because the national government requires states to meet (and generally pay for) certain national benchmarks in the area of education.

Though not included in the ACIR's definition of mandates, one of the most important types of mandate is a "pass-through" mandate whose ultimate fiscal impact is at the local rather than the state level. The first of these pass-through mandates was established under the Water Quality Act of 1965, and they have been emulated many times since. Essentially the act requires each state and many localities to develop enforcement plans that meet or exceed the minimum national standards of the law. A state that fails to develop a minimally acceptable plan forfeits its regulatory authority to the federal Environmental Protection Agency (EPA). While there is no doubt that the pass-through provisions of this act, especially those applying to waste water treatment, have imposed significant costs on local governments, compliance has been spotty, with some states enforcing compliance far more vigorously than others. The EPA itself has been slow in approving implementation rules, and many local governments have never been actually monitored. These different levels of enforcement and compliance make it virtually impossible to estimate accurately the real costs to state and local governments of unfunded mandates. "Estimating the costs to local governments of compliance with various environmental regulations— such as hazardous waste disposal and prevention of ground-water contamination—is compounded by the fact that many environmental mandates overlap."[22] Finally, the true costs of federal mandates are frequently obscured by the rather loose cost accounting systems of many municipalities.

Mandates have been imposed on the states throughout the twentieth century, with increased frequency beginning in the 1960s. It was not until the 1990s, however, that the concept became a hot-button issue in national politics. The costs of unfunded mandates were substantial. One reasonably prudent 1992 study put the total cost of compliance with such regulations at between $8.9 and $12.7 billion a year, and some politicians claim the costs were even higher.[23] Yet these costs would be higher still if the lost opportunity costs that derive from a wide variety of federal regulations, minimum standards and prohibitions, some of them as old as the Constitution, were included. For example, by prohibiting the states from levying tariffs on goods imported from overseas, the Constitution deprives a port-of-entry state such as New York of what could be a very lucrative source of revenue. Similarly, when the federal government required states to raise the drinking age to twenty-one, Congress cost New York untold dollars of lost tax revenues from the sale of alcoholic beverages (though in the long run the costs associated with alcoholism, drunk driving, and medical care might far exceed these short-term revenues).

While there had been some earlier interest in the concept of unfunded mandates among scholars and local government officials, "the number of newspaper articles discussing 'unfunded federal mandates' jumped from just 22 in 1992 to 836 in 1994."[24] As a result of increased attention, the Republican majority in Congress passed, and President Clinton signed into law, the Unfunded Mandates Reform Act (UMRA) of 1995. UMRA was the product of a campaign led largely by political conservatives who argued that unwanted federal mandates were "putting a stranglehold on state budgets."[25] UMRA was designed to sharply restrict the ability of the federal government to impose uncompensated financial burdens on state and local governments. Comprised of four titles, the act addresses proposed and existing mandates imposed on state, local, and tribal governments, as well as the private sector. In addition to requiring a set of reports that evaluate the impact of the proposed mandate, mandates also would be subject to a cost threshold of $50 million with annual adjustments for inflation. By 2006, the threshold had grown to $123 million. According to a recent report by the Congressional Budget Office, twenty-seven intergovernmental mandates were initiated between 1996 and 2005. Of the twenty-seven, twelve were enacted and fifteen failed, with five exceeding the cost threshold. During the same period, an additional eighty-one private sector mandates were initiated, of which thirty-three failed. Of the forty-eight mandates that passed or are still pending, twenty exceed the cost threshold.[26]

The growth of federal mandates can be attributed to many factors, including the role of congressional members as policy entrepreneurs, effective lobbying by public interests, the failure of states to solve multistate problems, and the general unpopularity of conditional grants-in-aid. Although it took an aggressive Republican majority in Congress in 1995 to significantly reduce the number of mandates, it appears that UMRA has been less successful in further reducing the total number of unfunded mandates. As Posner points out, "UMRA primarily covers only statutory direct orders, excluding most grant conditions and preemptions whose fiscal effects fall below the threshold. Statutory direct orders dealing with constitutional rights, prohibition of discrimination, national security, and Social Security are among those excluded from coverage."[27]

Compounding the problem—from a state perspective—was the Bush administration's very aggressive use of a doctrine known as preemption, which allows the federal government to claim that certain state laws are in violation of (or preempted by) overriding national rules. In 2006, for example, the Food and Drug Administration (FDA) added a provision to its rule on prescription drugs stating that FDA approval of a drug would henceforth preempt any state actions challenging drug safety. Even if a drug company, for example, failed to properly warn patients of potential side effects, no lawsuits against the company would be allowed. The legality of this rule—and of comparable rules issued by other agencies—is in doubt, with the courts and the Obama administration leaning increasingly the other way, but to the extent that any of these rules are sustained they would tip the scales of federalism very decisively in favor of national bureaucracies and against the states.[28] An even more extreme case concerns California and twelve other states, which have enacted laws setting higher standards for auto emissions than those required in federal law. Under the traditional interpretation of federal clean air rules, states must submit changes in their rules to the EPA to make sure that they meet *minimal* federal standards. In 2007, however, the EPA refused to consider the new state standards at all and then argued in court that because they had not been approved the new state standards were preempted by existing federal law. Despite federal district court rulings in California and Rhode Island in support of the new state standards, the issue remains in litigation. Whatever the outcome of these cases, it is clear that the Bush administration broke substantial "new ground in the nationalization and centralization of policy in areas that had heretofore largely been untouched by the instruments of coercive federalism."[29] Whether, when, and how many of these attacks on state power will be undone in the Obama years remains to be seen.

Local Governments and the State

Just as the federal government often has passed the bill for basic services to the states, so has the state of New York transferred a growing fiscal burden to its towns and cities. In 1948 journalist Warren Moscow wrote that "the state is not just a money-grubbing miser. It returns to the cities, the towns, and the villages a major portion of its revenues."[30] Zimmerman wrote in 1981 "New York devotes approximately 61 percent of its budget to aid local governments, the highest level of support among the 50 states."[31]

Today, however, New York requires its counties, cities, towns, and villages to shoulder more of the state's fiscal burden than does almost any other state. Depending on how the accounting is done (or who does it), the state could indeed be seen as Moscow's "money-grubbing miser." By no one's measure is the state's level of support among the nation's highest, as Zimmerman described it twenty-five years ago. Measuring taxes rather than expenditures, the most recent data from 2004 show that New York ranked last among the fifty states in terms of the state percentage of total state and local tax revenue. Nationally, state taxes accounted for 58 percent of all state and local tax revenue in 2004. In New York, the state government's share (45 percent) is even lower than Texas's (48 percent), and there is a comparable gap in spending.[32]

The general pattern is abundantly clear: New York, increasingly and more than almost any other state, relies on local taxes to finance the everyday operations of the government. It ranks forty-eighth among the fifty states in the proportion of state versus local funds expended on highways, fiftieth on corrections. New York, moreover, is a major user of the pass-through device, requiring local governments to administer and provide the matching funds for a variety of federal grant programs. It is one of only ten states, for example, requiring its local governments to share the costs of welfare and the only state to require a significant local share for Medicaid.

State "Mandates"

Beyond these deficiencies in state aid, local government officials in New York frequently fault what they regard as excessive efforts by the state to tell them what to do and how. Just as state and local officials complained about Washington's reliance on unfunded mandates, New York's county and municipal officials have leveled the same charge at Albany. Elected officials in New York City have been particularly critical of what they often describe as the state's tendency to micromanage the smallest details of city government.

> Legally it makes no sense to describe state laws regulating municipalities in the same terms that are used to describe federal-state relations. In legal terms, New York has a "unitary" rather than a "federated" form of government. State and federal courts have historically denied local governments any "rights" to perform functions not specifically granted to them by the state. They have adhered quite consistently to what is known as "Dillon's Rule" after an 1868 court case in Iowa by a Judge Dillon which argued that a municipal corporation possesses and can exercise the following powers, and no others: first, those granted in express words; second, those necessarily or fairly implied in or incident to the

powers expressly granted; third, those essential to the objects and purposes of the corporation—not simply convenient, but indispensable. Any fair, reasonable, substantial doubt concerning the existence of a power is resolved by the courts against a corporation, and the power is denied.[33]

While New York and the other states have granted varying levels of autonomy and home rule to local governments and agencies, they remain, following Dillon, "involuntary subdivisions of the state, constituted for the purpose of the more convenient exercise of governmental functions by the state."[34] No matter who actually puts up the money, "if a service is mandated, the funds come from the wallets of state taxpayers."[35]

Such legal niceties aside, New York is among the most controlling of state governments. One 1977 study conducted by the Legislative Commission on Expenditure Review counted 2,632 statutory mandates to counties alone. The commission identified three kinds of mandates to local governments. Type I mandates are those that simply and directly require specific activities: every community in New York State, for example, must provide a system of public schools that meets an elaborate range of requirements. Type II mandates are not legally binding, but they are so popular politically that few local officials can avoid them. As former Albany mayor Erastus Corning said of a law allowing (but not mandating) municipalities to exempt senior citizens from various property taxes, "Here the Legislature gives a municipality an opportunity to help senior citizens, so you're damned if you do and damned if you don't. It's not a mandate, but you look like a bum if you don't do it."[36] Finally, Type III mandates, in the commission's schema, are those that do not require particular services but set state standards for those that are provided. Towns and villages, for example, need not have their own police forces and may instead rely on county and state law enforcement officials, but if they do choose to have their own police officers, they must meet a long series of state standards as to training, equipment, and procedure.

As in our discussion of federal mandates, local governments in New York State have suffered as much from the *under*funding of established programs as they have from all three types of *un*funded mandates. While the state has followed the national trend of improving its public schools, it has put the fiscal burden of improved special education, computer training, higher teacher standards, and so on squarely on the shoulders of local government. The share of local school costs financed by the state fell to less than 38 percent in 2004–2005 from almost 42 percent in 2001–2002.[37] With schools accounting for nearly 40 percent of local government expenditures, the impact on some communities has been staggering. While property tax revenues increased by 50 percent between 1987 and 1992, state income tax revenues rose by only 22 percent, indicating the magnitude, in just five years, of a shift from income tax to property tax, a trend that has given New Yorkers some of the nation's highest property tax rates. When state aid declines, most local governments have no option than to either cut costs or raise real estate taxes. Under state law, "they can assess property for tax purposes on their own and set their own property tax rates, but most other policies either are strictly constrained or require explicit approval by the legislature. Counties only can impose sales taxes within limits established by the state, and cities, villages, and towns generally do not have this option."[38] In general, then, "if local communities do not want to cut their educational programs, they will have to increase local property taxes more than would otherwise be necessary."[39] A bill supported by Governor Paterson and passed by the senate in 2008 would have made even this option illegal by limiting increases in school spending to the inflation rate. It has been held up in the state assembly largely at the urging of the teachers' unions, which have argued that such a cap would forever preclude teachers' salaries from real increases in inflation-adjusted terms.

> As with many generalizations about New York government, New York City is different: The state legislature has authorized a full complement of taxes for New York City, giving it a tax structure more like that of a large urbanized state than other local governments in New York. The city has a large personal income tax with a progressive rate structure, a corporate income tax, a bank tax, and many other individual taxes. But even New York City can only do what the state legislature allows.[40]

The Tangled Web of Local Government

Cartoonist Rube Goldberg was famous for his comic depictions of elaborate machines that accomplished relatively simple tasks through incredibly bizarre mechanisms. His automatic sheet music turner, for example, began with a foot pedal that caused bellows to blow a whistle, which a goldfish was trained to regard as its dinner signal. By pulling on a worm suspended on a string in its bowl, the fish released a weight from a shelf on the wall that in turn activated a boxing glove on a spring. The glove hit an inflated punching bag into a spike, which forced the escaping air into a sail attached to the page of music needing to be turned. It would not be difficult to believe that Mr. Goldberg had something to do with creating the structure of local governments in New York. No state has a more elaborate, more expensive, or less efficient complex of local entities. Former Albany *Times-Union* columnist Dan Lynch was fond of pointing out that if you fired every single *state* employee in New York, leaving only local officials, there still would be more government employees per capita in New York than in neighboring Massachusetts.

This complex, often-redundant pattern has its roots in three strands of state history. The first strand, the "New England system, in which the town is the dominant unit of administration," was brought across Long Island Sound and over the Berkshire mountains into the early Yankee settlements on Long Island and along the Connecticut, Massachusetts, and Vermont borders.

> Its essential feature, perhaps, is its simplicity. . . . Confronted with the unknown dangers of the new land, they [the colonists] settled in enclosed areas sufficiently large to produce the food required for their sustenance and yet

compact enough to be adequately defended from hostile Indians. By the force of circumstances, the boundaries of their early communities were determined by their economic requirements.[41]

The second strand has its roots in the commercial and patroon systems of the Dutch, on the one hand, and the surprisingly compatible English county system on the other. Seen in most southern states, it is a system comprised of relatively large units of local government in which "townships exist in name only or not at all."[42] In this system, counties became the seats of the courts, law enforcement, and most government functions. Finally, local governments in New York have a western element associated with the Northwest Ordinance's creation of thousands of new settlements in the Adirondacks and Niagara Frontier. Counties in this part of the state were divided into townships of thirty-six square miles each, some of which were quickly populated and others which were not. Local government in these counties ranged from strong to nonexistent.

As if this mixed pattern of local governance were insufficiently complex, the rapid growth of New York City (and to a lesser extent Albany) led them to demand and receive special status. That special status continues to pertain in many cases only for New York City and in even more cases for what are commonly known as the "Big Five" cities of Buffalo, New York, Rochester, Syracuse, and Yonkers. In 1801, the legislature compounded the confusion still further by conferring the title of "village" on Troy and Lansingburgh, a designation that became increasingly independent of other boundaries to the extent that by 2000 there were seventy-seven "villages" located in more than one "town." A resident of the Village of Harriman thus pays local property taxes to the village, to Orange County, and to either the town of Woodbury or the town of Monroe.[43] More than 70 percent of the state's 1,548 cities, towns, and villages have fewer than 5,000 residents.

The picture becomes still more complex when we add to the mix the thousands of other government entities—school boards, water authorities, fire districts, highway and bridge authorities, park commissions, library commissions, development authorities, and so on—that sometimes overlap with other jurisdictions. Special districts for fire, sewers, streetlights, and water are commonplace in New York and often have their own taxing power. Authorities, though funded by revenue bonds rather than taxes, also play an important role in local governance. The Metropolitan Transit Authority (MTA), to use one prominent example, controls the subways, most of the bus routes, and the major commuter rail lines into and out of New York City, yet it is not a part of the city's governing structure. Like most public authorities, the MTA has its own governing board and the power to borrow on its own, is exempt from taxation and civil service rules, and is isolated, in many respects, from control by the mayor, governor, and legislature.

New York probably relies upon public authorities to provide government services more than any other state. Beyond the usual political and financial arguments for the creation of authorities rather than ordinary line agencies, in New York there are additional constitutional factors: the state constitution limits the number of state departments to 20; requires "full faith and credit" backing for state debt; and—very importantly—requires cumbersome statewide referenda for increases in state debt. The authorities escape these restrictions since they are separate, largely autonomous corporations that are not operating departments of the state.[44]

The Department of State counts 190 major public authorities with statewide significance, 68 other state authorities, 474 with local jurisdiction, and 8 with interstate or international jurisdiction—a total of 740 as of 2005.[45]

Finally, to confuse the picture still more, various state agencies and municipalities have established a variety of quasi-independent public corporations that are often granted, paradoxically, "more flexibility than the jurisdictions which establish them."[46] The research foundations of the state and city universities, for example, provide college administrators with funds for programs and supplies that are not within the bounds of their regular budget authority. Most of the state's large cities have local development corporations that can buy and sell property and broker deals between private corporations and mainstream government agencies. Many towns include special sewer, water, and other jurisdictions with the power to levy taxes or fees in exchange for a specific set of neighborhood services. All these local units, to be sure, are—following Dillon's Rule—creatures of the state and could, in theory, be abolished tomorrow. The political logic of localism, however, is as strong as its economic logic is weak. Attempts to streamline local government by eliminating small, inefficient units generally have failed. The state has for many years, for example, offered strong economic incentives for the merger of small school districts, but has found few takers. Small towns that could save money by contracting out police services from the county continue, pridefully, to provide their own police forces. Municipal consolidations are rarities, and it seems to be in the nature of New York politics to create more rather than fewer governments.

Judicial Federalism

In New York, as in all fifty states, a federal court system operates alongside and, in some senses, on top of a system of state and local courts. Although the U.S. Constitution seems clearly to define the Constitution, laws, and treaties of the United States as "the supreme law of the land," legal realities are more complex. As with issues of money and politics, federalism in the courts is a complex marble cake of conflict, accommodation, negotiation, and compromise. In both the state and federal systems there are two basic types of courts: *trial courts*, which hear the evidence in specific cases and apply the law to such matters as divorce, personal injuries, crime, and housing; and *appellate courts*, which deal with disputed interpretations of the law and get into the game only when the losing party appeals the trial court's procedures or legal rulings.

Questions of Jurisdiction

The U.S. Constitution established a Supreme Court that would function as a trial court in some extraordinary cases (such as those involving foreign diplomats) and as an appellate court with regard to virtually all other cases arising from the Constitution. The Constitution gave Congress the power and duty of defining the Court's appellate jurisdiction and of establishing any other federal courts. In the Judiciary Act of 1789, Congress refused to bestow on federal courts the entire jurisdiction to which the Constitution entitles them. At that time Congress was prepared to allow the state courts to handle a considerable part of what could have been federal court business. In particular, "federal question" suits were left to the state courts, and it was not until after the Civil War, in 1875, that the federal courts were authorized to exercise all the kinds of federal jurisdiction specified in the Constitution.[47]

Federal courts—the Supreme Court in particular—have tended generally to expand the scope of what they are likely to consider "federal questions." As early as the 1816 case of *Martin v. Hunter's Lessee*, the Supreme Court rather strongly asserted its power to review the decisions of state supreme courts. By slowly but steadily broadening its interpretation of the Constitution's commerce clause as to cover virtually any significant form of economic activity, the Supreme Court significantly expanded the legally sanctioned role of the national government and, by extension, its own jurisdictional reach. Similarly, the Supreme Court's use of the Fourteenth Amendment to apply the Bill of Rights to the states, begun during the later years of the New Deal and largely associated with the chief justiceship of Earl Warren (1953–1969), expansively interpreted federal authority with regard to racial equality, freedom of speech, and a wide range of issues involving state criminal procedures and the rights of the accused. Decisions during this period—particularly those in the area of criminal justice—expanded federal power into jurisdictional areas once patrolled almost exclusively by the states. These centralizing trends largely were preserved during the supposedly more conservative chief justiceship of Warren Burger (1969–1986). The Court began to move toward a states' rights position in the last years of William Rehnquist's 1986–2005 tenure as chief justice, with at least thirty-three federal statutes thrown out in the 1995–2005 period alone.[48] However, the court under Chief Justice John Roberts (2005–) seems guided less by a consistent theory of federalism than by the policy preferences of the individual justices. While a number of federal administrative rules—such as those approving drug and medical devices, banning the use of medical marijuana, and outlawing assisted suicide—have been held to preempt state laws, the Court also has used the doctrine of states' rights to prohibit federal regulation of the rights of state employees and business practices. As Justice Antonin Scalia, a self-described strict constructionist and supporter of states' rights, acknowledged in voting to override an Oregon law, the "legitimacy of physician-assisted suicide . . . ultimately rests . . . on a naked value judgment."[49] If there is any consistency in these decisions, it appears to be based less in an attitude toward federal and state powers than in a general tendency to oppose both federal and state regulations of business; to favor conservative preferences of both state and local acts in areas such as racial segregation, marijuana, guns, and women's rights; and to put the Supreme Court—rather than the states or Congress—in the position of drawing the boundaries between federal and state powers of regulation.

As a matter of general principle, when the issue is purely a state issue, when no important "federal question" is involved, the final say on issues of law resides in the state's highest court. Federal courts, moreover, will not normally intervene on a ruling based on state law unless it is clearly in conflict with federal law. In strictly legal terms, however, these limits on federal jurisdiction are permeable. All that the loser in a case decided by the highest state court needs in order to exercise an automatic right to appeal to the federal courts is a showing that the case involves a "federal issue." Given the scope of the Supreme Court's interpretations of the commerce power and the Fourteenth Amendment, the potential scope of this right is enormous. In practice, the range of issues the federal courts will treat as involving "federal questions," is not nearly so extensive. As Pritchett puts it:

> Federal legislation provides a right of appeal to the Supreme Court from any decision of a state court of last resort declaring a federal law or treaty unconstitutional, and also from any state court decision upholding a state law or constitutional provision against a substantial challenge that it conflicts with a federal law, treaty, or constitutional provision. While in theory the Supreme Court must accept such appeals, in practice most of them are rejected for "for want of a substantial federal question" or on other jurisdictional grounds.[50]

In interpreting state law, the federal courts are required to treat the rulings of the states' highest courts as definitive. They will not generally intervene in the absence of a clear and unambiguous conflict with federal law, though there are cases—as with the Oregon assisted suicide ruling—in which a more activist federal court may overrule state actions. State courts, in theory at least, have no discretion: they "must not only give precedence to federal law over state law but also interpret that law in line with rulings of the U.S. Supreme Court."[51] Despite the presumed supremacy of federal law, noncompliance does occur. There is sufficient leeway in the interpretation of federal court rulings that it would be erroneous to "conclude simply that the Supreme Court is the commanding officer and that a major state's highest tribunal is a usually obedient but occasionally recalcitrant private."[52] As with most questions regarding the relations between the federal government and the states, in other words, judicial federalism is less a matter of doctrine than of evolving practice.

Federal Courts in New York State

In large part because of New York City's role as a center of business and finance, New York State generates a disproportionate share of business for the federal courts. Only Washington, DC, has a higher ratio of lawyers per capita than New York. At the appellate level, the country is divided into twelve regions called circuits. New York, Connecticut, and Vermont make up the Second Circuit, which generally is one of the nation's busiest. There are four federal trial courts in New York State: the Northern District, with chambers in Albany, Binghamton, Syracuse, and Utica; the Southern District at Foley Square in lower Manhattan; the Eastern District in Brooklyn; and the Western District, which divides its sessions between Buffalo and Rochester.

The judges on these courts are appointed for life by the president of the United States with the advice and consent of the U.S. Senate. Through a long-standing tradition known as senatorial courtesy, the reality is that the president cannot appoint anyone to a district court who is unacceptable to the majority party's senior senator from the state or circuit in question. What this means in practice is that the real power of appointment is shared when senators and presidents are of the same party, but highly political when there is divided control or in the case of appointments to the appellate bench.

In addition to district and appellate courts, national legislation has created a rich variety of specialized courts and administrative agencies that function in some ways as if they were courts. U.S. magistrates relieve the burdens of federal district courts by dealing with the less serious cases. Bankruptcy courts are the courts of original jurisdiction in most bankruptcy cases, and immigration and tariff courts do pretty much what their names imply. Increasingly, the national government has worked to relieve the growing caseload burden of the federal courts by delegating both rule-making and adjudicating powers to various administrative agencies, with the result that so-called administrative law is one of the fastest-growing areas of conflict resolution at both the state and national levels. Although this trend has undoubtedly freed the courts from having to consider a large number of relatively arcane and technical issues that many judges are ill prepared to consider, the growing link of administration and adjudication has, as Jacob argues, troubled many observers. Because administrative agencies are at least one step removed from the political constraints inherent in popular democracy, their power holds frightening potential. Agencies' quasi-judicial functions give them additional powers that courts may be unable to control because of the volume of cases that flows through administrative channels. Unlike courts, administrative agencies are able to follow through on their adjudicatory decisions by implementing them without reference to another agency. Thus, executive branch administrative agencies have powers that neither a legislature nor a court can match. Those powers have the potential of transforming the legal system from a court-centered process to one that is administration-centered.[53]

The use of such administrative courts, at the same time, serves substantially to reduce the caseload of the federal trial courts, in itself a goal usually applauded. Increasing the number of federal judges, it has been suggested, is much like increasing and improving most highways:

They solve short-term problems, but over the long run they cause more conges-
tion. From a numerical and organizational perspective, the federal judiciary is
becoming more bureaucratic and much more complicated. As judge and staff
resources have increased over time, there has been an equal—if not greater—
growth in the administrative work imposed on the courts. And, ominously, the
pending backlogs of criminal cases and appeals have actually increased.[54]

Despite the rhetoric of decentralization currently in vogue, Congress seems rather
more than less inclined to nationalize criminal justice issues. Each of its recent attempts to get tough on crime by making various terrorist, drug-related, and violent
acts into federal offenses adds to the burden of federal trial courts.

This nationalization of the criminal justice process has enormously complicated
the prosecutory process. Let us take the hypothetical case of a citizen of the Bronx
who, unhappy with something he receives in the mail, shoots the postal service
worker who delivers it. Today, and throughout the history of the United States, a
murder of this kind would be treated as a crime against the people of New York
State. Following arrest, the perpetrator would be charged by a prosecuting attorney
from the office of the Bronx district attorney (DA) and taken before a Bronx County
judge for arraignment. Historically, the case would have proceeded from that point
through the state court system where—unless some extraordinary procedural question arose—it would have been resolved. Since the 1980s, however, it has been a
federal crime to murder a working government employee. Our enraged citizen, in
other words, could now be prosecuted twice: once in New York for the crime of
murder, again in federal court for the national crime of killing a civil servant in the
performance of her job. Since they are separate crimes, the rule of double jeopardy
does not apply. In practice, the Bronx DA almost certainly would consult with her
federal counterpart at the outset, and a decision would be negotiated as to which
track—state, national, or both—to follow. The nation's long tradition of deferring
to the states in the arena of criminal justice continues to prevail in most cases of
this kind, but there is no question that the tilt in recent years is in a national direction, particularly in areas tinged with so-called terrorism, where headline-seeking
federal prosecutors increasingly take cases out of the state system.

The State Court System

Despite the political imperatives that have led Congress and the president increasingly to nationalize the issue of crime, and in the face of the federal court's expansive
definitions of the commerce clause and Fourteenth Amendment, an overwhelming
proportion of legal issues, more than 99 percent by one count, continue to be resolved at the state level. Stumpf and Culver's 1992 estimate that New York's total
case filings alone exceeded those of all federal courts combined by a ratio of more
than ten to one is probably still on the mark.[55] The state court system, consequently,
is considerably larger and more complex than its federal counterpart, though its
basic structure is similar (Table 2.1).

Table 2.1

New York State's Court System

Court	Number of judges	How judges are selected	Term
Court of Appeals	7	Appointed by governor, with state senate consent	14 years
Appellate Division	Varies	Designated by governor from elected state supreme court justices	Varies
Supreme Court	327[a]	Elected	14 years
Court of Claims	32	Appointed by governor, with state senate consent	9 years
Surrogate's Court	33	Elected	14 years in New York City; 10 years in rest of state
County Court	119	Elected	10 years
Family Court	116	Appointed by mayor in New York City; elected in rest of state	10 years
Civil Court of New York City	120	Elected	10 years
Criminal Court of New York City	107	Appointed by mayor	10 years
District Court	49	Elected	6 years
City Court	167	Most elected; some appointed	Varies by city
Town Court	2,000 (approx.)	Elected	4 years
Village Court	570 (approx.)	Elected	Varies

Source: Adapted from New York Department of State, *Local Government Handbook*, 5th ed. (Albany: New York State, Department of State, 2000), Chapter 4, p. 3.

[a] Includes fifty-one certificated justices who have reached the mandatory retirement age of seventy.

At the apex of the system is the New York State Court of Appeals (New York and Maryland are the only states that do not call their highest courts "supreme courts"). The court of appeals, whose seven members are appointed to fourteen-year terms by the governor with the advice and consent of the state senate, is

New York's court of last resort; it handles cases only on appeal. Most of its cases come from one of the four appellate divisions of the state supreme court. These appellate courts consist of two seven-member courts located in Manhattan and Brooklyn, and two five-member courts in Albany and Rochester, supplemented by supreme court justices serving on temporary assignment. Like all appellate courts, these courts do not have juries, do not deal with the facts of the cases brought before them, and serve almost entirely to correct errors of legal procedure and interpretation brought to them on appeal from courts of original jurisdiction.

What New York calls its "supreme court" is its trial court of general jurisdiction. It is composed of 327 justices elected from twelve judicial districts, ranging in number from fifty-two (in the district covering Brooklyn and Staten Island) to ten in the Binghamton area. While these courts technically are empowered to handle most significant criminal and civil cases in their jurisdictions, they are, in practice, civil courts, largely handling disputes between private parties. Most important criminal cases (again, outside of New York City) are handled by the county courts. The city elects its civil court justices and has its criminal court judges appointed by the mayor, but when the criminal caseloads are high, civil court justices often are appointed (by the court administrator) to serve as "acting" criminal court judges. Upstate the system becomes more complex, with different parts of the state organized in different ways. In small towns and villages there are more than 2,000 town and village justices—who, in many New York jurisdictions, do not have backgrounds in the law—that handle most misdemeanor offenses, drunk driving cases, family disputes, traffic violations, and so on (see Box 2.1). The business of these "cafeteria courts," as they sometimes are called, "is to process large numbers of cases quickly and with an element of bureaucratic efficiency. . . . much of the work occurs in private—meetings between opposing counsel, conferences with the judges in chambers, and so on."[56] In New York City and many other large urban areas, these duties are usually parceled out among various specialized courts for traffic and parking violations, family disputes, probate, housing, and so on.

Despite the apparent complexity of New York's judicial system, its essential features are those characteristic of state judicial structures throughout the United States. Hurst's classic study of American legal history presents the features of the state judiciary. First is localism: virtually every community, almost on a neighborhood basis, has some sort of judicial presence, usually in the form of a justice of the peace or local magistrate. These are supplemented by trial courts, both criminal and civil, within a day's ride (usually at the county seat). Second, the state systems all tend to have both hierarchical and specialized components in which some courts are better staffed and deal with more significant cases than others, and in which there are rather clear jurisdictional distinctions between courts dealing with civil or criminal matters and, within these categories, legal specializations such as family law, small claims, and traffic. Third, there is a fairly clear judicial pecking order in which trial courts are considered "inferior" both in staffing and role to the "higher" courts of appeal. Fourth, and more than in any other nation, there is a proliferation

Box 2.1
New York's Justice Courts

"I just follow my own common sense, and the hell with the law," said one of New York's more than 2,000 town justices in describing how he decides cases.[1] New York is one of thirty states that continue to rely on independent, local tribunals to handle many aspects of its legal workload. The state's 1,277 justice courts operate in most of the state's small towns and even in suburban localities with over 100,000 residents. They collectively handle more than 2 million cases a year, nearly half the total caseload of the state system.

Seventy-two percent of the state's town justices have no legal education beyond six days of training and an annual refresher course. The test for qualification is reportedly so easy that only one applicant has failed since 1999,[2] and town justices are exempt from the rule requiring mandatory retirement at age seventy that applies to other state judges. While most of the cases adjudicated in these courts involve relatively trivial misdemeanors and traffic violations, the justices have the power to arraign all crimes committed in their localities and to determine civil cases involving less than $3,000. State law makes these courts creatures of their towns and villages, giving them "wide latitude to promulgate and implement their own policies in nearly every area of court operations, thus often frustrating the standardization, supervision and enforcement of statewide politics that the Constitution authorizes the State Judiciary to establish for the courts."[3]

In a series of articles on these courts in 2006, the New York Times "found overwhelming evidence that decade after decade and up to this day, people often have been denied fundamental legal rights. Defendants have been jailed illegally. Others have been subjected to racial and sexual bigotry so explicit it seems to come from some other place and time. People have been denied the right to a trial, an impartial judge and the presumption of innocence."[4] At the same time, many supporters of the system, particularly in rural areas, staunchly defend the flexibility, sensitivity to local mores, and personalized approaches to cases that the town justice system encourages. Their deep roots in the Anglo-American common law tradition, moreover, have stood the test of time.

A 2006 report on the system, prepared under the direction of Chief Judge Judith Kaye and Jonathan Lippman, chief administrator of the unified court system, called for a number of administrative and procedural reforms, but—not surprisingly—stopped far short of a major restructuring. Whatever their flaws, the state's justice courts are as strong politically as they are weak on formal legal training.

1. As quoted in Walter Glaberson, "In Tiny Courts of N.Y.: Abuses of Law and Power," *New York Times*, September 25, 2006.
2. Ibid., September 26, 2006.
3. Judith S. Kaye and Jonathan Lippman, *Action Plan for the Justice System* (Albany: Office of Court Administration, 2006), p. 8.
4. *New York Times*, September 27, 2006.

of the right to appeal. To this list, Stumpf adds, that there is a surprising resistance to change. As in most states, the basic structure of the judicial system in New York is pretty much what it was in colonial times, helping to produce a "paradox of unity and diversity": a system that despite its extraordinarily decentralized organization provides remarkably uniform outcomes.[57]

This uniformity of outcomes is attributable in part to the looming appellate jurisdiction of the higher courts. Even more important, however, is the Anglo-American common law tradition that makes precedent, *stare decisis*, the controlling paradigm of legal practice. Legal research in the United States is deeply steeped in a tradition of finding comparable cases. A ruling in the First District becomes a key point in the brief submitted by lawyers arguing a comparable case in the Eighth District. Rulings at the appellate level are more compelling, and rulings of federal courts still more so. Although there is no legal requirement that they do so, "the basic character of the American legal system encourages state supreme courts to consult and borrow from the decisions of sister courts."[58] Judges, defense attorneys, and prosecutors share an aversion to the time and expense of appeal; if the precedent is clear, so be it. On important issues of both substance and procedure, the congruence of laws between and among the several states is one of the system's most striking features. For example, a lawyer trained in California is not likely to find it particularly difficult to pass the bar exam in New York.

At the same time, there are few policy arenas in which federalism and local customs count for more than in the courts. There are whole categories of important cases that almost never move beyond the state level and in which the guiding principles of justice are set almost entirely by judicial precedent rather than statutory law. State courts, in effect, are the policy-making institutions in important areas such as divorce and child support, personal injury and medical malpractice, business contracts, real estate, and liability. Local courts, though theoretically constrained by precedent and the threat of appeal, are practically sovereign within their spheres. "The local judge who invariably sends drunken drivers to jail, the judge in the next county who throws the book only at youthful drug offenders, and the judge who sits in the courthouse making life miserable for errant spouses who have fallen behind in their child support and alimony payments—all are making policy."[59]

Other Intergovernmental Relations

Just as the courts frequently look to one another in deciding cases, governors, legislators, lobbyists, and bureaucrats pay considerable attention to what is happening in other states and localities. Organizations such as the National Conference of State Legislators and comparable convocations of governors, mayors, and attorneys general provide formal mechanisms of communication. More importantly, issue-specific groups—from welfare rights advocates to stockbrokers—frequently bring together lobbyists, legislators, and civil servants working in different states on the same issues. These issue networks, as they sometimes are called, are an important source of policy initiatives. Beyond the informal borrowing of ideas that constantly takes place at these and other forums, New York's governing bodies are involved in an enormous web of interstate and international institutions, arrangements, and formal agreements.

Most of the state's formal interstate relations involve agreements with the immediately adjoining states of Vermont, Massachusetts, Connecticut, New Jersey, Pennsylvania, and Ohio. In one way or another, however, New York has links with every state in the union. An alliance of states interested in protecting ocean resources, for example, connects New York with states as far away as Alaska and Hawaii. The Interstate Compact on the Placement of Children in Interstate Adoption includes forty-nine states and two territories; a the state has entered into numerous agreements with the adjoining Canadian provinces of Ontario and Quebec ranging from highly specific arrangements for the joint maintenance of bridges over the St. Lawrence River to complicated compacts governing the state's purchase of hydroelectric power generated in Canada.

The constitution of the United States contains three types of provisions on interstate relations. The first provides mechanisms for settling disputes between states and for establishing joint programs. The second governs the rights of citizens caught in conflicts of jurisdiction between differing state laws. The third gives the U.S. Supreme Court original or trial jurisdiction in cases involving suits between states. This last provision has been rather sparingly used in recent years as most states have been able to work out their disputes without resorting to the courts. Beginning with *New York v. Connecticut*[60] in 1789, it was rather frequently used in settling boundary disputes in the early years of the nation. Most recently, the handful of state v. state cases coming before the court have revolved largely around issues of water rights. Even in this sensitive area, however, it is the exceptional case that actually goes to court. Typically, New York State has resolved a number of water issues with neighboring states through the device of interstate compacts such as the Champlain Basin Compact (1966) with Vermont, the Great Lakes Compact (1960) with the eight states bordering the lakes, and the Delaware River Basin Compact (1961) with New Jersey, Pennsylvania, and Delaware.

Interstate Compacts

The Delaware River Compact is interesting because it was initiated by Congress, making the federal government a partner with four states to solve the problems of the river basin. In years with little rainfall, what New York's state and local governments do with the Delaware River—both in terms of extracting its water and using it to dump sewage—has a dramatic impact on downriver communities in Pennsylvania, New Jersey, and Delaware. Sporadic attempts by the states to negotiate water use agreements were largely unsuccessful until the federal government forced the four states to work together in 1961. The Delaware River Basin Commission, created at that time, is comprised of members from the national government and each of

---

Box 2.2
Interstate Compacts and State Law

In order to form an interstate authority, states must agree on a compact and have it approved by Congress. Getting out of a compact can be more difficult.

In 1940, New York and seven other states entered into a compact to control pollution in the Ohio River. To develop and enforce regulations regarding sewage, they created the Ohio River Valley Water Sanitation Commission, consisting of three at-large members and three members from each state. In 1949, West Virginia—one of the eight states represented on the commission—got into a fight with the commission over a ban on certain kinds of pollution and refused to pay its dues. The supreme court of West Virginia upheld the state's position, arguing that the 1940 compact could not supersede subsequent state laws. The case was appealed by the other seven states to the U.S. Supreme Court, where West Virginia lost. A compact, Justice Felix Frankfurter wrote for the majority, is after all a legal document. . . . It requires no elaborate argument to reject the suggestion that an agreement solemnly entered into between States . . . can be unilaterally nullified, or given final meaning by an organ of one of the contracting States. A state cannot be its own ultimate judge in a controversy with a sister state.

"That a legislature may delegate to an administrative body the power to make rules and decide particular cases is one of the axioms of modern government. The West Virginia court does not challenge the general proposition but objects to the delegation here involved because it is to a body outside the State and because its legislature may not be free, at any time, to withdraw the power delegated. . . . We find nothing in that to indicate that West Virginia may not solve a problem such as the control of river pollution by compact and by the delegation, if such be necessary, to effectuate such a solution by compact. . . . The Compact involves a reasonable and carefully limited delegation of power to an administrative agency."

West Virginia, in the Court's view, could not unilaterally withdraw from the compact once it was in force. This remains the prevailing law.

Source: State ex rel. Dyer v. Sims, 341 U.S. 22 (1951), 27B28.

---

the states adjoining the Delaware River. The commission has the power to regulate the river's flow by setting limits on how much water communities in each state can use and how. Similar federal-state compacts involve New York in the Appalachian Regional and Susquehanna River Basin Commissions.

The large role played by the federal government in establishing the Delaware River Commission is somewhat exceptional but, at the same time, illustrative of the enormous political barriers that commonly prevent the more widespread use of interstate compacts. The classic interstate compact is one initiated and administered entirely by agreement between the affected states. Compacts of this kind typically require tentative agreement between the cooperating states, enactment into law by each of the participants, and the formal approval of Congress. The key political actors are the states in question, and it has generally been their inability to reach agreement that has frustrated the widespread use of such compacts, particularly in recent years. One of the earliest and still most significant of these compacts is the 1921 agreement that created the Port Authority of New York and New Jersey. The Port Authority is an enormously wealthy and powerful institution, controlling more resources than many states.

What the Port Authority has been able to do, and what the states probably could not do on their own, is to coordinate a number of transportation alternatives to the benefit of the region as a whole. In overseeing the major airports—Kennedy, Newark, and LaGuardia—it has produced a reasonably equitable balance of economic benefits and air transit efficiencies that interstate rivalries never would have achieved. Critics argue that the Port Authority favors New Jersey, developing the area's maritime freight facilities at the expense of New York harbor. Like most independent authorities funded through bonds, the Port Authority of New York and New Jersey has not been a model of fiscal restraint. Completion of the World Trade Center in 1972 created a glut in the Manhattan real estate market that set the private sector back by a decade and significantly decreased the city's tax base. Because the Port Authority operates independently of the state, sewage from the World Trade Center, unlike that of any other building in lower Manhattan, flowed unfiltered into the Hudson River. The complicated web of deciding which units of government have responsibility for what aspects of the project continues to thwart progress on rebuilding the site of the twin towers destroyed in 2001. Having essentially paid off the bondholders who financed construction of the Hudson River crossings, such as the George Washington Bridge and Lincoln Tunnel, the Port Authority has become a cash cow whose revenues both New York and New Jersey covet. Even its sharpest critics concede, however, that the Port Authority has produced a level of substantial regional development that probably could not have been attained without a formal agreement.[61]

Despite the relative success of agencies such as the Port Authority and the Delaware River Commission, almost no significant interstate authorities have been created in the past three decades; the rush to sign such agreements appears to have peaked in the 1950s and 1960s. There are, to be sure, many less formal agreements between states, and numerous compacts that do not involve the kinds of separate governing bodies that the more prominent agreements involve. Numerous interstate compacts such as the 1965 Driver's License Compact, the 1960 Placement of Children Compact, and the 1977 Parole and Probation Compact, rather quietly operating at the agency-to-agency level, do much to facilitate relations between the states.

Full Faith and Credit

Many of the less visible interstate compacts, such as those governing driver's licenses, are designed to deal with problems that arise when different states have different laws. Rather than invade the prerogatives of the states by developing a national legal system, Article IV, Section 1, of the U.S. Constitution attempts to balance diversity with sufficient uniformity to facilitate commerce and exchange between the states. It establishes the principle of reciprocal recognition by stipulating that "full faith and credit shall be given in each state to the public acts, records, and judicial proceedings of every other state." A contract signed in Massachusetts, in other words, or a driver's license issued in New Jersey should be valid in New York. The "full faith and credit" section of the Constitution left it to Congress to "prescribe the manner in which such acts . . . shall be proved," but Congress has left the actual process pretty much up to the states and the courts.

An exception to the general unwillingness of Congress to involve itself in defining the full meaning of the full faith and credit clause occurred in 1996. When a gay couple in Honolulu brought suit against the government of Hawaii charging that its ban on same-sex marriages was illegal, Congress, alarmed by the possibility that the Hawaiian courts might sanction gay marriage, passed the Defense of Marriage Act, officially recognizing marriage between only a man and a woman. New Jersey, Connecticut, and Vermont recognize civil unions, while Hawaii, Maine, and Washington, DC, offer a range of spousal benefits. These laws raise few problems for other states, since such state benefits as disability insurance are not transportable. Yet since Massachusetts and California have allowed gays legally to marry, the question arises whether marriages performed in these states are valid in states such as New York. Governor Paterson's answer in 2008 was that the full faith and credit clause was binding, and although he refused to call for a law allowing gay marriages in New York, he called upon all state agencies to recognize the marital status of gays legally married in other states. In New York and elsewhere, there will be years of political accommodations and litigation before these issues are resolved.

Article IV of the Constitution also guarantees citizens the "privileges and immunities" granted by other states. A person living in New York, in other words, is as entitled to own property or do business in Vermont as is a native Vermonter. There are significant limitations on this right: a member of the New Jersey bar cannot practice law in New York without passing the New York bar exam, and it is perfectly legal for the City and State Universities of New York to charge higher tuition rates to students who are not legal residents.

Finally, the states also are expected to cooperate in enforcing one another's laws. Through a procedure known as extradition, the authorities in one state can ask another state to return a suspected felon for trial. Although such requests generally are honored, New York sometimes refused to return black defendants to southern states in the 1940s and 1950s when a segregationist system of justice made it unlikely that they would receive a fair trial. More recently, in 1994, Governor Mario Cuomo refused to extradite to Oklahoma a man who had been accused of murder there, but was already serving a life term for murder in New York. New York at that time, unlike Oklahoma, did not have capital punishment, to which Cuomo was philosophically opposed. One of George Pataki's first acts as governor in 1995 was to extradite the man in question to Oklahoma, where he was subsequently tried, convicted, and executed.

The Constitution, through the full faith and credit, extradition, and privileges and immunities clauses, imposes some loose degree of reciprocity and uniformity in state law. The realities of commerce and today's mobile lifestyle make such cooperation even more cogent; and the law has in many ways been nationalized. Since 1897, when West Publishing Company began indexing and compiling the decisions of state courts, legal precedents have flowed with growing frequency across state lines. Computerization has accelerated this flow, and federal statutes and court decisions have brought further uniformities to the judicial process. Yet, "the struggle between uniformity and diversity, between centralism and localism, goes on without let and without end. . . . The basic issue is power: where it is placed, and who should exercise it. The structural features of the legal system reflect the distribution of power, and, at the same time, influence or perpetuate power. . . . In short, decentralization does not vanish, even in the teeth of the master trend of American legal history."[62]

The Politics of Federalism

Former Speaker of the U.S. House of Representatives Thomas P. "Tip" O'Neill once said that "all politics is local," a phrase that has become an aphorism of American politics. What is equally true, though less frequently acknowledged, is that "all local is politics." It is not the Tenth Amendment, nor tradition nor philosophy, that sustains decentralization in American law and government so much as it is the localized nature of politics in the United States. Even the Supreme Court has acknowledged that, "State sovereign interests are more properly protected by procedural safeguards inherent in the structure of the federal system than by judicially created limitations on federal power."[63]

Professor Grodzins, in his essay developing the marble-cake image of federalism, argued that "the parties are responsible for both the existence and form of the considerable measure of decentralization that exists in the United States."[64] Whether parties continue to play as vital a role in sustaining federalism as they did three decades ago is not clear. What remains clear, however, is the local focus of so much of the dynamic of American politics.

3

Parties, Politics, and Elections

The total number of bills defeated on the floor of the New York State senate and assembly in 2007 and 2008 was zero. That's right: every bill and resolution that came to a vote in both houses—and the total was in the thousands—passed. This remarkable record of seeming consensus was not achieved because legislators agreed with one another on the issues. On the contrary, the 2007–2008 session was highly contentious. Rather, bills are not defeated in the New York legislature because, like the tightly disciplined "responsible parties" of Great Britain and many parliamentary democracies, the leaders of the majority parties have almost absolute control over the legislative process. Most of what happens on the floor of the assembly and senate in New York has been carefully orchestrated in the secret meetings of the party conferences.

As highly centralized as the political parties appear to be in the legislature, New York's parties are not truly analogous to those of Great Britain and fall far short of reform views of the kinds of "responsible" parties that can deliver what they promise. Horizontally, running across the three statewide elective branches, there is virtually no connection between the party systems that control, respectively, the two houses of the legislature and the offices of the governor, attorney general, and comptroller. As strong as assembly Democrats are in their chamber or senate Republicans in theirs, they have virtually no influence (or desire to be involved) in the politics of each other's elections or of gubernatorial races. Candidates for governor, attorney general, and comptroller seldom coordinate their campaigns with each other or with fellow party members in the legislature. Vertically, there is comparable fragmentation, with individual legislative campaigns revolving around local issues and personalities rather than the nuances of Albany politics. The six central campaign committees—the Republican and Democratic State Committees, the Democratic Assembly Campaign Committee, the Republican Assembly Campaign Committee, and their senate counterparts—play a steadily growing role in both bankrolling and managing key campaigns. Although they have become increasingly active in recruiting candidates and bankrolling their campaigns, the politics of primary elections is still largely local. Nominations are won and lost less by permanent organizations of the faithful than by what students of campaigns call candidate-centered coalitions, which—in a uniquely New York twist—frequently involve third parties.

The State Parties

The two major parties in New York—the Republicans and the Democrats—have essentially monopolized the state's key political offices, but minor parties play a much more important role in New York than in perhaps any other state. The Republican and Democratic parties in New York are allied in a loose sense with their counterparts in the other forty-nine states and with the national parties in Washington. Voters have been known to penalize and reward New York politicians on the basis of national policies over which they have relatively little control. Aside from national party rules governing presidential nominations, voting rights laws, and some rules regarding the conduct of elections, the rules of the game for elections in New York are set through state laws and state party rules. State laws give the parties a sort of quasi-legal status in which they remain private, self-funded organizations that must nonetheless follow a variety of specific government rules of organization and conduct. Officially, the election code defines a political party as an organization that polled more than 50,000 votes for its candidate for governor in the last election. The parties are then officially ranked, with the two whose gubernatorial candidates polled the most votes defined as the major parties, and the parties are listed on the ballot in subsequent state and local elections according to how well they ran in that campaign. Thus, based on the party votes for governor in 2006, Democratic candidates running for office throughout the state from 2007 through 2010 appear in column A of the ballot, Republicans in column B, Independents in C, Conservatives in D, and Working Families in E. These are the state's five official parties.

Two Parties, Plus

Perhaps the most important quirk in New York election laws is that which allows parties to "cross-endorse" candidates. In contrast with all but eight other states, New York law allows a party to nominate candidates already endorsed by other parties. In the 1994 gubernatorial election, for example, the Republican candidate, George Pataki, actually "lost" to Democrat Mario Cuomo by a vote of 2,156,057 to 2,272,903. Pataki, however, won an additional 328,605 votes on the Conservative Party line and 54,040 on a "Tax Cut Now" line, while Cuomo was able to win only 92,001 on the Liberal Party line.[1] In a very real sense, the Conservative Party could (and did) claim to have made the difference in getting Pataki elected.

Candidates frequently use the gimmick employed by Pataki in 1994 of creating a unique, cutely named party like Tax Cut Now to broaden their appeal. While it requires effort to get such parties on the ballot, some campaign strategists believe that voters are more comfortable crossing over from their normal vote to something more neutral than their usual party's main rival. Democrats who were disillusioned with Cuomo, for example, might have been reluctant to vote Republican or Conservative, but they could vote for Pataki on the Tax Cut Now line. Such parties appear and disappear regularly in New York. Their names, such as Taxpayers, Protect Seniors, or Save Medicare, may or may not have something to do with what they really stand for. Other small factions turn out year after year to secure the petition signatures necessary to put their candidates on the ballot. Like the third parties in most other states, such unofficial parties (unofficial in the sense that they have not reached the magic threshold of 50,000 gubernatorial votes in the previous election, as specified in the election code) as the Socialist Workers, Libertarians, and Prohibitionists seldom cross-endorse and, even less frequently, win. Two other small parties—the Right to Life Party and the Greens—lost their status as official parties when they failed to win the threshold 50,000 votes in 2006, but they retain solid cores of activists.

The most important and distinctive third parties in New York are those that have achieved more or less permanent ballot status, statewide organizations, and sufficient records of success to make them serious players in the eyes of the major party candidates. The parties that have enjoyed the official recognition that automatically qualifies them for places on the ballot are a varied and changing group. Two of these—the Conservative Party on the right and the Working Families Party on the left—style themselves as the "consciences" of the Republican and Democratic parties. Alex Rose, the longtime chair of the labor-backed Liberal Party, once described its task as "keeping Democrats liberal and Republicans honest."[2] Because the party, even though relatively small, could sometimes tilt the election to its candidate of choice (particularly in the city), it could reward its active members with commissionerships, judgeships, and all kinds of lesser offices. Former mayor Robert Wagner once implied that the Liberals held as many as "five hundred important positions" in his administration.[3] The Liberal Party reached the height of its influence in 1969 when John Lindsay was defeated in the Republican Party but nonetheless elected mayor of New York City on the Liberal line; it also played a key role in the election of Rudy Giuliani in 1993. As the Liberal Party became dependent on patronage, however, it shifted from backing the most liberal candidate to backing the one most likely to win. (The running joke was that it had become neither liberal nor a party.) By 2002 its ideological role was taken over by the Working Families Party, and, having backed too many losers to keep its job seekers happy, the Liberal Party has all but disappeared from the scene.

The Conservative Party, essentially a mirror of the Liberals, was established in 1962 by disgruntled Republicans who felt that the Rockefeller-led Republican Party had strayed too far to the center. In addition to the patronage and power the party gained by tipping the election to Pataki in 1994, the Conservatives are frequently able to tip the balance in elections upstate. The Independence Party is an offshoot of Ross Perot's national challenge to the major parties in 1996, when he won nearly 8 percent of the vote; its line was eagerly sought by a number of candidates for Congress and the state legislature. Although it is by far the largest third party in the state, with more than 340,000 enrolled voters (compared with 149,000 for the Conservatives and 36,000 for Working Families), its focus has never been clear. Many of those who registered to vote as Independents did so thinking they were proclaiming their independence of any party, and what little formal organization there is has been involved in a series of complicated power struggles.

Organizationally the minor parties are hollow shells whose executive committees, as one assembly member wryly puts it, "meet in a phone booth." Their power lies in their continuing ability to use the weapon of cross-endorsements to work with and against the candidates of the major parties. A few cases illustrate the leverage these minor parties can exercise:

- In 1980, a relatively obscure Nassau County Republican, Alfonse D'Amato, calculated "that he could win the Republican primary against Senator Jacob Javits, who was, as D'Amato's ads bluntly pointed out, seventy-six-years old, 'ailing and liberal.'"[4] The second and more difficult part of D'Amato's scenario—beating Democrat Elizabeth Holtzman in the November general election—became plausible when the Liberal Party backed Javits, who, having lost the Republican primary, stayed in the race on the Liberal line. Result: D'Amato—45 percent, Holtzman—44 percent, Javits—11 percent. Neither Holtzman nor her strongest backers ever forgave Javits or the Liberals for "giving" the election to D'Amato.
- In 1989, the Liberal Party was so disillusioned with New York City mayor Ed Koch that the party leader, Raymond Harding, began to court Republican Rudy Giuliani. Giuliani, in turn, began to fudge some of his more conservative positions, such as his previous opposition to abortion. Koch, meanwhile, lost the Democratic primary to David Dinkins, but Harding stuck with Giuliani, who lost. Four years later, however, the Liberals and Republicans stuck by their deal and Giuliani became the city's first Republican mayor in more than thirty years. (It is worth noting that the city's previous Republican mayor, John Lindsay, actually lost the Republican primary in running for his second term and won reelection running as a Liberal.)
- In 1990, no prominent Republican could be found to run against Democratic governor Mario Cuomo. The most enthusiastic candidate, New York University dean Herbert London, was far too conservative for most Republicans, who settled on the lackluster Pierre Rinfret as their candidate. The Conservatives nominated London, who was as articulate as Rinfret was inept. Cuomo won handily, and the Republicans came close to losing their status as a major party, with Rinfret getting only 22 percent of the vote to London's 21. Four years later, Republican leaders carefully consulted with the Conservatives before both agreeing to run George Pataki against a far less popular Cuomo. Pataki won.

Each of these cases illustrates the different ways in which the minor parties have been able to magnify their electoral impact by cross-endorsement strategies. One study, using data from all state senate races from 1950 to 1988, found that New York's third parties were a significant force in only about 3 percent of the elections,[5] but the above case studies show why they remain an important factor in the strategic calculations of candidates and party leaders. They derive disproportionate influence in no small part from the widespread perception that some third-party cross-endorsements are at least superficially decisive in electoral outcomes. Whether Giuliani could have beaten Dinkins for mayor of New York City in 1993 in a straight two-party contest we will never know, but the numbers clearly suggest that Giuliani won because of the votes he gained on the Liberal line. The widespread perception that such third-party votes are important sustains the minor parties in two ways. First, it leads major party candidates, particularly those in close races, actively to court cross-endorsements. In state assembly and senate campaigns in 2004, 72 percent of the Democratic candidates and 74 percent of the Republicans also ran on the Conservative, Independence, or Working Families lines. Second, third parties, as we have seen, frequently reap the rewards of patronage, thus giving some of their members a personal incentive to remain active. Liberal stalwarts long held numerous jobs in the city administrations of mayors Wagner, Lindsay, and Giuliani, and state Conservatives did quite well in securing patronage positions from Governor Pataki. These jobs, in fact, have been as important in sustaining the Liberals and Conservatives as were the ideologies reflected in their labels. "By 1980," as Scarrow puts it, "only Right to Life activists were known for their greater concern" for ideology as opposed to patronage jobs.[6] The Independence and Working Families parties seem less powertropic, but it is worth noting that seven of every ten third-party endorsements in 2006 went to incumbents. Table 3.1 (using data from 2002) shows that all six of New York's most important minor parties have cross-endorsed both Republicans and Democrats, with the Liberal and Working Families parties working most often with Democrats; the Conservative Party with Republicans; the Independence Party less reliably Republican; and the Green and Right to Life parties more independent. Only the Right to Life and Green parties have made a regular practice of supporting candidates with no major party backing, a strong indicator of their ideological orientation.

Patterns of Party Competition

Although third parties are more important in New York than in most other states, the real action takes place largely in clashes within and between the Republican and Democratic parties. Depending on how one looks at the question, New York has either one of the most competitive party systems in the country or the least. At least until the last few years, statewide elections were seldom landslides, and both parties were able to elect at least one statewide official in every election since World War II. The overwhelming statewide victories of Senator Charles Schumer

Table 3.1

Minor Party Endorsements of Major Party Candidates for New York State Legislative Races, 2006

Minor party endorsements	Democrats		Republicans		Other	
	No.	(%)	No.	(%)	No.	(%)
Green	9	(21)	1	(2)	33	(77)
Working families	104	(81)	16	(12)	9	(7)
Liberal	48	(72)	7	(12)	11	(18)
Independence	45	(30)	86	(58)	17	(11)
Conservative	42	(21)	126	(64)	30	(15)
Right to Life	1	(2)	19	(33)	37	(65)

Source: Adapted from figures compiled by Robert J. Spitzer, "Third Parties in New York State," in *Governing New York State*, 5th ed., ed. Robert F. Pecorella and Jeffrey M. Stonecash (Albany: State University of New York Press, 2006), p. 107.

in 2004, Senator Hillary Clinton in 2006, Governor Eliot Spitzer in 2007, and President Barack Obama in 2008 suggest that the state is becoming more reliably Democratic; and the fact that all its statewide incumbents—the governor, both senators, the comptroller, and the attorney general—are Democrats is not good news for the Republican Party. Yet to the extent that the state remains "competitive at the statewide level, it is equally true that most areas of the state are better described as being areas of one-party dominance."[7] The 2006 state legislative elections were relatively typical. In the state senate, party control changed in only one of sixty-two seats; in thirty-four of the remaining sixty, the winning candidate received more than 60 percent of the vote; and there were ten candidates who ran without major party opposition. In the state assembly, only two of 150 seats changed parties; 116 were won by margins exceeding 60 percent; and forty-two of these candidates had what amounted to a free ride. In 2008, despite Obama's overwhelming 63.5 percent victory, only four of 212 incumbent candidates for the senate and assembly lost.

These numbers have earned New York the dubious distinction of having some of the least meaningful general elections in the United States. In Rosenthal's tabulation of state legislative turnover from 1987 through 1997, New York's senate ranked last, its assembly forty-eight of forty-nine lower houses.[8] A long-term secular trend toward the Democrats has not made legislative races more competitive; it is still the rare incumbent who loses a legislative seat.

Regional Divisions

The traditional pattern in New York has been for the Democrats to win easily in New York City and some largely urban pockets upstate and for the Republicans to win everywhere else. "For much of the twentieth century," as the leading student of New York elections once wrote, "the bases of political parties in New York have been simple and clear. Republicans dominated upstate and the suburban areas around New York City. Democrats dominated New York City and a few upstate urban areas. The division reflected the long-standing hostility of upstate to New York City. New York was regarded as 'different.'"[9]

In the 1994 gubernatorial campaign, to cite an extreme but illustrative case, the winning Republican candidate, George Pataki, received 82 percent of the votes cast in rural Hamilton County (west of Lake George), the mirror opposite of his performance in New York County (Manhattan), where he won only 18 percent. Mario Cuomo carried four of New York City's five boroughs (losing Staten Island), but was able to win only one other county (Albany) in the entire state. Cumulatively, Democrat Cuomo won 71 percent of the vote in the city, 38 percent upstate. Twelve years later, Republican John Faso, running against Eliot Spitzer, got only 10 percent of the vote in Manhattan, but won Hamilton County with 54 percent. Cumulatively, he won only 14 percent in New York City, carried just four counties, and won only 35 percent outside of the city. In the 2008 presidential race, Barack Obama's best county was the Bronx, where he won almost 90 percent of the vote, but he too lost Hamilton County with just 36 percent.

Although personalities are important, and although the electorate is increasingly inclined to switch between parties and split its votes, two long-term trends are clear. First, the number of people refusing to register with any party has grown to 20 percent, or one in every five voters. This growth in the proportion of independents has come almost entirely at the expense of the Republicans. As Stonecash and Widestrom show,

> while Democrats have remained about 50 percent of all registrants, enrollment in the Republican Party has steadily declined since the 1950s. Perhaps most significantly, the problem is steadily getting worse for the party. County . . . files record the year that individuals register. It is possible to sort these files . . . and determine the percentage who enroll as Republican by the year of registration. The pattern for upstate counties is one of a continual slide in Republican enrollment. If this continues, and older registrants, who are more Republican, leave the state or die, Republican enrollment will be much lower in the future.[10]

A second, equally important long-term trend is the growing success of Democrats upstate. As frequently happens during periods of electoral realignment, the trend began at the national level. The overwhelming victories of Senator Schumer in 2004 (winning with 75 percent and carrying every county save Hamilton) and Senator Clinton in 2006 (winning with 68 percent) reflected a growing dissatisfaction with the increasingly conservative orientation of the Republican Party nationally. In 2006 and 2008, the trend continued with Democratic candidates for the U.S. House of Representatives scoring upset victories in three districts that had been solidly Republican for decades (see Box 3.1). The Republicans were able to maintain

Box 3.1
The New York Delegation in Congress
Upstate Goes Blue

In 2002, New York elected nineteen Democrats and ten Republicans to Congress. Eleven of the Democrats and only one Republican were from New York City, with the Republicans holding a narrow nine to eight margin in the rest of the state. When the votes were counted in 2008, the map of the state's congressional districts was almost entirely blue, with only three Republicans still in the House. The Republicans' reversal of fortunes was dramatic: looking at the 2002 returns, one would never have guessed that *any* of their incumbents would lose, since not one of them received less than 70 percent of the vote. District by district, here is how it happened:

　　3rd District (Long Island): Peter King easily won his sixth term in 2002 with 73 percent of the vote. In 2008 he won with 64 percent.

　　13th (Staten Island): Vito Fosella, who won with 71 percent in 2002, resigned in a 2008 scandal. A Democrat won easily.

　　19th (Westchester/Hudson Valley): Sue Kelly, who had held this seat since 1994, was defeated by John Hall in 2006. Hall won reelection with 58 percent of the vote in 2008.

　　20th (Hudson Valley/North Country): John Sweeney, who won with 75 percent in 2002, lost to Democrat Kirsten Gillibrand in 2006. Gillibrand won reelection in 2008 with 62 percent.

　　23rd (North Country): John McHugh, who was unopposed in 2002, won easily in 2008.

　　24th (Central): Shewood Boehlert, who won with 77 percent in 2002, retired and the seat went to a Democrat.

　　25th (Syracuse): After twenty years in the House, James Walsh retired and was replaced by a Democrat.

　　26th (Buffalo suburbs): Tom Reynolds retired, but the Republicans retained the seat.

　　27th (Southern Tier): Republican Jack Quinn won this district in 2002 with 71 percent of the vote. It went Democratic in 2004 and in 2008, the incumbent Democrat Brian Higgins raising his winning percentage to 77 percent.

　　29th (Southern Tier): In 2002, Amo Houghton won his eighth term with 77 percent of the vote. When he retired, Republican assemblyman Randy Kuhl replaced him. Kuhl was defeated in 2008 by few thousand votes.

　　What is perhaps most striking about these races is that in all but a few cases the districts went from being overwhelmingly Republican to just as strikingly Democratic. Voters shifted from Republican to Democratic in these districts by an average of 28 percent.

control of the state senate in 2006 largely on the basis on advantages—financial, political, and in terms of their control over election district lines—that could no longer block the tide in 2008.

　　New York Republicans retain some abiding strength in the state's unique regional splits. Although upstate-downstate differences are important in other states, the political shadow cast by the New York metropolitan area is unique. In Illinois, the Chicago metropolitan area contains more than 60 percent of the state's population, and Bostonians similarly dominate in Massachusetts, yet "when each metro region's percentage of its state's population is compared with the area's share of the winners in the contests for governor and senator, New York turns out to have the largest regional imbalance."[11] Upstate, outnumbered by more than 1 million votes, is also highly fragmented. It has, for example, four of the nation's fifty largest television markets in Albany, Buffalo, Rochester, and Syracuse, yet the four combined total less than half the viewers of New York City. For the statewide candidate seeking media exposure, upstate is "a series of airports" encountered in an all-day "fly-through" that will nonetheless yield less than half the media exposure of a single appearance in New York City. A local politician who makes the news in the New York City area "is regularly beamed into two-thirds of New York's households. His counterpart in Buffalo [the state's second largest television market] has his local accomplishments broadcast to only 9.8 percent of the state's homes."[12] As big a fish as he or she may be in the home pond, the upstate politician is a minnow swimming among whales when it comes to comparative media exposure. Small wonder that every single statewide public official in this century has been based in the New York City media market.

The state legislature has provided some balance. The Republican conference that had for decades controlled the state senate never drew more than eleven of its thirty-one to thirty-six members from downstate. Democrats gained control of the assembly only when they began regularly to win upstate seats (particularly in the large cities), and their successes in the 2006, 2007, and 2008 senate elections were divided between the city, its suburbs, and upstate. Candidates for statewide office who cannot draw a certain base vote upstate will lose. The very perceptive journalist Warren Moscow in 1948 criticized "a tendency to oversimplify the normal voting habits of the state electorate by explaining that 'rural' upstate, the fifty-seven counties outside the big city limits of New York, votes Republican and that New York City votes Democratic."[13] And there is some truth to Moscow's observation today. Within the city, Staten Island is competitive, with the Republicans often having an edge. The Bay Ridge section of Brooklyn, parts of the northeast Bronx, and many of the white neighborhoods of Queens are almost as Republican as some rural areas. Many of the city's suburbs are also highly competitive. Hostility to New York City, moreover, remains a staple of politics in upstate urban areas that might sympathize with its policy concerns, and the flogging of upcountry "hicks" is part of the ritual of New York politics even among politicians who know better.

More than in most other states, regionalism tends to distort the political de-mography of New York. Many working-class voters upstate who might normally be expected to vote Democratic (and who often do so in national elections) vote Republican for state offices out of hostility to the city. While the rest of the Northeast has moved rather decisively into the Democratic column, and New York is moving in that direction, upstate New York is far more Republican than states with similar demographic profiles. Even its upstate cities are more Republican than cities of equivalent size elsewhere in the country.

> The historically strongly Republican population of Upstate New York's mostly English, better-educated areas have also grown increasingly disenchanted with the national Republican party since the 1950s, probably for the same reasons found in most of New England. However, appeals to Southern voters emphasized opposition to civil rights measures, support for conservative moral positions, and the military threat posed by the former Soviet Union, which were not key issues in upstate New York local elections. State legislative elections have instead been dominated by another key issue for more than one hundred years—the antagonism between Upstate New York and New York City. For years, upstate voters have perceived themselves as paying high taxes to pay for New York City social services that were distributed by corrupt or incompetent city politicians.[14]

Affluent city voters, normally drawn to the Republican Party, vote Democratic based both on a feeling that Republicans do not understand their special urban problems and on a strong antipathy to what they see as the intolerant stands of national Republicans on social issues. "President Bush's appointments to the Supreme Court," one Republican state senator told us in a 2007 interview, "may have condemned New York Republicans to minority party status for a long time to come."

Partly as a by-product of regional cleavages, interparty competition for seats in the state legislature became something of a rarity in the 1980s and 1990s. Writing in 1994, Stonecash showed that "since 1900 the average margin of victory (percentage points by which the winner leads the loser) in legislative elections had steadily increased from a little over 20 to the current level of 54 percentage points."[15] That margin has been shrinking for the state senate since 2000 as the Democrats became increasingly competitive and eventually victorious (see Box 3.2). But it remains true that very few districts in either house have close elections in November. In fact, many legislators worry more about possible challenges in the September primary elections than they do about candidates of the opposite party in November.

The growing importance of primary elections has contributed to the growing fragmentation of the party system. Party discipline in the legislature exists despite rather than because of the parties' ability to control nominations. It is, at the same time, a legacy of the days when strong party organizations—both Republican and Democratic—very much dominated the electoral process.

Tammany Hall and Its Legacy

No organization better typifies the often-maligned urban political machine than New York City's Tammany Hall. At its late nineteenth-century peak, Tammany seldom lost control of city hall and was frequently able to elect governors as well. In the city its patronage powers extended to virtually all municipal jobs and contracts. If you wanted to work for the city, you went through Tammany. If

---

Box 3.2
Toward a One-Party State?

In 2007 and 2008, Democrats won two special elections to fill vacancies in the state senate, narrowing the Republican majority to 32–30. Both seats—one on Long Island, the other along the Canadian border—had previously voted Republican by comfortable majorities. Although the issues were largely local, the combined defeats suggested that perhaps the Republicans' senate majority was largely a function of incumbency that would disappear as the older Republican senators, seven of whom were over seventy-five, died or retired. Indeed, the Democrats not only retained both the seats they won in these elections, but unseated two more incumbents in 2008 to take a 32–30 Democratic edge.

The Republicans' long-term problems could have been anticipated by a close reading of trends in other seats. Three of the senate's powerful senior members—Finance Committee chair Owen Johnson, Education chair Stephen Saland, and Code Committee chair Dale Volker—are known for their outstanding records of constituent service, for example, yet all three have seen their shares of the popular vote decline rather significantly over the past decade.

Johnson, from the fourth district on eastern Long Island, won with 69.2 percent of the vote in 1998, was unopposed in 2000 and 2002, and dropped to 65.3 percent in 2004 and to less than 60 percent in 2006 and 2008. Over the same six elections, Saland, from the forty-first district in the Hudson Valley, registered victories of 72.4 percent, 67.6, 66.5, 65.2, 58.2, and 58.7. Volker, from the Buffalo area, won with 77.2 percent in 1998 and 74.9 in 2000, ran unopposed in 2002 and 2004, but dropped to 61.4 percent in 2006 and 55.6 percent in 2008. When powerful and conscientious legislators such as these all find their margins of victory dropping by more than 10 percentage points, it suggests that long-term trends beyond their control are at work; and the fact is that declining vote totals are difficult to reverse because weakened candidates tend to attract strong opponents. Like sharks smelling blood in the water, better-known and better-financed candidates increasingly come forward as incumbents falter. Should any of these senior candidates retire, moreover, the Republican Party will have real problems holding their seats.

The crucial election in determining the long-term balance of power comes in 2010, when the party that controls the senate will be in charge of drawing district lines for the next decade of elections.

---

you wanted to run for political office, you apprenticed in the organization, turning out the vote, organizing the community, and delivering services. Those who supported the organization with their work, votes, or money received their just rewards. Others did not. Critics of machine politics, and they are many, focus on the ethics of a political system based on trading favors. Through patronage, it was charged, key appointments and decisions were made on the basis of connections and kickbacks rather than merit. Votes were cast according to quasi-feudal loyalties to neighborhood leaders rather than rational appraisals of the issues and candidates. The machine, however, also served important positive functions. It brought politics into the neighborhoods; it provided channels of upward mobility for those ethnic groups excluded from more conventional pathways to success; it integrated immigrants into the nuances of a foreign culture; and it organized the dynamically changing political and economic life of the emerging industrial society. In other words, it helped make democracy work. And, as one of its latent functions, it made the cities governable.[16]

However one evaluates the roles of organizations like Tammany Hall, their influence pervaded New York State politics from the late nineteenth century well into the twentieth. Aside from Tammany, which dominated the city's Democratic Party for more than a century, the Albany county machine of "Uncle Dan" O'Connell and Erastus Corning effectively ruled that area from the 1920s until quite recent times.[17] Buffalo's Crotty organization similarly dominated Erie county politics well into the 1970s. Cohesive Republican organizations dominated the politics of both Syracuse and Rochester at the turn of century and were a major force in such upstate cities as Utica and Schenectady as recently as the 1960s.[18] And remnants of the patronage-driven Republican organizations in Nassau and Suffolk counties can still be found at the local level and in the continuing ability of the party organizations to control nominations.

Periodic reform movements succeeded, from time to time, in displacing the machines, and in the early part of the twentieth century, the reformers succeeded in enacting a number of state laws designed both to curb abuses of power and to weaken the party organizations. The most important of these reforms were those restricting the suffrage, establishing primary elections, and creating the civil service system. None of these changes in the rules of the game were to prove immediately fatal to the better-situated machines. Most students of American political history see the rise of the New Deal welfare state as far more corrosive of the party organizations' main bases of power. It seems likely, moreover, that curbs on immigration combined with other demographic changes, such as increased access to education, played an important role in the eventual demise of Tammany Hall and its counterparts. With or without civil service reforms, growing affluence made municipal jobs less attractive; the welfare state displaced the precinct worker as the friend of the needy; and a better-educated electorate preferred to make its own decisions about how to vote.

Party Structures and the Rules of the Game

Political machines and the reform laws aimed at the machines continue to leave important imprints on New York politics. The basic structure of the parties, as codified in the state election laws, is essentially that of the old machines. In its most elaborate form, Tammany Hall in the nineteenth century constituted, as Moynihan describes it, a massive party bureaucracy, which rivaled the medieval Catholic Church in the proportion of the citizenry involved. The county committees of the five boroughs came to number more than thirty-two thousand persons. It became necessary to hire Madison Square Garden for their meetings—and to hope that not more than half the number would show up as there wouldn't be room. . . .

[It was] a political bureaucracy in which rights appertained not to individuals but to the positions they occupied. "Have you seen your block captain?" It did not matter that your captain was an idiot or a drunk or a devout churchgoer who would be alarmed by the request at hand; the block captain had to be seen first. Then the election district captain. Then the district leader. The hierarchy had to be recognized.[19]

This essential structure is still embodied in the election code, which allows each of the state's approximately 13,000 election districts to select two members of each party in the primary election. Typically, a candidate who qualifies by getting signatures on a party petition will more or less automatically become the local representative of the party. If more than two candidates qualify, they will appear on the primary election ballots of their respective parties. The final fate of the machine in New York City was sealed in the 1960s and 1970s when reform Democrats won enough of these very local races to take control of the party machinery from Tammany Hall.

The individual precinct or election district (ED) is at the base—both in law and in practice—of the modern party organization as it was of the machine. Usually comprised of fewer than 1,000 registered voters, each ED elects two party leaders (one of each gender) for each party. These election district leaders (known in most areas as county committeemen and -women) are the building blocks of the party organizations. At the next rung up the ladder are the elected party officials variously known as ward leaders, district leaders, and town chairs. Typically, these party officials elect a county executive committee and a county leader. The modern county leaders are the lineal descendants of the old machine boss. Their power, like that of the boss, derives from their ability to maintain the support of those lower in the party hierarchy, although the term *hierarchy* seldom describes the relationship between leaders and led in organizations usually described as "porous," "ad hoc," and "permeable."[20]

Just as some bosses were more successful than others in keeping diverse factions under control, there are important variations in the ability of contemporary county chairs to control their organizations. Republicans in Nassau, Suffolk, and many upstate counties seldom experience competitive primaries and have been able, in general, to decide who can run as a Republican and who cannot. Similarly, in most of Queens, parts of Brooklyn, and in some upstate cities, the Democratic Party organization is as dominant in selecting candidates as Tammany ever was. The motivation of those who become party activists, particularly in the suburbs, has shifted toward ideology rather than dreams of patronage or other tangible rewards: "They use the party," as one study of Democrats in Westchester put it, "to achieve some version of their own visions of the future, playing the party's game to the extent that they agree with its goals."[21] As in the days of Tammany, the people who hold the party organizations together are those largely self-recruited individuals who toil at the election district and town committee level. They are at the base of organizations that are hierarchical in formal structure but loose, amorphous, and— quite frequently—democratic in their actual operation.

Parties, Campaigns, and Elections

New York, like most other states, has moved increasingly toward candidate-centered campaigns that bypass party organizations. At the same time, paradoxically, the state's major party organizations—the Republican and Democratic state committees and the assembly and senate campaign committees—are better financed and more professional than at any time in modern history. Stronger in their ability to channel resources into campaigns, they have been unable to establish consistent control over the process of recruitment. Nor have they been able to coordinate resources from one level of government to another or between and among the two houses of the legislature and the offices of governor, attorney general, and controller. One of the keys to the effectiveness of Tammany was its vertical and horizontal integration: once the organization decided its policy, it had the ability to put it into effect. The hallmark of the modern party system is fragmentation. Divided government—the state senate Republican, the assembly Democratic, and the governorship shifting—made it appear for forty years as if partisan warfare was the cause of deadlock; in fact, it was only a symptom of deeper splits in both parties that cut across institutional lines.

New York State election law provides that in addition to county committee members and district or county leaders, the parties in each county elect representatives to a state committee. The major parties' state committeemen and committeewomen constitute the governing bodies of the parties. They set party rules and endorse candidates for statewide office. Traditionally, the state convention of the Republican Party has been able to choose the party's nominees for statewide office with considerable regularity. Not so with the Democrats, whose endorsement by the party convention has been more a liability than an asset. Under the law, any candidate supported by a majority of the state convention automatically appears on the primary ballot. A nonwinner who garners at least 25 percent of the vote is not the endorsed candidate, but can appear on the ballot without going through the statewide process of gathering petition signatures. In the 1974 Democratic primary, the voters rejected the convention's choices for governor, lieutenant governor, and U.S. senator. Since that fateful year, it has become almost a kiss of death for a nonincumbent to win the convention endorsement. While many reformers celebrate the independent spirit of the voters manifested in such rejections of party leaders, others see the 1974 case as an important cautionary tale. Where the state convention had gone out of its way to put forth a balanced slate, primary voters selected one consisting entirely of candidates from New York City, all male, one of them black, and three Jewish. All but one (incumbent comptroller Arthur Levitt) lost in the general election.

Both the Republican and Democratic parties regularly face a tension between the preferences of their core primary voters and the candidate attributes most likely to win elections in November. Because only dedicated partisans turn out for primary elections in New York, Democratic and Republican primary voters are usually more polarized ideologically than the electorate as a whole. Primary voters are drawn from a narrow cross-section of the state electorate. In 1992, for example, there were 8,818,691 registered voters in New York State, 4,140,794 of them Democrats and eligible to vote in the competitive April primary for president. A little over 1 million actually did. Bill Clinton won the primary with 412,000 votes, about 10 percent of the state's registered Democrats, about thirty voters per election district. In the November general election, when there was little doubt that Clinton would win New York by a large margin, he received close to 3.5 million votes.

As one moves down the ballot to less visible races, the primary electorate shrinks still further. It is little wonder that the political machines were not particularly hurt by the introduction of the direct primary system. Indeed, the combination of primary elections and another turn-of-the-century "reform"—voter registration— made the machine's job easier by reducing the number of voters needed to win. In general elections in the 1880s, participation rates sometimes exceeded 90 percent statewide. Thirty years later, even before women's suffrage plunged the rate still lower by bringing millions of previously apolitical citizens into the fold, it had fallen into the 60 percent range. Between 2000 and 2008, it was closer to 50 per- cent in the November general elections for highly visible offices like president and governor, far lower in elections for Congress and the state legislature, and lower still in primaries.

The unwillingness of New Yorkers to vote in party primaries is quite re- markable, especially since those are the elections that are usually decisive. The 102nd Assembly District, covering parts of Columbia and Dutchess counties, is so safely Republican that in many elections no Democrat could be found to run against incumbent Patrick Manning. When Manning embarked on a brief campaign for governor in 2006, a local mayor decided to challenge him in the Republican primary for his assembly seat. Fewer than 6,000 voters turned out in the September primary, giving the upstart, Marcus Molinaro of Tivoli, the Republican line by a margin of just 2,770 to 2,539. Molinaro's opponent in the November general election was an unusually vigorous and articulate candidate, but despite lingering divisions in the Republican Party, she lost to Molinaro by a margin of 22,065 to 17,531. Molinaro spent more money on his primary cam- paign than he did in the general election, yet he received more than eight times as many votes in the less competitive November general election than he did in the more testing primary.

Box 3.3

Registering as an "Independent," or, How to Give Away Your Vote

In New York, as throughout the United States, a growing number of people prefer to think of themselves as "independents," unaffiliated with any organized political party. As in most states, voters in New York—when they register to vote—have the option of enrolling in any of the official parties or of declining to state a party preference. How they register has nothing to with how they vote in November: in the secrecy of the voting booth, a registered Democrat can vote for Independents, Republicans, or any other candidates on any other lines. New York, however, has a *closed* primary system, an election law that allows only the enrolled members of a party to vote in its primaries. This law is designed to protect each party from being "raided" by outsiders from rival parties seeking to choose the weakest possible candidate to run against. Thus a registered Conservative cannot vote in any primary election except that of the Conservative Party. Voters who declare themselves independent by not checking a party preference when they register cannot vote in any primaries. By registering as independents, in other words, they have effectively disenfranchised themselves in what is often the most important election.

What if voters change their minds? Suppose a person not registered in the Democratic Party had become interested in the Clinton-Obama primary race in 2008? Sorry, not this time: under New York law, voters who change their party registration must wait until after the next general election to vote in their new party's primary. Despite this rule, nearly 2 million registered voters in New York, more than 20 percent of the electorate, made themselves ineligible to vote in any party primaries in 2008 by refusing to state a party preference. In New York, political "independence" comes at a high price.

Who Votes and Who Does Not

The United States has one of the lowest rates of voter participation in the world; and New York State is increasingly distinguishing itself as a state in which voter participation rates are, even by American standards, unusually low. As far back as the 1920s and 1930s, New York ranked in the bottom third among northern states. The Voting Rights Act of 1965 was designed to give the federal government a role in helping people vote in areas where they had been previously disenfranchised. Aimed mainly at southern states whose segregationist policies had routinely prevented African-Americans from voting, the law targeted counties whose histories of nonvoting suggested systematic bias. New York is one of three nonsouthern states still under such federal jurisdiction. In the 2004 presidential election, it ranked forty-eighth in overall turnout. Whatever it is that depresses electoral participation in the United States operates with particular force in New York. More importantly, given the noncompetitive character of many senate and assembly districts, few states have a lower turnout in primary elections than New York.

Some of these figures may be deceptive. Because voter turnout is often measured as a percentage of the state's adult population, states like New York that have high proportions of noncitizens may actually have more politically robust participation rates than these figures indicate.[22] The fact that Hispanics, alone among New York's ethnic groups, vote at a slightly higher rate than the national average may be due simply to the fact that many of New York's Hispanics are already citizens by way of their Puerto Rican heritage. Many of New York's black residents, conversely, are citizens of Haiti, Jamaica, Ghana, and other countries; they cannot therefore register to vote in the state. Even among those immigrants who have become citizens, Berg suggests that some groups are unlikely to vote because "New York City is not viewed as their permanent or long-term home. Some immigrants plan on returning to their place of origin after having accumulated some wealth in the United States." It also may be, as Berg goes on to argue, that "lower voter turnout rates are in part due to a strong emphasis on work over other activities as well as an aversion to politics resulting from living in authoritarian political systems."[23]

Among all ethnic groups, poor and poorly educated people vote at dramatically lower rates than their wealthier and better-educated compatriots. And, up to a point, the older people are, the more likely they are to vote. These differences appear to be the combined product of three related variables. First, there are questions of motivation, mobilization, and efficacy. Poorly educated people lack the information to make politics salient; the poor, more generally, may lack a sense of political efficacy, or a feeling that their votes count, making them unlikely to participate in a process that seems remote from their everyday lives. Second, there are the costs of voting, which can be higher for some people than others. Using a rational choice model, some scholars have suggested that if the perceived benefits of voting seem to outweigh the costs, people vote; if costs outweigh benefits, they stay home. Emphasizing the cost side of the equation are those scholars who argue that nonvoting in the United States is largely the product of deliberately constructed impediments to voting such as difficult registration requirements, inconvenient times and polling places, and aggressive efforts to intimidate and threaten potential voters. Finally, as the third reason for not voting, it is important to look at the benefit side of the equation. If the political system is failing to offer meaningful choices to marginal voters, why should they be expected to vote? Stressing the failure of parties and candidates to reach out to the young and poor, the lack of meaningful competition in most elections, and the failure of politicians to address the real concerns of nonvoters, some scholars attribute nonvoting largely to the failure of groups like the Democratic Party and the union movement to reach out to their natural constituencies.

Increasingly, students of voting are moving toward a theory that stresses the complementary interaction of these three factors.[24] There seems to be a self-reinforcing triangle that increasingly has the effect of driving low-status citizens out of the voting pool. Less educated people are more easily intimidated and less likely to know how to file the proper papers to vote. Because the young and the poor are less involved in communities that are active politically, they are similarly less likely to be helped toward participation. Politicians, for their part, have little incentive to seek the support of such citizens or make it easier for them to vote; and the boards of elections, appointed under the patronage of these same politicians, seldom see their role as facilitating citizen participation.[25] Political campaigns are pitched toward the existing pool of registered voters, and those who run the campaigns are, as incumbents, leery of reforms that might dramatically alter the rules that have worked for them in the past. Nonvoters, for their part, correctly perceiving that politicians pay little heed to their communities, have still less incentive to become involved in the process.

A major consequence of this dynamic is the growing disenfranchisement of the poor. In 1994, the district-by-district analysis of New York's Voter Assistance Commission concluded that each increment of $10,000 in median income was associated with a 3.7 percent increase in voter turnout.[26] In New York City, the contrasts can be striking. On Manhattan's Upper East Side, the general election turnout in the affluent 65th Assembly District (AD) was 60,765 in 2004, more than double the vote cast in the impoverished 84th AD of the South Bronx, where only 29,545 voters went to the polls. The contrasts are less dramatic but still significant outside the city. The rural 118th AD, along the St. Lawrence River, covers parts of two of the state's poorer counties (Jefferson and St. Lawrence). It sent 48,507 voters to the polls in 2004, almost 25 percent fewer than the 65,899 who turned out in Long Island's 16th AD, one of the wealthiest in the state.

While income explains many of the variations in voting participation between different areas of the state, it does not account for the waning influence of New York City in state politics. The declining population of the city relative to its suburbs has significantly reduced its ability to control statewide elections. Much of this decline can be attributed to population movements that reduced New York City's share of the state's population from 55 percent in the 1930 census to 42 percent in 2000. But the city's political weight has declined even more precipitously: in the 2006 gubernatorial race, it cast less than 29 percent of the total vote. Voter turnout rates in New York City have consistently lagged behind the rest of the state, but while both rates have been declining steadily for more than fifty years, the gap between the city and the rest of the state grew from an average of 7 or 8 percent in the 1970s to 13 percent in 2006.

A surprisingly small proportion of this decline is attributable to immigration. Clearly, New York City—because its population includes a higher proportion of aliens not eligible to vote—could be expected to have a lower voting rate than the rest of the state. Because Latinos tend to have higher proportions of citizens below the voting age, moreover, a further drop in participation might be expected. But these differences are not truly significant: statewide, for example, "Latinos represent 12.31 percent of the total population and 11.20 percent of New York's voting age population."[27] Despite their formal eligibility to vote, however, few Hispanics have actually exercised the right. In 2004, 73.5 percent of white non-Hispanics voted, as compared with 34.3 percent of Hispanics. The figure for Asians, 35 percent, was almost as low. African-Americans had unusually high levels of registration in New York City in the 1990s, largely because Jesse Jackson's 1988 presidential campaign put a great deal of effort into registration drives, and the candidacy of David Dinkins for mayor in 1989 and 1993 sustained the effort. African-American registration levels actually exceeded those of whites in 1993 (76.8 percent to 73.6 percent),[28] but fell to less than 50 percent in 2008[29] before rebounding in apparent support for Barack Obama. Race still appears to be a less significant factor than class in predicting voter turnout. The key facts are that eligible New York City voters are considerably less likely than their upstate counterparts either to register or to vote and that throughout the state the gaps in voter turnout between rich and poor are substantial and growing.

The gaps between the New York City and upstate are in part the product of deliberate policy choices. The federal "motor voter" act required the states to provide easy access to voter registration forms for those applying for documents such as new driver's licenses. Although the law specifically mandated voter registration efforts in social welfare agencies, colleges, and high schools as well as motor vehicle offices, this part of the mandate was largely ignored in New York, and one of George Pataki's first acts as governor was to defund enforcement of the program. Since only half of New York City's voting-age citizens have driver's licenses, as contrasted with more than 90 percent outside the city, the predictable result has been a widening of the registration gap between the city and the rest of the state.

That neither Pataki nor the Republican state senate was enthusiastic about increasing voter registration is not surprising. The people least likely to vote are poor people from New York City, a demographic group that is inclined to vote Democratic. Although Governor Cuomo and the Democrats in the state assembly supported an expanded motor voter program, they did not fight very hard for it, and voter registration was not on Governor Spitzer's reform agenda in 2007. What seems to have been at work here was a reluctance of politicians to tamper with the method of election that got them where they are. New voters are wild cards, people who might support primary challengers or vote the wrong way—that is, against the incumbent—in the general election. Often there has been an unspoken bipartisan agreement not to risk whatever unpredictable consequences might flow from attempts to register the unregistered. Indeed, efforts by the Obama presidential campaign in 2008 to register new voters were not greeted with great enthusiasm by state and local Democrats. The Help America Vote Act, which Congress passed in the wake of the badly flawed presidential contest in 2000, has had the ironic effect of reducing the number of eligible voters by purging the thousands of people who made technical errors on their registration cards.

Districting and the Permanently Divided Legislature

Few things threaten incumbent politicians more than changes in the rules of the game. Changes regarding who can vote, how candidates are chosen, and what rules govern campaign finance have usually come only after long periods of public agitation. Few areas demonstrate this inherent conservatism more clearly than those surrounding the periodic redrawing of district lines.

One Person, One Vote

Every ten years, following the national census, the governor and the legislature must agree on a plan to redraw the lines of legislative districts to reflect changes in population. Even though the state constitution requires periodic reapportionments, it does not mandate districts of equal size. Indeed, the 1894 constitution (which is still in effect) was engineered by the upstate Republicans who controlled the convention to ensure that New York City would never be able to elect a majority of either house of the legislature. It managed this by guaranteeing sixty of the state's sixty-two counties at least one seat in the assembly and providing that "no two counties divided by a river—Manhattan and Brooklyn were in mind—could ever have half the Senate seats."[30] Demographic changes and the popularity of Democrats like Roosevelt and Lehman sometimes allowed the Democrats to overcome the bad hands dealt them by this malapportionment, but the decisive period in the history of New York's legislative elections had its dawn in a 1962 Tennessee case, *Baker v. Carr*, that was decided by the Supreme Court of the United States.[31]

The question before the Court in this landmark case seemed simple: although the constitution of the state of Tennessee—like that of the federal government, New York, and most other states—required the state to reapportion its legislative districts every ten years, it had not done so for more than sixty years. As a result, assembly districts in Tennessee ranged in population from a low of 3,454 to a high of 79,031. Baker, a resident of one of the larger districts, charged that such disparities diluted the voting power of city residents and thereby denied them the equal protection of the laws guaranteed by the Fourteenth Amendment. Precedent was on the side of the state. In the 1946 case of *Colegrove v. Green*, the Court had refused to involve itself in a similar case on the grounds that it was a political question: "Courts," the majority had argued in *Colegrove*, "ought not to enter this political thicket. The remedy for unfairness in districting is to secure state legislatures that will apportion properly, or to invoke the substantial powers of Congress."[32]

In *Baker v. Carr* the Supreme Court entered this political thicket. By ruling the Tennessee case justiciable and later enunciating the standard of "one man, one vote," the Court placed itself on a track that soon revolutionized the process of legislative districting throughout the United States. By grounding its opinion in the federal equal protection clause rather than the Tennessee constitution, the Court opened the door to challenges of the legislatures of almost every state. Baker was underrepresented because the Tennessee legislature had failed to keep up with population changes in drawing district lines. But what about a resident of New York City who was similarly underrepresented because the state constitution mandated it? In *Reynolds v. Sims*, Chief Justice Warren, writing for the majority in 1964, held that "the Equal Protection Clause requires that the seats in both houses of a bicameral state legislature must be apportioned on a population basis."[33]

New York's original efforts to meet the one-person, one-vote requirement failed to meet judicial scrutiny, and the 1966 legislative elections were conducted under a court-ordered reapportionment plan. By 1968 it was clear that the courts would tolerate virtually no deviations from a standard of strict population equality. The provisions of the state constitution that prohibit dividing counties in drawing senate districts and more generally disallow dividing towns and city blocks were rendered inoperative. Zimmerman and others have argued that ignoring these provisions in favor of strict population equality, while eliminating "rural over representation and urban under representation . . . made gerrymandering easier. . . . In other words, equally populated districts may have unfair district lines."[34] The term *gerrymander* originated in a journalist's description of a bizarrely shaped district designed in 1812 in Massachusetts by Governor Eldridge Gerry with the obvious intent of giving his party an advantage in the upcoming elections. In practice, the term is not easily defined. Oddly shaped districts most certainly predate the Supreme Court's reapportionment rulings, sometimes for nonpartisan reasons. Prior to *Baker v. Carr*, a legislature bent on gerrymandering could not only draw funny lines, but also make some districts artificially small (or large). But even with districts of equal size, one person's gerrymander is often another's equitable apportionment scheme. As former Assemblyman Peter Berle argues, for example:

> The urban interests of persons in a city are not represented if legislative districts are drawn in pie shaped sections with the center of the city at the center of the pie. This condition persisted in Syracuse, New York, under a number of apportionment plans. In such a situation, the core city area is divided into a great many small pieces, each of which is lumped with a much larger population of suburban voters. . . . The suburban interests which predominate in number will elect representatives who . . . may be in direct conflict with their city dwelling neighbors.[35]

Berle's argument makes sense only if one accepts the premise that there is such a thing as "urban interests." Are the differences between people residing in Syracuse so significantly different from those of people two miles away in Clay or Manlius that they deserve legislators of their own? Would a map that put suburban voters in a ring around the city be any less a gerrymander than one that mixed constituencies?

Ethnic Gerrymanders

This kind of question becomes justiciably significant when the issue is race and ethnicity. Syracuse, it has successfully been argued in court, may or may not be a community, but blacks, Latinos, and Asians are. Beginning with a series of reapportionments in the 1970s, the state legislature, particularly the assembly, began to create majority-minority districts; that is, districts in which minority groups were in a clear enough majority to elect more blacks and Latinos. This process was pushed from within by black and Latino members of the legislature and from without by the federal Department of Justice, which, under the Voting Rights Act, had the power to veto any changes in voting laws that might harm minority voters in historically underrepresented areas. The Justice Department became involved in 1974 when a federal district court ruled that the Bronx, Brooklyn, and Manhattan—because of their unusually low minority voter registration rates—were eligible for review under section 5 of the Voting Rights Act. In response to this suit, initiated by the NAACP Legal Defense Fund, the Justice Department voided the 1974 reapportionment and called for a new set of district lines. Although the new lines resulted in an immediate increase of only one new minority assembly member, taking the total from twelve to thirteen, the hidden hand of the Justice Department has been a player in every subsequent reapportionment deal.

Although the 1982 reapportionment plan pushed the number of majority-minority districts up to twenty, pressure from the Justice Department reached a peak in the 1990s. A Republican administration in Washington saw that by linking itself with minority aspirations for greater legislative representation it could also further its own legislative agenda. Since minorities, blacks in particular, tend to vote Democratic, any redistricting plan that concentrates minorities also concentrates Democrats. By conceding one seat to the Democrats by an overwhelming margin, the Republicans could remove enough Democrats from surrounding areas to virtually guarantee two, three, or even four surrounding seats to their own candidates. The districts created through this minority/Republican alliance served their dual purpose of substantially increasing the numbers of black and Hispanic legislators, on the one hand, and of Republicans on the other. One of the most misshapen districts created out of this alliance was a Hispanic district winding across four boroughs of New York City in a shape vaguely reminiscent of the cartoon character Bullwinkle. Challenges to these districts eventually caused the Supreme Court to abandon its traditional reluctance to rule on the shape as opposed to the size of legislative districts, at least in cases where race could be shown to be "the predominant factor" in producing district lines. "Shape," the Court held, "is relevant not because bizarreness is a necessary element of the constitutional wrong or threshold requirement of proof, but because it may be persuasive circumstantial evidence that race for its own sake, and not other districting principles, was the legislature's dominant and controlling rationale in drawing its district lines."[36]

Eventually, a challenge to New York's Bullwinkle district reached the courts and in 1997 it too was ruled unconstitutional: "all districting principles," a unanimous three-judge panel ruled, "must be applied in a race-neutral fashion."[37]

Protecting Incumbents

The Bullwinkle district's bizarre shape, the court made clear, was only one factor in making it constitutionally suspect: the whole legislative history of the redistricting process in 1992 "demonstrated that all traditional redistricting criteria were subordinated to race."[38] Thus, although the case of *Diaz v. Silver* was specifically limited to the 12th Congressional District, the reasoning of the court called into serious question more than one district in the state legislature, and there are currently no state senate or assembly districts quite as bizarre in shape as the congressional districts thrown out by the courts in 1997. There are districts, however, as Brian Murtaugh, one of the authors of this book, can personally attest, in which ethnicity was the primary factor considered in drawing the lines.

When the state legislature was redistricted in anticipation of the 1992 elections, Murtaugh's upper Manhattan district was little changed from the area he had represented for fourteen years. In June 1992, however, the Justice Department vetoed that part of the plan, including Murtaugh's heavily Hispanic district. Although the Legislative Task Force on Demographic Research and Reapportionment had provided figures showing that an overwhelming majority of the residents of the new district were of Dominican descent, the Justice Department ruled that a simple majority was insufficient. Because some Dominicans counted in the census are not citizens, because the percentage of Dominicans below the legal voting age is higher than among other groups, and because eligible Dominicans are less likely to vote, an effective majority-minority district in upper Manhattan would have to be at least 70 percent Hispanic to meet the test. So the legislature was forced to redesign the district's borders. By snaking new lines down from Washington Heights, seeking Hispanic blocks and buildings in central Harlem, and avoiding non-Hispanic blacks, whites, and Asians wherever possible, it was able to craft a district that met the Justice Department's criteria. The resulting key-shaped district, sixty-two blocks long and, for most of its length, no more than four blocks wide, was 77.7 percent Hispanic. Murtaugh was able, as an incumbent, to court a substantial Hispanic constituency and maintain a base vote in the few non-Hispanic election districts. He thus managed to discourage opposition in 1992 and to defeat a relatively inexperienced Dominican candidate in the 1994 Democratic primary. In 1996, however, overwhelmed by both demography and the emerging cohesiveness of the Hispanic community, he lost the seat by fewer than 300 votes.

The courts' new willingness to challenge majority-minority districts stands in rather striking contrast to their general unwillingness to look at other kinds of gerrymanders. After size and ethnicity, it seems clear that, "despite its conspicuous absence from any direct discussion, incumbency appears to have been the unacknowledged third-most-significant factor used when redistricting."[39] The New York constitution was amended in 1946 to incorporate compactness and respect for political boundaries into the factors that must be considered in drawing the lines for state legislative districts, but these guidelines have never been clearly defined, and the legislature has often created odd-shaped districts that—if not quite as high on the bizarreness scale as the Bullwinkle district rejected in 1997—are anything but compact. While some of these districts attempt to follow traditional community boundaries and others implicitly protect minority groups not covered under the

Voting Rights Act, the two kinds of gerrymanders most common in New York are those designed to maintain party advantages and protect incumbents in the state legislature. Since 1982, these two modes have largely coincided.

In its essence, the process of redistricting in New York during the four decades since *Baker v. Carr* boiled down to a system in which Democrats, who controlled the assembly, drew the assembly district lines, Republicans drew the state senate lines, and the two parties—almost as an afterthought—fought over congressional lines (giving due respect to the protection of key incumbents). This process—almost unique in the fifty states—has been firmly established in New York since 1982. Once beyond the court-ordered fluctuations of the 1960s and early 1970s, it was clear, following the 1980 census, that neither the senate nor the assembly could have its own way. Unable to agree on a reapportionment plan that could pass both houses and satisfy the courts, assembly speaker Stanley Fink finally proclaimed to senate majority leader Warren Anderson, "You don't quarrel with the way that I draw the Assembly and I won't quarrel with the way that you draw the Senate. I will pass a bill that has your version of the Senate if you will pass the same bill that has my version of the Assembly."[40] And that is the way it has been done ever since. Aided by newly developed computer programs, both assembly Democrats and senate Republicans have become remarkably adept at drawing district lines to maximize their respective party advantages.

While it is not always possible to predict how voters will divide in the future, party registration figures and past votes can be used as rough guides. The parties' ability to use these numbers is illustrated in Westchester County, where party enrollments have been increasingly Democratic (in 2006, for example, the proportions were as follows: Democrats, 44 percent; Republicans, 26 percent; no party, 25 percent; and others, 5 percent). In drawing their Westchester districts, assembly Democrats concentrated Republican voters into two districts, one overlapping with Putnam County, where Republicans usually win easily. By spreading their own voters more evenly around the county, Democrats have consistently won at least six of the remaining seven seats. Not to be outdone, senate Republicans consistently won four of the five senate districts they carved from the same electorate until they were finally ousted in the Yonkers area in 2006. By connecting the heavily Democratic areas of Mount Vernon to the South Bronx; building a donut-shaped, largely white, north Bronx/Westchester district around it; and extending part of another district into Putnam and Dutchess counties, the Republicans remained in control of Westchester's senate delegation even as their share of the vote slipped considerably below 50 percent. Repeated throughout the state, these partisan gerrymanders have produced a political map in which divided government, featuring a Democratic assembly and a Republican senate, was virtually a given of New York politics for almost four decades. Thus, even though the Republican Party's share of the major party vote for state senators slipped to just over 50 percent in 2004, it still won 60 percent (37 of 62) of the seats and retained a 34–28 majority in 2006 when its popular vote total was down to 45.6 percent. Not until the

Democrats won 57 percent of the vote in 2008 were they able to win a narrow majority of senate seats.

The Evolving Party System

For most of its recent history, the party system in New York has been relatively competitive at the statewide level, highly uncompetitive locally. While candidates for such statewide offices as governor and attorney general must be very much aware of both the other party's nominee and of the roles played by third parties, the only election that really matters in most legislative districts is the party primary. Once legislative candidates win their first primary election, moreover, it is only under exceptional conditions that the seat will be significantly contested again. One of these exceptional conditions is when district lines have been redrawn after a significant shift in population or a perceived need, as in the 1982 and 1992 reapportionments, to create new majority-minority districts. The other, and usually more interesting, exceptions occur during episodic periods of electoral instability when the attitudes of the electorate undergo major change.

Critical Elections in New York

Political scientists have used such terms as *partisan realignment* and *critical elections* to describe periods in which the dominant party has been displaced by a new constellation of political forces. Nationally, a critical election is typically followed by a long period in which the new coalition dominates both Congress and the presidency, not necessarily winning every election, but serving as the earth to the other party's moon for a long period.[41] The national election of 1932 was a classic realigning election, sweeping Franklin Roosevelt into the White House as the first Democratic president in twelve years and displacing Republican majorities with Democrats in both the House and Senate. Despite the elections of Republican presidents Dwight Eisenhower in 1952 and 1956 and Richard Nixon in 1968, the so-called New Deal coalition forged by Roosevelt and the Democrats in the 1930s dominated the system for decades.

The national realignment of 1932 began to manifest itself in New York in the 1920s. After winning the governorship in 1918, losing in 1920, and winning again in 1922, Al Smith saw his margins of victory grow with each subsequent election. His appeal to urban workers, particularly Catholics, transferred to Franklin Roosevelt in his 1928 campaign for governor. By 1930, Roosevelt's opposition to Prohibition, combined with the beginning of the Great Depression, helped him to one of the biggest landslide victories in state history. On top of the 71 percent he won in the five boroughs of New York City, Roosevelt won 61 percent in the fifty-eight counties outside the city, winning, most remarkably, 48 percent of the vote in the state's twenty-one rural counties. With Roosevelt at the top of the national ticket in 1932, Herbert Lehman won the governorship for the Democrats by an even larger margin, though his rural vote slipped, and neither Lehman nor any subsequent Democratic candidate until Eliot Spitzer in 2006 would approach Roosevelt's 1930 upstate performance. The New Deal realignment of the electorate was, despite Lehman's victory, only partially reflected in state politics, for although Democratic candidates for the state assembly received 2,374,000 votes to 1,793,000 for the Republicans, Republicans retained control of the legislature. There were, essentially, two reasons for continued Republican control of the senate and assembly. First, the 1894 constitution's anti-city strictures on apportionment and Republican-sponsored redistricting plans had made the legislature virtually immune to electoral change. Second, the New Deal realignment in New York, despite Roosevelt's temporary surge, proved a largely urban phenomenon. Building on Al Smith's enormous popularity as the first Irish Catholic from New York City to run for governor, Democratic enrollments among urban immigrants soared, both in the metropolis and to a lesser extent in upstate cities. Despite and in some ways because of these trends, most upstate voters remained solidly Republican. Even in Roosevelt's landslide victory over Herbert Hoover in the 1933 presidential election, he carried only five counties outside the city. Indeed, the only county outside the city that had a plurality of registered Democrats in 1932 was Albany.

The New Deal realignment, almost imperceptible upstate in 1932, began gradually to gather force, particularly in the urban centers, as both Lehman as governor and Roosevelt as president began to carve out new policy programs. As much as the Republicans schemed to rig the reapportionment of the legislature in their favor, by the 1940s "the Democrats had proved that they sometimes could win control of the Senate, if they are carrying the State by landslide or near-landslide proportions for other offices."[42] The growing weakness of the Republican majority was masked in part by the popularity of Governors Thomas Dewey (1943–1952) and Nelson Rockefeller (1959–1972), but their successes were built in no small part on their abilities to transcend and overcome the rural conservatism of the legislature's Republicans. The very ability of rural Republicans to use their opposition to urban programs for New York City as a means of securing their own reelection began gradually to produce a backlash in urban areas upstate. Outside of the city, its northern suburbs, and Long Island, there were six upstate Democrats in the senate in 1997, two each from Buffalo and Rochester, one from Syracuse, and one from Albany. In the assembly, there were nineteen upstate Democrats, thirteen of them from these same four cities.

Increasingly, in the years after World War II, the battle for party control in New York State shifted with the flow of population to the suburbs. Whether the exurbanites who fled the city were more conservative to begin with or whether their new neighbors and circumstances changed their perspectives, there seems little doubt that they did not bring their overwhelmingly Democratic voting behavior from the city to their new communities. At the same time, suburban voters have not been as reliable a bloc of Republican votes as one might have predicted, instead functioning as a swing group between the largely Democratic cities and the equally

Republican rural areas of the state. In the 2005 legislature, for example, the Long Island delegation in the state senate was entirely Republican, and there were only two Democratic state senators from Westchester, Orange, and Rockland counties, but eighteen of the thirty-one assembly members elected from these same areas were Democrats. In keeping with the theory of political realignment, the strength of the Democratic Party upstate grew, not gradually, but episodically in two critical elections.

The first of these realignments was in 1964 (see Table 3.2). As a rule, national politics have but a faint echo at the state level, particularly since ticket splitting—voting for candidates of different parties in the same election—has become more common. The 1964 and 1974 elections were exceptions to this rule. In 1964 the views of Republican presidential candidate Barry Goldwater, who was hostile toward Social Security and civil rights and apparently willing to use nuclear weapons, may have won the Republicans support in the South and West but were extraordinarily unpopular in New York. Many Republican candidates for Congress and the state legislature tried desperately to distance themselves from the top of the ticket, some successfully. But the magnitude of Goldwater's loss—he won just 31 percent of the total vote and lost every county in the state—was so great that districts that had not voted Democratic in living memory sent Democrats to Congress and the legislature. In 1974, after Richard Nixon resigned the presidency in the wake of the Watergate scandals, there was a similar drop in votes for Republicans at all levels. These so-called coattail elections, in which particularly strong or weak candidates drag fellow party members to victory or defeat, are becoming less common in American politics, but Goldwater's extremism and Nixon's ethical lapses put their fellow Republicans in difficult positions that many could not overcome. Some of the Democrats elected in these rather unusual contests were able to become something other than curiosities and actually hang on to their seats. One veteran Republican legislator described what had happened in an adjoining district that in 1974 had elected its first Democrat since the Civil War:

> Old X [the Republican] had been elected so easily so often that he had long since stopped kissing babies, campaigning or doing the things most politicians do. Essentially, he ignored his constituents. When the Democrat got elected, the first thing he did was to start touring the area in a mobile district office. He sent out newsletters, press releases and never stopped going door-to-door. Well, hell, said a lot of life-long Republicans, if this is the difference between a Democrat and a Republican, maybe I've been making a mistake. And they've been voting for that guy ever since.

When coattails do impact local elections, the effect is usually temporary, and the Democratic surge in 1964 had relatively trivial long-term consequences. But 1974 was different. Of the Democrats' net gain of nineteen assembly seats, fourteen were upstate. A decade later, eleven of these fourteen seats still were held by Democrats. "The 1974 transition," as Stonecash describes it, "was decisive. In subsequent

Table 3.2

Seats and Votes in the New York State Legislature: Democratic Percentage of Assembly and Senate Seats Won, and Statewide Democratic Percentage of Total Two-Party Vote, 1960–2008

	State assembly				State senate			
	Party division		Percent Democratic		Party division		Percent Democratic	
Year	Dem.	Rep.	Seats won	Popular vote	Dem.	Rep.	Seats won	Popular vote
1960	65	84	43.6	50.7	25	33	43.1	50.3
1962	65	84	43.6	48.9	25	33	43.1	48.1
1964	90	75	54.5	57.6	32	25	56.1	57.7
1966	80	70	53.3	51.0	26	31	45.6	49.5
1968	72	78	48.0	49.5	24	33	42.1	45.8
1970	71	79	47.3	49.5	24	33	42.1	48.2
1972	67	83	44.6	49.6	23	37	38.3	47.5
1974	88	62	58.7	55.9	26	34	43.3	53.5
1976	90	60	60.0	56.2	25	35	41.6	50.6
1978	86	64	57.3	52.5	25	35	41.6	48.2
1980	86	64	57.3	51.6	24	35	40.7	46.8
1982	97	52	65.1	58.4	26	35	42.6	46.5
1984	94	55	63.1	52.7	26	35	42.6	44.8
1986	95	56	62.9	54.5	26	35	42.6	45.0
1988	92	58	61.3	54.0	27	34	44.3	43.8
1990	94	56	62.6	52.8	26	35	42.6	44.2
1992	101	49	67.3	55.3	26	35	42.6	49.6
1994	94	56	62.6	51.5	25	36	41.1	40.2
1996	96	54	64.0	58.7	27	34	44.3	52.1
1998	99	51	66.0	57.6	25	36	40.1	49.1
2000	99	57	66.0	59.2	25	36	41.0	47.2
2002	102	48	68.0	57.2	25	37	40.1	40.5
2004	105	45	70.0	62.7	26	36	41.9	48.2
2008	109	41	72.6	70.6	32	30	51.6	57.0

Sources: Figures from 1960 through 1980 are calculated from the *Red Book* (Guilderland: New York Legal Publications, various years), which, unfortunately, stopped compiling vote totals. We are indebted to Professor Jeffrey M. Stonecash of Syracuse University for providing us with the aggregate popular vote totals from 1982 through 1994. More recent numbers are calculated from the website of the state Board of Elections.

years the Democrats were able to win even more seats upstate and expand their legislative base. The 1982 elections were particularly important. The Democrats increased their seats because they drew district lines as part of reapportionment. By 1991 they held 37 of 90 (41 percent) seats upstate. The Democratic party had become more of an urban statewide party than a downstate party."[43]

In the 2008 elections, the Democrats consolidated their emerging status as the dominant party by taking control of the senate as well. Winning 57 percent of the statewide senate vote (and an overwhelming 70.6 percent in assembly races), the Democrats overcame Republican advantages in both districting and incumbency to take two previously Republican seats, extend their victory margins in seats won in 2006 and 2007, and very nearly oust two other long-time Republican senators. Should the Democrats consolidate these gains in 2010, they will have the crucial power to draw the district lines for both the senate and the assembly.

The Norm of Divided Government

Divided government, with a chief executive of one party and at least one house of the legislature controlled by the other party, has become common both in Washington and in the states. It has been a particularly persistent phenomenon in New York. As can be seen in Table 3.3, every modern governor of New York, save Thomas Dewey in the years 1943 through 1954, Malcolm Wilson in 1973 to 1974, and David Paterson since 2009, has had to deal with a legislature with at least one house controlled by the opposite party. The roots of divided government in New York State extend at least back to the New Deal and in fact can be traced through much of the state's history. Al Smith compiled a remarkable record of legislative achievements as a Democrat between 1919–1920 and 1923–1928, yet the assembly in those years always was under Republican control, and the senate usually.

Whether divided government leads to deadlock and political stalemate is not as clear as conventional wisdom might suggest. At the national level, Mayhew's exhaustive analysis of the years 1946 through 1990 led him to conclude, in essence, that "unified versus divided control has probably *not* made a notable difference during the postwar era."[44] The competing demands of constituency interests, among other forces, can produce unpredictable alliances regardless of party alignments. An interesting case in New York occurred shortly after George Pataki assumed the governorship in 1995. Despite Pataki's vociferous opposition to a bill increasing the pensions of retired state and municipal employees, it passed both houses of the legislature by veto-proof margins, and the governor was forced to swallow it. While passage in the Democratic assembly surprised no one, even the governor seems to have been caught off guard by the enthusiastic reception accorded the bill by the Republican state senate and its new majority leader, Joseph Bruno. The main reason Bruno had unseated Ralph Marino to become majority leader, as one journalist put it, "was because the Senate's conservative Young Turks thought he was far more likely to do Pataki's bidding."[45] Yet here was Bruno, with strong support from the Young Turks, defying the governor before the honeymoon had even begun. The fact that Bruno himself came from a capitol-area district that included thousands of state workers may have been a factor in the senate's stand against the governor. Far more important, however, were the long-standing political and personal ties that the state's public employee unions had built with senate Repub-

Table 3.3

Divided Government in New York: Party Control of the Governorship, Assembly, and State Senate, 1933–2009

Years	Governor	Party	Senate majority	Assembly majority
1933–34	Herbert Lehman	Democratic	Democratic	Republican
1935–38	Herbert Lehman	Democratic	Democratic	Split[a]
1939–42	Herbert Lehman	Democratic	Republican	Republican
1943–54	Thomas Dewey	Republican	Republican	Republican
1955–58	Averell Harriman	Democratic	Republican	Republican
1959–64	Nelson Rockefeller	Republican	Republican	Republican
1965–66	Nelson Rockefeller	Republican	Democratic	Democratic
1967–68	Nelson Rockefeller	Republican	Republican	Democratic
1969–72	Nelson Rockefeller	Republican	Republican	Republican
1973–74	Malcolm Wilson	Republican	Republican	Republican
1975–82	Hugh Carey	Democratic	Republican	Democratic
1983–94	Mario Cuomo	Democratic	Republican	Democratic
1995–06	George Pataki	Republican	Republican	Democratic
2007–08	Eliot Spitzer	Democratic	Republican	Democratic
2009–	David Paterson	Democratic	Democratic	Democratic

Source: New York State *Red Book* (Guilderland: New York Legal Publications, various years).

[a]With a system of annual elections for the assembly, the Democrats won a majority in 1935, lost in 1936, recaptured control in 1937, and lost again in 1938.

licans. Twelve years later, Eliot Spitzer was to find that his fellow Democrats in the legislature were equally willing to assert their independence by ignoring the three candidates put forth by a gubernatorial screening panel and appointing their fellow assemblyman Tom DiNapoli state comptroller. "Eliot's problem," as one member of the assembly told us, "is that he believed those articles that said the legislature was dysfunctional. He'll learn."

The fact, as these cases illustrate, is that the major players in New York State politics have been accustomed to a playing field in which party control is divided; state legislators, in their turn, have become similarly accustomed to conditions of divided government. Although deadlock is sometimes a problem—chronically late budgets often are cited as symptomatic of a serious inability to govern efficiently—it can be argued that governing has become too ritualized in New York, that the parties are so used to accommodating themselves to each other that they have overlooked the real issues. There are ways, indeed, in which divided government served each party well, making them ritual enemies that used each other to shore up their own political positions. "One-house bills" were commonplace in two-party Albany. These were bills that passed either the Democratic assembly or Republican senate with no hope or expectation that they would become law. Bold new social programs, which even their sponsors knew the state could not pay for, emerged from the assembly together with equally irresponsible tax-cutting proposals from the senate. Democrats could thus take credit with their constituents for new initiatives and, while blaming Republicans for bottling them up, remain free of any need to find the money to pay for them. Republicans played the same games in reverse. In a similar fashion, every governor since Hugh Carey low-balled his budget request for education. Knowing that both houses of the legislature would fight to keep local school aid dollars flowing, governors were protected from the consequences of actually cutting the education budget, but gained bargaining leverage on other issues. Legislators, for their part, went home to the voters boasting of their success in restoring school dollars. Thus have politicians paved the road to reelection.

New York's Vanishing Marginals

Students of Congress have filled thousands of pages exploring the amazing ability of contemporary members of the House of Representatives to win reelection. "Marginal seats," districts in which challengers have a reasonable chance of winning, have all but disappeared. Similarly in New York, relatively few legislators have been at risk of losing in any given election. As with Congress, it is difficult to isolate a single explanatory variable for this decline in electoral competition. Indeed, evidence suggests that incumbents running for reelection in New York always have done quite well. As Stonecash notes, the "percent of incumbents (among those seeking reelection) winning reelection has remained in the 80 to 90 percent range since around 1900"; it has not dipped below 95 percent since 1982. Careerism, the tendency of legislators to seek reelection and make politics a career, "has increased dramatically in the last two decades."[46] Partisan gerrymanders, as we have seen, are an important factor. As in national politics, moreover, state legislators have more resources at their disposal: more staff, bigger printing and postage budgets to keep their names in front of the people, and the ability to deliver both symbolic victories (one-house bills) and real policies. Also, as the party loyalties of the voters decline, more of them seem likely to take incumbency as a guide on how to vote. Whether the continuing success of incumbents is due to their greater ability to raise money is not entirely clear, but it takes a constantly increasing amount of money even to think about challenging a sitting member of the legislature. "In the assembly in 1984 incumbents on average spent $22,625. By 2002 the average had increased to $108,625. In the senate, the average expenditure increased from $35,054 in 1984 to $328,228 in 2002."[47] This includes the spending totals of the many members who were running essentially unopposed. A competitive election, such as the 2008 state senate race in Long Island's third district, can cost more than $1 million. Before potential candidates can even think seriously about seeking the help of state party leaders in taking on an incumbent, they must demonstrate the ability to raise a minimum of six figures.

However each of these variables weighs into the equation, the two houses of the legislature have become increasingly isolated from swings in the party preferences of the electorate. Table 3.2 charts the fluctuating fortunes of major party candidates for the state senate and assembly. What is perhaps most striking about these figures is the sharp and growing isolation they show between swings in the popular vote and seats in the legislature. A dramatic surge in a party's vote—like the Democrats' jump from 48.9 percent of the total cast for assembly candidates in 1962 to the 57.6 percent they won in 1964—can produce a real change in the legislature. The Democrats' share of assembly seats went from 43.6 percent to 54.5 percent, taking them from minority status to a clear majority. Yet a jump of more than five points in the percentage of the electorate voting Democratic for senate candidates between 1990 and 1992 resulted in no change at all in the senate's party alignment. An even larger drop the next year—from 49.6 percent in 1992 to 40.2 percent in 1994—resulted in a net Democratic loss of only one seat. In 2006, when Democratic candidates for the state senate increased their overall share of the popular vote from 48.2 to 54.4 percent, their net gain in actual districts won was only one.

Aggregate figures such as these can be misleading. Legislative elections are won on a district-by-district basis, and variations in turnout and patterns of competition can be lost in statewide totals, but the data seem rather clearly to underscore the importance of incumbency on the one hand and of redistricting on the other. Reflecting the importance of incumbency, the party holding a majority of seats in the assembly or senate almost always has been able to capture a statewide majority for its own candidates. Particularly since the institutionalization of divided government in the 1970s, the percentage of voters supporting Democratic candidates for the assembly has exceeded support for Democratic senate candidates by an average of nearly 10 percent, and the gap is growing. In 1990, when Mario Cuomo was trouncing the hapless Pierre Rinfret and assembly Democrats were rolling up a 52.8 percent statewide vote, senate Republicans won more than 55 percent of the aggregate vote. In 1994, despite George Pataki's win and in contrast with a Republican margin of nearly 60 percent in senate races, Democratic candidates for the state assembly still won 51.5 percent of the aggregate vote. In Eliot Spitzer's landslide victory in 2006, the aggregate Republican share of the two-party vote for state senators decreased by 6 percent, but the Republicans lost only two seats.

New York City and the Cycles of Reform

In national elections, in most statewide contests, and in choosing its senate and assembly representatives in Albany, New York City has been overwhelmingly Democratic for the full century of its existence as a five-borough metropolis. For at least the past half century of that period, it has been almost as resoundingly liberal in its political orientation. Its members of Congress, state senators, and assembly members consistently receive high ratings from liberal groups and low ratings from political conservatives. Voters registered as Democrats have exceeded those registered as Republicans by a margin of at least three to one in every year but one since 1930, with 84 percent of those registering with a major party listed as Democrats in 2006. This quintessentially Democratic city, however, has had almost as many non-Democratic mayors as it has had Democrats. Even in the heyday of Tammany Hall, so-called fusion candidates, uniting dissident Democrats with Republicans and other outsiders against the machine, were a persistent, often successful feature of city politics. Some of the city's most famous mayors, including Fiorello LaGuardia, John Lindsay, and Rudolph Giuliani, began as outsiders and Republicans.

City Democrats and the Politics of Ethnicity

From the late 1950s through the early 1980s, the locus of reform politics shifted away from the traditional fusion model to a struggle within the Democratic primary. John Lindsay, who won his first campaign for mayor in 1965 as a typical fusion candidate running on the Republican and Liberal Party lines, depicted his main opponent, Democrat Abe Beame, as a tool of the old clubhouse bosses. Lindsay won by a narrow margin of just over 100,000 votes, polling 43 percent of the total vote to 39 percent for Beame and a surprising 13 percent for the Conservative candidate, the journalist William F. Buckley. While Buckley succeeded in cutting deeply into Lindsay's Republican base, the key to Lindsay's victory lay in his ability to hold a significant proportion of this vote and add to it a substantial bloc of voters (mostly on the Liberal line) traditionally loyal to the Democrats. In his reelection campaign, when it became increasingly clear that Lindsay would have trouble holding his Republican base, the mayor sought and received the backing of prominent Democrats and the leaders of the municipal labor unions. In the election, Lindsay won less than 20 percent of the largely Irish and Italian white Catholics but more than 80 percent of blacks. He and the Democrat, Mario Proccacino, split the Jewish vote, enabling Lindsay to win. A few months later, the mayor officially became a Democrat. So did many of his supporters.

For the next three decades, the real contests for mayor of New York tended to take place in Democratic primaries. With the party organization splintered between reform and regular factions, Democrats in the legislature passed a law in 1969 requiring a runoff in the event that no candidate received more than 40 percent of the primary vote. The idea was that a consensus Democrat was far less likely than one chosen by a small splinter to lose to a fusion candidate in November. Essentially that is how it worked in the 1970s and 1980s as the winners of Democratic primaries—sometimes with minor party help, sometimes not—became mayor. In retrospect, however, a more profound shift also began in the Lindsay years: the splintering along both ethnic and ideological lines of the old New Deal coalition that had made New York the quintessential liberal Democratic city. The alienation of white ethnics and many Jewish voters—particularly in the outer boroughs—and the growing isolation of blacks and Latinos was to become a persistent theme in city politics. "In the wake of the racial conflicts of the Lindsay era, many liberal

Box 3.4
Running to Lose

One of the most uncommon campaigns for mayor of New York City was that of magazine publisher William F. Buckley in 1965. The conservative Buckley, annoyed that Republican John Lindsay was as liberal on most issues as Democrat Abe Beame, sought the nomination of the Conservative Party in order to teach the Republicans a lesson by siphoning off enough votes to ensure Lindsay's defeat. Eschewing such traditional urban campaign tactics as shaking hands at subway stops, visiting ethnic restaurants, and seeking the endorsements of other politicians, Buckley focused almost entirely on the media. What was most striking about his candidacy was his candor in admitting that he was not in it to win. Asked at his announcement speech if he wanted to be mayor, Buckley replied, "I have never even considered it"; asked whether he had any chance of winning, he answered "No."

Later in the campaign, Buckley engaged in the following colloquy with a reporter:

Question: Why didn't you run in the Republican primary?
Buckley: Why didn't Martin Luther King run for Governor of Alabama?
Question: What would you do if you won?
Buckley: Demand a recount.

Source: Chris McNickle, *To Be Mayor of New York: Ethnic Politics in the City* (New York: Columbia University Press, 1993), p. 198.

whites, especially Jews, joined then-congressman Ed Koch in moving toward the more defensive, conservative positions already held by those who provided the social base for the regular Democratic clubs."[48]

As the reform movement that had united minority groups and liberal whites behind Lindsay began to splinter, the Republican Party began lurching to the right. Deserted by moderates like Lindsay and paralleling the rise of the party's Reagan faction in national politics, New York's Republicans became increasingly unlikely candidates for fusion. Moreover, whatever mass base the Liberal Party had ever had was gone. For the next four elections, from 1973 through 1985, the Democratic primary for mayor was, in essence, the only election that counted, and a badly splintered reform movement saw moderate and increasingly conservative candidates win relatively easy victories. Splits between blacks and Latinos and various factions of the reform movement led one liberal candidate for mayor to observe that "if reform Democrats were asked to form a firing squad the first order would be to form a circle."

The biggest of these circles was formed in 1977 when a record 900,000 primary voters narrowly selected Ed Koch as mayor over a field that included three members of Congress, a borough president, Mayor Beame, and a novice candidate from Queens named Mario Cuomo. The gap between Koch and the lowest vote-getter was less than 80,000 votes, with the candidates showing little ability to reach beyond their ethnic, ideological, or neighborhood base. By moving to the right, Koch was able to build a remarkably diverse coalition for his 1981 reelection campaign, winning the nominations of the Democratic, Republican, and Conservative parties. With his popularity seeming to cut across ethnic and ideological lines, Koch decided to run for governor and became the party's endorsed candidate against a man he had beaten for mayor five years before, Mario Cuomo. Despite Koch's statewide loss to Cuomo for the governorship, he rolled to an easy victory in the 1985 mayoral election. "His badly divided potential opponents were unable to put forward candidates who appealed strongly to their own constituencies, much less other constituencies."[49] Mollenkopf, dividing the city's assembly districts into five types, showed Koch, as expected, winning nearly 70 percent of the white Catholic vote and 65 percent of outer-borough Jewish votes. But even among white liberals (57 percent) and blacks (41 percent) Koch ran surprisingly well, particularly since he was facing both a black and a liberal white opponent.[50]

Then, as quickly and unexpectedly as Koch had risen to power, his coalition fell apart. "Within months," as historian Richard Wade puts it, "the euphoria of victory was replaced by unfolding scandals that spread throughout the administration and reached into the inner rooms of City Hall. The press was soon comparing the administration to the dark days of Jimmy Walker and Boss Tweed."[51] The 1989 election of the city's first African-American mayor, David Dinkins, seemingly restored the liberal Democratic coalition that had dominated city government for so long. Dinkins, benefiting not just from the scandals plaguing Koch, but also from a series of incidents seeming to reveal insensitivity on Koch's part to issues of race, ate into every part of the mayor's coalition. Most strikingly, Koch's support among blacks and Latinos dropped by more than 30 percent, and turnout in African-American districts was up almost 30 percent as well.[52]

Beyond Fusion: Rudolph Giuliani, Michael Bloomberg, and the New Republican Challenge

The general election pitted Dinkins against a former federal prosecutor, Republican Rudolph Giuliani. Unlike the typical fusion candidate, exploiting a split between the regular and reform wings of the Democratic Party, Giuliani seemed to have little chance of success. However, as Mollenkopf says:

> Race, and more specifically, racially based mistrust, provided a new basis for whites who traditionally voted for the Democratic nominee to defect from their party. . . . White liberals, blacks, and Latinos (and by definition more strongly partisan voters) figured less heavily in the general electorate than in the Democratic primary electorate. In the general electorate, Republicans, independents, and whites were more numerous. . . . These conditions opened the way for Rudolph Giuliani to seek to reconstruct the Koch coalition of white Catholics and Jews along somewhat more conservative lines than Mayor Koch had pursued.[53]

Dinkins prevailed, thanks in large part to a massive get-out-the-vote drive that was particularly effective in black neighborhoods. In ethnic and ideological terms, Dinkins's victory was a traditional coalition triumph cutting across a variety of cleavages. "The Dinkins coalition," as Mollenkopf concludes,

> resembled those that powered racial succession in other cities to the extent that it relied upon an extraordinary mobilization of his core constituency of blacks. But it differed from them in the degree to which it would have to rely on other constituencies as well. It had to include white liberals, Latinos, and indeed a significant number of the outer-borough Jews and white Catholics who had supported Mayor Koch. This black-led, biracial and multiethnic insurgent coalition constitutes a fundamentally new element in New York's political development, one that has few national counterparts.[54]

Giuliani's losing coalition was equally unique, and when Dinkins found himself embroiled in racially polarizing problems, the balance of power tipped enough to push him out of Gracie Mansion (the mayor's official residence) in 1993.

Although Giuliani had both the Republican and Liberal nominations, his was not a traditional fusion campaign. Unlike such classic fusion candidates as LaGuardia and Lindsay, Giuliani was not a champion of reform and did not campaign to the left of the regular candidate. It would be misleading to describe the shift from Dinkins to Giuliani simply in ethnic terms. Turnout declined slightly in black election districts and by a little more among Latinos, and there was some slippage in the mayor's support among white liberals. Turnout in white Catholic areas was substantially higher (particularly on Staten Island, where there was a concurrent referendum on secession from the city), and this helped Giuliani. But the shifts were small: having won by fewer than 50,000 votes in 1989, Dinkins lost by a comparable margin in 1993, a shift of less than 3 percent. In a nutshell, Dinkins's "difficulty was clearly related to the fact that many people, even among blacks and others who had supported him in 1989, had concluded that he had performed poorly as mayor."[55]

Giuliani's first term—marked by a boom on Wall Street and a striking drop in the crime rate—won generally high marks from the electorate, and he cruised to an easy victory in 1997. Because of a law limiting the mayor of New York to two terms, Giuliani was unable to run for reelection in the aftermath of the attacks on the World Trade Center; but another untraditional candidate, Democrat-turned-Republican Michael Bloomberg, was able to win. Bloomberg's victory on the Republican Party line marked the first time in modern history that New York had elected two Republican mayors in a row, and his reelection in 2005 made it appear as if a major realignment might have taken place. Noting that Democrats continue to dominate all other offices in the city, most observers doubt that there has been a significant switch. Bloomberg's willingness to spend more than $70 million of his own money in both 2001 and 2005 clearly contributed to his success, as did his relatively liberal stand on a number of issues. New York City's peculiar combination of ethnic, partisan, issue, and power politics results in a continuing kaleidoscope of shifting coalitions that are only tangentially related to state and national trends. Even in the first Dinkins campaign, arguably the most racially polarizing in the city's history, "what is interesting . . . was not their degree of racial polarization, which was to be expected, but the degree to which they were *not* governed by race alone."[56] The Giuliani victory in 1997 was similarly unusual in its ability to cut across traditional ethnic, partisan, and ideological boundaries. The mayor, despite a landslide victory, had no coattails—Democrats retained a forty-six-to-five margin in the city council, as they have in the Bloomberg years—and although the press enjoyed speculating about both Bloomberg and Giuliani's future in state and national politics, it is probably worth noting that no twentieth-century New York City mayor ever went on to higher office.

Berg offers the interesting theory that it is in some ways the very weakness of the Republican Party in New York City that accounts for much of its recent success in electing mayors:

> Divided by borough-based organizations and a large number of potential candidates now exacerbated by term limits for all city elected offices, the Democratic Party has found it difficult to coalesce around a single candidate for mayor. The Republican Party, given its lack of hierarchy and few potential candidates, has been able to seek out candidates who can run a credible campaign and draw votes away from the Democratic nominee. As a result of their lack of organization, the Republicans are not tied to candidates who arise from a decentralized and sometimes protracted process.[57]

The Dilemmas of the Parties

Despite the frequent successes of Republicans in winning control of Gracie Mansion, even the most popular Republican mayors have shown little or no ability to build the party's strength in New York City. The number of Republicans elected to other offices in the city has been and remains trivial. Except in such small pockets as Staten Island, the only elections that concern candidates for city council, judgeships, and seats in the state legislature are Democratic primaries. From a statewide perspective, the Big Apple remains the core of Democratic Party strength. Rural areas and the outer, more affluent suburbs are similarly central to the fortunes of state Republicans. Since 1974 the Democrats have expanded their city base to encompass urban areas in general and, to a lesser extent, some of the older, less affluent suburbs, but in statewide Democratic primaries the city continues to cast roughly 60 percent of all the votes.

Statewide, the Republicans are almost the converse of the Democrats: their primary electorate is, essentially, upstate, conservative, and white. So is their fading contingent in the state senate. The dilemma of both parties is the difficulty of escaping this inherent polarization, a task compounded by national trends. As long as the conservative, southern wing of the Republican Party controls its image, the party will have difficulty winning enough votes in urban areas to win a statewide majority. For the Democrats, the problems are at once ethnic and ideological: Jewish and other white city liberals together with blacks and other minorities have the votes to control most primaries, but the kinds of candidates they are likely to nominate will find it increasingly difficult to win statewide office. And the assembly's city-led Democratic majority has little interest in moderating its image, helping fellow Democrats maintain control of the senate, or working to elect statewide Democratic candidates.

Conclusion: The Roles of Parties in New York Politics

Potential candidates, surveying their chances of being elected in New York State, cannot ignore the historic and legal factors described here. To run for office in most parts of New York City, it helps to be a Democrat, and while being a Democrat was once a near-fatal defect upstate, times are changing. The support of the formal party organization, essential in most parts of the state during the heyday of the machine, is more peripheral today. There are four great contextual realities that define the parameters of politics in New York, distinguishing it markedly from most other states. First, the Democratic and Republican parties in New York are essentially three parties loosely joined by a network of local institutions and a formal framework of little real significance. The three Democratic and Republican party groups that count are those that compete for control of the state senate, the state assembly, and the executive branch, especially the governorship. Within each of the major parties, these three organizations operate independently of one another and of the local Republican and Democratic parties that contest for municipal, county, and judicial offices. These party systems, secondly, are supplemented and sometimes swayed by a unique array of satellite parties—Working Families and Conservative in particular—whose support is often significant enough to keep the major parties on their toes. Third, the kinds of demographic and economic variables that frequently explain electoral behavior lose their explanatory power in New York due to the continuing importance of region. More than in any other state, politics in New York is defined by a sharp line of cleavage that distinguishes New York City, and to some extent its suburbs, from everywhere else.

Finally, New York is different from most other states because its elected officials have worked deliberately to make it different. The fact that the New York State assembly has been as unassailably Democratic as the senate has been Republican; the highly unusual success rates of incumbent legislators winning reelection; the spectacularly low turnouts of voters in New York elections—all of these are the products not just of demography and change, but of a set of election laws crafted by incumbent politicians protecting their own interests. New York's election laws are by far the most complex in the United States, helping to account for the frequently cited fact that more than half of the election law cases filed in the courtrooms of the fifty states are filed in New York. Things that are relatively simple and straightforward in forty-nine other states can be quite complicated in New York—because the elected officials who make the laws that govern their own chances of reelection like it that way.

In his seminal works on state politics, the late V.O. Key described the study of political parties in terms of three distinct but overlapping circles: the party in the electorate, the party organization, and the party in government. As on the national scene, the party in the electorate is harder and harder to find in New York, where nearly one voter in five refuses to register with a party and where straight party voting is increasingly uncommon. Paradoxically, however, as one moves from voters to institutions, party lines are in many ways more sharply etched in New York politics than in most other states.

The party organizations are, in the aggregate, weaker than once they were. One statistical study, using a variety of quantitative indicators, rated New York's party systems as the fourteenth weakest among the fifty states.[58] But if the days of Tammany and its counterparts are past, there are strong party organizations in New York. At the statewide level, the Republican Party continues to control nominations, raise money, and contest elections with every bit as much vigor as it did in the heyday of Dewey and Rockefeller. Unlike the Democratic State Convention—whose endorsement has proven a virtual kiss of death for potential candidates—the nominees of the official Republican Party never have been rejected in a statewide primary election and almost never challenged. Potentially strong candidates have withdrawn in the interests of ticket balancing, as assembly minority leader John Faso did with his 1994 campaign for comptroller. And the party has been able to take virtual unknowns like Alphonse D'Amato and George Pataki and turn them into household names. The party organizations associated with the parties in the legislature, both Republican and Democratic, moreover, are considerably stronger than they have ever been.

Even in New York City, remnants of the old Democratic organization continue to exert considerable clout in the outer boroughs, where, to use Wolfinger's distinction, machine politics still are practiced in the absence of a well-organized machine.[59] As Mollenkopf puts it, "While they have much less influence over who wins the mayoralty than they once did, candidates supported by the Bronx, Queens, Brooklyn and Staten Island organizations typically win elections for lesser offices and can absorb most of the few insurgents who win elections against them."[60]

These kinds of individually strong party organizations are not reflected in the kinds of aggregate-level, statistical studies that attempt to compare state party systems largely by focusing on the state committees. Given the legislative party organizations and the continuing clout of many local leaders, the reality is that the parties as organizations in New York should be ranked in the top quartile rather than the lowest of the fifty states.

Finally, when it comes to the party-in-government, parties in New York have not declined in the slightest. As we shall argue in Chapter 6, party organizations—particularly in the legislature—have become central guidance institutions in the shaping of public policy in New York State. Where once party leaders in Albany relied upon county leaders to push legislators into line, today it is local leaders who come to Albany as supplicants. In few states are the parties in government as strong as they are in New York, and in no state are they stronger.

4

Power, Pluralism, Public Opinion, and the Permanent Government

For years, students of both local and national government were divided into two intellectual camps. Those described as *pluralists* emphasized the relatively wide dispersal of power in American politics, the existence of many competing groups and interests, and the role of government as an active arbiter of conflicts among competing interests. The *power elite* approach, on the other hand, viewed the system as essentially closed and tightly dominated by a small elite of powerful individuals who were in enough control of public officials that they could be described as a "permanent government."

Some of the force of the debate between these competing perspectives on power has been diminished by a growing recognition that the study of political power is incomplete when it focuses solely on governments. Private interests—business interests, in particular—play important roles in shaping society whether they control the institutions of government or not. *Structuralists* assert that the study of politics is incomplete to the extent that it focuses only on government institutions, which, whether pluralistic or elitist, must come to terms with key elements in the private sector. "Strong centrifugal forces," as Stone concludes in his study of Atlanta, "characterize modern societies. Fragmented into myriad special roles, these societies lack an overarching power of command. The formal authority of government is limited, and substantial resources are in private hands. Especially at the local level, the power of public officials may be dwarfed by processes and activities entirely outside government control."[1]

Even in the absence of an active power elite, certain interests—too dispersed and disorganized to constitute an elite—are too firmly embedded in the foundations of modern society to be defied. The very structure of a capitalist society forces all governments, especially local governments, to be deferential to the big mules that pull the economic cart. While these forces are neither as cohesive nor as omnipotent as early elite theories had suggested, they are more coherent and less visible than those described in the pluralist model of group struggle.

One thing the pluralist and elitist models have in common is a tendency to be dismissive of traditional "democratic" forces. In the extreme, some pluralists depict elections as instruments too crude to provide meaningful mandates, while public opinion in the aggregate is insufficiently informed to be meaningful. Only when their attitudes are channeled through their areas of special concern and knowledge— essentially through interest groups—are ordinary citizens likely to be a significant political force. Similarly, power elitists are dismissive of public opinion and electoral politics as essentially peripheral to real issues of power. While the people at large debate the trivial issues that the "real" power brokers assign them, major policy questions are resolved either by the ruling elite or the structural mandates of the prevailing economic order.

Most public officials and a growing majority of political scientists find it difficult to accept an overarching perspective on the nature of political influence. Economic realities and the interests of key business leaders do set significant limits on the range of policies government can responsibly consider. At the same time, the boundaries established by these structural elites are quite broad, broad enough for politics to be significant to most people. In the real world of politics, interest groups are important and power is, in many ways, specialized. But elections are also important: New York is a different city under Michael Bloomberg than it was when Rudolph Giuliani was mayor, the election of Eliot Spitzer in 2006 marked a significant watershed in state politics, and the people who made these changes possible are not entirely drawn from either the pressure system or the power elite. Finally, public policy continues to be influenced to a considerable degree by public opinion. Neither pluralist nor elite theory has a good explanation for the fact that New York's political leaders spend millions of dollars every year privately surveying public attitudes on the issues of the day. The mechanisms vary, and public attitudes matter more on some issues than others, but New York's conservatives—because they come from New York—will never be as conservative as North Carolina's. In sum, the forces that impinge on politicians in Albany are arrayed as a constantly shifting kaleidoscope of economic elites, competing interests groups, electoral forces, and general public attitudes.

Regime Politics in New York

Students of state politics have been largely peripheral to the debate between pluralists and power elitists. Textbooks on state and local government, while they frequently cite the debate in their discussions of local politics, seldom discuss its relevance to the states. Yet much in the argument clearly applies to politics in the state capitol. Every municipality in the state, moreover, has a power structure, or regime, that is not fully reflected in its formal governance. Governments, regardless of how they are configured, must be highly cognizant of the limits of their capacity to intrude forcefully on the key interests of the regime. In New York City, major corporations including Citigroup, Chase, and Verizon employ, on average, 22,000 employees. Whatever their ideology, public officials need not be reminded that the city's prosperity is deeply intertwined with the prosperity of these businesses. Even at the state level, companies such as International Business Machines (IBM) in Dutchess County and General Electric (GE) in the capitol region, two of the largest for-profit employers in the state, are so vital to economic prosperity that it would be almost unthinkable to challenge their core interests. As Pecorella writes:

> [B]ecause wealth production in the United States occurs largely in the private sector and because government at all levels depends on the producers of wealth for the resources it is charged with allocating, interests involved in large-scale wealth production are critically important to public officials. Such interests are particularly critical to officials at the subnational levels of government, where corporate mobility is often an option and operating budgets have to be balanced.[2]

Every New York politician knows, on the one hand, that many of the businesses that create jobs and fuel the economy could, if sufficiently unhappy, move to New Jersey (or elsewhere). Business leaders are not shy about threatening such moves. All politicians, on the other hand, also see the large, prosperous enterprises in their jurisdiction as potentially enormous sources of tax revenue. When a company closes down or leaves the state, it stops paying taxes, its employees stop paying taxes, and they stop buying goods and services from other New York companies that also pay taxes. When there is a collapse on Wall Street—especially of the magnitude of 2008—the state loses billions of dollars in income tax collections alone.

Rivals for Power

As solicitous of business interests as these forces make most politicians, there are countervailing powers at work, particularly at the state level. With an economy as complex as that of New York, no single group of industries or sector of the economy has the kind of disproportionate clout that, for example, the oil companies might have in Louisiana or the gaming industry in Nevada. While corporations in New York often have interests in common, they also compete with one another. New York, moreover, is a highly unionized state whose unions enthusiastically engage in politics. Real estate interests and land developers are well represented in New York, both state and city, but so are tenants. The reform coalitions that ended the rule of party machines also helped create government agencies—or bureaucratic "decision centers," as Sayre and Kaufman call them—that evolved into "new machines" centered around the protection and enhancement of their own roles.[3] The reemergence of community, the wave of decentralization that Pecorella and others have associated with "postreform" politics, fueled the emergence of ethnic interests, on the one hand, and a more general focus on community groups on the other. So-called not in my back yard (NIMBY) groups have shown increasing ability to frustrate powerful economic and political interests in the siting of roads, homeless shelters, stadiums, housing projects, and prisons. Finally, the general public, the mood of the state, the political culture—whatever one calls the usually inchoate set of attitudes, prejudices, media reports, and poll results that politicians believe to be reflective of reality—sets important limits on what political actors believe can and cannot be done.

Both pluralists and elitists, as noted, largely have ignored the states, and students of state politics have, by and large, returned the favor by ignoring the question. Not surprisingly, elite theories also have fared far better at the local level than the national. If, as most community power studies have suggested, New York City is more pluralistic than most cities, the most obvious explanation is rooted in size: New York is simply too big and complex to have a single governing interest or elite. At the state level, economic interests are still more highly diffused. Students of urban politics have given more attention to nongovernmental powers in part because private interests frequently do play more visible and significant roles in local as opposed to state politics. There are lots of company towns but few company states. Local governments, moreover, often have powers that directly challenge and confront certain kinds of businesses, such as real estate. Although a state government can tax, regulate, license, or subsidize an individual business enterprise, it must usually direct its policies at business as a whole, including a company's competitors. Both Coca-Cola and Pepsi were against New York State's bottle-return law, but neither suffered a competitive disadvantage from the requirement that they collect a five-cent deposit on every bottle. But when New York City denies Donald Trump a variance to build a particular building on land he owns, Trump's injury is both direct and singular. It affects no other developer, and it affects Trump absolutely. Not surprisingly, studies of community power in urban America almost always include real estate developers high on the list of power wielders. Yet these interests are not a major force at the national level and rank relatively low in most states.

The size and general liberalism of New York, both the state and the city, have long blended these forces in complex ways. Among students of urban politics, New York City usually has been depicted as unusually pluralistic. Paul Peterson's argument that urban areas must almost inevitably focus on promoting private investment while discouraging redistributive social services is persuasive *except* with regard to New York City, an anomaly that Peterson addresses.[4] Even to the extent that New York actually has been different, the fiscal crises of the 1970s forced the city to confront painful choices and at least make changes in the direction of Peterson's model. The Koch administration, as Mollenkopf shows, "vigorously promoted private investment in office building construction" and "de-emphasized redistributive spending." In the end, however, New York reaffirmed its unique style of urban governance, and, "in the final analysis the Koch administration did not pursue budgetary austerity.

After the early 1980s it rapidly expanded all components of city spending as well as social services."[5] What Mollenkopf convincingly shows is that the interplay between the economic realities supporting the so-called permanent government in New York City and the political pressures from interest groups and the general public is far more complicated than structuralist theory suggests. We argue that this is even more the case in state politics. With globalization impacting both cities and states, the role of economic elites in defining the parameters of public choice is not insignificant, especially in the wake of the events of 9/11, which, as Savitch and Kantor note, were not breaks from globalization but by-products of it.[6]

Despite increasing globalization, pluralists tend to overemphasize the importance of visible groups. Journalists too tend to focus their attention on the activities of organized interest groups because their lobbying efforts are most directly and obviously political; and because the focus of this book is on the political process, we follow that tradition. A strong argument can be made, however, that many groups are active in politics more because they are vulnerable than because they are strong. As E.E. Schattschneider observed in his celebrated 1960 work on national politics, "It is the losers in intra-business conflict who seek redress from public authority."[7] The ability of deeply established economic interests to escape adverse government action, thereby avoiding the need to lobby, has diminished since Schattschneider wrote his book. Government intrusions into previously "private" areas such as pollution control, health, worker safety, and consumer protection have forced almost all corporations to seek some form of political representation. Even if we confine our definition of public policy to decisions made by public bodies (such as legislatures, governors, mayors, and city councils), however, many of the most powerful interests in society have little reason to involve themselves in politics. Others can go for years with relatively few problems until suddenly confronting a major threat. All the major tobacco companies have become major players in Albany, a role they did not have to play before they were threatened by proposals to increase their taxes and ban smoking in various places.

New York is a less liberal state than public opinion polls might suggest, in part because its public officials, no matter how liberal they are, must honor the claims of more conservative key players in the permanent government. State and local politicians, as David Nice argues, compete with one another in seeking to attract jobs, investment, and affluent citizens. This competition is most acute at the local level because of the small geographic reach of local governments. An individual or company wanting to locate in a given area typically can select from several local governments in that area. Moreover, relocating from one local government to another is relatively easy for affluent families. From local to state to national governments, the difficulties associated with relocating from one jurisdiction to another increase. As a result, competition among governments for wealthy residents, business investment, and jobs is most acute locally and least acute nationally.[8]

States are, to be sure, less vulnerable on this account than localities, but the threat of relocation is an ever-looming reality. In the 1980s, Mario Cuomo began

---

Box 4.1
Group Representation in Albany

As in most states, lobbyists in New York are required to register. In New York, any lobbyist, group, or public corporation that spends more than $5,000 a year attempting to influence the legislature, the governor, or a state agency must register with the Commission on Public Integrity. Although the fines for non-compliance (a maximum of $25,000 per offense) are relatively trivial for large interests, no one wants the bad publicity that might accompany failure to report. For a variety of reasons, however, the list of groups and corporations registered with the commission is not particularly representative of the realities of group power. The state's largest employees are almost never among the most active lobbyists, and some, including Eastman-Kodak, Macy's, Sears, and Xerox, either have no registered lobbyists in Albany or are represented only part-time by a large firm.

At the other end of the scale are conglomerate enterprises, such as New York Telephone, that are vulnerable to government regulation and have multiple modes of representation. Over the years the champion of reported corporate lobbying groups was probably Phillip Morris, which—before it broke up into separate companies included its tobacco, Miller Beer, and Kraft Food divisions—had its own office, was represented by eight different professional lobbying groups, and was a member of at least five trade associations that were registered to lobby. This spreading of the action was undoubtedly a question, at least in part, of image (and became a factor in the company's breakup). Touting the health benefits of Kraft food products under the corporate symbol of a cigarette company was not a good idea. But companies in the tobacco and alcohol business are so frequently threatened by new taxes and regulations that they simply must have agents in Albany. Large conglomerates such as Phillip Morris and Verizon, at the same time, have diverse interests that sometimes may conflict with one another, forcing the corporate lobbyists simply to withdraw from the field. Trade associations also can have this problem. To play it safe, most groups that have significant interactions with the government are represented in more than one way.

---

cutting taxes on corporations and high-income individuals not out of ideological conviction—indeed, his rhetoric usually indicated great sympathy for redistributing income—nor as a result of any direct political pressure, but out of a real concern for the economic impact of such movements of wealthy taxpayers and businesses. Twenty-five years later, and for largely the same reasons, neither Eliot Spitzer nor David Paterson seriously entertained proposals to increase taxes on the rich as a means of sustaining support for the social services they espoused. In advocating low maximum taxes on personal income, none of these generally liberal Democrats were playing an electoral card or responding to the traditional kinds of political pressures associated with powerful lobbies. There was no "Citizens to Stick It to

Table 4.1

New York's Top Interest Groups Ranked by Reported Expenditures, 2006 and 2007 (in thousands)

	2006		2007
Healthcare Association of New York State	2,227	Verizon Communications	3,216
Forest City Ratner Companies	2,154	Trustees of Columbia University	2,261
New York State United Teachers	1,685	New York State United Teachers	1,685
Medical Society of the State of New York	1,520	Greater New York Hospital Association	1,562
Public Employees Federation	1,286	Healthcare Association of New York State	1,547
Greater New York Hospital Association	1,213	Medical Society of the State of New York	1,486
Yankee Partnership	1,125	Forest City Ratner Companies	1,160
Civil Service Employees Association	985	Trial Lawyers Association	960
United Federation of Teachers	890	United Federation of Teachers	877

Source: New York State Commission on Lobbying, *Annual Report* (Albany: Commission on Lobbying, 2007), Appendix H.

the Working Class" group lobbying on behalf of wealthy taxpayers in Albany. There did not need to be one.

The Power of Organization

There are some groups whose connections with government are so strong and enduring or whose legislative interests are so broad that their presence as active lobbyists is permanent. Public employees unions, teachers, health care associations, and local governments have lobbyists who are as well known in the halls of the Legislative Office Building as some legislators. Others are in and out of the system, depending on how they view the policy stream. Table 4.1 compares the amounts spent by the top ten groups in 2006 and 2007. Yankee Partnership (owners of the New York Yankee baseball team) appears on the list for the year in which it was trying to get state help with its new stadium. They are not normally on the list. Similarly the Forest City Ratner Companies is also on the list of top ten interest groups in both 2006 and 2007. Forest City Ratner, the nation's largest publicly traded commercial real estate development company, owns more than 8 million square feet of commercial property and sought to build a basketball arena for the Nets in Brooklyn. While it has continuing interests in politics, its appearance in the top ten was related almost entirely to its short-run interest in the new arena. Such cases aside, what is most striking about the list of big-time lobbyists is continuity: the same faces that showed up in 2006 and 2007, those representing public employees, local governments, teachers, and the health industry, have been making the list over and over again.

Five groups—the Healthcare Association of New York State, the United Federation of Teachers, the state Medical and Hospital Societies and the state's United Teachers—appear in the top ten in both 2006 and 2007. Organizations as diverse as the League of Women Voters and the Sierra Club, the Motion Picture Association and the Wine Institute maintain a relatively constant presence in Albany, both to keep politicians on their toes and to monitor those actions of state government that might affect the groups' members. Lobbyists for these organizations, together with a large group of higher-priced, for-hire professionals who make their livings representing a variety of interests, form a sort of surplus staff—a reserve army of researchers—for the legislature. Every day that the assembly and senate are in session, each member receives perhaps twenty memorandums from various advocacy groups touting their positions. While many of these memos quickly are discarded, a surprising proportion are read by members and their aides and often kept on file.

Just as shown in most studies of Washington lobbyists, legislators in Albany are more likely to feel helped by lobbyists than pressured. Politicians rely on lobbyists to indicate the concerns of key constituency groups and to provide guidance on technical policy issues. Lobbyists also play a vital role in fostering communication among legislators, at worst spreading rumors, at best bringing together people who might not otherwise realize that they had common interests. As one congressman said about Washington:

> A professional lobbyist becomes part of the woodwork here. He becomes a source of information. A lot of people talk about the invidious special interests, but we shouldn't engage in legislation without knowing who's affected by it, and usually the people who are affected by it are the best sources of information. There are a few guys up here who vote a certain way because they're bought, but most of us don't like to deal with people who only have a short-range interest in us.[9]

There are some important differences between Albany and Washington. The legislative community in Albany is much smaller and more intimate. It is not difficult for lobbyists to talk with the members themselves rather than being filtered through staff or given a cursory two-minute appointment. An Albany lobbyist can still buy a state senator a drink on State Street or join a group of assembly members for a late-night, after-session plate of pasta at Lombardo's or a plate of Buffalo wings at McGeary's. At the same time, the lobbyist's job is more structured in Albany, where the importance of party discipline makes the patterns of communication far less fluid. While no one totally ignores minority party members, lobbyists have little to gain by spending much time with either assembly Republicans or, until recently, senate Democrats. The dominating roles of party leaders, moreover, put most lobbyists a step away from the real decision-makers: lobbying an individual member on anything but a trivial issue essentially means trying to get the member in turn to lobby the party leadership to move the issue along.

Group Politics in Albany

Organization matters and lobbying works. While we have almost never encountered members of the legislature who would admit that their vote has been swayed as a result of organizational pressure, neither would they suggest that most groups that hire Albany representatives are wasting their money. Interest groups can be categorized in a variety of ways: single-interest, multi-interest, "good government," economic, and so on. Yet another way of classifying interest groups is by noting how they get paid. At one extreme are groups that are paid thousands of dollars and at the other extreme are the literally thousands of volunteer lobbyists who are unpaid. Traditionally, Tuesday is lobbying day in Albany and the halls of the Legislative Office Building (LOB, as it is commonly called) are thronged with busloads of citizens going from one legislative office to another to make the case for and against abortion, coyote hunting, increased funding for the arts, and all manner of issues small and large. These groups are rarely effective on their own: it takes a sound, experienced organization behind them to get the required numbers of people to Albany, to guide them to visit those legislators most likely to be influenced, to brief them on what to say. Unless they arrive in surprisingly large numbers (and keep coming back), these citizen lobbyists are seldom an important force. Indeed, most legislators welcome Tuesday lobbying days as opportunities to expand their own circles of potential electoral support. Legislators (and their staff assistants) tend to be good listeners and often appear sympathetic (or genuinely are so) even when they intend to do nothing.

The Lobbying Community

The difference between a professional lobbyist backed by large numbers of Tuesday amateurs and the go-it-alone individual unbacked by an experienced lobbyist was neatly encapsulated many years ago in Congressman Clem Miller's classic tale of the walnut growers and the chicken farmers. In Miller's story, groups of chicken farmers and walnut growers descended upon Congress to explain their dire economic straits. Both made persuasive cases for federal help and aroused considerable feelings of concern. But when the chicken farmers went home, they left the ball in the congressmen's court; the walnut growers, far fewer in number, left a professional lobbyist in Washington to follow up, to propose specific legislation, to remind the busy members of their concern with the issue, to make sure that things got done. Gradually the members, busy with other demands on their time, forgot about the chicken farmers. But the lobbyist for the walnut growers, constantly needling the members, kept the issue alive and got his clients what they needed.[10]

A number of voluntary associations, recognizing the importance of such follow-up activities, hire part-time lobbyists or have one of their members register with the lobbying commission (now known as the Commission on Public Integrity). While such part-time lobbyists are seldom Albany-based, they can help keep the momentum of lobbying alive. A step up from volunteers are professional representatives who "rep" a variety of clients on a contract basis. Individuals, companies, and law firms—often including one or more former legislators or staff persons—are paid on either an hourly or yearly basis to serve as a group's eyes and ears in Albany. Sometimes these professional reps handle a rich variety of group needs: a representative of the state's chiropractors, for example, may lobby on issues concerning chiropractors, organize the association's annual meeting and banquet, collect members' dues, maintain the mailing list, and produce a periodic newsletter informing individual chiropractors of new laws and regulations that might affect their practice. The same representative also may be performing similar services for a variety of other groups—funeral homes, window-covering companies, exterminators. The advantage of being repped by such professional lobbyists is, quite simply, that they are professional. As much as such lobbyists may be pulled by obligations to other clients, and as little as they may know about a chiropractor's particular problems, they are generally the most connected individuals in the Albany community. Bolton-St. Johns, for example, which represents such diverse clients as Erie County, the Long Island Lighting Company, a union of government employees, and a hospital association, became formidable by hiring such key partners as former assembly speaker Mel Miller; Norman Adler, once a top union lobbyist, campaign consultant, and adviser to Governor Cuomo; and Armand D'Amato, a former assemblyman and brother of a former senator.

As impressive as some of these lobbying firms are, many organizations prefer to have their own in-house lobbyists. Most major unions and a number of corporations have Albany offices whose staffers, presumably, combine political skills with a detailed knowledge of the organization's needs. Since lobbying in the capitol is not usually a year-round job, these in-house lobbyists frequently combine their political responsibilities with community affairs, philanthropy, and public relations. For some voluntary organizations, such as environmental groups and advocates for the poor, the executive director wears a lobbying hat when the legislature is in session and takes it off the rest of the week to focus on fund-raising and other organization-building needs.

An important part of the lobbying community consists of representatives from trade and peak associations. Groups such as the New York Restaurant Association, the Empire State Association of Adult Homes, and the Professional Fire Fighters Association serve the practitioners of these trades in a number of ways. The Restaurant Association, for example, keeps its members informed of changes in tax laws that may affect their business, provides them with signs to comply with a law requiring restaurants to remind their employees to wash their hands after using the restroom, and updates them on new products such as computer programs designed for taverns. It also lobbies on behalf of the industry. Many small businesses rely on such trade associations to keep them informed of new developments and represent their interests, though trade associations tend to be dominated by their bigger clients (McDonald's and Burger King, for example, in the case of restaurants). Peak associations such as the Business Council and the AFL-CIO represent a whole variety of businesses or trade unions, large and small. Some very large corporations and peak associations have New York offices that are part of a much larger network of offices in Washington, DC, and in other states. Anheuser Busch and AT&T, for example, are registered in forty-nine states, the Bankers Association in forty-eight.[11]

In New York, as in Washington, one of the most interesting developments in the interest group arena is the proliferation of intergovernmental lobbies, groups of officials at one level of government hiring representatives to influence officials at another level. Dand Nice cites studies indicating that the number of such groups in Washington increased from five in 1900 to eighty-six in the 1960s, and their growth continued.[12] The growth in this sector has been as remarkable in New York as it has been in Washington. Individual cities, the state and city universities, school boards, and counties all maintain Albany offices, as do a wide variety of public officials such as the State School Superintendents Association.[13] Some groups, such as the Committee for Modern Courts, are not really intergovernmental lobbies since they are privately funded, but they work at all levels of the government. All in all, by one count, "New York State has more registered lobbyists per legislator—a ratio of eighteen to one—than any other state in the country."[14]

The list of groups represented in Albany is by no means reflective of the range of interests with political concerns in the state. Some groups, as we have noted, are so unthreatened by government that they have no real need to lobby. Among organized groups, the pressure system clearly tilts against the poor. Not only are poor folks, students, welfare recipients, and so on likely to have no Albany representation at all, but the representatives they do have are likely to be poorly skilled, poorly paid, and part-time. Organized labor, to be sure, advocates for working people as a class; the Professional Staff Congress, which represents the unionized faculty of City University of New York, works hard to increase funding for the university and to keep tuition low; but the core concerns of groups such as these focus on their members. Forced, let us say, to choose between salary cuts for professors and tuition increases for students, there is no question where the Professional Staff Congress would stand.

So-called public interest groups that address issues such as consumer protection and the environment are growing in number. Often dismissed as do-gooders, they can be effective. In order to keep their members happy and to sustain contributions rolling in, such groups often confront a tension between the need to excite their members (often by trashing politicians or making outrageous claims) and the need to present a serious, responsible face to the people they have just dissed.

Until very recently, much of the literature concerning interest groups focused on these public interest groups. But a growing number of lobbies have no members. For example, the groups represented by Albany's biggest lobbying firm, Davidoff and Malito, include the American Museum of Natural History, Coca-Cola, the College of Podiatric Medicine, the Court-room Television Network, and the Long Island Jewish Medical Center. Institutions with interests, yes, but hardly a model of pluralistic representation described by group theory. These groups pay the state's most prestigious and powerful lobbying firm to represent them not only because they lack a formal base of support, but because their interests are not necessarily defined as "public interests."

Thomas and Hrebenar in 1994 used ten factors to rank the forty most influential interests in the fifty states. Their top five were schoolteachers' organizations (which were rated "most effective" in forty-three states), general business organizations (most effective in thirty-seven), utility companies (twenty-three), lawyers (twenty-six), and traditional labor organizations (twenty-two).[15] We asked a nonrandom sample of thirty-five legislators and staff aides which groups they regarded as highly influential in Albany. A majority of legislators mentioned the United Federation of Teachers and the Business Council. No other group was mentioned by more than three respondents, though most were able to offer examples of groups with considerable issue-specific power such as gun clubs, public employee unions, and the insurance industry. Republicans, interestingly, were more likely to see unions as powerful interests while Democrats were similarly more inclined to mention business groups.

The Changing Locus of Group Politics

In the rosiest view of early pluralists, the group struggle was depicted as a relatively balanced battle for representation between elections, a mechanism through which the rather crude mandates of the electorate could be translated into specific policy proposals. An election might provide a "mandate" for "reform," or for better schools, but it does not usually indicate just what kinds of reforms or educational programs people want. Here is where the policy experts, or lobbyists, step up. Few legislators at the state or national level report feeling pressured by lobbyists. Rather they tend to regard interest groups as service agencies that provide informed perspectives on important issues and, in an important sense, represent important groups. Who better to articulate the concerns of dairy farmers than lobbyists paid by dairy interests to articulate their concerns?

The further the analysis of group politics proceeds, the less this model seems reflective of political reality. While it is true that lobbyists can and often do effectively represent the interests of their clients, the pressure system is not, in the final analysis, democratic. The first problem with the pluralist model, as Schattschneider highlighted in 1960, is that the range of organized group interests fails to reflect the general population: "The vice of the groupist theory is that it conceals the most significant aspects of the system. The flaw in the pluralist heaven is that the

Box 4.2
Extreme Fighting
A Case Study in Lobbying

Extreme fighting, sometimes referred to as human cockfighting, puts two contestants into a ring where they pummel each other into a pulp until one of them becomes unconscious or surrenders or until a doctor stops the action. Head butts, kicks to the groin, and kidney punches are allowed. How New York in 1996 became the first state to allow this "sport" and then just as quickly ban it provides interesting insight into the sometimes murky legislative process.

In 1995, an extreme fighting match that had been booked for the Brooklyn Park Slope Armory was canceled by the mayor, who quickly rushed a bill through the city council banning the sport. The fans of extreme fighting promptly proposed a state law preempting such local ordinances. They then hired one of Albany's shrewdest lobbyists to take their case. James Featherstonhaugh, whose firm's clients included CBS, Goldman Sachs, Pepsi-Cola, and the Tobacco Institute, is particularly known for his close ties to the Republican senate leadership, though he is liked and respected on both sides of the aisle. Rather than overtly call for legalization, Featherstonhaugh drew up a bill to "regulate" extreme fighting by putting it under the auspices of the New York State Athletic Commission. Not many legislators liked extreme fighting, and there certainly was no large organized constituency for it, but the potential constituency in opposition was not organized, and few legislators wanted to go on record opposing the "regulation" of so brutal a sport.

Featherstonhaugh was able to get majority leader Joseph Bruno to push the bill on a fast track through the senate. The Democratic assembly leaders, seeing no organized opposition to block it, decided they could trade its passage for assembly bills that the Democrats favored but the Republicans were lukewarm about. So the extreme fighting bill was put on a "trade list" and passed without much debate during the end-of-session rush when many bills reach the floor during the late-night marathon sessions the legislature is famous for just before it adjourns for the session.

The members of both houses were not told that they were actually sanctioning this kind of fighting, only that they were allowing it to be regulated by the state. Few if any knew that the effect of their vote would be to make New York the first state in the country to sanction this kind of fighting, and since the bill was placed by the leadership on the so-called Consent Calendar, where noncontroversial bills go through with little or no debate, it passed without difficulty. The governor then signed the bill using the interesting argument that "there was a large majority for its passage, so it had to be almost veto-proof and therefore his veto would have been overridden,"[1] something that almost never happens in New York.

When a match was actually scheduled for the Niagara Arena, the media picked up the issue and a whole series of editorials, church sermons, call-in show rants, and letters to the editor showed a decidedly negative tone. Governor Pataki

(continued)

Box 4.2 *(continued)*

quickly introduced legislation to ban such fighting statewide and a companion bill to allow local communities a final say on the issue. Not coincidentally, the athletic commission (appointed by the governor) came out with its regulations, which required gloves and timed bouts, making the sport similar to boxing. Two weeks later the embarrassed legislature outlawed the sport entirely. Senator Bruno was reported as favoring legislation that would give localities the option to allow the sport, but it was too late politically for that. Most lobbyists claim that they can have little influence on an issue when the public is aroused, but when most people know little and care less, good lobbyists can earn their pay. The extreme fighting case was unusual only in that it showed both sides of this coin in one six-month period.

Interestingly, as the promoters of extreme fighting gradually implemented and even exceeded the regulations proposed in the original New York bill, and as the sport gained in popularity, the issue has reemerged. Whether a fan-based support group backing the industry lobbyists can reverse the ban remains to be seen.

1. *New York Times*, January 17, 1997.

heavenly chorus sings with a strong upper-class accent. Probably about 90 percent of the people cannot get into the pressure system."[16]

Though Schattschneider's essential point remains beyond serious challenge, his probabilities are dated. The chorus of pressure groups is both much larger than it was in 1960 and sings in more accents and keys. Far more classes and categories of people are involved in pressure politics than ever before. Whether they are effectively involved is another question, for even among the groups that are represented in the system there are serious questions about the legitimacy of the representative process. Almost a century ago, the Austrian sociologist Roberto Michels referred to the "iron law of oligarchy" to describe what he saw as the governing paradigm of Europe's supposedly democratic socialist parties. It was, Michels suggested, almost in the nature of voluntary organizations for the rank-and-file members to become increasingly disinterested in organizational business and for the staff to become correspondingly independent.[17] Michel's iron law applies with a vengeance to most contemporary interest groups. Most workers join unions either because company contracts require it or because they hope to advance their economic interests through collective bargaining. Most lawyers join the bar association so they can effectively practice law. The lobbying efforts of the union, the bar association, the medical society, or the farm bureau are not high on the agendas of their rank-and-file members. Increasingly, interest groups are run by paid professionals, expert lobbyists, and administrators who may never have lived the lives of those whose interests they represent. The leaders of most lobbying groups view themselves as career professionals, not as carpenters, teachers, dairy farmers, or doctors; it is precisely because they are professional lobbyists rather than farmers or workers that they were hired in the first place. Their desire to continue in these often well-paid positions combined with the apathy of their clients sustains Michel's iron law. Beyond oligarchy, however, is the greater threat of what Lowi calls "the iron law of decadence." Increasingly, he argues, in every "highly organized element in modern society, there are organizational characteristics that dictate organizational maintenance over every other possible goal." In established groups "the goals of the organization have become intertwined with the needs of maintaining the organization, until the two have become indistinguishable and self-reinforcing."[18] The growing number of institutional lobbies, those that essentially have no members, reinforces this tendency.

This institutionalization of group politics also has brought professional lobbyists into increasingly cordial relationships with their counterparts in government. Subgovernments—triangles of influence linking bureaucrats, legislative committees, and lobbyists—are less visible in New York than at the national level. Instead, group leaders in New York tend to link their fortunes increasingly to those of the parties in power. Much of this linkage is financial. Indeed, the nexus between money and power in the form of campaign contributions is so important that it receives separate treatment later in this chapter. The point here has less to do with the amount of influence generated by lobbies than with its direction. Not only have the established groups been caught in Lowi's law of decadence, but also they have become so enmeshed in their defense of the existing order of things that they are reluctant to call for change even when it would appear to be in their own interest to do so. They have, in a word, become powertropic, leaning toward the party in power as plants lean toward the sun.

Take, for example, New York State United Teachers (NYSUT), a union that appears frequently on the lists of the most powerful groups in the state. NYSUT's political action committee always ranks among the top campaign contributors in state elections. To whom does it contribute? In 2004, 175 of 209 incumbents running for reelection to the state senate and assembly received an endorsement and contribution. What did the union get in return for its support? In institutional terms it was and has been enormously effective. Its effectiveness, however, is defined almost entirely in institutional as opposed to programmatic terms. Like many groups in Albany (and in Washington), it has become what Aaron Wildavsky called a political aircraft carrier.[19] An aircraft carrier, Wildavsky would point out, costs, say, $10 billion to put to sea. Of that amount, $3 billion goes for sophisticated radar and sonar systems, double hulls and special plates to protect the carrier from attack. Of the $2 billion worth of planes on the carrier, roughly half are there to protect the aircraft carrier. Its guns—$1 billion worth—are there to protect the aircraft carrier. And it goes to sea with a flotilla of four other boats (cost, $3 billion) whose function is— are you getting the idea?—to protect the aircraft carrier. Net result: 75 to 80 percent of its resources are spent defending itself against potential attacks. NYSUT, to be sure, lobbies for better schools, but its real mission is to protect NYSUT: to fight against attacks on tenure that would make the jobs of NYSUT's senior members less secure, to oppose budget cuts or spending caps on school districts that would reduce the number of teachers (and NYSUT members), to protect the pension system of its dues-paying retirees, to protect the aircraft carrier.

We rather cynically single out NYSUT largely because of its size. Among major groups in Albany it continues, more than most, to fight for real policies and deeply held values. Like many other organizations represented in the state capitol, it is caught in the middle of a system stagnated by the institutionalization of divided government. In a system, like New York's, that has been dominated by strong parties, interest groups that want to be effective find it necessary to work through the parties to achieve their objectives. Groups with too strong an identity, in either ideological or partisan terms, can be frozen out of one party conference or another. There are, to be sure, a number of issues on which the parties have not staked out clear positions, and the array and tactics of interest groups in such areas are probably pretty much the same in New York as in most other large states. The general proposition that states (or countries) with strong party systems tend to have weak pressure systems is not entirely borne out in New York.[20] "The major parties in New York," as Cingranelli argues, "are not particularly ideological, and that fact increases the access that most groups have to the elected representatives of both parties. . . . Parties need to have the active support of interest groups in order to maintain and enhance their legislative majorities and to capture the governor's seat."[21] Yet a group that becomes too active in supporting one party risks so alienating the other that all its legislative victories are doomed to be one-house bills. Thus Thomas classifies interest groups in New York as "complementary," meaning that they "tend to have to work in conjunction with or are constrained by other aspects of the political system."[22]

While most researchers share the view that interest groups in New York are weaker than in other states and, in a general sense, more constrained by the strength of the party system, the study of state lobbying is in its infancy.[23] The so-called reputational approach, used in simply asking informed policy-makers which lobbyists they think are most powerful, runs the danger of mistaking rumor for clout. A strong reputation is nice to have, but it does not always win fights. NYSUT, for example, makes almost every New Yorker's list of powerful groups, yet it was beaten in the 1998 special session when the party leaders in effect bought the governor's approval of a legislative pay raise by passing a charter schools bill that the union had opposed. In bad economic years, such as 2009, it is able to ameliorate but not prevent significant cuts in school funding.

The Party System, the Pressure System, and the Locus of Power

In his famous discussion of agenda setting, John Kingdon uses the concept of a "policy stream" to describe how issues move onto or off the political agenda. "If

Box 4.3
School Tax Cap
Powerful Lobbies or Good Government?

Because of rising costs and diminishing state aid, local school property taxes—already the highest in the nation—have been rising rapidly in New York. In 2008 a special commission appointed by Governor Spitzer recommended a law that would disallow increases in school taxes exceeding the inflation rate or 4 percent, whichever was less. The bill was endorsed by Governor Paterson, and early public opinion polls showed that it was supported by as many as three-quarters of the voters. It died, however, in the legislature in 2008. (It will be debated again.) The governor blamed the bill's defeat on unnamed "advocates." Many newspaper editorials were more explicit in pinning the blame on the powerful lobbyists for the teachers' union.

But while NYSUT, with its 570,000 members, has long been one of the state's best-funded and most powerful lobbies, many members of the legislature—the assembly in particular—had their own reasons to be skeptical. "The average increase in school taxes approved by the voters in my district," one suburban Democrat told us, "was more than 6 percent. Of course people will tell a pollster that they want lower taxes, but when it comes to actual cases, the idea that teachers' salaries will never exceed inflation or that schools will be able to introduce new programs only if they get rid of others is simply bad government."

While NYSUT certainly can be influential in shaping education policies, "governors, legislators, and the Education Department also respond to broader public opinion, and to statistical and other indicators of school performance."[1] If NYSUT keeps the governor's tax cap from becoming law, the union will owe its success as much to its ability to harness these forces as to its raw political power. Ironically, however, both the teacher's union and its opponents have an interest in exaggerating the union's clout: the union because it keeps its dues-paying members happy, others because they can make the union a scapegoat for their own failures. And the press, loving stories of inside power, will oblige both sides.

1. Robert B. Ward, *New York State Government*, 2nd ed. (Albany: Rockefeller Institute, 2006), p. 369.

important people look around and find that all of the interest groups and other organized interests point them in the same direction, the entire environment provides them with a powerful impetus to move in that direction."[24] If there is conflict in the environment, conversely, there is almost invariably a reluctance to act. On major statewide issues, New York's system of divided government almost invariably traps some organizations into alliances that blend policy streams. Organized labor, for example, frequently finds itself in close alliance with the Democratic Party. In the 1996 fight to reform the workers' compensation law, labor and the Democratic majority in the state assembly were pitted against the governor and the Republican senate. For Democrats in the assembly, the streams merged: voting with labor, for workers, with their party, and in accord with their personal beliefs was easy.

The problem for labor was its allies. By linking the workers' comp issue with the budget, the Republicans in effect held other groups hostage. Teachers wanted more money for schools, advocates for the poor wanted more for social welfare, yet they had to deal with the Republicans by letting labor go it alone on this issue. Labor could win only by attaching itself to the Democrats, hoping to keep the assembly leadership from cutting a deal. In the end, the act could not be sustained: conflict in the environment—in this case, the budget needs of other groups—forced the Democrats to capitulate.

Many groups—NYSUT and the public employees unions in particular—are capable of a two-prong strategy dealing with both the senate and the assembly. But groups like the AFL-CIO, the gun lobby, and abortion advocates and opponents are locked into one party and one house of the legislature. This means that they usually can block legislation that can hurt them, but they have virtually no power of initiative and no ability to compromise. Interestingly, one study attempting to assess the relative power of interest groups in New York politics classified labor as less effective than some other groups during routine legislative sessions, but found that "legislators thought unions were the most effective interest groups as elections approached."[25]

Campaign Finance: Meeting Ground of the Party and Pressure Systems

New York's campaign finance laws are less restrictive than those of most other states and the federal government. Candidates for state office in both primary and general elections must file detailed reports with the Board of Elections listing all contributions of $100 or more. The maximum amount a single contributor could donate to a statewide candidate for governor or attorney general in 2008 was pegged at .025 cents per voter or $37,800 for the general election campaign, but that same contributor also could give as much as $94,200 to a party committee. In the primary, by this formula, the contributor would have been limited to donating about $17,000 to a Democrat, $14,500 to a Republican, and $5,400 to an Independent. In general election campaigns, candidates for the state legislature are limited to $7,600 in the assembly and $15,500 in the senate, regardless of party. Each donor must be clearly identified in reports filed regularly during the campaign with the Board of Elections. The state's reporting requirements, once notoriously lax, have been dramatically improved in the past few years.

To say that there were loopholes in New York's campaign finance laws is like saying there are holes in Swiss cheese. The so-called soft money scandals that have attracted media attention in the wake of recent presidential campaigns are more than matched by the less closely followed evasions of campaign finance rules practiced in New York. Until very recently, reporting requirements were easily evaded and both individual and group contributions could be made almost impossible to trace. Although most filings in New York are now computerized, the paper trails of some campaigns are at best confusing. One list produced by the Pataki for Governor Committee was alphabetized by first names instead of last. Candidates sometimes, quite legally, file reports under two or more different organizational names (a practice facilitated by third-party cross-endorsements). So-called in-kind contributions, by which unions, for example, donate phone banks, have not been effectively audited or regulated in New York. Incumbents in the legislature have access to very sophisticated maps of their districts. While technically they are available to the public, few people even know they exist. Employees of the legislature regularly work actively in election campaigns, though increasingly scrupulous about doing so in their spare time or on leaves of absence.

For wealthy individuals, it is relatively easy to avoid limits on contributions and the registration requirements and regulations imposed on lobbying groups. The wealthy conservative dilettante Ron Lauder, for example, was able to buy unlimited access to Governor George Pataki by paying the governor's wife an annual salary for twelve years of unspecified "consulting" services. Millionaire Tom Golisano in 2008 evaded contribution limits by setting up his own political action committee, Responsible New York, to funnel some $5 million into the campaigns of thirteen legislative candidates throughout the state.[26] A few months later, when the governor and senate Democrats met to negotiate the deal that made Malcolm Smith majority leader, Golisano was in the room, suggesting that his work in the campaign would be rewarded.

Without being unduly cynical, we see cases such as these as rather strong evidence that the campaign finance laws do little to prevent those with deep pockets from at least buying their way into the inner circles of political power in New York. When we look at the official numbers accessibly filed by campaign committees in New York, it is not really possible to say whether we are seeing nearly all, most, or only some fraction of the amount actually raised and spent in that election. From personal experiences and our conversations with a number of public officials, we would say that most—meaning 80 to 90 percent—of the funds spent in most campaigns are honestly and reliably reported. But it is also clear that the number and kind of evasions are numerous. What has improved, quite remarkably for those funds that are reported, is the record-keeping practice of the state Board of Elections. The Pew Campaign Disclosure Project moved the state's grade on accessibility from a C– in 2005 to an A– in 2007 and from an F to a C+ on usability in the same period. Its overall grade went from near the bottom nationally to sixteenth.[27] But it remains far from ideal.

The Role of Political Action Committees

Most interest groups have political action committees (PACs). Although the term *PAC* does not appear in either federal or state election law, it is generally defined

as a nonparty organization that accepts money from a number of individual contributors and then distributes the money to one or more candidates whose views
are compatible with the parent interest group. Frank Sorauf divides PACs into
"two broad types depending on their organizational structure: the connected and
the unconnected."[28] Connected PACs, in Sorauf's classification, are those that are
linked to a parent organization—frequently a lobby—and can solicit funds only
from members of the group. Unconnected PACs, including so-called leadership
PACs created by many party leaders, are free to solicit contributions from anyone
but must pay their own expenses out of those contributions. Most PACs in New
York are connected, and a sample of 2006 filings indicates that these organizations
account for considerably more than half of the money raised by most candidates
for the legislature.

Routinely members of the legislature now host a reception in Albany sometime
during the session. The asking price for admission to these yearly receptions has been
going up, with $250 being the floor and top policy-makers—such as the chairs of
important committees—charging as much as $1,000. Monday and Tuesday nights in
Albany find lobbyists and legislators doing the circuit from the Crowne Plaza Hotel
to the top of the Corning Tower to the "well" of the Legislative Office Building, sip-
ping soda water (you cannot start on alcohol too early when you have to attend six
receptions between 5:30 and 8 P.M.) and picking through the cheese plates and dips
trying to find any shrimp that are left. The key objective is to show your face. No
one acknowledges any kind of quid pro quo in these encounters, but it just would not
be smart for a lobbyist dealing with transportation issues not to attend a reception
for the chair of the transportation committee. A health lobbyist who has a Tuesday
appointment to talk about a bill with the chair of the health committee knows that it
is smart politics to be seen at the chair's Monday night reception.

There is not a lot of lobbying that takes place at these receptions. However,
the opportunities these receptions provide for networking, keeping up on the latest political gossip, and establishing and cementing personal relationships have
made them a favorite target of reformers. Since the invitation lists to these events
are culled almost entirely from the files of the Commission on Public Integrity,
it would be difficult to find a more blatant example of special-interest money at
work. Despite the ritualistic quality of these affairs and as much as both legislators
and lobbyists groan about the need to do the circuit again and again, the receptions
have proved highly resistant to being reformed away. For most legislators with safe
seats—and that means most legislators—these annual receptions provide most of
the funds they need to go to the receptions of other members and to fund their own
campaigns. For lobbyists, there are few better ways to make favorable impressions
on the right people and, at the same time, get to know key members.

Through connected PAC lobbyists, members can attend the important receptions, make contributions (within the legal limits) to individual campaigns, and
make contributions to other organizations such as the state committees, legislative
campaign committees, and various leadership PACs that funnel money (beyond the

legal limits) to individual candidates. Rosenthal summarizes the problems raised
by this system as follows:

> Reformers allege that even if money does not actually buy votes, it buys access.
> It gives the contributor the chance not only to speak with a legislator, but to be
> listened to as well. That is the least thing contributors get. . . .
>
> A campaign contribution, by offering support to a legislator in his or her time
> of need, creates an "attitudinal tendency," in the words of a former Ohio legisla-
> tor, on the part of a receiver toward a donor. . . .
>
> It operates in the interstices of the process at the margins. Under most cir-
> cumstances, a sense of obligation does not sway votes, but it probably earns
> from legislators the willingness to consider a case or even some slight change
> in their behavior.[29]

The amount of money it takes to mount an effective campaign in a competitive district is both enormous and growing. Perhaps the most important change in
campaign finance in the past three decades has been one of sheer magnitude: PACs,
legislative campaign committees, and incumbency are all more important quite simply because it is almost prohibitively expensive to go up against an incumbent.

Beyond these electoral effects, studies of campaign finance illustrate four other
types of relationships between money and politics. First, as Rosenthal suggests,
money buys access: it gives contributors at least the chance to make their case.
Second, as Rosenthal also suggests, money can buy a legislator's attentiveness, a
willingness to move from passive to active support of a cause to which the member
is generally sympathetic. In one study of Congress, it was clear that campaign contributions "bought time," increasing member activity in pushing legislation through
committees and on the floor.[30] Although the ability to gain such access and mobilization does bias the system in favor of the affluent, many scholars and politicians
regard this kind of bias as relatively benign. Even without campaign contributions,
a group with solid public support and a good argument can obtain similar access.
More troubling are two other kinds of relationships between campaign finance
and legislative politics, one in which members tailor their legislative interests and
activities in anticipation of their monetary value; the second in which a member
actually changes the direction of a vote. Twenty years ago it was uncommon for a
legislator to seek a committee assignment because it was a good place from which
to raise funds, or to introduce a bill in the hopes of attracting the interest of a PAC.
And if there were members who changed their votes with campaign contributions
in mind, almost none would admit it. Neither tactic is uncommon today. "I really
liked lobbying on the issues," one Albany lobbyist wistfully told us, "but now it's
just more and more about money."

Sometimes it is exclusively about money. The 2002 sale of shoreline development rights along the Erie Canal for $30,000—a deal that later turned out to be
worth millions—clearly was pushed through strictly on the basis of political connections. Calling it "highway robbery," the *New York Times*, joined in tone by most

other newspapers in the state called for the governor and the legislature "to open the doors to this cozy club."[31] Most attempts at significant reform have resulted in one-house bills that go nowhere or largely symbolic changes such as putting a limit of $75 on gifts that lobbyists offer to public officials.

Parties, Party Leaders, and Campaign Finance

Until the widespread proliferation of PACs, which began ironically with the first attempts at federal campaign finance reform laws in the 1970s, legislative campaigns in New York were funded largely by local party organizations, wealthy individuals, and a few key interest groups such as labor unions. Republicans had the additional advantage of having Nelson Rockefeller in the governor's mansion. When Rockefeller's money was no longer there, the party established the state's first legislative campaign committee.[32] The Republican Assembly Campaign Committee also was created, as one former speaker notes, because legislative leaders "didn't feel that the county organizations were giving us the right kinds of candidates or supporting candidates in the manner in which they should."[33] Soon there were four such committees, one for each major party in each house. Through these assembly and senate campaign committees, the process of fund-raising has become increasingly centralized within each house of the legislature.

The two manifest functions of these campaign committees are to reallocate contributions to campaigns that the leadership feels can best use them, and to professionalize campaigns throughout the state by offering electoral analyses, polls, help with newsletters and campaign brochures, issue research, research on the opposition, and so on. Their latent functions are to divorce special interests from individual candidates by pooling PAC funds so candidates do not know who—except the party committee—is actually funding their campaign; to allow the party leaders in Albany to control whose campaigns are going to be viable; and, by giving them that power, to make the speaker and majority and minority leaders even more powerful. Except for those with enormous personal wealth, it is almost impossible for a novice candidate to marshal the resources to run a viable campaign without the active help of a legislative campaign committee. How do the parties allocate their funds?

One strategy, as Stonecash suggests, is to enhance their own powers by directing PAC contributions to senior members, especially if they are facing any kind of potential challenge. The clear focus, however, is on helping "those in marginal contests" as well as "newer members, challengers, and those running in open seats," a strategy that, as Stonecash says, "could promote party unity and build the party."[34] The roles of the Democratic Assembly Campaign Committee (DACC), the Republican Assembly Campaign Committee (RACC), and their senate counterparts vary almost entirely according to electoral marginality. Safe-seat incumbents and those challenging safe-seat incumbents receive virtually no help at all. Other incumbents—except those from extremely marginal seats—are pretty much on their own unless and until they can show that they are really in trouble. One urban Republican who won a previously Democratic seat with active financial and strategic help from RACC was told two years later that she was on her own. Another member from a suburban area was told the same thing until he produced a poll showing that he was in danger of losing his seat. As a result, RACC not only provided needed funds but also sent campaign experts from Albany to work in his campaign. Little wonder that, as one party leader lamented to us, some members actually lie about how likely they are to lose and how good their opponents are.

There are some important differences among the four legislative campaign committees. In the assembly, as Stonecash shows, "the strategies of the two parties reflect their different situations. As the dominant party, the Democrats are concerned with maintaining that position. They have allocated more of their money to protecting incumbents because they must do so to retain power. The Republicans, as a party that must make some dent in the Democratic majority in order to regain control . . . cannot afford to devote money to incumbents."[35]

While we do not have the systematic data for the senate that Stonecash gathered for the assembly, the same logic apparently applies, with the majority Republicans adopting an essentially defensive, pro-incumbent strategy and the minority Democrats more aggressively backing insurgents. Both parties in 2008 invested almost all their centrally controlled funds in the races for the seats won by the Democrats in 2007 and 2008 by-elections, in two Republican marginal seats in the city (one won by the Democrats, the other narrowly retained by the Republicans), in one marginal district on Long Island (which went from Republican to Democratic), and in one upstate district where late summer polls showed the incumbent Democrat in trouble. What was unusual in 2008 was Governor Paterson's involvement in raising money for the Democrats in these marginal seats.

Centralization or Balkanization?

There is no doubt that party leaders, for many years, welcomed and embraced centralized fund-raising. One senior Democrat even lost his chairmanship of a major assembly committee because his friendly interactions with the groups interested in the committee's work had given him the ability to raise large sums of money both for his own campaign and for other Democrats. For Democrats, the centralization of fund-raising freed the assembly speaker and the senate majority and minority leaders from having to deal with county chairs in trying to put together legislative majorities. Republican speakers and leaders also welcomed such growing independence, which enabled them to establish greater independence from the governor and the state committee. Legislative campaign committees, as Daniel Shea concludes, "represent a means for legislative leaders to control external resources—to collect and control campaign funds, to free their members of damaging elements of the party, and to augment their caucus regardless of the party's status in other branches."[36] Many of the members we talked with, even some party leaders, expressed growing reservations about the system. To understand their reservations, we must briefly return to the "responsible parties" model discussed in Chapter 3.

The essential argument for strong parties is that by centralizing power parties become more responsive to voters. It is easier to ascribe blame or credit for changes in public policy because parties take a programmatic approach to governing. A strong party system, it follows, can prevent fragmentation into subgovernments, thereby sharply diminishing the often hidden influence of special interests. By clarifying differences between the parties, a strong party system brings issue differences before the electorate and thus facilitates what is called a "rational choice" model of politics. "At first glance," as Shea concludes, New York's legislative campaign committees appear to fulfill at least some of the conditions of this model. "But on closer inspection even this notion is tenuous. Units designed to capture seats only within one branch of a legislature, holding little or no affinity for broad-based or long-range activities, may strain even the most inclusive view of 'party.'"[37]

Money follows power. In a strong party state such as New York, this means that money flows largely to and through party leaders. To the extent that groups have ideological agendas, this tends to mean that as they cement relations with one party they destroy their ability to work with the other. Political action committees representing gun owners, real estate interests, and health insurers give vastly disproportionate amounts to Republicans. Many unions, similarly, are tied to the Democrats. In practice, what this tends to mean is that without a very strong push from the governor or from public opinion, these groups have veto power over policies that might affect them, but little or no ability to change existing law. Groups aligned with the Republicans can initiate or block bills in the senate, but they have no power in the assembly. Democratic groups are equally assured of success in the assembly and failure in the senate. To avoid these pitfalls, many of the most powerful groups in New York give heavily to both majorities. As Robert Haggerty, former director of the Republican campaign committee, said, "The major players in the money area don't play philosophical politics. They play majority politics."[38] Majority politics is almost by definition moderate politics. It is a politics that, like the politics of deadlock, produces few new initiatives. Although the locus of campaign giving is changing with the Democrats in control of both houses, this dynamic will remain essentially unchanged with the majority parties in both houses separated from each other and from the governor.

The Media in New York Politics

New York has about fifty-five daily newspapers and more than 650 weeklies, biweeklies, and semiweeklies. It has roughly eighty television stations and more than 500 radio outlets.[39] In the press offices in the Capitol, however, the pressroom is literally emptying out. As the *New York Times* reported in 2008:

> In 1981, the Legislative Correspondents Association, the organization of state-house journalists in Albany, had 59 members from 31 news outlets.

By 2001, the number of journalists had fallen to 51 and the number of news organizations to 29. At the beginning of this year, there were 42 journalists and 27 member organizations.

With the exception of Buffalo, Watertown and Albany itself, no city outside the New York metropolitan area has a newspaper with a dedicated, full-time correspondent in the Capitol.[40]

An overwhelming majority of New York's outlets thus are getting whatever stories they run either from wire services or from the press offices of politicians and interest groups. Even among statehouse reporters, there is widespread agreement that state politics in general and legislative politics in particular are not well covered.[41]

For the legislature, the problem of poor coverage is not unique to New York. Martin Linsky identifies four general sources of tension between journalists and state legislators that often result in gaps in understanding. First, there is the collective, unfocused nature of the legislative process that—even in a centralized legislature like New York's—makes it hard for legislators to give journalists the personalized, in-depth action portraits that tend to make interesting stories. Second, the legislators that politicians call show horses—as opposed to the workhorses who do most of the real policy-making—are easier to cover and tend to dominate the news with material that is really peripheral to the real work of the legislature. Third, the kind of compromise and bargaining that makes the process work rarely is interesting to write about: "Good legislating is often done without publicity, or else it would not, and perhaps could not, be done. . . . When good work is done that way, the result is sometimes very unappealing from a news perspective." Finally, "the mix between politics and the substance of legislation" sometimes gives legislators reason to avoid coverage if they can. The kind of flexibility that allows effective bargaining to take place is difficult to explain to the public.[42]

Beyond these general sources of tension, there are reasons specific to New York that make for bad coverage. One is simply that of competition. There are just too many things going on in New York for state politics to command ink. This is particularly true in New York City, where the city government is as large as that of most states and its politicians compete with Albany for ink. There are enormous variations between the various media and their coverage of state politics. Outside of the capitol district, television almost never covers state politics. Stations in Syracuse, Buffalo, and Rochester require a full working day for a news and camera crew to set up in Albany. Quite sensibly, their producers send a crew only when there is some certainty that a newsworthy event will take place: the governor's State of the State address, a major protest on the Capitol steps, final passage of the budget, or the vote on a major policy change. Newspapers vary in both the amount and kind of coverage they give state issues. In Morgan's study, the percentage of news space given to state as opposed to local, national, and international affairs ranged from a high of 52 percent in the Albany *Times-Union* to a low of 11.6 percent in the *New York Times*.[43] For the *Times-Union* and the very lively Time-Warner cable news channel in Albany, what happens in state government is in a sense local news. Reporters know that what they write probably will be seen by most legislators, their staff aides, and large numbers of civil servants whose jobs sometimes depend on government action. The *New York Times*, with a national audience and a tendency to view itself as the newspaper of record, weighs state issues against a flow of national and international events that tend to receive only cursory coverage in papers such as the *Times-Union*. At the same time, reporters from the *Times*, knowing that they have a more educated readership than other papers, devote more serious, thorough coverage to certain issues. In 1998, for example, both the *New York Times* and the Albany *Times-Union* gave rather extensive coverage to the revised budgetary process. Some other papers—the Syracuse *Herald-Journal*, for example—covered the change with particular reference to a local angle, but most barely mentioned it. As for the tabloids, as one reporter put it, "If it doesn't involve sex or the lottery we don't print it."

Weeklies and small local papers occasionally will run wire service articles on major issues, particularly if they have a local focus. Almost every paper in the state runs an article every year on the potential impact of various budget scenarios on local property taxes. Small papers quite frequently run press releases from local assembly members and state senators as if they were regular news stories. Whether they represent small towns or parts of big cities, getting mentioned in the press is an important goal of most legislators. For interest groups and bureaucrats with policy agendas, media attention is a major step on the road to influence. Because small town and neighborhood papers, weeklies in particular, do not have the staff resources to research the sources of press releases from politicians and others, such papers tend to be uncritical in their coverage, but tensions between journalists and public officials are very much a part of the system.

Perhaps the biggest source of frustration for Albany journalists is the essentially closed nature of the process by which legislators make key decisions. Journalists thrive on conflict, and as one told us, "it is rare that we have any drama around here." During typical budget negotiations, when a growing number of key decisions usually are made, twenty or thirty reporters of the Albany press corps sit on little metal folding chairs outside a room in which the governor, speaker, and majority leader are making deals that count. For perhaps two or three hours, the reporters chat about the Yankees, the weather, good restaurants—anything but what is going on inside: they are not "even doing spin control." From time to time a staff aide emerges, politely refusing any comment on the negotiations. Finally, the politicians emerge, sometimes only to go into equally secret conferences with their party colleagues, and you feel, as one newspaperman said, "as if you had gone through about the lowest form of journalism that you could get."[44] Because party discipline is strong, moreover, reporters usually cannot stir up a story—as they might in Washington—by going to a disgruntled member of the speaker's party or to a bureaucrat trying to protect an agency from rumored cuts. Few even try.

Managing the News

Politicians and journalists need each other, but they need each other for such different reasons that conflict is inevitable. There is a school of journalism that operates on the premise that all politicians are essentially corrupt and that it is a prime function of the media to expose that corruption to the public. Even journalists who know better are not above taking what legislators consider cheap shots at the institution and its members. Bill Passannante—who served more than thirty years in the state Assembly—took particular umbrage at the ritualistic articles, which almost every paper runs from time to time, blasting legislators as overpaid fat cats. Yet, at the fortieth reunion of his Harvard Law School class, Passannante discovered that he was the lowest-paid member of his class. City newspapers delight in making fun of rural projects, an upstate cheese museum being a favorite target, while upstate journalists invariably find something to outrage their readers in grants to city artists. Needless to say, the city papers seldom are as likely to hold art grants up to criticism as their rural counterparts are to criticize local dairy farmers. As much as the legislature often deserves to be criticized for late budgets, for the invariable sloppiness at the end of the session, for occasional corruption, and for excessive secrecy, "the degree of bad conduct by legislatures does not seem commensurate with the bad press and the low esteem in which the institutions are generally held."[45] There is nothing very newsworthy about competent legislators going about their job. There is a lot that is newsworthy about a legislator caught stealing or about the chair of the alcohol and substance abuse committee being arrested for drunk driving. Although such acts are far from typical, a public that receives most of its information from stories such as these may become unduly cynical about an important institution. The tone of the media's coverage of the state's chronically late budgets, for example, "was so hostile and aggressive that it largely precluded . . . reasoned deliberation," as Grant Reeher argues:

> Missing in particular was a recognition that politics is the arena in which claims about what society should collectively aim to accomplish and avoid are negotiated, and that a budget is the principal way in which this is done. New York, a large and diverse state, is rich with competing and conflicting claims, which are divided by a kaleidoscopic array of fault lines. . . . Adding to the tension is the fact that the amount of money at stake in the state budget is enormous. Instead, what readers encountered was the message that the correct answers to complicated political questions were readily available, and the legislators were simply incompetent and malicious in not arriving at them and implementing them quickly.[46]

Bureaucrats are perhaps the most abused of all public servants if only because they have almost no ability to fight back. Governors and other statewide officials, such as the comptroller and attorney general, get into interesting sparring matches with the press. Ever since the 1940s when Governor Thomas E. Dewey hired a press secretary, statewide officials have sought to put their own spin on stories out of Albany. Even in the legislature, press office staff are among the largest and best paid. Public officials, governors in particular, have long "sought and expected to get a large share of the credit for policy successes and tried to minimize their responsibilities for policy failures. . . . In pursuit of these goals, executive and legislative branches built up a highly professional public relations capacity that gave them, and especially the governor, maximum publicity. As seen by the press it also provided a potential for the manipulation of the media, or for their co-optation."[47]

No professional journalist likes to be the target of such manipulation, though that is what every politician would like them to be. Both Mario Cuomo and George Pataki were extremely sensitive about their coverage by the press. It is not an exaggeration to say that few Albany-based journalists were fond of Mario Cuomo. Cuomo, more than one reporter told us, would "call you in the office, call you at home, call your editor" if you did not report a story the way he wanted it reported. He would, apparently, refuse to recognize certain reporters at his press conferences or refuse to answer their phone calls after they had printed something he did not like. Rather than answer hostile questions, Cuomo often would lecture reporters on their manners, their syntax, or their motives. His press secretaries often spent hours working as go-betweens dealing with an angry governor and an individual journalist. What made the journalists' dislike for Cuomo particularly frustrating was the governor's Teflon-like ability to resist letting anything stick. No matter how serious his mistakes, he always came out looking good, particularly on television. Eliot Spitzer came to office with some of these qualities as well, which is why—in the peculiar ways of journalism—some people feel he was treated so harshly when he fell from grace.

George Pataki was, paradoxically, well liked, yet much less accessible. Where Cuomo courted coverage and seemingly read or watched almost everything the media said about him, Pataki's staff went to great lengths to distance the governor from personal encounters with journalists. The second floor of the Capitol, where the governor and his top staff people have their offices, became a protected enclave open by appointment only, with the elevator operators instructed not to stop there without prior clearance. Many journalists, even though they understand the changes wrought by the attacks of 9/11, find it ominous that both Eliot Spitzer and David Paterson have kept these offices similarly walled off. In dramatic contrast with Cuomo, however, Pataki always was affable, always personable when his staff allowed access to him in Albany. While Cuomo's press aides constantly were apologizing for the governor, Pataki played the role of good guy to his feisty staff. One journalist describes an incident in which he was attempting to get a more concrete answer to an embarrassing question than Pataki wanted to give. As the governor fumbled for words, his press secretary, Zenia Mucha, started yelling at the reporter and pushing the governor back toward his office. As the entourage of the retreating governor, his shouting press secretary, and a couple of dozen reporters moved down the hall, the reporter attempted to press his question. Finally, the governor stepped between Mucha and the reporters, apologized for *her* behavior, and tried to calm everybody down. "How," our reporter friend asked, "can you keep pushing a nasty question with a guy who has just done you a favor like that?"

For every incident in which politicians rebuff reporters, there are probably twenty in which they seek them out. The staffs of the governor and of legislative leaders are frequent callers and e-mailers to every newsroom. Most journalists identify legislative staff members as "more assiduous callers, though not more successful, than a variety of people who come from the agencies."[48] Interest groups, too, seek press coverage, if only because, as one lobbyist put it, "getting your argument in the right paper is like home delivery, you put it right in the hands of the people you want to see it." There also is a sense in which something that appears in the media is more authoritative than the same idea conveyed in a lobbyist's memorandum or a politician's letter.

Because their words tend to have this authoritative character, most journalists are acutely sensitive to being "used." There is a whole ritual of guidelines as to how certain statements from politicians should be reported: when politicians go "off the record," for example, it means that what they are about to say should not be part of the published story; statements issued "on background" may be used so long as they are not attributed to the person making them; statements "on deep background" can be used but only in such a way that most people could not discern who was making the comment. Specific terms and meanings differ from one state capital to another and across generations, but the nuances of the relationships between politicians and journalists that they suggest are a constant. A subtext of the "troopergate" affair, in which Governor Spitzer's staff allegedly overstepped its authority in order to expose majority leader Bruno's overuse of state aircraft, was whether the original story had been planted by the governor's office or dug up by an enterprising reporter.

The worst case, from a journalistic perspective, is one in which a planted story turns out not to be true. To admit to having been duped and used is almost worse that admitting you were wrong. The only defense, in the long run, is that a reporter once burned by a source is going to be very skeptical the next time. (Fool me once, an old saying goes, shame on you. Fool me twice, shame on me.) When a planted story is true, on the other hand, the source gains credibility, particularly if one reporter gets it as an exclusive. Through a long series of such transactions, politicians and journalists develop patterns of interaction that have generally served the public well in bringing important, politically sensitive issues to light. That Albany's downsized pressrooms make such interactions less common is likely to make this system work less well.

Albany correspondents do not always agree on what is news. Actions affecting the Erie Canal or the Adirondacks that get front-page treatment upstate may be ignored in New York City. Changes in the policies of the lottery or the Off-Track Betting Corporation that make the front pages of the *Daily News* and the *Post* likely are to be ignored by the *Times*. At its best, the tendency of most reporters to run the same stories reflects a true consensus on the nature of news. At its worst, in what its critics call "pack journalism," it reflects an ingrained laziness in which journalists follow the most obvious events to make sure that they are not being scooped by someone else. It is particularly easy for Albany journalists to fall into this habit because so much of the real conflict and compromise in New York politics takes place behind closed doors.

Media Biases and Roles

Building on the unquestionable fact that most of the people who own newspapers and broadcasting stations are well-to-do, elite theorists generally have depicted the media as lackeys to, or co-conspirators with, the powers that be. In their editorial policies, most of New York State's newspapers undoubtedly represent the relatively conservative leanings of their publishers. Frequently moderate to liberal on social issues, mixed on questions of equality and civil liberties, and pro-business on issues involving labor, taxes, and government spending, the state's media tend to reflect the old-family, largely Protestant, upper-income attitudes of their owners. Whether there is any truth in the countervailing hypothesis that the working press is hopelessly liberal and slants the news in that direction is a question of long-standing and possibly unresolvable dispute.

The most important fact about the media in New York is that they are media: they mediate between citizens, politicians, and power wielders, communicating facts, hearsay, opinions, and attitudes. Despite complaints from almost everyone involved in politics about the alleged biases of the press, the more serious problem is one of diversity. Whether because of pack journalism or the relatively closed nature of the state's political process, it is truly unusual for journalists in New York to go beyond ritualistic "exposés" of "overpaid" legislators, inflated "pork barrels," and "three-men-in-a-room" deals into really meaningful analyses of state politics. While this critique probably could be made in almost any state and in national politics as well, it is particularly damning in a state such as New York where state news seldom receives significant coverage. Whatever its ideological tilt, the tilt that matters most is toward the status quo: the press in New York seldom moves beyond party leaders and toward those stages in the political process where the essential decisions have been made. Too many journalists, as Stonecash suggests,

> don't like the conflict, politicians and the messy legislative process. Their hostility distorts their judgment. For whatever reasons, journalists have misled us with a myth. They have failed to explain how the legislative process works and why decisions are so difficult to reach. What is ultimately so unfortunate, and puzzling, is that in the name of saving democracy, journalists have continually failed to communicate how democracy works.[49]

The New Media

Some commentators argue that the spotty and sometimes distorted coverage given to Albany politics by the traditional media is increasingly being supplemented and even displaced by new and more diverse outlets. Blogging, social networking sites, and YouTube are the leading outlets, marked by user-created content. Of these new media, blogging merits further discussion.

Political blogs (web logs) are online diaries composed of written posts displayed in chronological order, from the most recent entry to the oldest. Identified by title, date, and author, posts typically offer commentary and analysis on a particular topic or issue. Photos, videos, and links to other blogs or websites are common. Among the top ten blogs rated by Technorati,[50] defined as those that receive the most traffic, eight are blogs that emphasize politics, public policy, and/or current events. The rise of blogging at the turn of the twenty-first century resulted in notable impacts on national-level politics largely attributed to bloggers. Two examples, the unseating of Senate majority leader Trent Lott and the resignation of Dan Rather following Rathergate, are especially noteworthy.[51]

The impact of blogging at the state level has not yet been examined, though its potential to influence state politics is arguably substantial. In small states, such as Rhode Island and Vermont, a few bloggers can dramatically impact local politics since networks are small and often are supplemented by face-to-face meetings that both smooth and explicate online conflicts and interactions. Characteristically, these states are marked by few media outlets, hence potentially increasing the influence political bloggers might have.

Somewhat perversely, large states also can be affected by blogging, though in not quite the same way as smaller states. In large states, connecting in person with like-minded individuals may not be possible due to geographical distance. Geography is largely rendered secondary among political bloggers, however, because blogging encourages individuals to coalesce around issues or ideology online. Political bloggers have organized online mobilization efforts on a wide range of issues across states regardless of size. One example of an online mobilization concerns gay rights, specifically the right to marry. This issue has received substantial attention in state politics through referenda and recent court decisions in California, Connecticut, and Massachusetts. Lesbian, gay, bisexual, and transgendered bloggers actively have mobilized around this issue online, which often translates into offline efforts. This case underlines the importance of issue salience within a particular community and the breadth with which political blogging might impact state politics and policy. Blogs facilitate political discussion and coordinated action, transcending state and local boundaries. That said, capturing media attention in a state such as New York is arguably difficult, since bloggers must vie for attention with other prominent media outlets.

New York enjoys a variety of political blogs devoted to state politics, Albany politics (legislative and gubernatorial politics, in particular), and regional politics. In November 2008, a cursory examination of political blogs in New York yielded a total of forty-four blogs emphasizing state and/or local politics (see Table 4.2). Of these blogs, ten focus specifically on politics in Albany, while a half dozen appear to emphasize state politics more generally. Somewhat atypically for political blogs, some of those that focus on state politics are connected to major area newspapers. The blog Capitol Confidential is an offshoot of the *Times-Union*, its

Table 4.2

Political Blogs in New York, November 2008

Long Island

http://nassaugopwatch.blogspot.com	Nassau GOP Watch
http://blogs.trb.com/news/local/longisland/politics/blog	Newsday: Spin Cycle

Upstate New York

http://polhudson.lohudblogs.com	Politics on the Hudson
www.cazpilot.com/cazpilot/index.php	Cazenovia Pilot
www.insideoswego.com	Inside Oswego
www.buffalorising.com	Buffalo Rising
www.fixbuffalotodayfortomorrow.org	Fix Buffalo
www.livingindryden.org	Living in Dryden
http://pudsandlosers.blogspot.com	Adirondack Musing
http://blog.jimostrowski.com	Political Class Dismissed
http://rochesterturning.com	Rochester Turning

capitol pressroom more specifically. Yet the vast majority of political blogs are written by individuals unaffiliated with a major media outlet. Unlike the mainstream media, bloggers are not beholden to an editorial board, and they typically are free of corporate sponsorship. Similarly, the entry costs associated with blogging are relatively low. Access to the Internet, time to blog, and a moderate knowledge of blogging software are the minimum requirements needed to create a blog.

Political blogs in New York State offer a variety of political perspectives. While mainstream media are supposedly objective, most political blogs offer a decidedly partisan perspective. For example, Red Albany and Albany's Insanity are right-leaning blogs that focus on the Republican Party and party politics in New York. Others, such as Politics on the Hudson and Fix Buffalo have a decidedly regional appeal, focusing on problems unique to their respective areas, while also placing them more broadly in the context of state politics.

In addition to blogs, social networking sites such as Facebook and MySpace and video sites such as YouTube gained widespread popularity during the 2008 presidential election. While social networking sites seem likely to have less utility in state politics, YouTube probably will play a prominent role in state politics, as it has in national politics. It is still too early to offer a definitive assessment of these new media, which are not yet a force in state politics. How and to what degree political blogs and the other new media will impact state politics remains to be seen.

Continuity and Exchange: Politics and the Power Structure

The desire to understand how politics "really" works can lead to penetrating insights or, with equal frequency, ridiculous distortions. The early pluralists made an important contribution to the study of politics both by underscoring the importance of interest groups and by showing that electoral politics and the politics of governing were not one and the same. Elite theorists demonstrated the existence of a "permanent government," a set of core economic interests, which makes both the group struggle and electoral politics more or less irrelevant to what happens on some very basic issues. Finally, if we can revert to the discussion of political cultures raised in Chapter 1, there is probably a case to be made for the general influence of public opinion in the crafting of public policies.

For politicians, all these forces are important. Politicians operate in a world of stimuli that is far more complicated than most citizens realize. So many incumbents in the legislature have safe seats that it seems almost ridiculous to imagine any of them worrying about the next election, yet almost all of them do. The leaders of all four legislative party organizations, Republicans and Democrats in both the assembly and senate, constantly survey public opinion, as does the governor; and the results of their opinion polls weigh strongly both in how they explain their stands and in deciding how they actually stand. Finally, as we have noted, there are certain key interests and certain economic realities that are so compelling that they need no organizational advocates. This field of forces within which politicians operate is not stable. Politicians themselves, moreover, have policy preferences of their own that serve as lenses through which they view their political universe.

Despite the complexity of this field of forces, what is perhaps most remarkable about politics in New York is the ways in which the forces coincide. The election of 1994 was as dramatically an unsettling event in state politics as the fiscal crises of the 1970s were to New York City, yet in both cases the policy consequences turned out to be relatively trivial. Events and elections pose new challenges to public officials, but as both pluralist and elite theories suggest, the underlying context within which politics takes place remains remarkable constant. Whether this turns out to be true of the far more dramatic economic shocks and electoral changes of 2008 remains to be seen. Although they were forced to respond to different circumstances, virtually all the legislators and bureaucrats who went to work in Albany in 2009 were the same people who had been there in 2008. The same lobbyists, with many of the same resources and concerns, came knocking at these same doors. More than two decades of divided government have given the major players in state politics growing disincentives to change the system to which they have become accustomed. Interest groups that, in ideological terms, "should" have supported Republicans found it easier and more convenient to make peace with assembly Democrats. For more liberal groups, the same game worked with senate Republicans. The incentive to show up the opposition, to make the other party look bad, to come up with new policy ideas that point up the differences between the parties is consequently less present in New York than the responsible parties model suggests it should be. Broad appeals to public opinion that might bring ideological concerns back into citizen consciousness are frustrated by a pressure group system that is afraid to shake the status quo and by a press that is rightly suspicious of posturing of any kind.

The elections of 2008 did produce changes in the process that almost certainly will prove significant in the long run. Fights over the budget in 2009—with the "three-men-in-a-room" all Democrats—were conducted under different rules of the game that will open the way for a very different dynamic in state politics. Before exploring these dynamics, however, it is important to understand the constitutional and legal structures within which these struggles for power take place. The Madisonian system of checks and balances has been so refined, elaborated, and convoluted in New York State that even the most dramatic of political changes can work its way but slowly through the system. In politics, as in sports, the strengths and weaknesses of the different teams are important, but so are the rules of the game.

5

The Living Constitution

The constitution of a state or nation usually is described as the fundamental document that defines the structure of government and the extent of its powers. In the narrow sense, it is a text—a folio of parchment or paper signed by appropriate dignitaries and ratified by some proportion of the populace—which guides succeeding generations of public officials. The true constitution of a political system, however, seldom is described simply by a text. It is instead a body of traditions, statutes, local laws, judicial opinions, and related texts that simultaneously reinforce, supplement, constrict, and sometimes even nullify the basic text.

As requirements for voting, the New York constitution sets the voting age at twenty-one, requires ninety days of residence in the state, and mandates literacy in English. In actual practice, the voting age is eighteen, there is no literacy test, and the required period of residence is thirty days. The superseding federal laws that mandate these requirements have not changed the *text* of the New York constitution; they have changed its meaning. Eighteen-year-old New Yorkers vote despite a constitutional text that still plainly states that they cannot.

In a related vein, the state constitution mandates a balanced budget. But while the state's highest court has recognized the obligation this rule imposes on the governor "to *propose* a balanced budget . . . at no time has the Court suggested that, once a plan is enacted, revenues and expenditures must match throughout the fiscal year. . . . There must in every year be either a deficit or surplus."[1] Thus, although the text of the constitution would seem to mandate a balanced budget, economic realities and the state's highest court have conspired to loosen substantially the seemingly inflexible language of the formal document.

Our description of the formal organization of the government of New York begins with its constitution, a text to be sure, but also a penumbra of custom, law, and political realities that constitute the true constitution of the state.

New York's Constitutional Tradition

The Constitution of the United States runs about 8,000 words. State constitutions, save that of Vermont, are more verbose. New York's, at more than 47,000 words, is a little above the national average. Frequent amendments and revisions of state constitutions have provided numerous opportunities to make constitutional policies that would appear in statutory form at the national level. By one count, the fifty states "have had 146 constitutions, for an average of nearly three per state."[2] Since its colonial charter was replaced by the constitution of 1777, New York has adopted three new texts, in 1822, 1846, and 1894. It has, moreover, held five other constitutional conventions—in 1801, 1867, 1915, 1938, and 1967—that, although they did not produce new documents acceptable to the voters, frequently resulted in significant amendments. The prevailing text of 1894 has been formally amended more than 200 times.[3]

Until the Revolutionary War, New York was governed under the terms of a charter granted by the king of England to his brother the Duke of York that gave the duke virtually dictatorial powers. Attempts by the colonists to liberalize the formal charter by giving some consultative local powers to an elected assembly were vetoed by the king, "but its rejection," according to Peter Galie, "did not prevent the principles and practices embodied in the charter from being implemented." Prudent governors found it increasingly convenient to consult with locally chosen officials, making the absolutism of the formal charter essentially a fiction or, as Galie puts it, "a 'charter' that was not a charter."[4]

In 1777, as it became increasingly possible that the colonies might win independence, the need for a new constitution could not be ignored. Some states, most notably Connecticut, had negotiated charters so tilted toward self-government that few or no changes were needed to adapt them to the needs of a sovereign polity. New York was at the other extreme. Although many of the traditions, institutions, and sociological factors favoring self-government were firmly established, especially at the local level, there was no text, no constitution worthy of an independent state.

The Constitution of 1777

At once a wartime legislature and a constitutional convention, the "Convention of Representatives of the State of New York" convened in White Plains on July 10, 1776. That it took nearly a year to produce a text is not surprising since British troops controlled New York City and the convention itself was forced to move up the Hudson to Kingston to keep ahead of the advancing British army. Compared with the constitutions of the other twelve rebellious colonies, most which had been adopted in 1776, the 1777 New York constitution was among the most conservative. It had no separate bill of rights, and the few rights specifically enunciated, such as trial by jury, were well established in the common law. The franchise was, even by the standards of the day, limited, with only white, male property owners allowed to vote. And at a time of rebellion against the Crown—when executive power was generally suspect—New York was alone among the thirteen original states in creating a strong office of governor. Unlike the New England states, moreover, the original New York constitution gave relatively trivial powers to local governments and made most local officials appointees of the governor.

If the structure created in 1777 both reflected and extended the powers of New York's landholding elite, the rise of political parties in the 1790s, particularly the somewhat more democratic Jeffersonian faction, made many of the gentlemen's agreements it embodied unworkable. A series of deadlocks between Federalists and Jeffersonians over the relative roles of the governor, the legislature, and a long-forgotten body called the Council of Appointment resulted, in 1801, in the call for a new convention. With the legislature that called the convention dominated by Jeffersonians, the successful referendum that brought the convention into being was, quite notably, based on universal male suffrage. Despite its democratic origins, the body itself was not particularly bold. After weeks of rather aimless debate it resolved the two main issues it convened to deal with—reapportionment and the role of the Council on Appointment—and then adjourned.

Nineteenth-Century Roots of the Modern System

After a series of false starts in the early 1800s, the question of whether to have another, less narrowly focused convention was put on the ballot in 1820 and passed by a vote of 103,396 to 34,901. This time, reflecting the restricted suffrage laws in force, the vote represented roughly 10 percent of the state's population. The 1821 convention, nonetheless, was the one that marked the full emergence of the state from its colonial heritage.[5] The convention clearly delineated a separation of powers between legislative, executive, and judicial branches; adopted a bill of rights; nearly doubled the eligible electorate; and made thousands of local offices elective. Although it did not go as far as some states in expanding the suffrage or increasing the power of the legislature, it produced a constitution that was, compared with the document it replaced, reasonably democratic. Numerous checks on popular sovereignty, including a still very limited electorate, are found throughout, but what is more significant, in Galie's words, "is the extent to which the 1821 Constitution was modeled on the United States Constitution in both its structure and its essential theory."[6]

A series of amendments between 1821 and the Civil War gradually extended the suffrage to virtually all adults save women and African-Americans. More important, an 1846 convention produced what has been called the "people's constitution," both because of its broad-based membership and its devolution of power to the voters. Under its terms, the powers of local governments were greatly increased, and virtually all significant state and local offices—from judges to sheriffs, from the state attorney general to court clerks and canal commissioners—were to be chosen by popular election. Despite the convention's refusal to extend the suffrage to African-Americans or women, there is considerable truth to Galie's suggestion that "the 1846 Constitution represents the apogee of participatory democracy in New York."[7]

The Constitution of 1894

Since 1846, the constitution has required the question of whether to have a constitutional convention be put to the voters every thirty-two years. Following the failure of an 1867 convention to produce an acceptable text, the voters again chose to convene a convention in 1894, and it was this convention that produced the basic document under which the state is still governed. Subsequent conventions have offered important new provisions, many of which were adopted by the voters, but they have not substantially modified the fundamental structure of the text.

Although the convention of 1938 did not alter the basic structure of government erected in 1894, it did attempt some interesting changes. Students of the convention have characterized it largely in terms of its domination by interest groups and by its moderate to conservative ideology.[8] It also was notable in going beyond both national policy and the constitutions of most other states in guaranteeing a new set of social and economic rights. Because of its work, New York remains the only state with a constitutional guarantee of "the aid, care, and support of the needy." The convention also marked the first constitutional affirmation of a public role in housing. Its guarantees of labor's right to organize and of a state role in public health also went far beyond existing national policies or those of most states. Finally, the 1938 convention expanded the bill of rights. Long before the U.S. Supreme Court interpreted the Fourteenth Amendment's equal protection clause to protect racial equality, the New York constitution specifically prohibited discrimination on the basis of race, color, or creed. The 1938 convention also added language, similar to that of the federal Constitution, prohibiting unreasonable searches or seizures and made New York the first state in the United States specifically to recognize wiretaps as a potential threat to liberty. Unlike most previous (and subsequent) conventions, the 1938 gathering submitted its work to voters as a series of amendments rather than in the form of a new constitution, and the bulk of its recommendations were passed.

Numerous amendments to the state constitution, approved by voters since 1938, have done little to alter the basic text. A 1967 convention offered a number of significant revisions, but when put to the voters as a complete package it went down to overwhelming defeat. Two of the convention's recommendations were particularly controversial: one was the repeal of a provision in the 1898 constitution known as the Blaine amendment, which prohibits the use of state money by religious schools; the other, infuriating fiscal conservatives, would have eliminated the requirement that state debt extensions be approved by the voters. Some of the convention's proposals have been added as amendments, most notably a conservation bill of rights, a reorganization of the courts, and a provision allowing the legislature to call itself into session. Others have simply faded away, such as an article requiring the state to pay for college tuition for all state residents.

Box 5.1
New York's Landed Aristocracy

Unlike the New England colonies, settled largely by corporations and religious dissidents, New York inherited and built upon the Dutch patroon system in which an aristocracy of large landholders dominated both the economy and the government. Although many of the freeholders on Long Island and what is now Westchester established self-governing villages like those in New England, most of the colony's rural inhabitants worked as tenant farmers. When the British ousted the Dutch from New Amsterdam, "New York was a colony of conquest; to the victor went the right to establish political ground rules."[1]

New York's seventeenth-century royal governors recognized and extended the patroon rights of the wealthy and took some for themselves. Thomas Dongan, appointed governor in 1683, added a total land area larger than Manhattan to the existing manors of the Van Renselaers in what is now Columbia County and the Van Cortlands in the Bronx. He also added 250,000 acres to Livingston Manor and established new family estates in what became known as Pelham Manor, Cassilton Manor, Lloyd's Neck, and, of course, Dongan Hills. Dongan and his successors did concede such basic English rights as jury trials to the colonists, and representative assemblies continued to meet in many towns, but the manors of the Livingstons, Van Renselaers, and Schuylers were essentially medieval fiefdoms "over which their 'lords' received quasi-feudal legal and governmental powers subject only to the authority of the governor."[2]

The men (no women allowed) who drafted New York's first constitution were anything but a representative cross-section of the population. The convention essentially brought together those wealthy landowners who supported the cause of independence, and the document they drafted—though remarkably progressive in extending the suffrage, guaranteeing basic civil rights, and separating church and state—was deliberately protective of their interests. Only the wealthiest landowners, for example, could vote for governor, and the powers of the more democratically elected state assembly further were checked by a senate, a council of revision (with the power to review and veto legislative bills), and a council of appointment. Not surprisingly, the manor system survived well into the nineteenth century.

1. Alan Tully, *Forming American Politics: Ideals, Interests, and Institutions in Colonial New York and Pennsylvania* (Baltimore: Johns Hopkins University Press, 1994), p. 15.
2. Edwin G. Burrows and Mike Wallace, *Gotham: A History of New York City to 1898* (New York: Oxford University Press, 1999), p. 92.

New York's Constitutionally Strong Governors

In colonial days, during the War of Independence, and now at the start of the twenty-first century, New York has had strong governors. Even if the written constitution did not provide the office with significant formal powers, the preeminence of the state almost automatically confers upon its chief executive an aura of influence. The governor of New York virtually is assured of being treated by the media as a potential president, and in fact, ten of the state's fifty-three governors have been major party candidates for the presidency, four (Van Buren, Cleveland, and the two Roosevelts) have won, and six have served as vice president.

In comparing state constitutions, political scientists have long distinguished between strong and weak governors. Strong governors, the literature suggests, are armed with the following key powers:[9]

- First, they are elected for four-year (as opposed to two-year) terms and can run for reelection as often as they choose. A majority of the states restrict their governors to one or two terms. New York is one of only twelve states with no restrictions. While only two states now have elections every two years, New York still is among only thirteen states with unlimited four-year terms.
- Second, the governor is one of only four statewide elected officials. Aside from the lieutenant governor, comptroller, and attorney general, the governor appoints—and can fire—all cabinet members. New York's governors almost always have been relatively free of potential rivals for executive power; nationally, the states elect an average of 10.2 executive officials.[10]
- Third, New York's governor has the power not only to draft the executive budget, but also to veto specific items added by the legislature. Most states now grant both of these powers to the governor, but there are few in which the process has become so deeply institutionalized as in New York.

Beyle has quantified various aspects of these institutional powers, comparing governors on a scale of one (*very weak*) to five (*very strong*). With an overall score of 4.1, New York's governors were tied for second among those of the fifty states in 2004.[11] In most important respects, the formal powers of the governor in New York closely parallel those of the president in Washington. They include the powers to "take care that the laws be faithfully executed"; to grant reprieves and pardons; and to appoint—with the advice and consent of the state senate—members of the court of appeals, the appellate division of the supreme court, and most important executive agencies. As with the presidency, moreover, the powers of the governor are checked and balanced by the legislature's ability to override vetoes (by a two-thirds vote), to approve major appointments, to reorganize the executive branch, and, of course, to make the laws. New York's governors also have the ability, long craved by American presidents, to single out individual lines and items in the legislative budget for executive veto. This "line-item veto power," as it is known, was recently extended by the court of appeals. Under these rulings the programmatic language used by the governor in his budget to describe how various funds are to be spent cannot be amended by the legislature; it only can be voted up or down.[12] While the legislature's ability to negotiate these program issues is always there, its bargaining position vis-à-vis the governor has been weakened by these decisions. As in Washington, of course, the real powers of real governors in Albany flow largely from their abilities to use effectively the parchment powers granted them by the formal constitution.

New York's Really Strong Governors: The Exercise of Power

Even before the court of appeals expanded the ability of governors to prevent the legislature from amending their programs, governors of New York have had resources at their command that significantly extend and enhance formal authority. "The second floor"—the governor's office in the Capitol building—houses 180 directly appointed members of the governor's personal staff (not counting the budget division). This is the third largest such staff of any governor, far exceeding the national average of fewer than fifty-nine.[13] New York's governor, moreover, directly appoints more than 2,500 high-level officials and has considerable influence in the selection of thousands of other bureaucrats classified as "exempt" (from civil service regulations). The ability of New York governors to shape their own administrations is not only extensive but has tended to be remarkably free of legislative impediment. In 1977, when the Senate Committee on Corporations, Authorities, and Public Utilities voted not to confirm Governor Carey's nomination of Republican-turned-Democrat Peter Peyser to a position on the Public Service Commission, it marked the first time in memory that a nomination did not sail through the normally perfunctory confirmation process. While the process of confirmation became less automatic in the Cuomo years, none of Governors Pataki, Spitzer, or Paterson's nominees were rejected. It remains largely true, as Zimmerman wrote in 1981, that "one of the unwritten rules of Empire State politics is that the Governor is free to pick the top members of his administration provided they are competent and honest."[14]

A second source of informal power for New York governors derives from their almost unique access to key media. They play in the home parks of the *New York Times* and the *Wall Street Journal*; of Howard Stern, David Letterman, and *Saturday Night Live*. They, together with the governors of California, are the ones most talk-show hosts and late-night comedians read about in their morning papers. Like the governors of California and Texas, they are national figures simply by virtue of the size of their electoral constituencies.

Third, candidates for governor in New York typically run expensive, highly visible campaigns: Eliot Spitzer, for example, raised $41 million in 2006 and had already raised another $3 million for 2010 by the time he was forced to resign in 2007. The size and wealth of the business community remains unmatched, and while it certainly tends to be heavily Republican there is a strong progressive element as well. For Democrats, moreover, the state's high rate of unionization ensures a steady flow of campaign dollars. By the time they are elected, most New York governors are well known to the voters.

Fourth, party discipline in the legislature has more than a faint echo in the governor's mansion. As long as the governor's party maintains more than one-

---

Box 5.2
Nelson Rockefeller and the Modern Governorship

Few New York governors introduced more social and political innovations than Al Smith, and Thomas Dewey was perhaps the quintessential party leader, but none loom larger in the history of the state than Nelson Rockefeller. Whether or not he was, as one of his biographers asserts, "the best governor in New York's history," his sixteen years in Albany defined the modern governorship.

Whether Rockefeller was a "liberal" or a "conservative," what best describes his politics was a desire to get things done—above all, to get things built. The Empire State Plaza that dominates downtown Albany commonly is described as a fitting monument to Rockefeller's "edifice complex," but also he transformed the State University of New York (SUNY) from a collection of teachers colleges into a major university. He once described his attitude toward governing to a small uptown audience as follows: "You could plop me down in a town of two hundred people, and the first thing I'd do is to start solving their problems." A few days later he got a letter from one member of the audience saying, "Thank God our town is too small for you plopping."

Despite the growing hostility of conservative Republicans, particularly at the national level, Rockefeller never lost his ability to win upstate votes and work with the most conservative Republicans in the legislature. What best defines his governing style, however, was his ability to reach across the aisle and make deals with Democrats. Using a blend of personal charisma, media appeals, and raw power, Rockefeller seldom lost a legislative fight. He especially was proud of his ability to horse-trade. Once, needing two Democrats' votes to get a bill through the legislature, Rockefeller promised them high-level jobs in his administration. A few months later, when the appointments were publicly announced, an aide to the governor was asked if they were the products of a political deal pushed by Rockefeller. The answer was simply, "Of course."[1]

1. Joseph E. Persico, *The Imperial Rockefeller* (New York: Simon & Schuster, 1982), pp. 200–201, 210.

---

third of the seats in one house of the legislature, it has proven almost impossible to override a gubernatorial veto. Arguing that it could only embarrass the whole party, Democrats and Republicans alike have been able to keep their troops in line to protect the tradition of letting vetoes stand. Sometimes, as we shall see, legislative leaders extract their price, and governors must be careful not to push their veto power too far, but the remarkable fact is that only two gubernatorial vetoes were overridden in the entire twentieth century. Not until George Pataki pushed too far, in what was widely perceived as an attempt to bolster his conservative credentials for an ill-fated presidential campaign, has the legislature ever used its override power effectively. Even then, the deck clearly is stacked in favor of the governor. In 1997 Governor Pataki refused to negotiate the budget until certain other policy goals were met, and then he vetoed some 1,300 separate articles. It was the legislature that was widely blamed for producing a late budget, and the usually irrelevant assembly Republicans—by backing the governor—made the task nearly impossible. As Rosenthal notes:

> To override Pataki's line-item vetoes, the legislature would have had to summon up a two-thirds vote in both the assembly (100 of 150 members) and the senate (41 of 62 members) on each line that was struck by the governor. And the governor would be able to target legislators and apply pressure trying to win over the votes he needed to deny an override.[15]

This is just what the governor did. He was less successful in 2003, when the Democrats held a two-thirds majority in the assembly and cooperated with the senate in overriding 119 of Pataki's item vetoes, but this session remains highly exceptional and perhaps unique.

An equally important, somewhat paradoxical consequence of party control in the legislature is the parallel line of control it extends to the governor and the bureaucracy. Centralized power in the legislature prevents the kind of fragmentation, common in most American legislatures, which allows individual legislators and committees to establish the strong, enduring links with key bureaucrats that enable them both to elude central direction. Beyle combined a variety of measures, including standing in the polls, electoral margins, and a 1994 survey of elite opinions, to compare the personal (as opposed to institutional) powers of governors. As in his rankings of institutional powers, New York's governors came out near the top, scoring four on a scale of five, among the fourteen strongest in the fifty states.[16] Since these figures were compiled during the last, fading lights of the Cuomo governorship, they serve vividly to underscore the comparatively strong role of New York governors in the system. Much of this strength derives, quite simply, from the qualities of leadership that such individuals as Mario Cuomo, Nelson Rockefeller, and Franklin Roosevelt brought to Albany. These strengths cannot be measured in a study such as Beyle's, though they derive in no small part from the power that inheres in the office itself. Because for so long it has been the nation's commercial and legal center, the state has never been short of talented men and women. That they can be tempted to leave positions of great power in the private sector or in public affairs in order to run for governor is in part due, as Nelson Rockefeller once suggested, to the fact that the formal powers of the governor "comprise a substantial grant of authority. And because our governors possess this authority, we have enjoyed leadership that has established New York as a pioneering, innovative, and eminently successful state."[17] From a broader, national perspective, one 1982 effort to choose ten members of an all-time, all-state, gubernatorial hall of fame would have listed five New Yorkers were it not for a deliberate attempt to achieve geographic balance. As it was, three of the ten governors selected (Al Smith, Thomas Dewey, and Nelson Rockefeller) were New Yorkers.[18]

The Governor's Rivals for Executive Power

In some states virtually the entire cabinet is separately elected. Running in the same statewide constituency as the governor and able to cultivate strong support among the groups whose interests their departments affect (such as farmers in the case of an agriculture commissioner), these officials often emerge as the governor's key rivals for power. Because they cannot be fired and because they have their own electoral bases, separately elected department heads tend to diffuse gubernatorial authority. New York's governors are characterized as strong governors in part because they have few such rivals for power.

The Lieutenant Governor, Comptroller, and Attorney General

In New York, only the comptroller, the attorney general, and the lieutenant governor are, as statewide elected officials, the governor's potential rivals. One lieutenant governor in recent history (Mary Ann Krupsak) ran in the Democratic primary against the man (Hugh Carey) who had been her running mate just four years earlier; another (Betsy McCaughey Ross) ran, on the Liberal Party line in 1998, after having been George Pataki's Republican running mate in 1994. Although most of them eventually back off, it is almost a reflexive action to put the sitting attorney general and comptroller—both of whom have demonstrated the ability to win statewide elections—on the short list of potential candidates for governor. Given this logic, one of the interesting paradoxes of New York politics is how *infrequently* the state's other statewide elected officials actually have run for governor. Part of the reason probably is rooted in historical accident. For a cumulative total of forty-four years, the offices of attorney general and comptroller were held, respectively, by Republican Louis Lefkowitz and Democrat Arthur Levitt, neither of whom seemed to have higher political ambitions. They not only established a tradition of keeping the offices out of a career track aimed at the governorship, but they conducted their offices in such as way as to avoid policy decisions that might bring them into conflict with the governor, a tradition that essentially endured until Eliot Spitzer used his position as attorney general as a launching pad for his run for governor in 2006. A second reason for the comparative insignificance of these officers as rivals to the governor inheres in the written constitution, which uncommonly is spare in defining their powers. The comptroller's constitutional power is defined largely in terms of the unglamorous accounting chore of approving all state vouchers and auditing state and local government accounts. While such audits can be embarrassing to a corrupt or incompetent administration, in the normal order of things they carry little political weight. Similarly, the comptroller's role as guardian of the pension plans of almost 1 million present and former state and local employees is an awesomely important job that receives little public attention.

If the state constitution is terse in its definition of the powers of the comptroller, it virtually is silent on the powers of the attorney general. Aside from putting the office at the head of the department of law and requiring the attorney general to report to the legislature on the legal implications of proposed constitutional amendments, the constitution defines no formal power inherent to the office. In practice, the legislature and more aggressive occupants of the office have substantially expanded the role and size of the law department. Robert Abrams, who served as attorney general from 1979 through 1990, vigorously expanded the office's reach into areas such as consumer protection, prosecuting white-collar criminals, and using litigation as a tool for fighting environmental pollution. Some of the law department's expanded activities, such as its pursuit of certain kinds of criminal activities, were founded in powers long latent in the office; others—particularly in areas such as consumer protection and civil rights—were expanded as a result of Abrams's lobbying the legislature to give his office new powers. Eliot Spitzer's exploitation of these powers, particularly in pursuit of illegal trading practices on Wall Street, gained him national publicity and vaulted him into the office of governor in 2007. From the moment of Spitzer's election, moreover, his successor as attorney general, Andrew Cuomo, has been widely regarded as next in line to run. The Department of Audit and Control (the formal name of the comptroller's office), by way of contrast, seldom has produced aspirants for higher office. It has been less able to expand in large part because article 5 of the state constitution specifically provides that the legislature may not assign additional duties (beyond those of audit and control) to the office, and its existing duties are seldom the stuff of headlines.

Commissioners and Department Heads

Because the New York constitution limits departments to twenty in number, there are only twenty appointed executives with the formal title of commissioner. In practice, many units not called "departments" are located in the "executive department" and are of comparable importance. The executive department's division of housing and community renewal, for example, has a larger budget than many of the formal departments. The divisions of human rights, parks and recreation, and the state police are departments in all but name. Whatever they are called, the centrifugal forces pulling agencies away from the center is strong. As policy problems become more complex and technical, the ability of career experts to isolate themselves from control by elected neophytes expands. Most career civil servants are highly protective not just of their own jobs but of their agencies' missions as well. Unionized employees—most New York state civil servants are union members—have the extra organizational clout of the union movement behind them. And every agency has strong supporters in the private sector, in the legislature, and in parallel federal agencies. In describing the federal government, Louis Galambos expresses what most informed observers believe to be true in Washington. Although nominally in charge, Galambos says, the president's grip on the executive branch is weaker than most Americans think. He can place his own political appointees in departments and agencies, but where well-entrenched administrative officers are in charge of programs specifically authorized by statute, even the president can do little to influence their performance. Moreover the bureaucracies have in some instances acquired a virtual monopoly on expertise, on knowledge about their specific programs and their implementation. . . . Bureaucratic decisions have in many cases replaced legislative or executive decisions as the key factor shaping the specific content of our national policies.[19]

The size and complexity of New York government make a substantial degree of bureaucratic discretion almost inevitable. The decision how best to combat AIDS or to neutralize a toxic waste site is not likely to be centralized in the office of an elected politician. Many state bureaucrats, moreover, have access to a number of pass-through powers derived from federal rather than state law: the air resources division of the New York State department of environmental conservation is a state agency with important responsibilities under the state's clean air compliance act, but also it is responsible for enforcing federal rules in New York State. Since New York's air quality standards often match or exceed those of the federal government, this is a less important source of bureaucratic discretion than it might be in a less liberal state. One of the defining characteristics of New York State government, moreover, is the extent to which most day-to-day issues of governance *are* centralized. Whatever its formal position on an organizational chart, the typical department or division is firmly under the governor's control. While the senate has the power to approve or disapprove initial appointments, the governor alone has the power to dismiss. Appointed bureaucrats, in other words, serve at the pleasure of the governor. The governor's office on the second floor of the Capitol—known officially as the executive chamber, more frequently as "the chamber" or "the second floor"—has a number of less stringent mechanisms in place for controlling and coordinating administration policies. Different governors emphasize different mechanisms and display different styles of leadership, making it difficult, as one study put it, to describe a "generic administration."[20] But both the formal structure of the governor's office and the realities of New York politics combine to give the chamber a degree of influence over the bureaucracy that is perhaps second to that of no other governor and certainly far stronger in relative terms than that of the president.

There are three formal institutional mechanisms through which policy direction radiates from the second floor to the agencies. Every year, usually in the early fall, each agency must clear its legislative agenda through the program office under the guidance of the director of state operations. These proposals are circulated for comment among other agencies that might be affected and then checked, as one program officer put it, "to make sure that these bills support, or at least don't work counter to the Governor's priorities."[21] Agencies also are expected to check regularly with the program office on their routine activities. The Cuomo administration regularized this form of management control by requiring one-quarter of the agencies to submit monthly reports to the second floor each week. Finally, the Division of the Budget (DOB), though not formally a part of the executive chamber, plays a significant role in monitoring agency policies. The DOB's primary role is developing the executive budget, but also has its own lines of access to the governor and the agencies. The line between money and policy is thin, and the policy of recent governors has been to bring them closer together. Robert Margado, secretary to Governor Carey, claims to have "brought the first floor up to the second floor. That was difficult. I made the Budget Division part of the central policy process, a participant in the executive process. I forced them to understand the political judgments as well as financial judgments in ways they were not previously prepared to do."[22] This "politicization" of the budget division, as its critics call it, was intensified by Governor Pataki, who brought the DOB firmly into the executive process where it remains today. Indeed, the DOB has been very much a part of the policy process and a very strong force in enhancing the chamber's control over agency programs.

New York's budget is more policy focused than that of the federal government or that of most states since it makes no real distinction between program authorization and appropriations. In Washington and in many states it is—technically at least—illegal to legislate in an appropriation bill: that is, legislators cannot budget funds for an agency or program that has not already been established in a separate law. In New York it is commonplace for the governor and legislature to create all kinds of new policies in the budget. Thus, even before Governor Carey brought the DOB "up to the second floor," it was, almost by definition, a very important part of the policy process that has become, arguably, almost the only game in town. The 1997 budget, in particular, was a sort of legislative black hole, a celestial phenomenon that the governor packed with a rich array of nonfiscal policies that stalled the budget process for months even as it rendered the rest of the legislative session nugatory.

Governors still have one other device for influencing the flow if not the substance of policy. By reshuffling components of the executive chamber or by getting the legislature to authorize the full-scale reorganization of executive departments, a governor can refocus the level and nature of administrative attention that a policy proposal is likely to receive. Most administrative agencies, if they cannot be independent of everybody else, want to be as close to the top as possible. Divisions of the executive department, such as the arts council, the division of criminal justice services, and the division for women are thought to have greater visibility and access to the governor than they would if located further down the hierarchy in a traditional department. Under Carey and Cuomo, a number of offices were created in the executive chamber whose functions closely paralleled those of existing departments. The commission of quality care for the mentally disabled located in the executive department, for example, had a different set of responsibilities from the department of mental hygiene, yet there is sufficient overlap between the two that the governor could, if he chose, play one against the other. Carey and Cuomo apparently were more comfortable with these kinds of overlapping jurisdictions than was Pataki, who consolidated a number of such units, to the manifest annoyance of advocates for those groups who saw their access to the governor weakened.

Within the first four months of his inauguration, Pataki abolished the state energy office, the office of voluntary service, the division for women, the Martin Luther King commission, the office of gay and lesbian concerns, and the offices of black affairs and minority affairs. It does not take an astute student of electoral politics to see something more than a desire to streamline government in these choices: just as Carey and Cuomo had created chamber offices to facilitate the access of important supporters such as gays and blacks, Pataki felt no particular obligation to continue them. For the same reasons, many of these same offices were recreated when Eliot Spitzer moved into the governor's office in 2007. Spitzer, on the other hand, retained Pataki's most ambitious reorganization effort that consolidated the numerous divisions, agencies, and semiautonomous public authorities and corporations whose purposes are to attract or keep businesses in the state.

Quasi-Independent Authorities, Commissions, and Boards

One of the interesting and ironic aspects of Governor Pataki's consolidation of economic development activities was its being undertaken under the aegis not of a line department or an executive office but, rather, by a semiautonomous government corporation. The irony of this use of a government corporation to consolidate governing authority is that most such independent agencies were created to *isolate* them from political control. "It is clear," says Keith Henderson, "that authorities are not held to the same standards as general-purpose governments. As in other states, the legislative and gubernatorial intent to establish 'business-like' agencies with the power to issue tax-free bonds has resulted in a profusion of authorities removed from direct accountability to the public." Ironically, as Henderson continues, those authorities that "have taken advantage of their position" to "directly thwart the public will" usually have done so "with the collusion of the governor."[23]

There is a continuing danger that such independent authorities will become rogue elephants capable of trampling lesser creatures. Because their finances do not, as a rule, go through the standard budget process, they are little influenced by the DOB, and because they often have self-perpetuating boards of directors, they frequently can free themselves from control from the second floor more generally. Nonetheless, the incentive to create such independent agencies is strong. By limiting the number of departments to twenty, the constitution prohibits the governor and legislature from expanding the cabinet. More importantly, the constitutionally mandated balanced budget makes it almost imperative to put capital-intensive agencies such as the thruway authority and the Empire State Development Corporation off budget; that is, in a position to raise their own funds through borrowing and fees. The Rockefeller administration particularly was fond of creating new authorities whose total operating budgets were "nearly half the size of the state's own budget for operating its departments and agencies."[24] Some of the more ambitious of these independent agencies came to grief in later years when a shrinking state economy made them unable to pay back their accumulated debts. On the day he was sworn in as governor in 1975, Hugh Carey was faced with the imminent collapse of the state's urban development corporation and forced to devise a bailout plan. Carey and his successors, moreover, have found it difficult to exercise firm control over many of these corporations and authorities. As Benjamin and Lawton have written:

> Though firmly controlled by Rockefeller, the governor who created them and made the initial appointments, the board members of some of these agencies who serve fixed terms, were less responsive to Governors Wilson and Carey. Although Mario Cuomo has had nearly twelve years to put his own stamp on New York's authorities through appointment and reappointment, his control has yet to approach that exercised by Rockefeller.[25]

The Pataki administration's use of some authorities to reward political allies led to a series of minor scandals in the waning years of his administration. Calling them "patronage dumping grounds" in his 2007 State of the State address, Spitzer proposed a series of reforms that would have eliminated nearly 200 of the state's 733 independent authorities and brought the remaining boards under the same financial controls as other agencies. The bill passed the assembly in 2007, died in the then-Republican senate, and then faded from view when Paterson replaced Spitzer later that year.

New York was one of the first states to make extensive use of independent authorities and government corporations, but it has been slower than others to privatize or contract government services out to nonpublic agencies. The movement to reinvent government, to bypass state bureaucracies and to leave the task of implementing public policies to the private sector, has gained few victories in New York in part because the state's highly unionized public employees have had enough allies in the legislature to resist. A growing number of local governments in New York, conversely, have turned to private corporations for such functions as trash collection.

One unique New York institution that merits special attention is the board of regents of the University of the State of New York (USNY). As described in a press release from the board:

> USNY is perhaps the most comprehensive educational organization in the world, including within it all public and nonpublic elementary and secondary schools; all postsecondary institutions including the State University of New York, the City University of New York, and all independent and proprietary schools; vocational education entities serving individuals with disabilities; all museums, libraries and historical societies, and jurisdiction over 38 licensed professions.

Unlike the other independent agencies, the state education department is subject to budgetary controls. The governor and legislature, in other words, can tell the regents how much they can spend each year on what. In most other ways the board is free from gubernatorial control. Its sixteen members are elected by the legislature, sitting in joint session, with one member from each of the state's twelve judicial districts and four at large. The board of regents, in turn, appoints the commissioner of education, who sits at the pleasure of the board.

The Legislature

The constitution requires that the laws of the state must pass both houses of the legislature, an assembly of 150 members and a senate of sixty-two. The constitution of 1777, though less focused on the legislature than were the constitutions of the other twelve emerging colonies, provided for a strong, independent legislature. A long series of scandals in New York and other states brought the institution into growing disrepute. When the distinguished student of American politics Lord Bryce wrote in 1906 that "the state legislatures are not high-toned bodies," he was expressing both the prevailing public view and the concomitant reality.[26] The response over the past two centuries has been a series of amendments and redrafts of the constitution that gradually eroded the powers granted to the legislature in 1777 or that imposed procedures designed to check specific kinds of abuse. In 1847, for example, the senate was stripped of its power to sit as part of the court of final appeals. Also added to the constitution were a number of procedural rules such as the requirement that local and private bills be confined to one subject to prevent the legislature from sneaking special provisions into otherwise innocuous laws. The constitution also lists fourteen kinds of local bills the legislature cannot enact and—by the terms of the so-called Blaine amendment—forbids public assistance to religious institutions. Bills in the legislature—unless given a special waiver by the governor (called a message of necessity)—must "age" for at least three days before a final passage. Most important, the power to initiate the state's budget was transferred in 1927 from the legislature to the governor.

Partly as a result of these changes in formal rules, partly as a consequence of electoral politics, and partly because strong governors—Smith, Dewey, and Rockefeller in particular—tended to dominate the system, the legislature by the middle of the twentieth century was not a strong institution. In the 1950s Dewey sometimes would wait until just a few days before the deadline to submit his budget to the legislature, which usually passed it virtually unchanged. Rockefeller, it sometimes was said, owned one house of the legislature and had a long-term lease on the other. No change has been more striking in recent New York politics than the reemergence of the legislature as a key policy actor. With no significant changes in the written constitution, the rise of the legislature as an equal branch has been remarkable.

The Institutionalization of the Legislature

In a widely reprinted 1968 essay, Nelson Polsby delineated three characteristics of what he called an "institutionalized" legislature. Referring to the U.S. House of Representatives, Polsby suggested that an organization achieves institutional status to the extent that it is differentiated from its environment, it is relatively complex, and it has fixed rules and procedures that shape its behavior into relatively predictable patterns.[27] The institutionalization of the House was manifest most clearly between 1890 and 1910; similar patterns can be discerned in Albany largely between 1950 and 1970, when the contemporary legislative system flowered.

The Establishment of Boundaries

"In an undifferentiated organization," Polsby writes, "entry to and exit from membership is easy and frequent."[28] In the U.S. House of Representatives, more than 40 percent of the members elected in most years prior to 1890 were in their first term. Since 1910, the percentage of freshmen has seldom exceeded 25 percent, and the average number of years served increased from four to six years in the nineteenth century to more than ten years by the 1950s. There has been a similar change in Albany. The percentage of freshman legislators in the assembly declined from 56 percent in the 1890s to 26 percent in the 1920s to 13 percent in the 1980s. In the senate it went from 59 percent in the 1890s to 30 percent in the 1920s to 10 percent in the 1980s. Although legislative salaries remained low, "the legislature became a very attractive place to return to by around 1930,"[29] and it apparently has become even more attractive since. By 2000, the average New York state legislator had been in office for 12.7 years,[30] and most legislators had come to consider membership as a career. Instead of the citizen-legislators who moved in and out of the legislature to resume their "real" occupations as farmers, lawyers, or businesspeople, "there is not a very high proportion [today] who have full-time occupations outside the legislature."[31] In their biographies "in 1964 not a single member of either house listed their occupation as 'Legislator' in the official guide to state Government. . . . By 1988, however, more than two-thirds of Assembly members and more than half of Senators were describing themselves not as lawyers, businessmen, or consultants but as legislators."[32]

Another sign of the legislature's growing sense of itself as a distinct institution has been manifested in growing control over its own leadership and governance. The first speaker of the assembly to serve for more than two consecutive terms was S. Frederick Nixon, who served from 1899 to 1905. Four to eight years has been the norm in recent years. In the senate, between 1880 and 1920, sixteen men served as majority leader, only one for more than two terms. In a comparable time span of fifty-four years between 1954 and 2008, six men held the same job, with Warren Anderson (1973–1988) and Joseph Bruno (1994–2008) holding the post for thirty of those years. More important, the legislative parties in both houses have chosen their own leaders. An important source of Nelson Rockefeller's legislative power was the influence he was able to exert in the elections of party leaders in both houses, even, in one case, in the Democratic Party. Other governors, prior to Rockefeller, actually may not have involved themselves in the process of leadership selection, but the legislative leadership clearly viewed its role in subordinate terms. Many participants cite a 1981 fight over the financing of the metropolitan transportation authority as marking a crucial turning point in defining the independence of the legislature. In the words of a former speaker:

> When this major institution was on the verge of collapse, and an Executive attempt to solve the problem was abandoned, I believe that [senate majority leader] Warren [Anderson] and I jumped into the breach. . . . We put the budget together that year, and I think that this gave birth to the sense that the Legislature had finally achieved the capability of developing its own financing plans and had the courage to put into place unpopular taxes when people said no one could do it. I think that the whole MTA era was a turning point in Executive-legislative relations.[33]

Also contributing to the autonomy of the legislature, as noted in Chapter 3, was the decline of party machines. In comparison with the legislator of the 1950s and before, members were free to serve as autonomous actors rather than as delegates of local bosses: free, in effect, to work with each other in the legislature rather than in lockstep with a myriad of diverse external organizations. Most important, perhaps, was the professionalization of the legislature, which came in the wake of completion of a separate legislative office building in the Empire Plaza. Stonecash shows that in constant dollars the budget of the legislature increased tenfold from 1900 to the 1980s, with the bulk of the increase coming after 1950. Also, he notes, "during the Rockefeller era the legislature . . . was incapable of making policy initiatives in most areas. It was more often in a position of responding to gubernatorial initiatives than proposing its own."[34] In the contemporary legislature, each member has a district office with a minimum of two paid assistants and an Albany office with a minimum of one. Each committee has both its own counsel and staff aides plus the help of a counsel appointed by the party leader. The central research staffs of the party leaders, the financial experts on the assembly ways and means and senate finance committees, and the central staffs in such specialized offices as the bill drafting commission make the New York legislature one of the best-staffed legislatures in the world.

The Growth of Internal Complexity

Growing staff has made the legislature a far more complex organization. In Congress, one of Polsby's key indicators of complexity was found in the proliferation of subcommittees and party leadership positions. In New York, there has been a similar trend, with the balance tilted far more heavily in the direction of party leaders than committees. While committee work is not trivial in New York, the party leaders overawe all. The result, as former Republican speaker Joseph Carlino once said, is that "the Legislature is more highly organized than any other in the world—bar none. Never once in the fifteen years since I've been there have we failed to get a Republican majority for a 'must' piece of legislation. We Republicans have a tradition of discipline. Any new member is immediately schooled in that tradition of Republican control."[35]

The combination of staff resources and centralized leadership is at the core of the emergence of the legislature as the coequal of the governor: "The party conferences within the legislature serve as vehicles for policy positions. The legislative staff generates information and studies to support party positions. . . . All this has allowed the legislative parties to participate in and structure policy debates within the state. . . . The legislature is now a full partner in the political process."[36]

One consequence of this new partnership is that it takes longer to get things done. The budget passed in August 1997 was the latest in the state's history, 126 days after the constitutional deadline. The press makes much of late budgets, which were, throughout the Cuomo and Pataki years, almost chronic. What has been less frequently noted is that these budget delays were "part of a larger long-term trend of longer decision processes in Albany"[37] that reflect the growing complexity of the legislature and its growing willingness and ability to confront the governor with its own set of policy preferences. "It doesn't take long," as one veteran assembly member puts it, "to be a rubber stamp."

As in Washington, the state legislature has moved irregularly but inexorably toward the creation of more and more policy-relevant titles and positions. In 1981, when Zimmerman published the first edition of his textbook on New York politics, there were thirty standing committees in the assembly and twenty-six in the senate.[38] Today the respective numbers are forty-one and thirty-two, the largest total among the fifty states. In the senate, this means that there are thirty-two committee chairmanships available to the thirty-two members of the majority party and thirty-two ranking minority positions on committees to be divided among the Republicans: counting the majority and minority leaders, party whips, and so on, there are more than seventy-five "leadership" positions for sixty-two senators. In the assembly, there are only eighty-two committee leaders among the 150 members, but, as in the senate, there is a rich variety of other positions to satisfy member ambitions, such as assistant, deputy, and deputy assistant party leader, majority and minority whip, assistant whip, and speaker pro tempore. There are also legislative commissions and task forces, joint committees, and party committees. Whether substantive power actually flows from these positions is another question; but the point, quite simply, is that the New York State legislature has become a large, highly differentiated, complex organization. Measured in terms of its workload, staff, facilities, and resources, today's legislature would have been unrecognizable fifty years ago.

Fixed Rules and Procedures

As Polsby defines institutionalization, an important part of the process involves a shift from the personal to the routine, from discretionary procedures to fixed rules. Borrowing from classic sociological concepts, Polsby looks in particular at the seniority system and the treatment of contested elections in an effort to show that established methods of allocating resources have displaced more purely personal considerations. New York's strong legislative party system makes comparison with the U.S. Congress difficult. When Joseph Bruno beat incumbent Republican leader Ralph Marino for the position of senate majority leader in 1995, Marino did not slip to second spot on the totem pole of power: he went from first to last. When the speaker is unhappy with an assembly committee chair, she simply removes him.

The power of party leaders, while at one level intensely personal, is at another level a sign of institutional strength. As former assembly member Arthur Kremer notes: "In the 1960s the County Chairmen were the ones to consult when there was a tough issue, when they needed the votes."[39] Today, the bargaining takes place entirely within the institution: the rules may not be fixed, but the boundaries are. County leaders, lobbyists, and governors have to deal less with individual personalities than with representatives of the institution; that is, the elected party leaders. Instead of the highly complex rules that give Congress its institutional identity, the New York legislature has essentially one rule: legislators who can gain and maintain control of the majority party are beholden only to their supporters in the legislative party caucus.

In keeping with Polsby's analysis, however, the power of party leaders in the state is institutional, not personal. That Ralph Marino went from first to last in the rankings is testimony to the fact that power inhered in his institutional role. In Congress, institutionalization is reflected in the growing complexity of norms such as the seniority system, which serve to isolate the institution from outside influence. In the New York legislature, the centralization of power in the party leaders performs the same essential function.

Strong Parties, Strong Committees: The Pathways of Power

The fox, an old adage says, knows many things, the porcupine only one; but the porcupine knows it very well. There is, to put it in porcupine terms, only one route to power in the New York State legislature; to know it well is to get ahead. Even in parliamentary systems, where party discipline governs political survival, there are few legislatures in the world that are more leadership-oriented than New York's. Power in the New York State legislature follows a strict hierarchical ranking: at the top of the heap are the elected leaders of the majority parties, the speaker of the assembly and the majority leader of the senate. Inner circles of their closest allies in the majority party come next, followed by committee chairs. Rank-and-file Democrats in the assembly and Republicans in the senate have some legislative influence proportionate to their skills and efforts and, in particular, their closeness to the leadership. The leaders of the minority parties in each house are sometimes consulted, particularly in the senate. Rank-and-file minority members are almost never a factor. "If the issue is purely local," one assembly Republican told us, "that is, if it only affects my district, I can sometimes get something done. And if I have a really good idea that I'm willing to let some Democrat take credit for, I can sometimes have some influence in committee. But by and large members of the minority party around here are not part of the law-making process. We just don't count."

The Speaker

Article 3, section 9, of the state constitution provides for the election of a speaker of the assembly and empowers the body to establish its own rules. Article 4 recognizes the speaker as third in line, behind the lieutenant governor and president of the senate, in the event of the death, impeachment, or resignation of the governor. These are the only two constitutional references to the office. Its powers and duties derive almost entirely from rules adopted by the assembly.

Election of the speaker is, as a rule, the first item of business following the governor's State of the State address. Usually, the outcome of the vote is known in advance as party caucuses already have met to choose the Republican and Democratic party candidates. Under the unity rule, commonly enforced by both parties, all party members are pledged to vote for the candidate receiving the most votes in the party conference. Thus the nominee of the party with the most seats is an almost sure winner. We say "almost sure" because the unity rule does not always work. In 1965, for example, a split in the Democratic Party produced two Democratic candidates for speaker, creating a deadlock (discussed in Chapter 6) that paralyzed the legislature for months. In 2008, after the Democrats seemingly swept into power in the senate, four party members refused to accept the unity rule, thus putting themselves in a position to bargain with both parties for special benefits. No legislator likes to give the governor the kind of leverage with the speaker that the 1965 fight gave Rockefeller, nor do members of the majority power like to let the opposition become involved in choosing a leader; there are times, however, when the stakes for some members are high enough that they will risk deadlock. When individual legislators vote for a new speaker or majority, they are doing a good deal more than electing a party leader who will set the ideological tone and strategic direction of the party: they also are choosing the person who will, for the foreseeable future, control their careers.

In a study of legislative leadership in the American states, Jewell and Whicker place New York among the strong leadership states. In institutional terms, the New York legislature confronts a strong governor, but is otherwise independent and supported by strong party rules and traditions. Party leaders are independent of outside control and command highly cohesive, polarized parties. All the important tools of leadership, from complete control over committee assignments and staffing to access to campaign funds, are abundantly available in New York.[40]

So strong are party leaders in New York that forces that in other states have produced a fragmentation of power actually work to strengthen the hands of New York speakers and majority leaders. In many states, for example, the professionalization of the legislature has given individual members greater independence. As Alan Rosenthal argues:

> The natural state of a legislature is fragmentation. But in a number of respects, the legislature is even more fragmented today than twenty years ago. Earlier, leaders were truly in command, and power was tightly held. Partly as a consequence of modernization and reform, legislatures have become democratized. Resources are more broadly distributed, and the gap between leaders and other legislators is broader.[41]

Increased staff, in this analysis, gives an individual legislator the tools to stake out an individual policy position and gives a committee the resources to act on its own.

In New York, however, most of the important staff people are, in effect, agents of the party leaders. Each important committee has its own counsel, appointed by the committee chair, but also it has a counsel or program staff person appointed by the party leader. The real heavy lifting in policy research on important issues routinely is conducted less by committee staff members than by the program staff people appointed by, and responsible to, the party leaders. Committees are not trivial in New York, and there are rank-and-file members whose staff members have considerable influence, but the pervasive source of all real power, the people who count in the crunch and whose preferences prevail in cases of conflict, are those closest to the leadership. In New York, unlike almost every other state, in other words, the growing professionalism of the legislature has served to further centralize rather than disperse power.

Another factor cited by Jewell and Whicker as important in affecting the powers of party leaders also seems to have worked differently in New York. The decline of "the strong urban party machines that existed in many northeastern and midwestern states," they plausibly argue, "had a significant impact on state legislative institutions. . . . Some of these organizations instructed their legislators on how to vote, contributing to legislative party discipline."[42] Such instructions were not at all uncommon in New York. Instead of increasing party discipline, however, the urban (and rural) machines tended to erode it by using their voting blocs in the state assembly and senate to cut deals. Speaker Travia's inability to unite his Democratic colleagues in 1965 was due largely to the ability of the Brooklyn machine to hold out in favor of its own candidate. Even after their election, speakers prior to the 1950s often served less as party leaders than as brokers cutting deals between the real party leaders back in the districts. In New York it was the decline of powerful local organizations that gave the legislative party leaders their power.

One final source of leadership power derives from the speaker's nearly complete control over the agenda. Only the governor can issue a so-called message of necessity that allows bills to be considered late in the legislative session, but in all other matters of scheduling the authority of the party leadership is complete. Technically, the assembly rules committee controls the flow of business, as does its senate counterpart: it decides which bills get to the floor of the assembly and when. On paper, the rules committees are committees. In fact, until they were reformed in 2005, they seldom met. "Rules committee?" one former speaker told us in 2001: "I was the rules committee." While this is no longer technically true, because both the senate and assembly rules committee consists of the party leaders' most trusted colleagues, they almost never have been known to make a difference.

Other party offices in the assembly vary in importance largely as a function of the personal style and preferences of the speaker. Generally, the majority leader is the only other member of the majority party whose formal position betokens real clout. Usually a close confidant of the speaker, the majority leader is officially next in line to become speaker in the event of a vacancy, but Stanley Fink is the only majority leader since the 1960s to have actually won the speakership. What has happened in recent years is that the Democratic majority has tended to balance New York City's lock on the office of speaker with a corresponding tendency to award the majority leadership to upstate. Although Daniel Walsh of Franklinville, majority leader from 1979 through 1987, and James Tallon of Binghamton, who served from 1987 through 1993, were both viable candidates for speaker, both lost and soon retired from politics. Despite these failures, Walsh and Tallon, as well as Michael Bragman of Cicero (majority leader until he unsuccessfully challenged the speaker in 2000), were clearly second only to the speaker in party power. All three served as the party's official spokespersons and as floor leaders, as does Ron Canestrari of Troy, Bragman's successor. The speaker rarely appears on the assembly floor, and the majority leader—whose seat on the aisle is directly wired to the podium—typically conducts the day-to-day flow of assembly business.

The Senate Majority Leader

Technically, the lieutenant governor, identified in the constitution as president of the senate, is the presiding officer in the upper house, with the majority leader carrying the official title of temporary president. In fact, the rules of the senate give all real power to the majority leader, who as effectively controls the senate as the speaker does the assembly. When Hugh Carey's first lieutenant governor, Mary Ann Krupsak, sought to name the person who would preside if she was not present, majority leader Warren Anderson took her to court. He won. His explanation of why he began the case is instructive. "I didn't care," Anderson claims,

> who was actually presiding. That wasn't the point, though she thought it was. If we didn't like the ruling by Mary Ann or any other Lieutenant Governor, we could move to overrule the position of the chair. I was concerned that if she was the only person with the power to name the one to preside in her absence, she could, by not naming anybody to preside, keep the Senate from meeting or acting at all. She didn't agree, so we took her all the way to the Court of Appeals and they decided in our favor. That's why I'm the Temporary President.[43]

That also might explain why—knowing that he would lose in the long run—David Paterson, when he was lieutenant governor, ruled against his fellow Democrats in their 2007 effort to force a recorded vote on a package of reforms opposed by majority leader Joseph Bruno.

The constitution gives the minority party two potentially enormous points of leverage that, in recent years, have applied particularly to the senate. First, budget bills require a live quorum of 60 percent: they cannot be passed, in other words, in the absence of more than 40 percent of the members of either house. Second, a variety of local bills require the consent of a two-thirds majority. Since senate Republicans seldom have held a 60 percent majority, the Democrats seemingly should be able to exert bargaining leverage either by refusing to vote for important local laws or absenting themselves from budget votes. There are conflicting perspectives on the importance of these provisions. One aide to a senate leader told us that they was an important, though often overlooked, source of minority party influence in the senate. Another veteran staffer claimed that he had never seen it used. And a former assembly leader, recalling the days when Democratic majorities were thin, called it "nonsense. The majority always will support the ruling of the chair." Former senate majority leader Ralph Marino probably put the issue in perspective when, reflecting on his relations with minority leader Manfred (Fred) Ohrenstein, said that although he could not recall a case in which Ohrenstein had threatened to invoke either provision, he was aware of them. "But those are crude instruments," Marino argued. "If Fred really wanted to pressure me he could do it far more effectively by working through the governor or the speaker."[44]

The differences between party leaders in the senate and assembly are almost exclusively a function of size: dealing with at most forty followers, senate party leaders rely more on informal, face-to-face negotiations than do their assembly counterparts. The formal structure of the party organization is less elaborate and usually less meaningful. In particular, the role of the deputy majority leader—though clearly second in command—is not as clearly institutionalized as that of the counterpart majority leader in the assembly.

In both houses, the particular leadership style of the assembly speaker or senate majority leader says more about the distribution of power than any organizational chart. A table listing and describing such offices as deputy speaker, majority whip, and conference chair could be highly misleading. These party officers sometimes have real power and—not insignificantly—often are paid more than rank-and-file members, but the methods that party leaders use to communicate with party conferences have virtually nothing to do with organizational charts, titles, or formal rules. The official party whips, legislators technically responsible for whipping party members into line, sometimes actually play that role. As one assembly Republican told us, people who are known to be close to the leader are at least equally influential: "whether you get hit by the whip or the whap, it means the same thing."

Within the two houses, individual senators are more important than individual assembly members. This is only in part a function of size: because there are fewer than half as many senators, it would figure that each of them would, in a certain sense, be at least twice as important. As in the U.S. Congress, however, there is also a more individualistic tradition in the state senate, a tradition that extends even to the minority party. On important issues, to be sure, senate minority members are as far out of the loop as their assembly counterparts, but a tradition of reciprocity gives them a voice and vote that minority members in the assembly often envy.

Politics reinforces and, in no small part, explains this tradition. The Democratic majority in the assembly is, arguably, as diverse as the long-time Republican majority in the senate was; but it also is larger. For two decades the assembly leadership has had a majority large enough to allow individual members to vote their districts on some issues; senate leaders have not had that luxury. In 1997, to give an example, senate majority leader Joseph Bruno attempted to make the abolition of rent control a major issue. Only six of the thirty-five members of his party conference (as opposed to twenty-two out of twenty-six Democrats) were from districts where rent control was an important issue, but tenants' groups were mounting effective campaigns that could have threatened the reelection of all six. Facing a unified Democratic bloc of twenty-six votes, Bruno needed at least two of the six to cast a vote that might lose them their seats. There were, as we shall argue in Chapter 6, other forces operating on this vote, and there is little doubt that Bruno could have won in the event of a senate showdown, but the numbers are instructive. The senate is different.

Committees

Every Republican senator is either a committee chair or a party leader. Every one of them, in other words, earns a "lulu" of $5,000 or more on top of the base senate salary of $79,500. (A "lulu" is short for compensation received "in lieu of salary.") Only about 40 percent of the Democrats in the assembly similarly are blessed. Ranking minority members—senior members designated by the minority leaders in both houses to sit opposite the chairs—also receive lulus.

A party leader's ability to appoint all committee chairs, and indeed all committee members, often is cited as a key source of power. It also can be a source of considerable tension: "It was," said one leader, "the hardest thing I had to do." In order to avoid hurting colleagues or making enemies within their own parties, most party leaders closely follow seniority rankings in choosing committee chairs. "There have been very few times," said one speaker, "when the people whose seniority turn came were, in fact, passed over." Another insisted that he had "never" once violated seniority even though he actually had dismissed two chairs: "but," he added, "they both got promotions." What he meant was that both chairs were given positions of party leadership that carried bigger lulus than their chairmanships. Their new positions, it should be pointed out, were meaningless in terms of power.

Despite the centralization of power in New York's party leaders, the standing committees of the senate and assembly play a surprisingly important role in the crafting of public policy. Many committee chairs and quite a few rank-and-file members have developed a considerable degree of expert knowledge in the areas of their committees. Some committees, of course, are more important than others, and complaints about being bypassed or ignored by party leaders are not uncommon.

But committees in New York have an almost unique gatekeeping role. In California and many other states, all bills referred to committees must be reported back to their parent bodies. Thus, a bill referred to the senate transportation committee, no matter how ridiculous, must be brought back to the senate floor. It comes from committee with a "do pass" or "do not pass" recommendation, and most "do not pass" bills are killed in a matter of seconds, but they do get to the floor. In New York, as in the U.S. Congress, most bills referred to committees die there, and a bill that cannot command a majority in committee is highly unlikely ever to be seen again. Most referred bills, 90 to 95 percent at least, die in committee, but in Congress, unlike in the New York legislature, a determined majority can force a bill to the floor. In New York, only the leadership has the tools it needs to bring back a bill.

The Many Systems of Local Government

More than one-quarter of the New York constitution is devoted to local governments. No state, save perhaps California, has more units and more types of units of local government than New York. New York's 1777 constitution continued the charters of local governments conferred by the king of England, and also it continued the practice of granting the governor (and legislature) the power to appoint local officials. The constitutions of 1841 and 1846 granted increasing powers to local governments, but still in the context of central control. Not until 1867 did the concept of home rule emerge as an operative doctrine. "The meaning of home rule," as Galie rather dryly but accurately notes, "depends on the context in which it is used. Broadly conceived, it refers to the ability of local government to perform functions and activities traditionally undertaken by these governments without undue interference by the state. Home rule powers refer to the constitutional and statutory powers to enact local legislation and carry out the duties and responsibilities of the local government."[45]

Few issues proved more difficult to resolve at the 1867 convention than those arising over the concept of home rule. The tensions manifested there between the proponents of home rule and those who saw the extension of state power as a necessary antidote to municipal corruption were to remain prominent well into the twentieth century. As noted in Chapter 2, New York's almost unique mix of local government traditions—an amalgam of Dutch and British traditions overlaid with the township provisions of the Northwest Ordinance—established a complicated grid of towns, villages, cities, counties, townships, and boroughs that few states can match. The sizes and shapes of the state's towns, villages, and cities have less to do with any kind of constitutional plan than with historical circumstance. Some local governments, such as those of New York City and Albany, can trace their roots to colonial charters granted as early as 1686. Counties, which also predate the Revolution, were created to build such public facilities as courthouses and orphanages. Until the U.S. Supreme Court ruled that legislatures must be based on a system of equal representation, most counties were governed by boards of supervisors consisting of one delegate from each town. Some county boards of supervisors still meet, with each town supervisor casting a weighted vote, but most counties have adopted a system in which there is a county legislature, elected by districts of equal population, and an elected or appointed county executive.

Most cities in New York are governed by a mayor-council form of government, usually with what is known as a "strong" mayor (i.e., a separately elected official with clear budgetary and executive powers). The council-manager form, which enjoyed a wave of popularity at midcentury, replaces the mayor with a professional city manager who serves at the pleasure of the elected council. Towns, despite the usual connotation of the name, are not necessarily small. The town of Hempstead, for example, is larger in both size and population than the cities of Buffalo, Rochester, and Syracuse. Towns are governed, as a rule, by a council elected at large (rather than by districts, as in most cities) and a town supervisor who sits on the council and performs various administrative duties. In some counties, the town supervisors collectively constitute the county board of supervisors.

Villages add a more complicated level to the mix since they often overlap the jurisdictions of towns and cities. Historically, villages were formed to perform special functions such as zoning or providing police and fire services. Governed by an elected board of trustees, they typically are limited in their powers to the purposes for which they were created. While many villages continue to exist— and a new one was created by the legislature as recently as 1998—their functions largely have been supplanted by a bewildering variety of special districts. In the nineteenth century, the drive to create new units of local government was based partially on demographic changes. As previously underpopulated areas became more densely settled, the demand for the kinds of public services provided in other areas increased. The increasing need for centralized water and sewage systems and for such newly developed functions as electricity and mass transit produced concomitant demands for the creation of local service agencies.

By the Great Depression, most New Yorkers lived in incorporated communities, or, to put it the other way, most inhabited areas of the state were contained in officially organized towns, villages, or cities. Yet new local governments were created at an accelerating rate. The reason for this surge is found in a dramatic increase in the number of special district formations, which occurred for essentially two reasons. First, politicians—strapped for resources as tax collections slowed— increasingly needed to borrow funds to provide essential services. By the early 1930s many local governments were already at the maximum level of borrowing allowed under the constitution. One way of evading these limits was to create new units of local government that could tap new lines of credit. The federal government added a second incentive for the creation of special districts by passing a variety of laws that required the creation of bond-funded local housing authorities and soil conservation districts in order to be eligible for federal matching funds. First as governor and later as president, Franklin D. Roosevelt was a particularly enthusiastic proponent of special districts as a way to avoid municipal defaults

---

Box 5.3
New York's Changing Court System

Judith Kaye, almost from the day she became chief judge of the court of appeals in 1993 until her retirement in 2008, pushed a strong agenda of court reform. Although her master plan for simplifying the overall structure of the system repeatedly stalled in the legislature, she did succeed in creating a series of specialist courts, some in collaboration with the independent Center for Court Innovation. These courts include drug courts in the criminal court system, community courts for juveniles, domestic violence courts, and some very innovative drug treatment courts in the family court system. The court system now is developing a statewide system of mental health courts.

The concept underlying courts such as those dealing with drug addiction is that the judiciary should take an active role in dealing with the root problems associated with criminal activities. In drug courts, those accused of drug-related crimes are entered into treatment programs instead of prisons. The same judge continues to see each person, and, aided by a staff of addiction specialists who act as case managers, follows each case closely. The district attorney, defense attorneys, and usually the local department of mental hygiene cooperate using a series of "graduated sanctions" as a response to relapses. Successful completion of treatment usually means dropping the charges, while dropping out of treatment results in an immediate start of the jail sentence. The system has proved a good inducement for drug users to stay in treatment.

The family drug treatment court uses the same cooperative concept to maximize a mother's chances of successful recovery and the elimination of any neglect charges stemming from her addiction. Dropping out of treatment means that her children will be made available for adoption earlier. This concept is vastly superior to the present court practice of telling the woman to find treatment on her own, reviewing the case about nine months later, and punishing her if she has failed to negotiate the labyrinth of treatment facilities to find the one suitable for her. There were only fourteen family treatment courts in the country just five years ago, and two of them were started in 1998 in New York State. Now they are found throughout New York and in at least twelve other states. While Judge Kaye has been unable to effect the complete overhaul of the court system that most observers agree is overdue, small innovations such as these are constantly changing the nature of the state's judicial system.

---

during the Depression; in 1934 he sent a letter to governors urging them to create public corporations that could employ revenue bonds. He urged the creation of water, sewer, and electric light and power districts. He explicitly argued that these governments should be used to circumvent debt limits and referendum requirements for the issuing of bonds. He also dispersed model enabling legislation for housing authorities and soil conservation districts.[46]

The pattern continues. While the national number of townships, counties, and municipalities has remained virtually constant since the 1940s, the number of special districts soared from about 8,000 in the 1940s to 18,000 in the 1960s and nearly 30,000 in the 1980s.[47] New York alone has more than 10,000 local entities not including the literally thousands of public and interstate authorities that are governments in all but name (see Box 5.3). It is important to recognize that none of these structures are etched in stone. Home rule notwithstanding, local governments remain the creatures of the state: what the legislature giveth it can take away. Despite the work of a commission appointed by Governor Spitzer showing how much could be saved by consolidating some local entities and abolishing others, the chances of significant reductions are slim. Home rule, like federalism, is more about politics than about constitutions.

The Judiciary

The constitution of 1777 created a highly decentralized court system that relied heavily on state trial courts (known collectively as the supreme court) and local justices of the peace. In 1821 the supreme court was divided into trial and appellate jurisdictions. It was not until 1846 that New York created a single court of last resort equivalent to the supreme courts of most other states, but known in New York as the court of appeals. The court replaced a rather odd, House-of-Lords-like institution known as the Court for the Trial of Impeachments and Correction of Errors, described by one journalist as an institution "as cumbersome as its name."[48] Originally comprised of eight elected judges, the court of appeals now consists of seven judges appointed by the governor, with the consent of the state senate, to fourteen-year terms. The chief judge—until 2008 Judith S. Kaye of Manhattan—presides over the court and serves as chief administrator of the state court system as a whole. In this latter role, the chief judge is assisted by an administrative board consisting of the four presiding justices of the appellate division and a chief administrator of the courts, whom the chief judge appoints. Since 1977, all of New York's many state and local courts have been administered and funded by the state.

The unified court system, as noted in Chapter 2, is a four-tier system with the appellate division of the supreme court hearing appeals from the legal rulings and procedures of the trial courts. The trial court system in New York is as complicated a structure as one can find in the United States. As in most states, it includes two levels of trial courts of general jurisdiction. At the higher level are the county courts and the trial division of the supreme court. Not counting those assigned to the appellate division, the supreme court consists of 323 justices elected to fourteen-year terms from each of the twelve judicial districts of the state. Supreme court justices are paid $136,700, among the lowest relative to cost of living in the states.[49] Although a move from bar to bench represents a substantial cut in pay for a New York lawyer, it is a sacrifice many appear willing to make, and the quality of the attorneys willing to forgo higher incomes for the status of a judgeship generally has been high. Quite another story prevails at the lower levels of the system. Town magistrates, who handle such low-level offenses as petty larceny, simple assault, and drunk driving, need have no legal background in order to serve. Elected by the voters largely on the basis of party affiliation and personality, they are, to put it mildly, a mixed bag.

Court Reorganization

As chief administrator of the state courts, chief judge Judith Kaye followed her predecessor, Sol Wachtler, in taking a strong interest in reorganization, and she was successful in implementing a number of small reforms. Computerization has reduced the backlog of criminal cases substantially, as has the creation of special drug treatment courts in a number of jurisdictions. Experiments with a variety of quasi-judicial panels also have proven effective in replacing formal trials with less contentious, cumbersome, and costly arbitration sessions. Also a jury reform program eliminated exemptions from jury service, raised the daily stipend, and ended mandatory rules on sequestering. But the larger, widely recognized structural problems of the system— many of them requiring constitutional amendments—have remained untouched. The constitution's establishment of a unified court system remains, as one former chief judge described it in 1974, "a constitutional fiction. New York has an inheritance of a colorful but confused and sprawling mass of eleven trial courts"[50] that are generally agreed to be among the least efficient in the country (Table 5.1).

Despite numerous calls for reform, neither Governor Cuomo nor Pataki was willing to confront the political difficulties of steering a meaningful restructuring plan through the legislature. The *New York Times*, in a particularly biting editorial, attributed these failures largely to narrow partisan motives:

> The urgency of this task is attributable in no small measure to indifference by . . . George Pataki. Although he periodically gave lip service to making improvements in the courts, occasionally following through, Mr. Pataki generally shied from expending the necessary energy or political capital to persuade the State Legislature to go along. To the extent Mr. Pataki led in this sphere, it was mostly by bad example. His misuse of the governor's judicial appointment power to play politics—even to the extent of packing Manhattan's appellate court with upstate Republicans—has left a legacy of mediocrity and cronyism.[51]

In fairness to Governor Pataki, the partisan division of the legislature has made court reform particularly difficult. With the two houses of the legislature in the hands of different parties, "the major roadblock to reorganization and rationalization of the structure of the courts has been the issue of how the various judicial officials are selected. While many of the relevant actors profess an interest in simplifying the organization of the system, none seem willing to give up their role in choosing the various judicial officers who populate the current system."[52]

Table 5.1

Local Governments

General purpose local governments: 1,607
- Counties: 57[a]   Largest = Suffolk: 1,419,369   Smallest = Hamilton: 5,379
- Cities: 62   Largest = New York: 8,008,278   Smallest = Sherrill: 3,147
- Towns: 932   Largest = Hempstead: 755,924   Smallest = Red House: 38
- Villages: 554   Largest = Hempstead: 57,000   Smallest = West Hampton Dunes: 11

Special purpose local governments: 1,811
- School districts   685
- Fire districts   867
- Library districts   181
- Other special districts   78

Local public authorities: 991
- Local development corporations   618
- Housing   123
- Industrial development   116

Town special districts: 6,525
- Lighting   1,783
- Water   1,436
- Sewer   1,110
- Fire protection   953

Sources: 2006 New York State Statistical Yearbook; various reports of the New York State Commission on Local Government Efficiency and Competitiveness, www.nyslocalgov.org.
[a]Not counting New York City's five boroughs.

A breakthrough in this roadblock may have been started with the enthusiastic acceptance of a 2006 report by the Special Commission on the Future of New York State Courts, appointed by Chief Judge Kaye. Governor Spitzer backed most of the commission's major recommendations in his 2007 State of the State address, and it was well received by legislative leaders in both houses. The commission's proposals would, in essence, merge a number of specialized courts into a supreme court with commercial, family, probate, and criminal divisions, and a district court system with limited jurisdiction over criminal and civil matters. Such specialized courts as the court of claims, the surrogate courts, family courts, and New York City's civil and criminal divisions would be folded into this unified system. More controversial is a long-standing proposal to equalize the appellate workload by creating a fifth judicial department for Long Island. A similar proposal passed the 1967 convention but has never been enacted, thanks to New York City Democrats who fear they would lose judgeships to Long Island. As the Long Island caseload grows, however (and as Long Island becomes less solidly Republican), opposition to the new district has waned. City legislators are under particularly strong pressure to support a restructuring of the major trial courts in which nearly half the judges serving in the supreme court in New York City are acting judges, often from upstate, serving on temporary appointments to these chronically underserved courts.

Reorganization proposals have failed in the past when they have been folded in with efforts to remove more judicial positions from the electoral process. Judge Kaye, with the support of key legislators, insisted on decoupling the issues of court reorganization and election, and hearings held by both the senate and assembly judiciary committees over the past ten years have shown widespread support for the general reorganization plan. But agreement in principle has not meant agreement in fact: tangential issues—such as legal representation for the poor in the 1998 legislative session—have repeatedly prevented the issue of reorganization from moving through both houses of the legislature. By carefully balancing aspects of reform favored by both parties, Spitzer's presentation of the commission's recommendations seemed better positioned than its predecessors. Thus, although it seems increasingly likely that the legislature will pass a proposed amendment on to the electorate sometime in the near future, Governor Paterson seems to have neither the will nor the power to provide this needed push to get the assembly and senate to agree on a mutually satisfactory plan in the two consecutive sessions as the constitution requires.

The Rights of New Yorkers

Among the original thirteen states, New York was one of the last to adopt a formal bill of rights; in modern times it has been a trailblazing state in both formally protecting and generally respecting individual liberties. There is, in a sense, no paradox here. As the most ethnically, religiously, and culturally diverse of the thirteen original states, New York has long been among the most tolerant. Its early constitutions were based on the premise that a government of limited powers could not and would not intrude on individual liberties. The 1777 constitution specifically guaranteed only a limited right to vote, the right to a jury trial, and religious liberty. As experience showed the need for further protections, each succeeding constitution has expanded both the substantive and procedural rights of state citizens guaranteed in the written constitution. Even where the state constitution is silent, moreover, or where its provisions are essentially identical to those of the federal bill of rights, New York's courts have tended to be relatively liberal in deciding questions of individual liberty.

Substantive Rights

Students of constitutional law often distinguish between such "substantive rights" as freedom of speech, which pertain to what the state must allow people to do on their own, and "procedural rights," which define, in effect, how things are done by the state. With respect to the most fundamental rights of individual freedom, article 1 of the New York constitution differs from the national Bill of Rights in two important respects. First, it covers a substantially broader range of protected liberties, including the right to vote, to belong to a labor union, to be educated at public expense, and even the right to a decent standard of living. Long before the U.S. Supreme Court began its assault on racial segregation and Congress passed its first civil rights laws, the 1938 New York constitution stated, "No person shall, because of race, color, creed or religion, be subjected to any discrimination in his civil rights by any other person or by any firm, corporation, or institution, or by the state or any agency or subdivision of the state" (article 1, section 11). Second, New York's bill of rights, unlike the nation's, is stated largely in positive terms. Thus, while the U.S. Constitution's First Amendment *prohibits* Congress from enacting laws abridging speech, freedom of religion, and so on, New York's locates these rights in the people. Section 3, on religion, for example, begins with the words: "The free exercise and enjoyment of religious profession and worship, without discrimination or preference, shall forever be allowed in this state to all mankind." This positive wording contrasts with the more circumspect phrasing of the federal First Amendment: "Congress shall make no law respecting an establishment of religion, or prohibiting the free exercise thereof."

Not surprisingly, given its liberal tradition, New York State has tended toward a more liberal interpretation of questions involving individual liberties, even when the language of the state constitution is not substantially different from the federal Constitution. In the words of a New York Court of Appeals ruling:

> Freedom of expression in books, movies and the arts, generally, is one of those areas in which there is a great diversity among the states. Thus it is an area in which the Supreme Court has displayed great reluctance to expand Federal constitutional protections, holding instead that this is a matter essentially governed by community standards. . . . However, New York has a long history and tradi-

tion of fostering freedom of expression, often tolerating and supporting works which in other States would be found offensive to the community. . . . Thus the minimal national standard established by the Supreme Court for First Amendment rights cannot be considered dispositive in determining the scope of this state's constitutional guarantee of freedom of expression.[53]

Interestingly, the state's courts have not been so expansive in applying some of the constitution's more distinctive guarantees. The state's 1938 provision against discrimination (section 11) was not only among the first such guarantees in the United States, but also unique in prohibiting any *private* "person . . . firm, corporation, or institution" from violating an individual's civil rights. In 1948, however, when an African-American couple was denied housing in Manhattan's Stuyvesant Town apartments, the court of appeals held to the very narrow argument that housing was not one of the civil rights protected in the state constitution. "Since," as Galie summarizes the court's ruling in *Dorsey v. Stuyvesant Town* (1949), "there was no statute recognizing the opportunity to acquire real property as a civil right, the court concluded that the section could not apply to individuals in the appellant's situation. . . . In effect the court said the clause is not self-executing; for its prohibitions to be effective, legislation is necessary."[54] Similarly, New York's famous section 1 of article 17, which seemingly establishes a state obligation to provide for the "aid, care, and support of the needy," has been effectively rendered meaningless by the courts' rulings that it is up to the legislature to decide who is really needy.

Procedural Rights

In the days when Earl Warren was chief justice of the Supreme Court of the United States (1953–1969), the Court substantially expanded its interpretation of the Fourteenth Amendment to make a number of federally protected rights applicable to the states. States were required, for example, to provide even the poorest defendants with the right to counsel, local police were required to warn defendants of their rights before questioning them, and states were expected to avoid unreasonable searches and seizures. These court rulings were, and in some cases continue to be, highly controversial. They are, however, less controversial in New York than in most other states because New York either has a similar guarantee in its constitution or because its court of appeals already has inferred such rights. To put it bluntly: if you are formally accused of a crime, you have a better chance of defending yourself in New York than in almost any other state.

Although the rights of criminal defendants are better protected in New York than in most other states and, indeed, more than federal guidelines require, the differences are subtle. Most of the time, it would make little difference in the twenty-first century whether you were arrested in New York or Mississippi. In both states, the police—following the U.S. Supreme Court's ruling in the case of *Miranda v. Arizona*—must read you your "Miranda" rights, advising of your rights to remain silent and to seek the help of counsel. In both states, following federal guidelines, you have the right to counsel, to be free from unlawful detention (habeas corpus), to be informed of the charges against you, to not be unreasonably detained without indictment, and to confront key witnesses against you. While all these rights pertain today in all fifty states, most of them date back in New York to the 1821 or 1846 constitutions, when such guarantees were less common.

What probably accounts for New York's liberal reputation in the area of procedural rights is its weighty history of case law founded in state—as opposed to federally mandated—constitutional rights. New York's 1821 constitution, for example, contains wording identical with the due process clause of the federal Fifth Amendment: "No person," it reads, "shall be deprived of life, liberty, or property without due process of law" (article 1, section 6). The federal due process clause was only recently applied to the states and has generally been held to apply only when there is so-called state action. The state due process clause, through more than 185 years of case-law development, "has been construed to provide broader rights than the federal provision."[55]; and it is arguably broader than that of most other states, particularly those whose due process rights derive solely from federal court imperatives.

One of the most interesting areas of procedural rights in New York—its provisions regarding search and seizure—is particularly instructive as to the real meaning of the constitution. Prior to 1938, the state had no constitutional guarantees against unreasonable searches. The amendment adopted then (section 12) is almost identical in wording to the federal Fourth Amendment, but it adds an interesting and progressive set of restrictions on wiretapping. Strictly speaking, however, the New York constitution falls short of federal practice because it does not include the so-called exclusionary rule adopted by federal courts in 1961. In fact, New York's 1938 convention explicitly rejected a proposal, "supported by Governor Lehman and others, to prohibit the use of unreasonably obtained evidence" in court.[56] What the delegates declined to do, however, the state court of appeals went ahead and did anyway. By conflating emerging federal doctrine, a little case law, and a whole lot of its own thinking on the issue, the court essentially added the exclusionary rule to the constitution, which did not originally include it. We return to our original point that the constitution of a state is not simply a text: it is a living corpus of formal parchment, statutory and court interpretations, and actual state practices.

Changing the Constitution

Although the U.S. Constitution formally has been amended twenty-seven times, most scholars agree that legislative and judicial interpretations of the basic document have been more important sources of fundamental change than written amendments to the text itself. Change of this kind, as we have seen, is not unknown in New York, but because state constitutions tend to be far more detailed and specific, the formal processes of revision and amendment loom larger at the state level. The New York constitution adopted in 1938 formally has been amended 137 times in the intervening years.

Change Through Formal Amendment

The process of amendment in New York is designed, as it is in most states, to make changing the constitution considerably more difficult than passing an ordinary statute. The federal constitution requires a two-step process of amendment involving, first, passage of the proposed amendment by a two-thirds majority of both houses of Congress and, second, ratification by three-fourths of the states. Alternatively, the states may call for the convening of a constitutional convention to revise the whole document. In seventeen states, citizens may bypass the legislature by placing a proposed amendment directly on the ballot if enough registered voters sign a petition to do so. This process, known as the citizen initiative, is not allowed in New York, where only the legislature can authorize a referendum. In twenty states, a majority of both houses is all that is required for the legislature to propose a constitutional amendment; about the same number require a two-thirds vote, though some of these allow simple majorities to act if they pass identical resolutions in two consecutive years. New York is one of eight states that requires a three-fifths majority in both houses.

Generally speaking, the legislature and the voters have been on the same page with regard to most amendments. Looking at the period from 1967 to 1993, Benjamin and Cusa found the voters approving 41 of the 61 amendments proposed by the legislature (67 percent). As the authors note:

> No more than a quarter of the constitutional amendments passed by the legislature in the twenty-six years under study involved fundamental changes in the structure of state government. The three amendments concerning the state judiciary passed in 1977 and approved by the voters were most important. . . . Five other amendments adopted during the period, several based on ideas developed at the 1967 Constitutional Convention, were of some structural significance.[57]

The public seems most likely to reject amendments that invoke such key words as *taxes* and *borrowing*. Its record of accepting major changes in the process of governance, on the other hand, is strong.

Change Through Practice and Experience

Because of its unusual specificity, the New York constitution has not changed as much through practice, statute, and judicial interpretation as has the U.S. Constitution, but a number of significant changes have occurred through such means. Most important, the rise of the legislature as a coequal of the executive in policy power has taken place without significant change in the written constitution. Many of the most important extensions of civil rights and liberties have occurred either through federal rulings that supersede those of the state or through rulings of the court of appeals. Historically, judicial and legislative action has been a less significant source of constitutional change at the state than the national level, but the courts have shown a growing inclination to reinterpret the basic text.

It is also true, in New York as in almost all constitutional democracies, that the living constitution is effectively amended almost every day by the acts of elected officials, bureaucrats, and even ordinary citizens. What Gross and Schneier have called "social vetoes" take place every day when citizens exceed the speed limit, discriminate in a hiring situation, or cheat on their taxes.[58] More significantly, public officials frequently defy the constitution or interpret it in light of their own policy preferences. Some of the most significant characteristics of state politics and government, moreover, are extraconstitutional. The rules of the legislature that vest extraordinary powers in the hands of the majority party leaders, for example, are based on only the vaguest of constitutional provisions.

Constitutional Conventions

The constitutional requirement that the question of whether to call a constitutional convention be put to the voters every thirty-two years adds an interesting dimension to the process of constitutional revision in New York State. When the issue came up in the 1997 elections, it was rejected by a margin of better than 3 to 2. Although it was favored by most newspapers, former governor Cuomo, and a number of other dignitaries, incumbent politicians were sharply divided, and most of the state's important labor unions came out against it. Interestingly, almost no one argued that the constitution was in no need of change. Opponents of a convention argued instead that it would be a costly waste of time, potentially dangerous, poorly representative of majority opinion, and unlikely to solve the problems of gridlock that seemed to concern the voters most.

There is no doubt that such conventions can be expensive. With each of its 198 delegates receiving the same salary as a member of the legislature, a per diem expense account of $89, travel allowances, and a staff allocation of $15,000 for each delegate, the minimum cost of a convention would run about $15 million. Assuming, however, that the convention were to operate for more than twenty-four weeks, hold public hearings around the state, and print records of its work, some estimates of a convention's real costs ran as high as $60 million. Although election night polls showed that these cost considerations troubled many voters, other arguments were equally telling. Liberals tended to oppose a convention because the method of election—founded in the Republican gerrymandered districts of the state senate—tended to favor conservatives. Some "good government" groups were opposed because the ballot access laws, deciding who could run as delegates, were highly restrictive; also, the convention process gave less time for reflection and discussion than the regular process of amendment, with its requirement that a proposal pass two sessions of the legislature before going to the voters. And the prospect that all would be in vain, that the 1999 convention, like its 1967 predecessor, would have its ultimate work rejected by the voters, probably was a factor as well.

Most scholars agree that the state's constitution is unnecessarily detailed and out of date in a number of not too significant respects. The essays collected by the

Temporary State Commission on Constitutional Revision offer numerous concrete, often exciting possibilities for change. With the exception of the judiciary, however, few of these proposed reforms relate to issues of basic structure. There are few advocates of a weakened legislature, fewer still of a weakened governor; while some would strengthen home rule and devolve more power to local governments, others favor consolidation and centralization. Few, if any, suggest that late budgets and other problems of gridlock that the public finds troublesome can be solved by structural as opposed to political change. Most agree, in the final analysis, that the "important ends of government can be declared and effectuated by statute."[59]

Conclusion

To the extent that New York differs from, say, New Jersey or Nevada, the major differences are not found in their formal constitutions. It makes a difference whether a state's constitution creates few or many electoral rivals to the governor and whether it gives the office a line-item veto. It matters how much home rule is written into the constitution and whether there is a unified court system. Bills of rights are not just rhetoric. In most important respects, however, a state's living constitution may or may not coincide with the text it calls its constitution. If the social welfare provision of the New York constitution is the strongest in the nation, it does not mean that "the aid, care, and support of the needy" actually "*shall* be provided by the state" (author's emphasis) as it says in article 17. What it means is that advocates for the poor have a somewhat stronger base for arguing their case than would their counterparts in states without such a constitutional provision. The constitution, like the federal system described in Chapter 2, the party system discussed in Chapter 3, and the pressure system described in Chapter 4, is part of the context within which the policy-making process takes place.

6

Struggles for Power, Position, and Access

In the jargon of Albany, the first step on the road to political influence is to become a "player." This circle of players shifts over time and often from one issue to another. As noted in Chapter 4, there are few generally effective lobbyists, and even the most powerful groups tend to be issue-specific. With the exceptions of the governor and the majority party leaders in the senate and assembly, this is true of the executive and legislative branches as well. Major shifts in power tend to have long gestation periods. The most effective lobbyists, legislators, bureaucrats, and even judges build their reputations brick by brick. Particularly in the legislature, there is a continuous weighing of character: whose word can be trusted, who has access to whom, who knows what. Former speaker Stanley Fink argued that "people gain power, particularly in the legislature, by the accumulation of knowledge—it is, in my opinion, the single surest way that one can gain influence and power."[1] The knowledge Fink was talking about was not just knowing the substance of an issue, but knowing how things work and whom you can rely upon for what.

It would surprise most individuals who are not politicians to learn how much these evaluations boil down to questions of trust. Politicians usually do not lie to each other. Those who do almost certainly are going to pay for it. As much as they might fudge their positions in public, exaggerate their records during campaigns, and avoid direct answers to difficult questions, the only real leverage most of them have with each other is their credibility.

In the long run, credibility, knowledge, and skill are the resources that tend to separate the players from the herd. But there are short-term events—elections and their financing, indictments, and scandals, most notably—that can strike like lightning to destroy the strongest leaders overnight. Eliot Spitzer, after eight notable years as attorney general, prosecuting cases involving corporate white-collar crime, securities fraud, and environmental protection, won the governorship in 2006 by the largest margin in recent history only to be felled by a sex scandal just fifteen months into his term. Mel Miller, one of the shrewdest speakers in the modern assembly, was forced to resign after just four years when a 1994 lawsuit—later dismissed—tarnished his image.

Many players in the system and many aspects of the system, at the same time, endure. Apart from a twelve-year period from 1995 through 2006, when Republican George Pataki occupied the governorship, New York has had Democratic governors since 1975, and the Democrats have controlled the assembly for the same period. Sheldon Silver, who assumed the position of speaker after Saul Weprin's death in 1994, has been in power longer than any other speaker in assembly history. And save for a one-year period in 1965, and until 2009, the senate was primarily Republican since the 1920s. Joseph Bruno served as the senate majority leader from 1995 to 2008, being reelected to the position five times. One source indicates that majority party leadership in the New York legislature has been more stable than that of any other state save Tennessee.[2]

Legislative Party Leadership

There are few more revealing events in the legislature than those revolving around changes in party leadership. Because the powers of legislative party leaders are so extensive, those legislators who are out of favor with their parties are generally without influence. These legislators retain the trappings of the office and whatever impact on public opinion they can exert through press releases and outside activities. Their votes on issues might sometimes be sought, but a legislator who is out of favor with the leadership is not a player.

Formally, the speaker of the assembly and the senate majority leader are elected by the full membership of each house, though the majority party conference usually controls the vote. When a newly elected legislature takes office every other January, choosing the new leaders is the first order of business, even if it is only a ritualistic reaffirmation of the existing power structure. Shortly after the November election returns become official, the respective parties in each house caucus in Albany to choose their leadership candidates. On the first Tuesday after the first Monday in January, the newly elected legislature convenes and the members respond to the roll call by stating the name of the person they support.

Party Leadership Fights

In the assembly, the elected speaker is escorted to the podium by the most senior member of the majority party and presented with the gavel symbolizing the formal position of presiding officer. The person with the second largest number of votes is declared the minority leader. The process is less formal in the senate, where the lieutenant governor officially presides. Rules to govern each house are adopted, usually in a routine carryover from previous sessions. The process of maneuvering that precedes these votes, though barely visible to the public, is one of the most fascinating in politics. Leadership is a position that is won essentially by accumulating sufficient individual commitments from party colleagues to win a majority vote in the caucus—in recent years, fifty to fifty-five Democrats in the assembly, seventeen to twenty Republicans (or Democrats) in the senate.

The process is not necessarily confined to the party conferences. In 1964 Democrats won the majority of both houses for the first time in almost a century. A revolt over the choice of the senate majority leader spread to the assembly and soon became a fight between the Democratic county chairs in New York City and Mayor Robert Wagner. This fight tied up the legislature for months. With no elected leaders and no committees appointed, no legislative business could be conducted. The impasse finally was broken when Republican governor Nelson Rockefeller cut a deal in which the Republican minorities voted for Democrats Anthony Travia for speaker and Joseph Zaretzki for majority leader. The specter of this fight still haunts state legislators, putting strong pressure on the party caucus to reach some kind of consensus lest they lose control of the process entirely. It has become an unwritten rule that no matter how severe the party's internal divisions, its members will agree to support the winning conference candidate in the full house, but it is seldom an easy process, and the wounds from a prolonged battle can be slow to heal. The deal forged by senate Democrats in 2008 was as much the beginning of a continuing struggle for control as it was a resolution of the conflict: together with the fight in 1965 it may well stand as a model of how not to choose a leader.

For individual members, there is nothing more terrifying or exhilarating than a leadership fight. Being on the winning side can turn an also-ran into a player overnight, and vice versa. With county leaders no longer able to deliver blocs of votes, personal friendships, regional and ideological differences, and chances for individual advancement play stronger roles. Groups such as the Black and Hispanic Caucus—and even some county delegations—may enhance their leverage by negotiating as blocs, but in the final analysis each lawmaker is both alone and nervous about how the outcome might change the direction of his or her career. Although assembly Republicans in 2002 elected Charles Nesbitt minority leader by secret ballot, there was no secret which members were behind the campaign of his opponent John Flanagan. Flanagan, who lost the leadership position by just one vote, also lost his position as ranking member of the ways and means committee and soon retired from the legislature. His campaign managers soon retired as well. In most leadership races, the voting is not in secret, and as much as members may try to avoid firm commitments, there comes a point in the meeting when they—knowing it may affect their future in the legislature—must stand up and declare a choice.

The Rules of the Game

The politics of leadership succession is divided into two scenarios: one in which there is sufficient lead time for bloc-by-bloc coalition-building, and a second, more frenzied scenario where the actual or impending death or resignation of the party leader dramatically compresses time and deliberation into a flurry of hurried conversations among party members. In the latter case, the field of potential candidates narrows rapidly, and perceptions of power and of having the necessary votes become more important. This scenario tends to favor the inner circles of the departing leaders: the day that senate majority leader Joseph Bruno announced his retirement in 2008, for example, one senior member began calling his friends to ask for support, but it became almost immediately apparent that deputy majority leader Dean Skelos was next in line. There was no contest. Similarly, when Thomas Reynolds retired as assembly minority leader to run for Congress in 1998, there were two possible candidates to succeed him: George Winner, after four terms as deputy leader, was expected to move up, but he quickly stepped aside when Governor Pataki made it clear that he preferred John Faso, the ranking member of ways and means. The contest was over before it began.

Generally speaking, only senior members are viable candidates. Seniority alone is not decisive, but a successful candidate must have a record of credibility and competence that others have learned to trust. The assembly majority leader, deputy leader in the senate, and the chairs of the assembly ways and means and senate finance committees are almost always in the mix if only because they can influence legislative outcomes and, in some cases, make campaign funds available to their colleagues. Since 1975, there have been twenty leadership changes in the two houses. In half of these cases, the incumbent leader has been replaced either by his top deputy in the party leadership or by the chair or ranking minority member of ways and means or finance. More subtly, candidates are invariably members who have been looking (discreetly, of course) at the job for years and quietly building up collegial relationships and a core of close supporters. As one Wisconsin speaker summarizes the rules:

> The decision to support one colleague instead of another for a leadership post can be based on many seemingly logical reasons. These include ideology, geography, gender, race, past favors (such as helping raise money), prospects of future favors (such as committee assignments), and even whether the person is good on TV. But these reasons are not important considerations when compared with friendship. . . . That's the base.[3]

The struggle for leadership begins with the tightest of friends and hopefully spreads like ripples on a pond—or maybe not. When Stanley Steingut was defeated in a Brooklyn Democratic primary in 1978, majority leader Stanley Fink was widely regarded as his likely successor, though he refused to campaign before the election was over. One less cautious senior member rallied his friends, but quickly abandoned his campaign when one of the first people he called not only refused to support him, but also called Fink to tell him what was going on. In 1986, conversely, Fink's announcement that he would not run for reelection set off a wide-open fight for the leadership. There was an upstate candidate (the majority leader, Dan Walsh), a Brooklyn candidate (Mel Miller), two from Queens, one from Manhattan, and ways and means chair Jerry Kremer of Long Island. By securing a firm base in his home borough of Brooklyn, the largest county in the state, plus a scattering of upstate and Long Island friends, Mel Miller was able to scare some of the weaker candidates into dropping out and supporting him. By the time Kremer, who as chair of the ways and means committee had built a base rivaling Miller's, began to build similar coalitions, it was too late.

Speaker-elect Miller made sure that no leadership positions or committee chairmanships were announced until after the official vote in January. In a bow to upstate and the party's more conservative wing, he retained Dan Walsh as majority leader, but Kremer was replaced as chair of ways and means and left the legislature soon after, as did Walsh. Within a short period of time an entirely new leadership team was in place, a transition duly noted in a body where even minor shifts of power are carefully weighed. Not one of the five once-powerful assembly members who ran against Miller was still in the legislature three years after nearly reaching the top.

Challenging Incumbents

In the 1990s the rules of the game seemed to change with a series of quick successions. When Mel Miller was indicted in 1991 on charges that were sufficiently ambiguous that many people dismissed them as the political ploy of an ambitious Republican prosecutor, the party caucus refused to take formal action against him, and majority leader Jim Tallon decided neither to campaign for speaker nor to allow any of his friends to work on his behalf, a pattern common in situations involving a sitting speaker. As long as members believe the leader is likely to win, they do not want to support anyone else and risk ending up on the losing side. In most states it is unusual for presiding officers or legislative party leaders to be challenged, and it is rare for them to be defeated. On occasion a leader will jump before being pushed, choosing to retire in the face of growing dissatisfaction and the emergence of one or more potential challengers.[4]

Ways and means chair Saul Weprin—older than Tallon and with less to risk—began quietly to line up support for a campaign. When Miller was actually convicted (though he was later found innocent) and resigned his seat, Tallon went to work, but a series of frantic phone calls to the membership made it apparent that Weprin's campaign had paid off. Majority leader Tallon was not replaced, but he resigned his seat months after Weprin was elected. Two early Weprin supporters were appointed as part of a new leadership team. Sheldon Silver became the chair of ways and means and Michael Bragman (Syracuse) majority leader. There were no reprisals against Tallon supporters, but some did not fare well in a reapportionment plan passed later in the year.

When Weprin died in office in 1994, it was clear that Sheldon Silver was the natural choice for speaker if only because he had the almost solid backing of New York City Democrats. Majority leader Bragman remained as Silver's majority leader, a

Box 6.1
Fending Off an Attack on the Speaker
The Tools of Party Discipline

As state Democrats convened in Albany in May 2000 to nominate Hillary Rodham Clinton as their candidate for the U.S. Senate, rumors began circulating about a challenge to the leadership of assembly speaker Sheldon Silver. By the next morning, Thursday, May 18, it seemed clear that the majority leader, Michael Bragman of Syracuse, not only intended to challenge the speaker but that he had the fifty or more votes he needed to win in the Democratic conference when it met the following Monday. By the time of the actual vote (on a procedural motion to bring the leadership issue to the floor), however, only eighteen Democrats actually stood by Bragman.

What happened between Thursday and Monday is not a matter of public record; but the decline in Bragman's support from the fifty-three pledges he thought he had on Thursday to the eighteen who actually stood with him on Monday neatly illustrates the powers that are inherent in the office of the speaker and explains why sitting party leaders are so seldom challenged. In a speech to his colleagues following his defeat, Bragman charged the speaker with using the following tactics to convince people they should support him and not Bragman:

- stripping committee chairs of their posts and telling others "they have 5 minutes to express their support to the speaker or they would lose those chairs"
- saying to the child of a member who answered the phone, "Tell your father that he has 15 minutes to call the speaker and change his position or he will lose everything he has ever cared about in this assembly"
- telling members that if they did not support the speaker "their districts would be reapportioned and they wouldn't be able to win an election again"
- threatening those whose districts had strong party organizations that "their petitions wouldn't be circulated and primaries would be run against them"
- threatening not to provide, or offering to provide, campaign contributions from the Democratic Assembly Campaign Committee
- encouraging "specially connected lobbyists" and union leaders to lobby "the members and tell them who they ought to vote for and what the consequences would be if they didn't"[1]

Because two Bragman supporters lost their committee chairmanships, we know that Silver used at least some of these tactics, and it seems likely that he used them all. The fact is that most party leaders, facing similar challenges, would have used them too. The day after the vote, Bragman was evicted from his large ninth-floor office and moved to one normally allocated to minority party freshmen; his staff was cut from the third largest in the assembly to the minimum. Of his declared supporters, only two remain in the legislature, and one of them—despite high seniority and a long record of hard work—has no leadership positions to this day.

1. New York State Assembly, *Record of Proceedings*, May 22, 2000, pp. 26–28.

choice viewed by many observers as an acknowledgment of upstate interests rather than of close ties between the two. Indeed, as early as 1998 rumors circulated that Bragman was plotting a coup. Despite the persistence of such rumors during the next two years, most Albany observers were surprised in May 2000 when Bragman actually attempted to unseat the incumbent speaker (see Box 6.1).

Bragman's unsuccessful challenge to Silver illustrates why incumbents rarely are challenged. Unless the opponent has the votes locked up or has decided to gamble that the speaker will resign (as Weprin did with Miller), there can be no public campaign. Coups against the leadership only can begin with very discreet conversations with close friends and political allies, but the challenger may soon reach a member whose loyalty to (or fear of) the incumbent will serve to expose the incipient candidacy. Unless this point is reached after the challenger has enough commitments to win, both challenger and supporters are susceptible to sanctions. Thus, when Bragman's challenger was flushed into the open and two of his supporters stripped of their committee chairmanships, most of his other commitments disappeared. It is unlikely that Bragman—a shrewd insider—would have set himself up for failure without having private commitments from a majority of the members of the caucus: Silver was not that popular a speaker, but in the end Bragman had only twenty announced supporters and eighteen actual votes.

In contrast with the assembly, the senate has seen two successful challenges to incumbent leaders. One April day in 1988, Governor Cuomo, senate majority leader Warren Anderson, and speaker Stanley Fink emerged from the governor's second-floor office to announce that they had reached a budget agreement. Normally, when the "three-men-in-a-room" reach their agreement, it remains only for the staff to iron out the details before an almost automatic vote of approval. But the 1988 budget was lean, and the increases in school aid it proposed did not keep up with inflation in affluent suburban districts. A few hours after the leaders' press conference, Ralph Marino—a state senator from Long Island and normally a close ally of Anderson's—informed the majority leader that there were not enough votes to pass the budget. Unless school aid was substantially increased, Marino warned, every Republican senator from Long Island would vote no. Faced with a solid block of opposition in his own party conference, Anderson was forced to go back to the speaker and governor with the embarrassing admission that he could not control his own party. A few months later, Anderson announced his retirement from politics and Marino—virtually without opposition—took his place as majority leader. Until his dying day, Anderson insisted that the budget debacle had nothing to do with his retirement. Marino, likewise, insisted that his only motive in leading the Long Island rebellion was to get more money for schools, but insiders remain skeptical. To challenge and embarrass the majority leader is risky business, though doing it on an issue directly linked to the needs of a member's constituency is to at least present a plausible rationale. Marino could test his strength by implying that Anderson was losing touch with rank-and-file members and secure his base for a campaign without directly challenging the majority leader.

Whether the 1988 fight over school funding was the opening gun of a campaign for party control, the differences between Anderson and Marino were not basically ideological. In their study of state legislative leaders, Jewell and Whicker suggest that "a tension is likely to develop between the members and those individuals who serve long tenure in leadership. . . . One reason that some Speakers and presidents retire or run for another office is that they are sensitive to the problem of *leadership ladder gridlock*."[5] Such gridlock, where there are few opportunities for advancement, is most likely to occur in a legislature, like New York's, dominated by career politicians. It is worth noting that Ralph Marino, despite twenty years in the senate, was not even second in line for the chairmanship of the key finance committee. When Marino became majority leader, he moved the aging chair of the committee to a meaningless but high-paying position in the party leadership and installed a more junior member. Other chairmanships were shifted in ways significant enough to suggest a change in generations rather than ideology or political orientation. Whether Marino had deposed a sitting party leader or merely replaced one who was planning to retire anyway, the 1988–1989 transition was one that had leadership gridlock written all over it. In 1995, Marino himself fell victim to a similar coup, but a great deal more than gridlock was involved.

Shortly after George Pataki's upset of Mario Cuomo in the 1994 election, the governor-elect, his political patron—U.S. senator Alfonse D'Amato—and the chair of the Republican state committee, William Powers, decided that Marino could and should be taken down. For Pataki, it was perhaps a question of revenge: Marino had not only opposed Pataki in his first run against an incumbent senator in 1990, but had been adamant in attempts to find a more moderate challenger to Mario Cuomo in 1994. Powers's and D'Amato's motives were murkier, including ideology, ambition, and a strong sense of what they felt was right for the Republican party. But the bottom line, as Marino put it, was that it was "three against one." Whether the governor made any direct contacts with former senate colleagues we may never know, but D'Amato and Powers were clearly manning the phones and there was little doubt which side Pataki was on. Joseph Bruno's ascension to the leadership was not simply a question of internal politics. For the first time since Nelson Rockefeller "owned" one house of the legislature and "had a long-term lease" on the other, a governor was overtly involved in a leadership contest. In 2008, a split in the new Democratic majority once again brought the governor's office into a legislative leadership contest. Although Governor Paterson was present at the 2008 meeting in which the so-called gang of three agreed to give the senate party leadership to Malcolm Smith, it was not the kind of factional fight that gave the governor leverage (see Box 6.2).

Although minority party leaders have fewer goodies to distribute, they too are seldom openly challenged. Numerous leadership changes among assembly Republicans have come about largely because party leaders have tended to use their public positions as springboards to other office—for example, a failed bid for comptroller in the case of John Faso, a successful run for Congress in the case

Box 6.2
Democratic Leadership and the Senate's "Gang of Three"

Within hours of learning that the Democrats had won enough seats in the 2008 elections to control the new senate, minority leader Malcolm Smith scheduled a party conference to choose the party's candidate for majority leader. His hasty move to cut off an attempt by a potential rival to mount a campaign was undercut when four senators from New York City refused to attend. Smith was able to make peace with one of the dissidents, but three—Pedro Espada and Ruben Diaz of the Bronx and Carl Kruger of Brooklyn—threatened to vote with the Republicans.

At a meeting in early December—with Governor Paterson, two borough political leaders, and (rather oddly) the maverick millionaire Tom Golisano in attendance—Smith negotiated a deal: splitting the usually joined positions of majority leader and president pro tempore, he took the latter title for himself, making Espada majority leader and Kruger chair of the finance committee. Diaz apparently was promised that the issue of gay marriage would not be brought to the floor. The deal was lacquered over with a gloss of "reforms," one real—allowing committee chairs to bring bills directly to the floor—and one rather silly, arranging senate seats on the floor alphabetically instead of by choice and leader allocation.

A week later, a long, reportedly animated party conference ratified the agreement, but apparently forced Smith to modify its terms, thus causing the gang of three to again back off. The dance continued into the 2009 session. As in 1965, when a split in the Democratic Party made the conference unable to choose a majority leader, Smith emerged from the fight with his leadership sharply diminished. Unlike the deal brokered by Nelson Rockefeller in 1965, the winner in 2008 was not the governor, who—in negotiating his 2009 budget—could never be sure that the senate leader du jour was really in command of his troops: the process came to involve "three men in a room plus the three outside" (and maybe a few others to boot).

Leadership fights *always* involve power-sharing deals—sometimes explicit, as when a candidate offers a particular committee chairmanship in exchange for support, but usually implicit, as in the expectation that a speaker from the city will choose someone from upstate as majority leader. What was unusual about the contest in 2008 and 2009 was the way in which these deals were played out in public, exposing the complicated web of issues, personal ambitions, regional splits, and ethnic rivalries that color every leadership contest but are seldom so visible.

of Tom Reynolds. Revolts in the minority ranks have most commonly come in the wake of disappointing elections when the case can be made that the incumbent leader's style (or lack of it) was in some way responsible for the party's electoral misfortunes. Since Clarence Rappleyea retired in 1995, after twelve years as minority leader, the Republicans have had changes in their leadership five times, twice because their leaders have gone on to more interesting jobs, and once, in 2009, when Jim Tedisco's congressional campaign left him vulnerable to the charge that he was neglecting his duties as minority leader. Senate Democrats, after twenty years under Manfred Ohrenstein, have had only three changes. The only case of a successful challenge to an incumbent was when David Paterson, then deputy to senate minority leader Martin Conner, successfully challenged Conner in 2002.

Consolidating Leadership Control

Running for a leadership office is part of the process of learning to be an effective leader. As Loftus puts it, "it is the campaign for the job that teaches a leader how to ask and how to distinguish a yes from a no. It is the campaign that teaches the leader how to get a vote."[6] Despite the awesome powers of the office, all party leaders know that their continuing ability to exercise these powers derives from their continuing ability to maintain the confidence of a conference majority. In the words of one former speaker:

> Leadership is a two-way street. I think a leader in the legislature these days in New York would be foolish to underestimate the collective power of individual members. . . . People want to have an opportunity to be heard and take part in the process. . . . I used to hold Democratic Conferences where all members were given an opportunity to be heard and no one was cut off. . . . After . . . giving everybody the opportunity to be heard, I generally was well aware of the parameters of what I could or could not negotiate on behalf of this group of men and women.[7]

Generally, the most successful leaders are those who communicate most effectively with their fellow party members, though different leaders use different channels. Some meet frequently with the entire conference; others make regular use of party steering committees appointed with an eye toward the representation of all significant factions in the party. Some meet regularly with committee chairs (or the ranking minority members of key committees), and others rely primarily upon an informal network of personal allies. Most leaders work at cultivating face-to-face connections through devices such as "the development of club-like atmosphere, the exchange of amenities, the building of personal relationships based on shared experiences, and assistance to lawmakers in their nonpolitical problems."[8]

Most rank-and-file members appreciate and rely upon the ability of party leaders to facilitate communications. As Rosenthal puts it, "Only a legislative leader—such as the Speaker or the president—could get four or five important people to a meeting on short notice. . . . Getting people to show up at a meeting may not appear impressive, but it attests to a leader's power."[9] Sanctions also are available, from refusing to move a member's bill to taking away committee chairmanships or other perks. Because the party leaders' ultimate powers derive from their ability to command majorities within their conferences, carrots are more frequently employed than sticks and persuasive efforts more than either. In actual practice—as noted in Box 6.2—the distinction between rewards and sanctions is not as clear as it might seem.

Most party leaders, while they cannot give everything to everybody, measure their own effectiveness in terms of their ability to deliver political payoffs: "The most important techniques are . . . of a political character, such as assistance to members in legislative matters (such as passing local and private bills), giving members meaningful debate assignments, granting them extra lulus on staff allotments, interceding with the executive branch on behalf of members or their constituents, and so on."[10] As one Vermont speaker wrote of his willingness to cater to party colleagues, "My criteria to judge how far I would go to help a member were simple and straightforward. As long as it wasn't against the law, didn't require that I go to confession, or wouldn't break up my marriage, I did it."[11]

On most issues, party leadership involves neither sanctions nor rewards. Essentially it flows up from the basic coherence of the party conference. Party cohesion is neither a function nor even a symptom of party discipline. No matter how you phrase the question, members of the New York state legislature seldom can cite instances in which they have felt pressured by party leaders to vote one way or another. The rank-and-file often complain about how issues are framed and presented or about questions of timing and emphasis, but they almost never suggest that they have been forced to vote contrary to their political values. The emphasis in political science on party discipline may indeed have it backward: instead of asking how leaders hold members in line, the more appropriate question, which arises with greatest clarity in leadership selection contests, is "How can backbenchers discipline leaders and get them to promote policies and positions that are to the backbenchers' liking?"[12] This job, in general, begins in committee.

Committee Leadership

The work of the legislature is too complex for one person to control. Leaders have no choice but to delegate many of their powers. Some rely on their personal staff, some on other party leaders, and some—particularly in the smaller conferences of the senate and the assembly minority—on the entire conference. All give considerable influence within their spheres of expert knowledge to the members and chairs of the standing committees. It is important to note that the party leaders have nearly absolute control over all committee assignments. In the New York legislature, unlike the U.S. Congress and most other state legislatures, committee membership does not carry over from one session to the next. Every other January, members of the senate and assembly anxiously await the pronouncements from the ninth floor telling them who will serve on which committees and who will be honored with committee chairmanships. Party leaders do, of course, take such factors as seniority and previous service into account—some committee chairs, such as Joseph Lentol on assembly codes and Kenneth LaValle on higher education in the senate, held their positions for fifteen years or more. But the party leaders' virtually unfettered ability to manipulate the committee lists remains a hallmark of leadership power in both houses of the legislature.

Interactions between party leaders and committee leaders reflect a dynamic, sometimes intensely personal process of trust-building and shared perceptions. In return for the powers entrusted to them, the chairs of important committees are expected to be unusually loyal to the party leader.

Events sometimes upset established patterns of committee work, such as when a previously obscure issue gets on the agenda as the result of a gubernatorial initiative or a change in federal policy. Generally, however, there is defined ordering of committees in which some are more important than others. Overshadowing all others are the assembly committee on ways and means and its senate counterpart, the committee on finance. Unlike Congress, which separates the legislative process of raising money from that of appropriating it, many state legislatures house all money issues in a single pair of committees. Thus any bill that spends or raises money must go through ways and means in the assembly and finance in the senate. Quite frequently it is "dual referenced"; that is, sent both to the committee with substantive jurisdiction (such as higher education) and the money committee. Under a rule adopted in 1975, the chair of the assembly ways and means committee can require the dual reference of any bill determined to have fiscal implications. The chair of senate finance has the same power. Given the jurisdictional reach of their committees, the chairs and ranking minority members of ways and means and finance are clearly among the most powerful legislative leaders in Albany. They are assumed to be next in line for advancement and—with the occasional exception of majority leaders in the assembly—the second most powerful members of their respective parties.

The codes committee is the second most important committee in both houses, again because of dual referencing. Any legislation that imposes a criminal penalty—whether a drug bill reported out of the alcoholism and substance abuse committee that imposes longer sentences than those in existing law, or a bill from the housing committee that imposes fines on abusive landlords—must be dual referenced to codes. But the codes committee also must deal with issues, like the death penalty, that tap emotions in the electorate that many members would rather avoid. A large part of the committee's work deals with very tedious issues of legal reasoning. Thus some members, though fully understanding its powers, would just as soon not be appointed to codes. As we move down the list of preferred committees, these kinds of conflicts become increasingly important. Quite obviously a committee such as agriculture, which might be enormously appealing to someone from Chautauqua County, would not be ranked nearly so high by someone from Brooklyn. The judiciary committee—which deals with issues such as crime that are visible and important—has a particular appeal for lawyers. The senate judiciary committee, with the added power of screening judicial appointments, is a particularly attractive assignment. Members of both houses are drawn to the education committees because they deal with issues of universal concern. The health committees are increasingly attractive for the same reasons.

Party leaders try to accommodate member preferences, especially when they are good for the members' electoral fortunes. They know that in the long run maintaining and building their party's electoral base is what distinguishes being in the majority from being in the minority. "Top leaders," Rosenthal notes, "prefer to have committee chairs upon whom they can rely"; and they prefer to give their committee chairs members with whom they can work effectively. "But leaders are not always free to appoint trusted allies. They have to consider some of the factors that govern the appointment of committee members including seniority, geography, other committee service, and qualifications."[13] In New York, key committees must balance upstate and New York City for Democrats, rural areas and the suburbs for Republicans. Democrats must consider ethnic balance and gender as well, and for both parties ideology is a factor. The preferences of interest groups, sometimes given weight—particularly if they are major campaign contributors—are not likely to be controlling because party leaders do not like involving outsiders in what they consider inside business. One chair of the assembly labor committee was stripped of his position, it was widely believed, because he had become too close to the unions that were the committee's major clients.

Power and the Perquisites of Office

The senate and assembly formally rank leadership positions by an ascending scale of financial allowances for serving as "officers." Augmenting their regular salaries, committee chairs and party leaders receive supplements ranging from a low of $9,000 for the ranking minority members of committees such as tourism, consumer affairs, and mental health, to $34,000 for the chairs of senate finance and assembly ways and means, to $41,500 for the speaker and senate majority leader.[14] In Table 6.1 we list the top majority party members in 2008, their pay, and their seniority ranks within both the assembly and senate. We also indicate which of the more senior members were appointed to the committee on rules, generally considered to be composed of those senior members closest to the leadership. While there is no seniority rule in Albany, party leaders generally give considerable weight to length of service in doling out offices carrying special allowances. In the senate in 2008, there were enough offices providing supplemental pay to give lulus to every member. The Republican majority allocated these extra funds pretty much according to seniority, but actual positions of power were quite different. Indeed, the second and third most senior members had pay titles that carried no real influence, and neither vice president Frank Padavan nor assistant majority leader for house operations Caesar Trunzo had a committee chairmanship. Trunzo's age (he was eighty-two in 2008) and a certain lack of vigor (the leading newspaper in his district once called him a "perennial nonentity"[15]) explain his case. Not coincidentally, Trunzo lost his seat to a Democrat in 2008. Padavan, one of the last holdouts in Joe Bruno's challenge to Ralph Marino, fell from fifth to fifteenth in pay rank immediately after Bruno won. But Republicans from New York City generally have trouble entering the inner circles of power in the Republican Party because the nature of their districts forces them beyond the party mainstream. Party leaders generally are understanding of their members' electoral needs, but there are limits as to how much latitude they will allow. When one Republican senator voted with the Democrats against a casino gambling bill, the majority leader was quite candid in explaining why he was disciplined: "Members," Bruno told the *New York Times*, "know that when they take a position that isn't reflective of the leadership, that there is a downside." Such a defector "knows it might make his life less comfortable."[16]

In the assembly, seniority is far less controlling than it is in the senate. Conservative Democrats, such as Robin Schimminger, Dov Hikind, and Anthony Seminiero, are slightly lower paid than others of comparable experience, though all three moved up after they supported Silver against Bragman's challenge. Indeed, it was only after the 2000 contest that Hikind received his first pay bonus. He remains the only member of either party who has no committee assignments. Seminiero is no less conservative, but has fared better because, in Albany parlance, he is more likely to "give you a vote"; that is, to go along with the leadership if his vote is needed. Many members develop considerable expertise and become comfortable with a particular chairmanship. With extensive knowledge of substance abuse and a growing interest in the issue, Brian Murtaugh, for example, would not have given up his chairmanship of the alcohol and substance abuse committee for a minor increment in salary and prestige. Only a major promotion to codes or ways and means could tempt most long-tenured chairs to give up special influence and connections in an established area.

Another symbol of party status is membership on the rules committees of each house. The rules committees, in theory, schedule the business of the legislature. By formal rule, indeed, no bill can go to the floor in the final weeks of the session without first getting special permission from the committee on rules. Until quite recently, however, the rules committees were whatever party leaders made of them. "The rules committee? I was the freaking rules committee," one former speaker told us, and he went on to describe an occasion when the speaker, needing time to do a little arm-twisting among his senior colleagues, recessed the assembly in order to convene a meeting of the rules committee. His unexpected move threw the members into consternation as they scurried about trying to find out who was on the committee and who was not. Until a package of reforms adopted in 2005 and strengthened in 2007 took effect, no bill, not even one approved by one of the other standing committees, could be scheduled for floor consideration after a certain date without going through rules. Since that date typically passed before the legislature was finished with the budget, the upshot was that the rules committee (i.e., the leader of the majority party) decided which bills would get to the floor and which would not.

The party steering committees, like the rules committees, are whatever the party leaders make of them. Never a factor in the smaller senate or the Republican Party in the assembly, the assembly Democratic steering committee once played a key

Table 6.1

Top Republican Senators and Democratic Assembly Members Ranked According to Seniority With Key Titles and Extra Pay Allowances, 2008

Member	Seniority	Highest title(s)	Extra pay allowance	Other committees
		Senate		
Johnson	1	Chair, finance committee	$34,500	Rules
Padavan	1	Vice president pro tempore	$34,500	Rules
Trunzo	1	Assistant leader for house operations	$22,000	Rules
Volker	2	Chair, codes/Assistant leader for conference operation	$25,000	Rules
LaValle	3	Chair, higher education/Chair of majority conference	$25,000	Rules
Farley	4	Chair, banks/Program development	$25,000	Rules
Skelos	5	Majority leader	$41,500	Rules
Seward	6	Chair, insurance/Whip	$20,500	Rules
Maltese	7	Chair, cities/Conference vice chair	$20,500	Rules
Libous	8	Chair, transportation/Senior assistant majority leader	$34,000	Rules
Hannon	8	Chair, health/Deputy whip	$20,500	Rules
Larkin	9	Chair, racing/Conference secretary	$20,500	Rules
Saland	9	Chair, education/Chair, steering committee	$20,500	Rules
		Assembly		
Gottfried	1	Chair, health	$15,000	Rules
Lentol	2	Chair, codes	$18,000	Rules
Farrell	3	Chair, ways and means	$34,000	Rules
Silver	4	Speaker	$41,500	Rules
Lafayette	4	Deputy speaker	$25,000	Rules
Schimminger	4	Chair, economic development	$18,000	
Jacobs	5	Assistant speaker	$25,000	Rules
Seminerio	5	Chair, majority program committee	$15,000	Rules
Weinstein	6	Chair, judiciary	$18,000	Rules
Greene	7	Speaker pro tempore	$25,000	Rules
Parment	8	Chair, committee on committees	$22,000	
Brodsky	8	Chair, corporations	$15,000	
Gantt	8	Chair, transportation	$15,000	Rules
Hikind	8	Deputy majority whip	$16,500	
Nolan	9	Chair, education	$18,000	Rules
Lopez	9	Chair, housing	$12,500	Rules
Brennan	9	Chair, cities	$15.000	
Clark	10	Assistant majority whip	$15,000	
Abate	10	Chair, government employees	$12,500	
Pheffer	11	Chair, consumer affairs	$12,500	
Sweeney	12	Chair, environmental conservation	$12,500	Rules
Hooper	12	Deputy majority leader	$19,500	Rules
Canestrari	13	Majority leader	$34,500	Rules

role as a sounding board for the leadership, though it essentially fell into disuse under speaker Silver. The strengthening reforms of the rules committee has made membership on the steering committee even less relevant to the point where its only function appears to be that of providing an extra pay billet for its powerless chairperson. Membership on the rules committee, by the same token, has become more desirable, and a lot can be inferred about the standing of members with speaker Silver by their membership on the rules. One of the Democrats on assembly rules (Earlene Hooper) had fewer than ten years of service when first appointed to the committee, while five of the most senior members are still not on it (see Table 6.1). Majority party membership on senate rules is based almost entirely on seniority, but it is interesting that when Dean Skelos jumped seniority to a position on rules in the 1990s, there were already rumors that he was the majority leader in waiting.

One recent test of how senior members stood with their respective party leaders came with the 2007 appointment of conference committees to work out interhouse differences on the budget. These appointments generally confirmed the patterns shown in Table 6.1. Thus the assembly members included speaker Silver, majority leader Ron Canestrari, ways and means chair Herman "Denny" Farrell, speaker pro tempore Aurelia Greene, and minority leader James Tedisco. In the senate, the members were majority leader Bruno, finance chair Owen Johnson, then deputy leader Dean Skelos, assistant majority leader Thomas Libous, and minority leader Malcolm Smith.

Party leaders also appoint the chairs of the relevant substantive committees to the appropriate conference committees, and both Bruno and Silver's appointments to the nine joint budget subcommittees reflected leadership preferences as well as seniority. Daniel Burling—an assembly member for just ten years—was picked ahead of members with more than twice his seniority. Because senate Republicans have more positions to fill than people to fill them, several members were asked to serve on two committees. Bruno, interestingly, gave some of these double assignments to one of the party's freshman senators (Joseph Griffo) and to two in their second and third terms respectively (Joseph Robach and Martin Golden). It is not unlikely that Bruno was looking toward the 2008 elections in giving junior members something to boast about.

Leadership Styles

Political leadership, as every text on the topic avers, is highly contextual. "Through their roles strategizing, negotiating, building consensus, and getting the votes," as Rosenthal argues in his study of legislative leadership, "leaders certainly appear to be at the head of the parade. But what leaders are doing, except on special occasions, is leading the parade on the route the members want to take."[17] An interesting aspect of elected leadership is how the leaders discern the wishes of their members, communicate with them, and maintain their trust. At the most fundamental level, party leaders must have sufficient support in their party conference to avoid becoming—like Ralph Marino—the target of an active opposition campaign. Particularly in the case of divided government, however, the ability of party leaders to sustain the support of their own party conferences must be balanced against the sometimes conflicting ability to negotiate effectively with other leaders, in particular the governor and the party leaders of the other house. One of the reasons for Marino's downfall, ironically, is that he was perceived by many of his fellow Republicans as being *too* good at working with the Democrats. The most effective leaders—and both Bruno and Silver have been reputed to be masters of the art—are able to use the professed preferences of their respective party majorities as negotiating tools in dealing with each other, while simultaneously using these negotiations as leverage within their own parties.

The Party Conference

Perhaps the most obvious place to look for the ways in which legislative leaders communicate with party colleagues is in the party conferences. All four conferences meet almost every day that the legislature is in session and frequently when it is not. In their basic outline, party conferences are "closed door sessions held off the floor on a regular basis for legislators only. In those sessions, members are free to make arguments about policy directions the party should take. The leadership is then generally free within those limits to negotiate with the other house and the governor over policy."[18]

How much freedom leaders take from conference instructions varies. Some conference meetings are agonizingly specific. During session, for example, the parties frequently recess, going into conference, often in the middle of debate on a bill. This happens when party leaders sense that there is unhappiness in the ranks. On rare occasions, should it become apparent that the unhappiness is widespread, a bill will be pulled from the floor either to be redrafted or to die. Sometimes, particularly at the beginning of a session, discussions in conference are wide-ranging and almost philosophical in tone, though different leaders have different styles. Former assembly minority leader Tom Reynolds's conference meetings, for example, were tightly scripted, with discussions dominated and directed by a small circle of his most trusted party allies. Sheldon Silver also is said to maintain tight control, using party conferences for disseminating information and setting the party line rather than as a mechanism for building consensus. In contrast, the very narrow leads Bruno, Skelos, and Smith have held in recent years in the senate have forced them to lead more cautiously and collegially.

The Inner Circles

Most modern party leaders have had as their closest advisers a fairly predictable set of relatively senior colleagues. Both former majority leader Joseph Bruno and speaker Sheldon Silver have concentrated power in their offices on the ninth floor of the legislative office building. Silver, in particular, relies heavily on his personal staff and on the party's program staff for important issues. As more than one member says, "Shelly plays his cards close to the vest," and while most Democrats agree that some degree of secretiveness is important, it also has caused considerable grumbling. Former majority leader Michael Bragman exploited these discontents in his nearly successful challenge to Silver in 2000. "The leadership style must change. Members must be informed and participate in the process," Bragman argued. "This must be a member-driven Conference. This must be a member-driven House. It cannot be a body where non-elected members of the Speaker's staff dictate the activities of lawmakers."[19] A number of key bills have been drafted not in committee, but by the leadership-dominated program staffs of the assembly. A major education bill in 1997 was drafted entirely by central staff and presented to the chair of the education committee only days before it was formally introduced. And the negotiations between the key interests involved in Medicaid reform were conducted entirely on the ninth floor. "Damn it," the chair of the health committee burst out, "if I'm supposed to be changing my stand on an issue, I'd like to know about it before the lobbyists."

While there is bound to be grumbling in the ranks when committee chairs feel they have been insufficiently consulted or when leaders bypass their conferences, party leaders must balance strategic calculations against such member concerns. Until 2006 Silver had been the lone Democrat among the big three in Albany; forced to deal with both a governor and state senate under Republican control, he had sound political reasons to be circumspect. In Jewell and Whicker's typology of leadership styles, he is clearly a "command" as opposed to a "consensus" or "coordinating" leader. He tends, according to the typology, "to suppress conflict . . . minimize participation by rank-and-file legislators, and . . . use party caucuses to disseminate information and to inform members of decisions already made. . . . [Command leaders] are likely to apply more pressure on members to support positions taken by the caucus. Command leaders limit access to key information."[20]

There have been few "consensus" leaders in modern New York history. As long as there is divided government, few legislators would be willing to trade the benefits of unity for the uncertainties of too much internal democracy. Consensus leadership, which "emphasizes debate and discussion, even at times at the expense of action,"[21] is, we suspect, seldom found in states such as New York that approach the party government model. This does not mean that the rank-and-file cannot be consulted, especially if the discussion is kept within the boundaries of the party conference. Speaker Stanley Fink loved the give-and-take of lengthy conference sessions, often running them "almost like graduate seminars," as one member put it; he was like "the conductor of a symphony seeking harmony in the ranks," said another. Yet for all the discussion, Fink was still very much the conductor.

Jewell and Whicker label their third type "coordinating" leadership, in which leaders have a "moderate need to control others and they focus on the outputs of public policy."[22] According to former senator Seymour Lachman, Governor

Paterson's style of leadership when he was senate minority leader in 2002 is best characterized as coordinating. He worked closely with three or four of the top Democratic leaders to iron out positions on policy issues prior to conference meetings. Paterson was also willing to meet individually with senators, unlike his predecessor Martin Connor.[23] It is worth noting, at the same time, that Paterson was dealing with a Democratic conference of at most thirty members in contrast with the more than 100 in Silver's assembly.

Axiomatically, leadership involves strong elements of reciprocity. A leader's continuing power is a function of the trust accorded by party colleagues. The ability to inspire such trust, however, is in part based on the ability effectively to press party positions in the outside world. Party leaders, as they deal with their counterparts, have a strong interest in presenting a united front; their fellow party members share that interest. One important function of the party conference is to develop a sense of unity or, if that is unobtainable, at least the image of not being divided. Combine the strong norm of party government with the persistence of divided party control, and it seems unlikely that either party will substantially increase rank-and-file participation. The luxury of in-house democracy is likely to emerge only if and when one party is firmly enough in control of the assembly, the senate, and the governorship. It is worth noting that Mike Bragman, the only candidate for party leader in either house who made decentralization an issue in a campaign, lost in 2000.

Leadership Goals

A second dimension of Jewell and Whicker's leadership typology focuses on leadership goals, and here the differences—though more difficult to classify—are as pronounced in New York as they are elsewhere. Legislative leaders are classified in this schema as to whether they are motivated primarily by an orientation toward power, policy, or process.[24] Surprisingly, few legislative leaders in New York manifest the ambitions typifying power-oriented leaders. Perry Duryea, who served as speaker from 1969 through 1974, was the only sitting leader of either house who actually ran for governor since Al Smith in 1919, though John Faso ran in 2006, years after he had left the legislature. David Paterson was senate minority leader before his election in 2006 as lieutenant governor; but these are the exceptions. The contemporary New York legislature is perhaps too partisan to serve as a hothouse of political ambition: the very ability to compromise yet remain combative that makes a party leader effective may be just the combination that makes for weak statewide candidates. Power-oriented leaders, in this typology, also may be too willing to defer to outside interests, too pragmatic in their approach to governors and interest groups to serve the needs of their party conferences.

In the assembly, the evolution from Stanley Fink to Sheldon Silver has clearly moved, in Jewell and Whicker's terms, from policy to process. Fink had a clear programmatic agenda. With his base in the liberal wing of the party, he not only put liberals in positions of power but also fought his own party's governor, Mario Cuomo, when Cuomo began moving to the right. Although subsequent speakers similarly have been drawn from the party's city wing, their ideological leanings have been more difficult to discern. Silver, in particular, was unusually pragmatic in his approach to issues under Governor Pataki. Rather than directly confront a conservative governor, Silver countered Pataki's policy proposals with scaled-down alternatives. Expanding upon a survey research operation institutionalized by Mel Miller, Silver relied on frequent public opinion polls to guide both strategic and policy decisions, often using poll data to convince party liberals to go along with many of Pataki's proposed budget cuts. During Spitzer's brief administration, it is interesting to note how few of the legislature's conflicts with the governor involved substantive policy issues. Despite a looming budget gap of nearly record proportions, the big fights in Spitzer's first few months involved who would be appointed to replace the comptroller and whether the governor had abused his powers by ordering the state police to investigate majority leader Bruno's use of state helicopters.

If trends in the senate majority and in both houses' minority parties are less clear, the long-range developments are the same. In both houses, in both parties, frequent polling has become a hallmark of contemporary legislative leadership. The parties have confronted each other less along ideological lines than through emotional and symbolic issues such as "partial birth abortion," a dramatic surgical procedure that is almost never used, and whether illegal immigrants should be able to get driver's licenses.

Courting Party Leaders

Of the roughly 20,000 bills introduced every two years in the assembly and senate, few are expected to go beyond the introductory stage. When there is serious interest in changing public policy, the locus of power shifts to a much wider road, a road that leads invariably through the tollgates of the majority party leadership. To pass either house of the New York State legislature, a bill must be acceptable to the majority party leadership; to become public policy, the bill must have the leadership's active support. How do legislators go about marshaling such support?

Committees

Party leaders are not equally accessible to all members. Clearly, they listen almost exclusively to members of their own party. Even within their party conferences, however, some members gain considerably more access than others. Other things being equal, senior members have an advantage. Through long-standing acquaintance, they are known commodities in the eyes of party leaders, and—because of their seniority and perhaps friendship—more difficult to avoid. Most of them, moreover, have built up substantial backlogs of knowledge and connections with outside groups that make them important gatekeepers of information through the committee system.

Most members of the assembly sit on anywhere from two to six committees, senators on as many as nine. While seniority, party loyalty, and constituency concerns play a role in committee assignments, party leaders generally attempt to give most members what they want. Unlike the U.S. Congress, however, where stability of membership is a key factor in explaining the powers of standing committees, turnover in New York is substantial. With certain key exceptions—the ways and means committee in the assembly and the finance committee in the senate, most obviously—members, the more junior members in particular, tend to sit lightly in their committee seats. Rapid turnover is as much a function of individual preferences as it is of the leadership's need to put together the jigsaw puzzle of committee assignments. As in Congress, committees range from the highly desirable (e.g., ways and means or finance, health, education, and—for most members—codes and judiciary) to those whose value varies according to where the member is from (e.g., agriculture, housing, transportation) to those that are more duty than privilege (e.g., ethics, election law). Attendance at the meetings of minor committees is low, and turnover from one session to another is fairly high. Having the children and families committee on your résumé does not hurt, but the reality is that the committee seldom handles an important bill, and membership on it is not highly prized. What is prized, and quite highly, is the chairmanship of even a relatively unimportant committee. And it is not valued just for the extra money. What Rosenthal says of state legislative committees in general is true in New York as well:

> In many respects, the chairperson *is* the committee. This is because participation by other members is often sporadic; they may have their own committees to chair or are spread thin among many assignments. Increasingly, practically all returning majority-party members have a committee . . . to call their own; that is where they focus their energies while playing a more nominal role in the affairs of other units on which they sit. The more important the committee, the likelier it is that members will be involved.[25]

Almost every Republican senator and more than one-third of the Democrats in the assembly has either a chairmanship or regular assignment to a major committee; most other majority party members specialize in no more than two or three areas.

In 1981, Francis and Riddlesperger sent a questionnaire to the members of all ninety-nine state legislative bodies. One of their goals was to compare legislatures according to the degree that key decisions were made by party leaders, in the party conference, in committee, on the floor, and so on. Not surprisingly, committees ranked relatively low in importance in New York State, where, presumably, most members would have cited the central role of party leaders and the party conference. In the Francis and Riddlesperger ranking, New York's assembly committees were thirty-ninth in their "centrality" scores, senate committees still lower at forty-seventh.[26] Nancy Martorano's more recent study similarly found New York's committees on the low to middle end of committee system autonomy.[27] Committees in both houses, though more so in the assembly than the senate, do play a traffic cop role, exercising some control over the flow of bills through the party conferences to the floor. Committees in New York, unlike those in other state legislatures, have no significant subcommittees, hold relatively few public hearings, and do not mark up or amend bills. But if the committees as institutions are peripheral to the process of lawmaking, committee members—chairs in particular—are not.

Committee chairs have considerably more access to party leaders—on bills within their jurisdictions—than do other members; majority party committee members, working through their chairs, are next in line. There are, as we shall see in Chapter 7, formal mechanisms by which members can request serious committee consideration of their bills, but the reality is that committee membership is the best guarantee that a bill will be heard. Because this is true, lobbyists tend to focus their efforts on committee members (chairs especially) who deal with their issue areas. Regular interactions with these lobbyists tends to build familiarity with the issues and to plug individual members into networks of lobbyists, bureaucrats, local officials, academics, and constituents concerned with those issues. Committee chairs, moreover, are given staff allowances that permit the hiring of at least one professional staff assistant, sometimes more.

Typically, during the course of a legislative career, members gradually will narrow their focus to a limited set of issues. The members of the assembly belong, on an average, to five and a half committees each in their early years in the legislature, compared to fewer than four committees after they have served more than twenty years. Senior members are considerably more likely to stay with the same set of committees from one session to the next, particularly after they have secured an important chairmanship and/or a seat on the ways and means committee. Although the speaker controls the central research staff, long-serving chairs simply know more of the details of their issue domains than can any party leader. Committee staff members, moreover, though they must work with central staff, are appointed by and responsible to the committee chairs.

Committee chairs seldom find it difficult to control their committees. In the final analysis, party discipline can be invoked against a dissident bloc. The more difficult problem faced by committee chairs in New York is maintaining control over their own turf. The first dimension for evaluating the strength of standing committees, Rosenthal suggests, "involves the extent to which the jurisdiction of committees is respected and committees are referred bills. If many bills, or the most important ones, bypass committees, then the strength of the committee system is in doubt."[28] The problem for committee chairs in New York is not at the referral stage. As in Congress and in most state legislatures, most bills, including the most important ones, are properly referred to the appropriate committees.[29] The problem faced by committee chairs in New York is that of having bills taken over by the leadership either for a redrafting by central staff or by folding them into the budget. The latter problem surfaces increasingly as a source of rank-and-file frustration in both houses. A bill is introduced and referred, for example, to the committee on energy. Supported by the chair and a committee majority, it is reported out of committee, but before it ever gets to the floor, the speaker or majority leader uses it as a bargaining chip in negotiations with his or her counterpart and the governor. The relatively trivial problem with having a bill co-opted in this manner is that the legislators do not receive full credit. As a budget item, it no longer carries the member's name as sponsor. More seriously, it may not emerge in exactly the form that the member imagined it would have as a statute. Yet since you got essentially what you asked for, it is difficult to complain.

What political scientists call agenda control, the arrangement and structuring of the choices available to members when a bill comes to the floor, flows, in the regular order of things, through the committee and—again, in the regular order of things—is under the firm control of the committee chair. Ninety-six of every hundred bills introduced in Albany will die a silent death at the hands of one committee or another. And if there are competing approaches to the same problem, it is the committee that decides which one to report. If the majority party leaders have strong preferences, however, there is no regular order of things: agenda control—more than in almost any other U.S. legislature—is firmly in the hands of speaker in the assembly, the majority leader in the senate. While there are procedural means by which the leadership can overrule a committee—by folding the issue into the budget, for example—usually the process is straightforward and direct: the speaker or majority leader simply tells the committee chair what to do. And should the message not get through, there are ways in which committee chairs can be reminded. In 2008, for example, a committee chair in the assembly worked with some Republican members to report a bill that was not the version preferred by speaker Sheldon Silver. The speaker then appointed majority leader Ron Canestrari and two other Democratic Party leaders to the committee, which, at its next meeting, voted to reconsider the issue and substitute the bill favored by the speaker. The next day—the message having been sent—the committee's three new members resigned.

To Get Along, Go Along

"To get along, go along" was the slogan that Speaker of the House Sam Rayburn passed on to every new member of the U.S. House of Representatives under his leadership. It applies with particular force in New York, where a key test of the legislators' status as players lies in their willingness to "go along" with the party majority even when that vote might go against their conscience, constituency, or judgment. Most of the time, members have wiggle room. With a majority as large as the one that assembly Democrats have enjoyed in recent years, the speaker usually is prepared to allow a few of his party colleagues to vote with the minority. In fact, a member who might face serious reelection problems—such as a rural

Democrat on a gun control bill—sometimes will be encouraged to vote against the party position. Generally, senate Republicans have enjoyed smaller majorities and therefore less freedom of action, but often there are defections in the other direction that allow most members to vote as they like most of the time. Almost all legislators, however, have at some time or another been asked to cast a vote that they would rather not. The leadership usually will try to bring the issue to vote in a form that makes most party members comfortable, but the time will come when they will be asked to "fall on their sword."

There are times when the leadership wants a show of strength, and the blood flows freely. In 1995, Sheldon Silver had to push very hard to gain conference acceptance of the budget deal he reluctantly negotiated with Governor Pataki and the senate. Huge increases in tuition for the city and state universities, drastic cuts in health and welfare, and tax cuts targeted largely toward the wealthy were a bitter pill for many New York City Democrats to swallow. Discussions in conference were heated. A handful of liberals held out to the end and voted no on the floor, an act that won applause from liberal voters in New York City, but made few friends in Albany. Those liberals who unwillingly agreed, for the sake of the party, to support their speaker were particularly annoyed with what one described as "cheap grandstand votes."

Since the speaker got the votes he needed, there was no direct confrontation with the dissenting members, but these are the kinds of votes that are noted. A willingness to "go along" with the leadership is, in the long run, an important measure of how well a member will "get along" when it comes to committee assignments, help with campaign funds, reapportionment, staff allowances, and so on. It is also, in the long run, a key standard by which members are judged by their colleagues. A willingness to go along should not be confused with a member's voting record. Under normal conditions, a party leader "enforces discipline on as few of his members as possible, for there is no point in imposing further political costs once he is over the top. But often he does not know how many he can 'let off the hook' until the minority members vote."[30] The way this usually is done is to hold a few votes in reserve until the final tally becomes clear. Whether or not switches are prearranged in conference, the process is not always this smooth. For example, on an assembly vote one Democrat refused to shift his vote unless and until the majority leader switched first. "If the leadership won't take a fall," he explained, "how can they ask me to?" While his logic might not have been appreciated at the time, it is—as a general rule—the senior party leaders who are asked to switch first.

Tactics

Once, near the end of session, assembly member Murtaugh needed the leadership's help in encouraging senate action on one of his committee's bills. Already on the list for a formal appointment about another issue, Murtaugh decided that an informal encounter might suffice. When the party went into conference, he positioned himself, ready with a carefully rehearsed speech, on the only available aisle. As the session broke up, he deftly maneuvered himself into the speaker's only line of exit. But the speaker, in a move worthy of a professional football halfback, managed to slide two chairs out of the way, vault the third row, and make his escape.

End of session perhaps encapsulates the problem of access for rank-and-file legislators. There is only so much money to go around, only so much the party leadership can ask of the governor and the other house, only so much time available. During the final weeks, everyone, it seems, wants to get to the speaker, the majority leader, or the governor. If you are an assembly Democrat, you do it through the speaker. Senators work through their majority leader. Lobbyists go where they can. Minority party members, by and large, work through their party leaders' contacts in the other house, though with the Democrats in control of both the senate and the assembly, Republicans can hope only to find sympathetic Democrats to make their case. The later in the session it gets, the more difficult access becomes. As noted earlier, members are "ranked," not in any formal sense, but in the sense that the speaker or majority leader will give priority to those who have earned credibility. Factors such as seniority, committee chairmanships, and records of reliability help. In both majority party conferences, there is a particular advantage to being from a marginal district. A Democratic assembly member from a normally Republican area, for example, is far more likely to get a sympathetic hearing than one from a safe Democratic seat if only because the party and its leaders need these marginal district members to maintain their majorities.

While the kind of informal contact Murtaugh sought at the end of conference can be useful for small favors, the two most common channels for communicating with the leadership are through formal appointment and in conference discussions. Any member of the majority conference can schedule a meeting with the party leader's top aide, who seldom makes direct commitments. The aide normally will get back to the member later or schedule an appointment with the party leader. Here too it often is difficult to get a direct answer because the important requests usually necessitate further deals. "I'll see if I can get it in the budget" or "Well, let's move it through the assembly and I'll talk with the majority leader" often is about as strong a pledge of help as anyone can hope for.

In order to promote positive action from the leadership, an idea must be pretty well fleshed-out, if not in the form of a bill, at least as a concrete proposal for action. Moreover, as one former top aide put it, "An idea has to make sense. It has to be something that is not going to cause a problem for the other members of the majority. There is an evaluation of individual ideas and a meshing of the different things that the members of the conference would like to do, a placing of priorities on them."[31] If a proposal is likely to help the party in the polls, in raising funds, in helping a marginal member win reelection, it will get a hearing; if it is good public policy, so much the better. The more easily the leadership can sell it to the governor and to the other house, the better its chances. Thus it helps to have support in the other house, to have the same or a similar proposal pending in committee or on the calendar, or to have it passed in different form. It does not hurt for the speaker, majority leader, or governor to hear from more than one member on the same issue, and the backing of an interest group with strong ties to the party can be a big plus.

A lot of the real work in Albany, the detailed political crafting of policy proposals, takes place in the party conferences of the majority party. This is where the speaker and majority leader "listen to the members . . . , discern their positions, mesh those positions, conceptualize policies which were responsive to those distilled and reconciled positions, enunciate those policies back to the members, get their reactions, and finally modify those policies, as appropriate, based on the reactions of the members."[32] Wise members pick their spots in conference, commenting only when they have important insights to impart. Committee-based specialization plays a major role, with committee chairs—those who are respected for doing their homework, at least—getting the most attention. At the same time, overspecialization—seeing every policy issue as involving the legislator's own field, whether health, schools, substance abuse, or whatever—can turn an expert into a "one-trick pony," whose response to every issue is predictably tied to one answer. In the assembly's Democratic conference, regionalism plays a strong role, with New York City Democrats deferring to suburban and upstate colleagues on many issues, and vice versa.

In the new world of a one-house legislature, members of the Republican minority are relegated largely to the role of critics. A member with a policy proposal that might become law can get a serious hearing only by working through—and giving credit to—a Democrat. You can have the satisfaction of having had a good idea that went nowhere, or the private pleasure of seeing your idea become law in someone else's name.

Most party conferences go smoothly. Although the party may be split, most of the time the real enemies are "out there." Emotions, however, can erupt, and individual members sometimes feel so strongly about particular issues that they ignore the concerns of other members. A chair of the assembly higher education committee, for example, once threatened to vote against the budget if the speaker agreed to a proposed elimination of a college in the city university system. His strong stand worked in this case, and the speaker went back to the governor and majority leader in order to rework the university budget, but as the chair himself conceded, "you can't use that kind of tactic too often."

Governors

One of the most salient features of national politics has long been what President Woodrow Wilson called "the imperious authority of the standing committees" of Congress. Aided by the seniority system, many committee and subcommittee chairs develop close, usually friendly, long-term relations with their counterparts in the executive branch and affected interest groups. The resulting "whirlpools of influence," "subgovernments," or "iron triangles," as they are called, are remarkably resilient to challenge either by party leaders in Congress or by the White House. The autonomy of these subgovernments allows—indeed, encourages—end runs around central authority. Federal agency heads who feel their programs are being slighted take their cases to their allies on the relevant congressional subcommittees. Aided by the lobbying efforts of subgovernment friends in the private sector, they frequently see their programs restored by a Congress that respects a degree of decentralization that New York's legislative leaders would not tolerate. While committee chairs in New York frequently have cordial relations with their executive branch and interest group counterparts, the tradition of central command is far stronger in Albany than in Washington. Few New York agency heads would even dream of the kinds of end runs around the governor that are commonplace in Washington and in many other states. Few chief executives in the other forty-nine states are as firmly in control of their executive agencies as are the governors of New York.

As in all bureaucracies, however, there are strong centrifugal forces in New York State's government. Most agencies have clients, often politically powerful groups, that take a strong, continuing interest in what the agencies are doing. Environmental groups closely monitor the department of environmental conservation, and EnCon bureaucrats know and regularly work with group representatives. Civil servants, moreover, tend to become protective of their missions. Those who work for the state library are trained as librarians, work as librarians, and tend to believe that what they are doing is worthwhile. A governor whose program calls for cuts or changes in the mission of the state library is likely to encounter resistance. Despite the relative weakness of subgovernments in New York, the ability of state bureaucrats and their interest group allies to resist a governor, to end-run his directives by appealing to the legislature, the press, or the courts, is not insubstantial. The powers of a governor are not simple powers of command.

Personal Influence

Political power demands skill as well as formal authority. Some of the factors that bolster political effectiveness are not entirely under a governor's control. Those who face a legislature at least partially in the hands of the opposite party, as have all recent New York governors before David Paterson, operate under significant constraints. Each governor, nonetheless, brings to the job a set of personal and political attributes that can make the formal powers effective or not. The essential problem of all chief executives, as Richard Neustadt argues in his classic study of the presidency, is "how to be on top in fact, as well as name." Neustadt's exploration of presidential power is so brilliantly articulated that it diverts the eye from the conceptual sparseness of his analytic framework. Indeed, most studies of leadership are stronger in anecdote than intellectual rigor, more art than science. But what Neustadt teaches a generation of political scientists is that the formal powers of public officials cannot be explained simply in terms of formal roles: "outcomes are not guaranteed by advantage."[33]

Some governors come to office with what the press and some sectors of the public perceive as significant electoral mandates. As Thad Beyle puts it, "The premise is that the larger the margin of victory the stronger the governor will be in the view of other actors in the system. Governors with a wide margin can use that margin politically by declaring that the people overwhelmingly wanted him or her in office so that a particular goal could be achieved."[34]

Because statewide elections in New York tend to be competitive, few of the Empire State's governors have come to office with the kinds of mandates that command such immediate attention. George Pataki won his first election in 1994 by a relatively slim margin of just 4 percent. But his victory was recorded in the context of a strong national showing by the Republican Party that had deeply shaken many Democrats, particularly a number of upstate and suburban assembly members who had seen their victory margins narrow. Instead of trying to work with them, Pataki went on the attack with a series of television commercials targeted at these marginal Democrats. The short-run results were impressive: the governor was able to pass a death penalty bill, lower high-end tax rates, and substantially cut the budget. By the next session, however, assembly Democrats had regrouped and many of these changes were undone. Even after winning by a true landslide in 1998, Pataki never regained a position of strength vis-à-vis the legislature.

In 2006 Eliot Spitzer was elected governor with nearly two-thirds of the vote. Like Pataki a dozen years before, Spitzer came to Albany determined—in a phrase that would come back to haunt him—"to fucking steamroller" the legislature. Mounting a personal attack on majority leader Joseph Bruno, trying to block the legislature's power to appoint one of its members as a replacement for comptroller Alan Hevesi, who had been forced to resign, and then campaigning against Democrats who opposed him in that fight, Spitzer was soon without a friend in Albany. Far from a steamroller, Spitzer himself was rolled within in a matter of months. Whatever grades observers might give Cuomo, Pataki, and Spitzer, the one comment that would probably appear on all their report cards is "does not play well with others." In part because the legislature in New York gets such bad press and in part because it deserves it, all three governors had underestimated the legislature, a mistake that soon dissipated whatever electoral mandates they might have had.

Staff

Sophisticated studies of political leadership do not offer simple formulas for success. It would have been impossible for a George Pataki to have replicated the rhetorical skills of Mario Cuomo, and he was not foolish enough to try. Few governors have been able to exude the personal charm and charisma of a Nelson Rockefeller; none have had his kind of money. All of the successful ones, however, surrounded themselves with talented aides, marshaled their resources effectively, responded effectively to crises, and were able to articulate a policy agenda to the legislature and the public. New York's governors have an unusual degree of formal freedom to choose their governing teams. The law provides them with large personal staffs, generously paid to attract top-flight people (many earn more than $150,000 a year), and the power to appoint most agency and department heads. A tradition of legislative deference allows the governor wide latitude in deciding whom to appoint.

In reality, there are political constraints that encumber the power of appointment. While patronage is not nearly so controlling a force as in the days of machine politics, there are invariably groups and individuals with more or less legitimate claims to recognition. These range from such abstract considerations as gender and ethnicity to very concrete demands to include particular individuals or group members in important policy positions. Labor unions, for example, expect to be represented in a Democratic administration as business groups do in a Republican one, not necessarily demanding the appointment of specific individuals, but expecting some sort of general recognition of their importance in a winning electoral coalition. The sometimes pivotal role of minor parties in New York politics adds still another facet to the range of attributes governors must consider in filling the thousands of jobs exempt from civil service rules. For example, it was a given that George Pataki would consult with Conservative Party leaders and follow their general and specific recommendations in making a number of key appointments. In every administration, a sorting process takes place through which certain individuals—regardless of formal titles—begin to emerge as key players.

These general political constraints seldom limit effective control. There are offices with nice titles and salaries but little effective responsibility to which untrustworthy or incompetent but politically important individuals can be appointed. Conversely, reliable appointees may hold technically minor positions: Rockefeller appointed William Ronan and Carey appointed Robert Morgado as the governor's personal secretary, both of whom emerged as virtual surrogate governors. With Cuomo and Pataki the inner circle expanded to three or four key players; one of Cuomo's key people, his son Andrew, did not even occupy an official position. Governor Paterson's staff, carried over to some extent from his days as senate minority leader, has given him unusual leverage with the legislative branch if only because they are extremely understanding and appreciative of the legislature's role.

Lower-ranking aides and department heads (called commissioners in most departments) drift in and out of the governor's personal orbit. The governor's cabinet—the collective body consisting of the heads of the major departments—seldom meets and has never been an important unit. Some department heads are considerably more important than others. When Hugh Carey became governor, he brought his personal physician, Dr. Kevin Cahill, to the second floor as an unpaid special assistant for health care. Carey's first health commissioner was little more than an administrator, but when Cahill picked Dr. David Axelrod for the position and became less active himself, there was a visible shift in power. Axelrod, who continued as commissioner under Governor Cuomo, became an extremely influential adviser to both governors, unusually free to run his own department and even to extend its influence into areas previously under strong local control. It is rare for commissioners to achieve this kind of independence, even within their own departments, as a too-powerful commissioner threatens the governor's chain of command.

Equally threatening are attributes such as stupidity, ethical insensitivity, and overt disloyalty. Both Pataki and Carey had troubles with their lieutenant governors: both of them—Mary Ann Krupsak under Carey and Betsy McCaughey Ross under Pataki—actually running against their former patrons. Some of Pataki's early cabinet appointments, accustomed to the looser standards of the business world, embarrassed the governor by using their aides as personal assistants, using state cars for their private use, and running up large expense accounts. These cases, idiosyncratic as they may be, illustrate a general dilemma all governors face in putting together governing teams. Appointments have symbolic loading. It is politically important, as a rule, to balance the governing team in terms of gender, region, and ethnicity. When it comes to governing, however, qualities such as loyalty also are crucial; governors need an administration that, if not in full sympathy with their program, is at least reading from the same page. An administration that is "balanced" is generally difficult to control, but this tends to be less true in New York than in most other states.

What makes New York different in this sense is that the intervening layer on the second floor—the governor's personal staff—is far larger than that of any other governor. Whether or not the governor personally runs the bureaucracy in New York, the executive office does. Especially through the division of the budget, the executive office is large enough, professional enough, and imbued with a tradition of control that makes it virtually impossible for state officials to take significant actions without clearing them through the second floor. The 2008–2009 budget counts 184 full-time employees in the governor's chamber plus another 365 under his direct control in the budget division. And these figures do not include a number of miscellaneous offices and special committees that report directly to the second floor.

Controllers and Controllees

Although it is a problem most other governors would gladly take, the size of New York's executive office presents a challenge of a different sort. More than seventy years ago, when a special commission proposed a major expansion of the president's personal staff in Washington, some wise students of public administration warned against too strong a faith in what became known as "salvation by staff." The problem is twofold. On the one hand, the larger the executive staff, the more time the executives have to spend hiring, firing, monitoring, and motivating their own people. This leaves less time for working with legislators, journalists, commissioners, and the public. A large staff, on the other hand, is also more difficult to motivate and control and can become "institutionalized" in the worst sense of that term. Few agencies of executive power are potentially more potent than those with real budgetary authority, but as Alan Schick once wrote about the old federal Bureau of the Budget:

> As it became the institutionalized presidency, the Bureau became separated from the President. With a 500-man complement, the Bureau was just too large and too remote to be the President's own. . . . It could not be quick or responsive enough for an activist President who wants to keep a tight hold over program initiatives. . . . Over a period of decades, the Bureau had become a rigidified institution. . . . The routines of budgeting and legislative clearance, had been solidified by years of tradition-building and practice, not easily changeable. It was a labyrinthine task to make even minor modifications in the procedures for budget preparation and review, and in fact, few changes were made.[35]

New York's budget office is neither so large nor unwieldy as the federal agency, but Schick's point applies. By appointing a strong budget director, a governor can set the administration's general tone. But from the budget office down to the lowest levels of the bureaucracy, a tremendous amount of inertia is built into the system. As Martha Weinberg concludes in her excellent case study of Governor Francis Sargent in Massachusetts, "gubernatorial intervention is limited and not even-handed for all agencies. In agencies where there is no crisis, there is often no management on the part of the governor."[36]

As much as New York's governors are empowered by large staffs, control is diminished by filtering it through a second layer. Governors are not precluded from dealing directly with their commissioners—as Carey and Cuomo did with Dr. Axelrod—but they risk sending conflicting signals unless they bring their own executive office on board at the same time. On a comparative basis, no governor has more tools at command for managing the executive branch; no governor has a more confusing and complicated a system within which to work.

Credibility

In dealing with staff, governors have the ultimate sanction at their command, the ability to fire those who refuse to go along. Like most powerful weapons, it is best used with care. Whatever George Pataki gained from the announcement that McCaughy Ross would not be on his ticket in 1998, he paid a price in bad press, a perception that he was insensitive to women, and a general feeling among insiders that he was not really in control. All agency heads know that they hold their jobs at the pleasure of the governor. They do not usually need to be reminded, but a governor who gets to the stage at which firing is the only option is probably already on the margins of trouble.

Most of a governor's other powers are grounded less in command than in re-

Box 6.3
Carrots or Sticks
Member and Leader Perspectives

Most academic studies of political leadership emphasize its collegial, reciprocal nature. "Punishment," as Alan Rosenthal puts it, "is the exception, even when members refuse to go along with their legislative party on an issue."[1] All the present and former party leaders we talked with went out of their way, repeatedly, to make the same point. Phrases such as the following appear throughout our notes of these conversations: "I never demoted anybody." "Why would I want to hurt a member of my own conference?" "Ultimately, the only real power you have is the power of persuasion." Most governors would probably say the same kinds of things.

Many of the journalists and legislators interviewed presented a very different view, emphasizing the toughness of these same leaders and telling stories of members who had faced the speaker's anger or aides who suffered from the governor's rebuke.

These different perspectives reflect the real-world elusiveness of the concept of sanctions, which, like nuclear weapons in the military theory of strategic deterrence, are most effective when they are not actually used. When Sheldon Silver looked Brian Murtaugh in the eye and said, "Brian, you can't do that," Murtaugh was not inclined to ask why not. Silver was no doubt convinced that he had "persuaded" Murtaugh not to act; to Murtaugh it felt like sanctions. Stanley Fink enjoyed the give-and-take of the party conference, but what Fink might have seen as hard bargaining or making a tough argument easily could have been perceived as threatening to a member dependent on the speaker for favors. When the speaker's counsel or a top aide to the governor summons you to his office and asks why you are doing something, it is not unnatural to think that you are being asked to stop doing it.

If, in fact, formal sanctions are seldom used, this in no way negates their importance in shaping the relationships between party leaders and the rank-and-file in the legislature, or between the second floor and various agency heads in the executive branch. Sanctions, rewards—the whole panoply of inducements available to party leaders and governors—are given to the members by their leaders in order to advance party and policy goals. Resources are finite: legislators and bureaucrats know that not all of them can get what they want. What they ask of their leaders is not that they be yea-sayers but that they be fair in saying yes and no. As much as every bureaucrat and every member of the senate and assembly knows and understands this fact, it still feels like a sanction when the answer they get is no.

1. Alan Rosenthal, *The Decline of Representative Democracy* (Washington, DC: Congressional Quarterly Press, 1998), p. 276.

spect. Even the power to fire aides is not much of a threat if the aides believe that they have less to lose from being fired than from going along. A governor who is doing poorly in public opinion polls or who has a reputation for indecisiveness or for backing down in the face of adversity is more likely to be challenged than one who is riding high. Skill is respected in Albany; it is part of credibility. By the end of his eight years as governor, Hugh Carey's personal problems had made him the butt of many jokes and negative editorials, but his shortcomings generally were compensated by his command of difficult policy issues and willingness to make difficult decisions. The mismatch between Carey's public image and his standing among insiders led his biographer to label him "a Rolls Royce engine in a Studebaker body."[37] More recent governors seem to have had exactly the opposite problem. Just a year out of office, George Pataki's standing was so low among his fellow Republicans that he was not even invited to serve as a delegate to the party's 2008 national convention. "Pataki's insouciant leadership," as one disgruntled supporter puts it, "and his administrative mismanagement, incompetence, and corruption have not only hurt New York but have crippled New York's Republican Party."[38]

A governor's political reputation—like a president's—is grounded in forces not wholly in his or her control. If the state economy follows a national trend into a recession, there is little that governors can do to prevent their poll ratings from following the economic indicators down. What they can control, conversely, is their own personal reputation: "the men he would persuade must be convinced in their own mind that he has the skill and will enough to *use* his advantages."[39] When the press revealed Eliot Spitzer's dalliance with a prostitute, many of his supporters believed he could ride the scandal out: after all, they reasoned, his personal failings had nothing to do with his ability to govern. What they had failed to understand is how little credibility Spitzer had left. If only because Spitzer himself had moralistically prosecuted others for the same offenses, there was no place he could hide. A few weeks later, when Governor Paterson admitted that both he and his wife had had extramarital affairs, the story disappeared from the newspapers in a matter of days. Paterson's explanations of his indiscretions were credible; Spitzer's were not.

Public Prestige

A governor has two very distinct constituencies. The first we might label an "Albany" public of political insiders, including legislators, journalists, lobbyists, and other politicians; the second is the general public. What plays with one of these constituencies may not play at all with the other. Mario Cuomo, at the peak of his power, was one of the state's most publicly popular governors, revered not just in New York but also throughout the nation. In the Albany community, however, he had few friends, some grudging admirers, and numerous (silent) detractors. In our interviews with Albany insiders, we found only two (both on the governor's staff) who really liked him. In our interview with the late Ralph Marino he called Cuomo a "bully," a perspective shared by many of those we talked with. Similarly, Spitzer was well liked by the public, but few Albany insiders admired him and many described him as arrogant and out of touch.

Affection may or may not be related to prestige. One of the most enduring questions raised by Machiavelli in *The Prince* (nearly 500 years ago) was whether it was more important for a leader to be feared or loved. Although Machiavelli came down largely on the side of fear (on the grounds that it is the more enduring emotion), the situation is a bit more complicated in a democracy where the ability of a governor to inspire fear in the Albany community may be directly related to the ability to engender the love of the voters. Legislators, as a general rule, hate it when a governor appeals a policy dispute directly to the public. The ability of a popular governor to mobilize the legislature through public opinion is enormous, particularly in the age of television. Much of Eliot Spitzer's fleeting power vis-à-vis the legislature derived from the fear most legislators had of his ability to go directly to the public and make them regret their opposition to his positions. Much of his inability to overcome scandal was equally based in his inability to make such appeals.

Dealing With the Legislature

Little of consequence changed from the 1950s through the 1990s in the formal powers of the governor. And it would be difficult to make a case that Thomas Dewey or Nelson Rockefeller was smarter, was more skillful, or had better staff than Hugh Carey or Mario Cuomo. Looking historically at New York politics during Dewey and Rockefeller's time at Gracie Mansion or further back to the administrations of Al Smith, Franklin Roosevelt, and Herbert Lehman, it is clear that *their* powers, relative to those of legislature, were overwhelming. Even Averill Harriman, a relatively weak governor in terms of skills and popularity, got pretty much what he wanted from the legislature. The rise of the legislature as an equal partner in the process revolutionized the nature of New York politics. Under Rockefeller, as Norman Adler—political scientist, lobbyist, and gubernatorial aide—puts it, legislators were "like the Harlem Globetrotters playing against the Saugerties Little League. They were giants with enormous resources. . . . That's simply not true anymore."[40] The professionalization of legislatures, combined with divided government, has been the hallmark of state governments in the twentieth and twenty-first centuries, giving legislatures an upper hand. Neither George Pataki nor Eliot Spitzer was especially adept at dealing with the New York state legislature, the former due to economic difficulties in the state, further exacerbated by 9/11, and the latter having an especially contentious relationship with the leaders, indicated earlier in this chapter. The fact that all three of the state's most recent former governors have had difficulty in getting their budgets enacted is instructive. In the words of former majority leader Bruno:

> The problem that we have with the budget is, in my mind, the process has been totally politicized. It is so politicized that we deal with it in the media. You almost lose track of the merits of everything. It's, "How will this go?" "How will this sell?" "What will the editorial be?" That's what's wrong with our budget process. And any person, Silver or myself currently, or the governor, can stop a budget from happening.[41]

Since 2004, however, the legislature's power essentially has been limited to blocking the governor's budget. Legally, in the wake of a key court of appeals decision,[42]

> The Governor-as-legislator has extensive and unreviewable discretion to make policy decisions when drafting the annual budget and when exercising any vetoes. The Legislature, in stark contrast, is explicitly circumscribed in reacting to the policy embodied in the Executive Budget. Thus, the power of the purse, traditionally a legislative power, is no longer the plenary, or even the primary, domain of the legislature although enactment of the budget remains with the legislature.[43]

Symbolic Politics

It would be misleading and wrong to portray the contest between legislatures and executives as one in which the growing power of one comes simply at the expense of the other. In New York, as in national politics and in most states, both executive and legislative powers have grown as central governments and governments in general have become more important in the lives of the people. Many issues once resolved privately or at the local level have been politicized, particularly in the years since Franklin Roosevelt became president in 1933. Astonishingly enough, it is still within the memory of living Americans that the governments of neither the United States nor the state of New York had any significant role whatsoever in key areas such as health, welfare, and environmental conservation. In many areas, a general expansion of government power results in increased powers for both the legislature and the governor.

A good deal of the seeming conflict between governors and legislators, moreover, is more symbolic than substantive. Particularly in a state like New York, where both executive and legislative powers are centralized, certain kinds of conflicts have taken on an almost ritualistic character. Throughout the Carey and Cuomo years, for example, the legislature never had enough votes to enact a statute allowing the death penalty in New York. Both governors made it clear that they would veto any capital punishment bill, and there was always a large enough bloc of anti–death penalty assembly members to sustain the veto. Thus, although there was usually a majority in both houses for capital punishment, its proponents could never marshal the two-thirds majority needed to override a veto. Every year, however, the senate, sometimes joined by an assembly majority, would pass some form of death penalty bill and send it to the governor for his ritualistic veto. Both sides, of course, would issue numerous press releases, with the Republicans' point being to embarrass a Democratic governor and assembly majority on a crucial issue with voters. To underscore the point, the Republicans usually would package their proposal around the most heinous crimes imaginable—what one assemblyman called "the lurid crime of the month bill"—mandating capital punishment for such crimes as planting a bomb on an airplane or torturing and murdering a child.

Similarly, governors frequently propose programs they know will not pass. In

1989, for example, the *New York Times* counted almost 150 new program proposals in Cuomo's State of the State address. As Rosenthal asserts, "With so many initiatives it was virtually impossible for the governor to build much legislative support. Nor did Cuomo really try; his style was not that of courting and cajoling. From a legislative point of view, his political leadership was wanting. Cuomo laid out an agenda and then abandoned it."[44]

When governors propose bills they have no intention of pushing, they are not necessarily playing games. Cuomo's eloquent speeches, it could be argued, though not intended as blueprints for that year's public policy, were politically sincere, significant statements of aspiration. In academic terms, governors attempt to set the policy agenda, using their visibility as a means of initiating a dialogue about new priorities. It is, in Polsby's terms, "the politics of inventing, winnowing, and finding and gaining adherents for policy alternatives before they are made part of a program, and likewise the politics of moving alternatives from the unlikely to possible or probable candidates for inclusion on an agenda for enactment."[45] There are times, to be sure, when a governor's motives are suspect, when the intent is less to initiate policy change than to reap partisan advantage from emotional appeals to the voters. Whatever the motives, no player in New York politics is better situated than the governor to play an agenda-setting role. Whether their intentions are seriously to develop new policy directions or are largely political, access to the media makes all governors—whatever their formal powers—players.

The governor is aided in these efforts by being the ceremonial leader of the state. In this ceremonial role, governors gain and maintain visibility by opening county fairs and new highways, appearing in ads touting the state's tourist attractions, welcoming presidents and foreign dignitaries to the state, and so on. They also use this nonpartisan role as a means of giving a subtle push to certain kinds of issues, as when they march (or choose not to march) in a gay rights parade, give a speech (or not) at the annual dinner of the American Civil Liberties Union, or visit a newly opened wildlife refuge. Moreover, however governors choose to play a leadership role, they are the preeminent member of their political party in the state.

Party Leadership

How serious various governors have been in attempts to change the policy agenda is not always clear. Sometimes attractive policy proposals are put forward less to move them onto the agenda for enactment than to get good ratings from the public. Policy proposals, particularly those contained in the governor's budget message to the legislature, also can be strategic in intent; that is, governors will propose something they know the legislature will not accept in order to trade it later for something else. School funding has almost always been such an issue. Every recent governor has sent the legislature a budget that, if enacted, would result in cuts in state aid to many local school districts. The governor knows that the legislature will restore the cuts, but hopes to obtain something in return.

Whatever its purpose, the usual focus of symbolic politics is the wider public. Republicans pushed the death penalty in the 1970s and 1980s to make Cuomo, Carey, and Democrats in general appear to be out of step with public opinion. Similarly, Spitzer's controversial proposal to allow undocumented immigrants access to driver's licenses was arguably an example of symbolic politics with little chance of being passed. In the ideal party government, the purpose of these symbolic battles is to underscore, for the benefit of the electorate, the philosophical differences between the parties. Purists might argue that most of these appeals are demagogic and misleading, but there is little doubt that they can be effective in forcing legislative action.

In theory, the governor is the leader of a political party. In the responsible party model, governors and their fellow party members in the legislature present a program to the public, attempt to enact it, and run for reelection on their records in office. That model has never worked particularly well in New York. Governors Dewey and Rockefeller certainly dominated the Republican Party. For two decades, they were able to control both the executive mansion and the Republican contingents in both houses of the legislature. Through adroit uses of patronage and centralized campaign fund-raising, they were able to overwhelm even the strong county organizations. Unfortunately for the advocates of responsible parties, the Democrats were seldom able to provide a cohesive opposition. While members understood the value of party unity *within* the legislature, there were few career incentives for the kind of party unity that cuts across institutional boundaries. Governor Pataki and senate majority leader Joseph Bruno frequently agreed on the issues, and Bruno probably would not have become majority leader without Pataki's help. But Republican senators have both the ability and the motive to maintain a certain level of autonomy. Mario Cuomo almost took pride in *not* becoming involved in legislative campaigns, and some observers actually were surprised in 2008 when Governor Paterson actively worked to elect a Democratic majority in the state senate.[46]

The picture we are drawing of six distinct party systems, gubernatorial, assembly, and senate for both Republicans and Democrats, while not inaccurate, minimizes the role of the governor as party leader. While governors no longer control the career fortunes of legislators as they often did in the 1940s and 1950s, they still have an extraordinary power to set party agendas—that is, to define issues in their terms rather than those of legislative majorities—and especially to use their control over the budget to create new law. Because Carey and Cuomo opposed the death penalty, most voters assumed that assembly and senate Democrats were against capital punishment also. While it is true that the crucial one-third of the votes to uphold a veto came almost entirely from Democratic ranks, the issue lost much of its partisan loading when Pataki was elected and the death penalty sailed through both houses.

The Power of Provision

Some sources of power—particularly those based on reputation and credibility— can be incubated and multiplied; others are scarce—once used they are gone. A governor can dangle a possible appointment to the court of appeals before four attorneys and perhaps hold some of them in thrall, but once the appointment is made, the governor has created, as an old saying has it, three enemies and one ingrate. When resources are declining, as they were in Pataki's last years as governor, his failure to provide continuing or growing levels of support for various constituency groups produced an almost perceptible erosion of power. When resources are relatively abundant, power, used effectively, builds power; that is, the greater your reputation for acting effectively and delivering as promised, the more people are likely to believe that you will continue to do so in the future. Judiciously used, patronage is a potent resource; so is money.

New York, in a tradition little changed from the days of boss rule, has given its elected officials an abundant array of goodies to distribute. While civil service reform took most of the operating bureaucracy outside party control, the number and variety of patronage positions for the politically connected remain substantial. There are literally dozens of obscure boards and commissions that pay decent salaries, provide pension credits, and almost never meet. The government is a major customer of everything from prison food and pencils to iron bars and printing presses. Construction jobs and supply contracts are awarded through competitive bidding, but there are ways of writing specifications or reviewing capabilities that can clearly tilt a job to a politically favored company. In addition, state budgets traditionally provide both the governor and the legislature with large discretionary accounts. Depending on party, seniority, electoral needs, and clout, an individual legislator may be able to distribute as much as half a million dollars in the assembly and a million in the senate in virtually unrestricted grants to local groups. The press enjoys poking fun at the legislature's so-called member items, special pockets of money cleared through legislative party leaders for special local purposes, such as providing computers for Baruch College, promoting Long Island seafood, or supporting a farm museum in Queens. Member items also are subject to attack from partisan politicians. The *New York Times* once quoted an upstate Republican assembly member, John Faso, on the uses of these funds for essentially political purposes: "Say with a senior citizens' center in New York City. Those centers become almost local political clubs for the member who got the money," Faso charged. The *Times* went on to note that Faso distributed a newsletter in which—under the heading "John Faso: He Listens and Leads"—he boasted of the $22,000 grant he had been "instrumental in securing" for a senior citizen's center in Ravena.[47]

Assemblyman Faso no doubt thought his senior citizens different from those he was criticizing, just as New York City journalists are likely to be critical of upstate items, and so on. But for all the attention given to these relatively small pockets of money available to legislators, it is surprising how little attention is focused on the really large discretionary accounts available to the governor. These come in five primary forms. First, the budget almost invariably puts wiggle room into the funding for most agencies. These discretionary accounts are expected to be used for unexpected changes in mission as, for example, when an unusually hard winter forces the highway department to spend more than was planned on snow removal. In many cases, such as heavy snows, these expenditures are event-driven; but they are—whatever the nature of events—discretionary accounts that the governor controls. Thus, in 1998, when Governor Pataki was under fire for vetoing a popular item in the community college budget, he simply restored it by shifting discretionary funds.

A second large pocket of unallocated money is available to the governor in certain parts of the capital budget. In 1996, for example, the voters approved a large environmental bond act that allowed the state to borrow money primarily devoted to clean water and clean air. In Albany, two churches near the governor's mansion are being restored with money granted from this fund by the governor. What does the restoration of two landmark buildings have to do with clean water and air? Not much. What is the value of the governor's ability to move capital projects around the state? Priceless.

Closely related is a third form of gubernatorial power, the ability of the governor to move existing jobs from one part of the state to another. Just as Democrats Hugh Carey and Mario Cuomo moved jobs to largely black and Hispanic neighborhoods in Harlem and the Bronx, so did George Pataki move jobs out of Albany and New York City into the lower Hudson Valley. In both cases, supporters of the moves cited motives of efficiency and community development. Critics pointed to the tendency for the Bronx and Harlem to be heavily Democratic and the Hudson Valley, Republican.

Fourth, governors and legislative leaders frequently set aside special slush funds of their own, particularly in election years. Although member items in the legislature must be cleared through the leadership—and party leaders take their own district-oriented shares—most budget agreements provide them with additional discretionary funds. The 1998 agreement went further than most in this regard, allowing Pataki, majority leader Bruno, and speaker Silver to divide nearly $1.5 *billion* (roughly 2 percent of the total budget) for unspecified purposes. As the election approached, each of these officials managed to find good uses for their shares of this substantial resource, and the policy of dividing these funds in relatively strict proportions not only continued but also has been augmented through what are known as State Personal Income Tax Revenue Bonds. More than $3 billion of these bonds were issued in the wake of 9/11, ostensibly to cope with the recession, but in fact a fiscal gimmick to use the state's borrowing power—normally reserved for capital projects—as another source of discretionary operating funds.

Finally, there is the Empire Development Corporation (EDC). Once known as the Urban Development Corporation, which went bankrupt in 1975, the EDC's mission "was refocused," as Wikipedia puts it, "to finance other ambitious state projects and has been used frequently by governors to implement projects that circumvent formal Legislative or voter scrutiny." Indeed, its projects are so cleverly concealed that it has largely escaped its own scrutiny. Referring to its enterprise zone projects, for example, EDC director Patrick Foye acknowledged, "We have no way of knowing how many jobs have been created or retained."[48] One upstate survey looked at thirty grants totaling $57 million that had reportedly created or served 1,294 jobs (that would be $44,000 per job), but there are no real records available to confirm these estimates.[49]

The Judiciary

Scholars have paid considerable attention to swings of power between the legislative and executive branches, paying considerably less to the role of the judiciary. Perhaps taking a cue from Alexander Hamilton's description of the courts as "the least dangerous branch," critics have demonstrated a widespread, though diminishing disinclination to look at the judiciary from the perspective of power politics. The image of justice as a blindfolded woman is designed to suggest blindness to bias and a sense of being above everyday conflicts. In reality,

> although some judges deny it, courts occupy a significant position in the policy-making process by ratifying choices made by legislatures and governors, by interpreting their policies (and thus adding or subtracting to their substance), and by vetoing policies when the courts declare them unconstitutional. Moreover, they routinely exercise discretion as they impose the norms specified by statutes and administrative regulations while ruling on the disputes brought before them. Thus judges are very much the kinds of officials who might be held responsive to the electorate.[50]

Selecting Judges

Even in large towns and cities, many judges are elected to the civil and criminal courts less for their legal talent than for their political skill. The question of whether judges should be elected or appointed has been debated throughout the history of the state. Opponents of the electoral system argue that some of the best-qualified attorneys are the kinds of people least likely to subject themselves to the vagueries of a political campaign and that some of those most successful at campaigning are least likely to have judicial temperaments. While judicial temperament is difficult to measure, most studies of state courts do not show that judges elected in partisan elections differ much from those selected through gubernatorial appointments or nonpartisan elections.

A more telling argument against the election of judges is that it is unseemly. The ethical codes of the New York State Bar Association prohibit campaigns based on issues, and candidates usually avoid indicating how they might rule on specific cases. Interest groups, however, are under no such constraints, and clever advertising campaigns can bring opinions in by innuendo. Many lawyers still remember with distaste Jacob Fuchsberg's campaign for a seat on the New York State court of appeals in 1973. The campaign cost the then shocking sum of more than half a million dollars, and its emotional television commercials narrowly skirted bar association rules on issue advocacy. Although Fuchsberg turned out to be a better judge than expected, his campaign so alienated many people that the state constitution was amended to give the governor power to appoint judges of the court of appeals from a list of candidates selected by the State Commission on Judicial Nomination, with the approval of the senate.

Although the commission generally has been successful in screening out incompetent candidates and ending demagogic campaigns, its work has not been without controversy. In 2008, when the commission sent its list of possible replacements for retiring Chief Judge Judith Kaye, the list included no women and only one minority group member, and Governor Paterson vowed to find a way of further changing the process. Not incidentally, four of the twelve members of the commission were Pataki appointees.

Various attempts to amend the constitution and make other judgeships appointive have failed although, ironically, the argument for depoliticization may well be strongest at the lower levels of the system. Perhaps the outstanding example of deficiencies inherent in the system of electing judges is found in New York City's system of surrogate judges. The county (or borough) surrogate's job essentially is probating wills, normally a routine task. When someone dies without a will, however, the surrogate appoints a lawyer to handle the estate. Since the lawyer in question can be paid as much as one-third of the total inheritance plus fees for service, the business can be quite lucrative. Now it is true that under the provisions of the Code of Judicial Conduct, a judicial candidate is forbidden to know the names of campaign contributors (though candidates can certainly see the people in the room at a pricey dinner), but there is no way to enforce this rule. Surrogate campaigns in New York City are financed almost exclusively by lawyers who specialize in probate. These lawyers, in turn, receive almost all the probate assignments.

The nexus between campaign support and judicial decision-making is seldom so clear, though there is little doubt that, throughout the system, the major contributors to judicial campaigns are lawyers. There is, on the other hand, a strong argument to be made for local electoral control of the judiciary. As the most democratic system of selection, it provides some assurance that the judiciary will reflect local community norms and social values. The system, whatever its defects, has worked quite well, producing a history of fairness, efficiency, and even distinction. If party hacks, mountebanks, and charlatans occasionally slip past the voters, there is no guarantee that appointed judges—appointed, in the final analysis, by party politicians—will be any better.

The records of the parties in choosing judicial candidates vary enormously. In New York City's borough of Manhattan, where the Democratic nominee is virtually sure of election, the reform Democratic clubs have long insisted on a screening of candidates by a panel of supposedly nonpolitical lawyers. Ever since these reform clubs took control of the organization in the 1970s, the caliber of judicial candidates has improved and the quality of the bench has been higher in Manhattan than in the outer boroughs. Politics is still very much a part of the process, deals are made, and the voters seldom have a real choice on Election Day. But very few really bad judges slip through the screening process. As one study of the screening panel system concluded, "merit selection produces a younger, more representative, better educated, highly qualified and more politically diverse judiciary."[51] Since 1993, the state bar association has been lobbying for a modified version of the Manhattan system statewide. "Fundamental reform," the state association of lawyers argues, "requires that we eliminate political considerations from judicial selection—that we keep the clubhouse out of the courthouse—and focus solely on merit."[52]

Critics of the merit system argue that the system serves simply to change the nominating elite by transferring real power to the bar associations and elite lawyers who compose the screening panels. Party leaders may no longer be in control, but neither is the electorate. Much the same thing happens in many upstate counties where the party organizations frequently cut deals to cross-endorse a bipartisan slate of judges. Each party agrees to nominate only its negotiated "share" of potential judgeships (for example, one of the three seats up that year). In areas where one party dominates, the effect of such deals is to take control away from the electorate and lodge it in the hands of party leaders.

While it may be true that the electorate serves as an ultimate check on the worst of these insider deals, the fact is that judges are seldom actually chosen in competitive elections. The system is essentially a fraud, which is why most legal scholars are more comfortable with the present system of an appointed court of appeals. Whether the system can be changed at the lower levels is entirely another question. Attempts to establish fewer elected judgeships have been popular neither with legislators (some of whom aspire to run for the bench someday), lawyers (ditto), and ordinary voters. Generally speaking, selecting judges is a controversial process be it through elections or otherwise.

Politics and the Courts

An appointed judiciary can be every bit as political as one that is elected. Indeed, a case can be made that almost everything judges do is in some sense political. What the system of justice tries to sustain is a courtroom environment in which decisions are made according to the participants' perceptions of the facts of the case and the relevant laws. If this process were as automatic as it sounds, few cases would come to trial, far fewer than the more than 4 million cases filed each year in New York State.

The United States is one of the most litigious societies in the world, and New York has more lawyers per capita than any other American state. The reach of the courts in crime, business, housing, family relations, health, and almost all aspects of daily life is enormous and growing. But as much as the role of the courts is expanding, their proportionate share of government power has been in steady decline. New York, like all the other forty-nine states save for Louisiana, is a common-law state. Judicial rulings are based on a long series of precedents dating back through pre-revolutionary colonial courts to those of seventeenth-century England. The history of the law in New York, however, is one of growing codification. More and more, courtroom procedures, rules of evidence, criminal sentences, and the definitions of criminal behavior are determined by statute rather than litigation. At the time of the Revolution, most crimes were so-called common-law crimes; that is, the meaning of such offenses as assault, rape, manslaughter, and murder was derived through the principal of *stare decisis* from a long string of precedent cases. By the end of the nineteenth century, virtually all these rulings had been embodied in or superseded by statutory definitions; that is, by laws enacted by the legislature and signed by the governor. These laws defined, often in considerable detail, the various shades of meaning of offenses such as murder, voluntary and involuntary manslaughter, reckless endangerment, and depraved indifference to human life. The penal code of 1891 actually abolished the concept of common-law crime. No act, it read, "shall be deemed criminal or punishable, except as prescribed or authorized by this Code, or by some statute of this state."[53]

Codification of the civil law was a bit slower in reaching the legislature, and common-law traditions continue to play a somewhat stronger role in civil as opposed to criminal cases. What has happened in both arenas is clear. The power to define what the law is has moved steadily if not decisively from the courts to the legislature. This move coincided with two complementary aspects of modernization, the professionalization of the legal system and the depersonalization of the legal process. In colonial days, most trials truly involved juries (and judges) of one's peers: they were community events involving people who usually knew each other well. Questions of guilt, damage, and liability were decided by considering both the legal issues and the people involved. An upstanding citizen could almost always get away with more than the village ne'er-do-well, and strangers and outsiders were likely to be treated harshly. In many large communities, "less than half of all felony defendants went to trial . . . in others they were 'tried,' but in slapdash and routine ways, in trials that lasted a few hours or a few minutes at best. And most were convicted."[54] The move toward codification and away from common-law crimes was fueled, in Friedman's words, "by that pervasive feature in American legal culture, horror of uncontrolled power. Lawmakers believed that courts should be guided—ruled—by the words of objective law, enacted by the people's representatives; nothing else should be a crime."[55]

Almost all major modifications of the statutory code are made at the appellate level because these are the courts that focus on interpretive rather than factual questions. Indeed, a case can, as a rule, reach an appellate court only when the losing party in a trial alleges that the judge has either misinterpreted or misapplied the law. How much latitude the judges should have in ruling on these questions has been the source of many arguments, with those surrounding recent nominations to the U.S. Supreme Court often becoming quite heated. Terms such as *strict constructionist* generally say more about a potential jurist's ideology than about his or her faithfulness to the written law, but there are important issues at stake.

Judicial Power

Statutes passed by the legislature, signed by the governor, and codified in *McKin-ney's Laws of New York State*[56] form the backbone of both criminal and civil law. They create the entitlements, crimes, prohibitions, and penalties that give rise to legal disputes. Those disputes that cannot be negotiated are brought to the courts, which must interpret the ways in which the laws in the code apply to the particular case. Sometimes, governors and members of the legislature are not pleased with these interpretations and a whole new round of lawmaking takes place in which the legislators try to restate their "true" intentions. This new statute becomes what is known as a "pocket insert" in *McKinney's* (literally a page or pamphlet inserted in a pocket in the back of the relevant volume to update the law between editions of the full volume), and it becomes the starting point for future legal disputes.

A judge who wishes to change the direction of the law must operate within the constraints of a system of separated powers. Judges must recognize the importance of balancing legislative and judicial policies. Courts that reach too far in revising statute law are likely to find their rulings effectively overruled by subsequent stat-utes. Mindful of the ability of the governor and the legislature to revise the code and even to alter the structure of the courts themselves, even the most activist judges tend to practice some form of what scholars call judicial self-restraint. With regard to the Supreme Court of the United States, most scholars would agree with William Lasser's argument that "the modern Court has achieved its power and influence by distancing itself from precisely those issues capable of creating full-scale crises and thereby revealing the limits of its political strength."[57]

In a similar manner, New York's court of appeals has largely avoided an activist role in policy areas that might most threaten its relations with the governor and legislature. As noted in Chapter 5, for example, the court has refused to give teeth to the state constitution's seemingly clear guarantee of the "aid, care, and support of the needy," holding instead that it is up to the legislature to decide who is needy. The appeals court similarly managed to dodge the fight over equity in educational funding for nearly two decades, defining it again as a largely political question, until the evidence of substantial inequalities became overwhelming. Even then, the court found it virtually impossible to enforce its decision. Despite repeated lawsuits and seemingly unambiguous court decisions, neither the Pataki administration nor the legislature made a serious effort to respond. Not until Eliot Spitzer made the issue his own in 2007 did the court's opinion have any impact. The failure of the Campaign for Fiscal Equity to translate its victory in the courts into immediate policy change underscores both the limits and potentials of judicial power.[58] The inability of the court, one the one hand, to enforce its 2003 decision stands as a cautionary note to those who would urge a more active judiciary. It can be argued, on the other hand, that the court's reasoning and example played a strong role in pushing Governor Spitzer and the legislature to act.

Whatever the ability of the courts to effect policies of this kind, there is little doubt that the Campaign for Fiscal Equity case was exceptional. In playing its activist role primarily in the areas of criminal procedure and civil rights, while leaving economic issues largely to the governor and legislature, New York's courts essentially have followed the national pattern once described by Supreme Court justice Lewis Powell:

> The irreplaceable value of [judicial review] lies in the protection it has afforded citizens and minority groups against oppressive or discriminatory government action. It is this role, not some amorphous general supervision of the operations of government, that has maintained public esteem for the federal courts and permitted the peaceful coexistence of the countermajoritarian implications of judicial review and the democratic principles upon which our Federal Government in the final analysis rests.[59]

New York chief judge Sol Wachtler once expressed much the same kind of thinking, though expressing it in a more positive vein, when he argued, "There is a place for judicial restraint. But the protection of such things as individual and privacy freedoms is a uniquely judicial obligation and responsibility. Judicial restraint should not be confused with judicial abdication."[60]

Most judges, however strong their personal feelings, operate in an atmosphere of enormous restraint. They fear the possibility of arousing not only legislative, gubernatorial, and public disapproval, but also the negative judgments of their judicial peers. Judges do not like to be reversed by higher courts. Most of the time, the cases that confront judges—even at the appellate level—do not raise profound policy issues. Indeed, it is a rare case that matters much to anyone but the people in the courtroom. Taken individually, few court cases involve anything more than dispute resolution; only in the aggregate, over time, do they produce important changes in public policy. Even trial courts, in the long run, make policy. Indeed, one of the ironies of judicial policy-making is that its most profound impacts may come in areas attracting the least public attention. Tarr cites the shift in child custody cases as an example of such change. From an automatic assumption that the best interests of the child could be served only by awarding custody to the mother, judges in divorce cases have increasingly weighed a number of other variables in the decision and given fathers an increasingly important role.

> In sum, then, cumulative policymaking occurs when the courts, by deciding a series of essentially similar cases, in effect define policy in a given area. Although legislation or rulings by appellate may circumscribe the range of judicial choice, trial judges often retain considerable leeway in deciding individual cases. In exercising this discretion, judges rarely announce broad policy standards. Indeed, they may give little consideration to the broader policy their decisions are creating. Nonetheless, the results of their decisions constitute the state's policy.[61]

When courts do strike out into new areas, the savvy jurist recognizes the importance of what might be called the doctrine of seeming restraint. The more dramatic the decision—and this is a rule that applies to legislators and governors as well as lawyers and judges—the more important it is to be sure of the facts and meticulous in marshaling them. In his halcyon days on the court of appeals, Sol Wachtler was, in the words of his biographer, "a consummate coalition builder. . . . willing to compromise for the sake of presenting an image that the court was cohesive, even when it wasn't." Criticizing his predecessor as chief judge, Lawrence Cooke, for his failure to compromise, Wachtler once argued that "when you go into new areas of law, it is important that the imprint be a strong one. The perception out there when you had a 4–3 decision is . . . that the decision was tentative and could be overturned in a couple of years. I thought it very, very important that . . . the new court come out as unanimously as possible."[62]

The Who of Policy-Making

Judge Wachtler's emphasis on consensus reinforces a theme that has persisted throughout this chapter. Power in politics derives largely from the ability to build enduring coalitions, to convince other people in politics to make the necessary deals in order to get at least part of what they want. People skills are a very important part of political leadership, which is, in no small part, the ability to bring people together.

Political power is also a function of knowledge. Cases often are won in court because one lawyer presents a better argument than the other. Court decisions are more likely to stand when they are well argued. Although our discussion of power in this chapter has focused largely on the manipulative aspects of the power struggle in New York, it should not obscure the fact that many legislators, governors, and judges gain power through rectitude: they succeed because other people believe that what they are doing is right.

Politicians and government officials, judges not excluded, seek power. Few people run for public office for the money; some do it for prestige; most do it because they want to change the way things work—they want to be players rather than spectators. The road to being a player—whether as lawmaker or bureaucrat, judge or governor—involves, perhaps more than anything else, an ability to sense where you and your goals fit in with your environment. It also is essential to know the rules of the game, the how as well as the who, what, and why of the game.

7

Making Public Policy

The legislative process in Albany flows, like a deep river, on two levels. Below the surface there is a steady stream of relatively trivial legislative activity: crafting laws to bring New York into compliance with new federal guidelines, to allow local governments to merge, or to take account of a new medical procedure. These laws are trivial only in the sense that they seldom attract the attention of the media, the general public, or even most members of the legislature. They are important, in the cases cited, to those who live in the affected communities or need the new medical procedure. A lot of what happens in Albany, in Washington, or in most state capitals is this kind of ordinary, routine business. Closer to the surface of the legislative river are bigger, more controversial issues that may even be covered on the nightly news: fights over the budget, immigration, and rent control. This stream of legislation in New York concerns a broader public and evokes a different kind of legislative politics, a flow that is far more centralized, usually more visible, and frequently more partisan than that which runs at the lower depths.

What has happened in Albany over the past few decades, and at an accelerating rate since the Pataki years, is that the strong currents of partisanship and centralization have deepened, cutting increasingly into the normal flow and markedly centralizing the process. With more and more items brought to the surface, logjams and delays have become increasingly commonplace. The policy space has become more crowded: policies keep bumping into each other. Party leaders link policies together not because they have any tangible relationship to one another, but to secure bargaining points. Both Mario Cuomo and George Pataki put a growing number of often-controversial issues into their budgets rather than submitting them as stand-alone bills, often with the result of making budget negotiations with the legislature more contentious. Even though the governor (because of his line-tem veto authority) enhances his or her power by folding items into the budget, Eliot Spitzer briefly reversed the trend; but the 2009 process seems to have reverted to form with Governor Paterson not only packing most of his legislative program into the budget, but also leaving the Republicans out of the negotiating process.

This chapter divides the policy-making process into a series of stages that move from agenda setting through decision-making, implementation, and enforcement. As useful as these signposts are, it is important to remember that the actual process is less sequential than continuous. Today's decision often becomes tomorrow's agenda. One legislative aide described a transportation bill she helped draft in 1988. In consultation with various interest groups, local officials, and experts in the Department of Transportation (DOT), the bill went through three or four drafts before passing both houses of the legislature and being signed by the governor. In drawing up the detailed regulations (the "regs," as they are commonly called in Albany) to implement the law, officials in the DOT discovered technical flaws that were corrected in a new law, passed by the legislature and signed by the governor in 1989. By 1992, with both enforcement officials and the affected groups agreeing that the law was not accomplishing all that had been intended, it was revised again. By 1997, a somewhat different constellation of affected groups was back before the legislature arguing for still further changes in the law which, when enacted, produced yet another set of revised DOT regulations that finally were completed in 2002.

If an issue such as this were controversial enough, it might lead to demands not just for new policies but for new political configurations as well. A distinction between politics and policy-making can be as misleading as the attempt to divide the process into artificial stages: contests over leadership positions are seldom without policy implications, and vice versa. Transportation groups, if they were upset enough about the policy in question, might try to change the lawmakers involved by making appropriate campaign contributions, lobbying for leadership changes, or seeking to change the DOT's powers or personnel. They also might try to shift the battlefield away from the legislature and into the courts by bringing various kinds of lawsuits challenging aspects of the program.

The Normal Legislative Process

The governor's annual budget bills go directly to the legislature from the second floor. All other bills must be sponsored by legislators. Even a governor's program bill, which may embody a major policy of the administration, must be introduced by a state senator and a member of the assembly, usually by the chairs of the appropriate committees. There is no requirement that such bills be introduced at all, and some are not. In 1985, for example, eighteen of the 105 program bills proposed by Governor Cuomo were not introduced.[1]

Once introduced, legislation follows a fairly predictable track. Most legislation goes nowhere, or rather is held in committee, where it is said to have died. To become law, a bill must get out of committee in both the senate and assembly, be passed in both houses in the exact same form, and be signed by the governor.

In recent years, members of the senate and assembly have typically introduced more than twice as many bills as are introduced in the next most prolific state: Massachusetts. Many of these bills are redundant; indeed, some are exact copies of each other, and many refer to purely local issues that would not require legislative action in other states. Most, however, are largely symbolic, relatively cost-free vehicles for individual legislators to show the flag. On average, about 900 bills are favorably reported by assembly committees, slightly fewer in the senate. Almost all reported bills pass their respective houses. One-quarter of these bills will pass only one house of the divided legislature. Somewhere between 500 and 750 bills will pass both houses in the same form and be sent to the governor, who will veto as many as 20 percent. Thus in 2007, a total of 16,072 bills were introduced, 562 were sent to the governor, he vetoed 115, and none of his vetoes were challenged. Of the 562 bills passed by both houses, 299, or 53 percent, originated in the assembly. For the statistically inclined, a bill introduced in New York State has about one chance in thirty of becoming law.[2]

The Origins of Legislation

Members' motives for sponsoring legislation vary, as do members' attitudes toward legislative activity. Some members—minority party members in particular, but also those whom Barber classifies as "spectators"—focus primarily on constituent services and play little active role in the policy-making process.[3] For others, as one assembly aide put it, "constituent service and all that is important; but legislators like to score points, and you score more points with legislation." Many bills are introduced with no real legislative intent. A bill can be, as one member put it, "a great way to get people off your back." Even if doomed to failure in this session, a bill serves as a publicity device aimed at future legislators or as a statement of principles designed to contrast with other bills. In a typical session of the Democratic assembly, majority party members will introduce nearly twice as many bills as Republicans, with senior members, committee chairs, and party leaders the most active.[4] A handful of Republican bills, essentially those dealing with local issues, had a realistic chance of passing the assembly; most were introduced to make a point. Democrats were similarly marginalized in the Senate. But the symbolic importance of introducing bills is underscored by the fact that minority party members—knowing that their bills are unlikely to become law—are actively engaged at this stage of the process.

A bill that does not pass in one session must be reintroduced in the next or it will be dropped, but most show up again: old bills, it seems, never die. One of the first functions of a legislator's staff at the beginning of session is to dust off last year's bills for reintroduction. This process is so routine that one member, when asked about a bill he had introduced for twelve years, promptly sent a note to the chair of the committee to which it had been referred asking that it be withdrawn: "Oh my god," he said in our interview, "is that turkey still around?" Sometimes members copy bills from one another. One new member, who had narrowly defeated an incumbent in the Democratic primary, instructed his staff simply to reintroduce all of his predecessor's bills.

Fortunately for this member as for most, the laws of copyright do not apply to legislation. Frequently the copying flows across state lines, with the result that "statutory precedent grows as case-precedent grows. . . . Legal sciences call this the doctrine of *stare decisis*. The legislative process is similar. For example . . . Connecticut adopted a statute relieving the operator of a motor vehicle from liability to a guest except for 'willful or wanton conduct." Twenty-three states followed that lead. Described in juristic language, the legislatures have followed the rules of precedent, the statute has been copied. The result is the same.[5]

The proportion of bills borrowed from other states (Horack uses the phrase *stare de statute* to describe the process) has increased in recent years, in no small part because of the proliferation of national associations of state legislators connected both by annual meetings and the Internet. Interest groups and the press also play a role in bringing bills from one state to another. Businesses that operate across state lines have a strong interest in statutory uniformity, and the national meetings of environmental groups, unions, and so on are a fertile source of legislative cross-fertilization.

However, legislators need not look to other states for ideas when they can find them closer to home. In Schneier's study of the bills in the state assembly, 11 percent of the bills considered were borrowed, received, or simply stolen from other members; another 6 percent came from the senate.[6] Only one of the bills transmitted from one assembly member to another came as a gift, in this case from a committee chair to a freshman Democrat from a marginal district. Muggings were far more common. Indeed, bill theft has the status of a fine art in some offices. One majority party member who shared a media market with a legislatively active minority party member developed a source in the printing office who would provide advance warning of his rival's legislative initiatives. Taking advantage of a little-used rule that allows a member to "reserve" certain bill numbers, the majority member not only stole his rival's bills, but also gave them a lower number, thus giving the impression that he was the victim of theft rather than the thief.

Agenda-Setting and Initiation

Tracing the true parentage of a bill is a tricky enterprise because participants in the process often lie. Staff persons and lobbyists often try to hide their true roles even as politicians generally exaggerate theirs. In any case, the path of innovation is frequently complex. Many bills have parents, godparents, foster parents, midwives, and guardians, many of whom might claim credit. Most basically, there is a distinction between an original source of agitation and the actual initiator of legislative action. The distinction here is similar to that made by Anderson and other students of public policy between "agenda setting," which establishes the general parameters

Table 7.1

Source and Legislative Parent of 100 Legislative Proposals in the New York State Assembly, 1985–1986

Legislative parent	Original source of the idea for legislation						
	Member	Staff	Lobby	State	Local	Other	Total
Member	16	3	5	3	15	10	52
Legislative staff	0	2	1	3	3	0	9
Lobbyist	0	0	11	1	0	0	12
Governor/state agency	1	0	0	5	5	0	11
Local official/ constituent	0	0	0	2	9	2	13
Other	0	0	0	0	1	2	3
Totals	17	5	17	14	33	14	100

Source: Edward Schneier, "On the Origins of State Legislative Issues: The New York State Assembly, 1985–86," paper delivered at the 1987 Annual Meeting of the Southwestern Political Science Association, Dallas, Texas, March 18–21, 1987, p. 15.

of policy problems, and "initiation," which is the "development of appropriate and acceptable proposals for ameliorating" these agenda issues.[7]

In many instances, the distinction between agenda setting and initiation is moot. In 1985, for example, a member of the assembly—ordered by his physician to reduce his salt intake—was frustrated to discover that few food labels provided the necessary information. Acting as both initiator and agenda-setter, he introduced a bill requiring sodium labeling. Even in a seemingly simple case such as this, others were involved. To draft his bill, the assemblyman found an existing law requiring sugar labeling and simply substituted the word *salt* for *sugar* every time it appeared. Clearly a twofold scheme overlooks the role of other important forces that are sometimes involved in the development of legislative issues. Since all bills have a starting point—the point at which someone says "there ought to be a law"—and a point at which they become concrete proposals, these are the points analyzed in Table 7.1.

What this table shows most strikingly is the extent to which legislators themselves are policy entrepreneurs. They think in terms of making laws. In the 1985–1986 session, 17 percent of the ideas for new legislation came from members themselves, and more than half the legislative solutions crafted to meet these problems and others were devised by legislators. The second most common source of legislative issues was local government officials, a finding that—given the nature of state-local relations—is not surprising. Every time a local government wishes to change its boundaries or tax rate, the only recourse of local officials is the legislative process. If there are surprises in Table 7.1, they arise in connection with the limited roles of interest groups and the executive branch.

Low levels of interest group activity in initiating legislation contradict traditional theories that quite consistently overstate the importance of lobbyists. Groups are an important source of ideas for legislation, but even allowing for the reluctance of either legislators or lobbyists to acknowledge their true roles, failure to find more than one bill in five originating with lobbyists points up the essentially defensive nature of most lobbying. Business groups in particular are more concerned about staving off government action than encouraging it. Many groups, moreover, recognizing that close identification with a special interest can be a kiss of death, prefer to work with agendas devised by others.

The Role of the Governor

More striking than the relatively small role of interest groups (sources of only twelve of the 100 bills) was the surprisingly small role played by the governor and executive agencies in initiating legislation. Fourteen bills had their sources in executive actions, but in half these cases the bills were designed to overturn executive actions rather than to fulfill program requests. These figures are misleading in that the sample did not include budget bills, in which governors have tended, with increasing frequency, to place many of their key programs. The fact is that neither the governor's office nor the bureaucracy has been a major source of policy innovation. Governors, like presidents, tend to be involved "at the margins" of legislative gestation, and even those who have appeared dominant "were actually facilitators rather than directors of change."[8] Most governors come into office, particularly in their first terms, with agendas based on promises made during their campaigns. Spitzer's promise of campaign finance reform, for example, made it an issue in the 2007 session, but even a change-oriented governor such as Spitzer could not get his actual proposals onto the Senate floor. Even when a governor does produce a large portfolio of program bills, his legislative agenda is often more symbolic than concrete.

Ideas for legislation are seldom in any real sense "innovations"; most changes in public policy involve incremental shifts in existing law.[9] Frequently the ideas for such changes come from those most affected by existing policies: constituents and local government officials in particular. Bureaucrats tend to be more cautious, preferring to work around laws that are working badly than to propose new laws. Most people with ideas for changes in policy take their problems right to the legislature, where most legislators like to introduce new bills and do so frequently.

The Art of Drafting

Each lawmaker is assigned a bill drafter to put legislative concepts into proper form. The bill drafting offices of the two parties in each house are staffed by valued professionals whose skills at the least can inoculate against legal problems if bills become law. Although the professionalism of these offices is beyond question, bill drafters do work for the leadership: unlike the legislative counsel offices in Washington, they are not bipartisan. Even if they do not always put the leadership's spin on issues, they can be slow to draft bills that go against party policy, and they may keep the speaker or majority leader up-to-date on bills that might cause problems. Tensions between bill drafters and politicians are common. As one bill-drafter wrote:

> Our drafting conference proceeded smoothly as long as the discussion centered on the broad objectives to be accomplished by the new legislation. But, as always, there were subordinate policy issues of which the committee had not thought until the draftsman raised them and requested the committee's instructions. Which of two administrative bodies should be entrusted with enforcement of the statute, or should an entirely new authority be created to carry the policy into execution? How severe should the sanctions be, and what procedural rights would be guaranteed to persons affected by the statute without interfering too much with its administration?[10]

These tensions do not normally arise when a bill is introduced for symbolic reasons, and many bills are introduced with little prospect of becoming law. Even when a member is simply trying to float an idea for discussion, the relationships between central staff and individual legislators reflect party control. One junior legislator worked with a lobbyist to develop a new approach to school funding. His assigned bill drafter and five other central staff people kept pointing up the complexities of the issue. For months the proposal languished in bill drafting until quite suddenly a leadership bill, only slightly different in its approach, emerged. The junior member stopped pushing for his own. Had he been more senior and secure in his relationship with the speaker, he might have been offered something in return for going along—leadership, as noted in Chapter 6, is a two-way process—but the essential fact is that bill drafting, as much as any part of the process in Albany, flows through party leaders.

This is especially true for minority party members, who soon learn that if they want their programs to have a chance they must recognize that the bill will not go anywhere with their name on it; instead, they need to find a member of the majority party who will agree to shepherd it through. Often, when legislative party control was divided, they relied on the help of a member of the other house to make the needed contacts. One newly elected Republican assemblyman, for example, took a list of bills useful to his district to a senior senator. "We sat down and went through them," he said,

> and he agreed to help, especially with those bills where he had a long working relationship with the Democratic committee chairman in the assembly. But there were four or five bills where he said I was on my own. "What is this," I thought, "a test?" And I'm still not really sure if that's what it was; but I went around to the Democrats and found someone for every bill. And some of them were actually quite helpful, though of course we both knew that the bill—if it passed—would have their name on it and not mine.

Since 2009, when the Democrats secured control of both houses, the task of a Republican policy entrepreneur has become more difficult. Minority party members are now almost entirely on their own.

The Asking Price

Program supporters must address a number of strategic questions. First is the asking price:

> When a person thinks of selling a car, three figures usually come to mind: the price one would like; the price one expects; and, finally, the asking price. If sellers ask too much, they run the risk of frightening off would-be purchasers. If they ask too little, there is no room for bargaining. Framers of a bill face the same problem. In the case of appropriation bills, agencies do not usually request all the money they feel they could profitably use. At the same time, it is important not to ask too little. If you don't do some "padding" or leave room for bargaining, you find, in the colorful words of one official, that "you get cut and you'll soon find that you are up to your ass in alligators."[11]

The problem does not apply only to money bills. Many activists in the right-to-life movement would prefer a ban on all abortions and contraception as well. Although some states once had laws of this kind, New York would be highly unlikely to ban contraceptives or all abortions. Rather than fight battles they know they will lose, activists in the movement have focused on popular proposals like banning late-term abortions and requiring parental consent, which offer a better chance of success and serve as levers for raising the public's conscience.

Packaging

The state legislature is allowed to consider multisection, nonfiscal bills. That means that a lot of laws can be amended in one overall bill, sometimes called an omnibus bill. Bill drafters take care to determine which section of the existing law should be amended first as that can determine which committee has jurisdiction over the bill. More important, since the governor's line-item veto extends only to bills increasing expenditures, it is possible for a clever bill drafter to hide controversial changes in larger packages of popular proposals. The advantage of a narrowly drafted bill is that it focuses attention on the issue and limits the list of potential groups whose opposition might be aroused by a broader measure. The more limited the scope, in other words, the less the chance of being dragged down by peripheral fights. If, on the other hand, the goal is to push a controversial idea, it may be best to surround it with a package of more popular items in an omnibus bill. This strategy often is used to please both sides in a difficult bargaining situation. In 1997, for example, the governor's proposal to cut local school taxes was not popular with assembly Democrats, who objected to its caps on school spending; the governor was not pleased with Democratic attempts to extend prekindergarten classes and reduce class sizes. Since neither side quite trusted the other, the solution was to put both the tax cut and the proposal for smaller classes in the same omnibus bill. The packaging of bills is more important in New York than in Congress or most other state legislatures. This is because the assembly and senate have a long tradition of not amending bills, either in committee or on the floor. Indeed, senate rules do not allow a committee to amend a bill in any way. Provisions buried in an omnibus bill must be accepted or rejected as part of the package. This is true as well of budget bills and is one of the reasons that party leaders have tended to load more legislative language into the budget.

Whatever the package it comes in, the sponsor of legislation also must decide how specific to be in detailing what actions will be covered, who will enforce the policy, and so on. Leaving it to the administration to develop the specific rules (the "regs") is fine if the legislator trusts the administrators. Vagueness also can make it easier to get a bill through the legislature. The less said about how, when, and where, the easier it often is to get agreement in principle. More serious problems arise when trust breaks down. Both Warren Anderson and Ralph Marino frequently skirmished with Mario Cuomo, but they generally trusted him—once an agreement was reached—to follow through. Assembly speaker Silver did not, by most accounts, have that kind of trust in Governor Pataki, and neither Silver nor Bruno had much confidence in Eliot Spitzer. Governor Paterson, having served in the senate, is better known (and better liked). Some of the problems causing late budgets in the past decade derived from an insistence by the leadership on carefully detailing how allocated funds would be spent.

Relation to Existing Legislation

Another key decision a legislative draftsperson must make is whether to create a new statutory title or amend existing language. The problem is confounded by the fact that many existing statutes have been substantially modified by subsequent regulations and court rulings. In some fields of policy, the revised statutes and regulations are so dense that it is almost impossible to add to them without repealing some old rules and revising others.

Every bill must be accompanied by a memorandum explaining the bill's general provisions and, if necessary, including a "repealer" section showing just which existing laws will be eliminated. There is, however, no legal requirement that these memos be true or, in fact, that bills themselves be clearly written; some bills, in fact, are quite misleading. While most of these errors are probably unintentional, deliberate deception is not unheard of. A classic case of deceptive bill drafting was once perpetrated by Robert Moses, head of the Long Island Park Commission. The story, as told by Robert Caro, is as follows: in 1924, Moses drafted a bill defining the commission's powers. Buried in the bill was a clause empowering the commission to acquire land by condemnation and appropriation "in the manner provided by section fifty-nine of the conservation law." To most legislators, the word *appropriation* meant simply "an allocation of funds by the legislature," and none of them thought there might be anything worth checking in the 1884 laws. But Moses knew, as Caro writes,

> that in that section "appropriation" had quite a different meaning. Worried in 1883 about incursions by lumbering companies into the Adirondack forests, the legislature empowered the Conservation Commission to condemn the forests to preserve them. But during that year, between the start of condemnation proceedings and the actual transfer of title, the lumbermen stripped the parcels of their trees. In 1884, therefore, the legislature passed section fifty-nine of the conservation law empowering the state to "appropriate" the forest lands and defining "appropriation" as a procedure in which a state official could take possession of the land by simply walking on it and telling the owner he no longer owned it.[12]

The growth of legislative staff makes it far less likely that a contemporary Robert Moses could pull so blatant a power grab, and some forms of deceptive bill drafting are prohibited by newer rules. Indeed, the requirement that every bill be accompanied by an explanatory memo has its roots in such abuses. But the growing complexity of policy issues increases the likelihood that new statutes will impact on old ones in ways that even their sponsors may not have predicted. New York's court of appeals has established an office to deal with legislative relations, and both the governor and the attorney general have shown growing interest in the question, but many areas of law have become so complicated that confusion is built into the process. Unlike many other legislatures, moreover, New York's senate and assembly committees do not file explanatory reports with the bills they file, leaving members with only the sponsor memo (and perhaps the advice of a friendly lobbyist) to guide interpretation.

Sponsorship

The next big decision about a bill is who should be the lead sponsor. The lead or prime sponsor is the person who "carries" the bill and will lead its debate if the bill reaches the floor. Sponsorship is critical. Most legislation, other than home rule legislation (bills dealing with purely local issues at the formal request of local governments), should be introduced by a majority party member if it is to have a serious chance of passage. Under divided government this can be tricky since it requires finding a Republican in the senate and a Democrat in the assembly. It is even better to have the appropriate committee chairs as the bill's prime sponsors.

The question of cosponsorship then becomes important. Cosponsorship of difficult legislation is a sign of political support that can be used to convince the leadership to allow a bill to the floor. In New York, there are two forms of cosponsorship. Any cosponsor, accepted as such by the bill's prime sponsor, can claim part of the credit for the bill if the governor signs it into law. Being listed as a coprime sponsor is a step up that can win a member not only partial credit, but also a "pen certificate" as a trophy if the bill becomes law. (Governors use a lot of pens at bill-signing ceremonies.) Sometimes the coprimes are the most important sponsors, whose work is essential to getting the bill passed. Many senior committee chairs will give routine departmental bills (that is, bills—usually technical in character—drafted by state agencies) to junior members of that committee to carry as the prime sponsor. The junior member is the lead debater on the bill if it is debated and gets the "chapter," as successful legislation passed into law is sometimes called. (Most legislation is introduced as a chapter amendment to existing laws.) The committee chair will then become a coprime sponsor, just to send a signal to other members that the bill—despite its humble origins—really is important, and to join the floor debate if opposition appears. In some cases, a member can gain a measure of immortality by being a prime sponsor. While few modern co-op owners know anything about former legislators Alfred Lama and MacNeil Mitchell, they know that they live in what everyone calls "Mitchell-Lama housing."

When Brian Murtaugh first became an assemblyman in 1980, it was common to cast a wide net in seeking cosponsors. A bipartisan list of cosponsors, sometimes even including coprimes, was considered an asset in the assembly and, more important, in gaining senate cooperation. This is seldom true today. Indeed, it is unusual for an assembly Democrat or senate Republican even to request support for a bill by sending a "Dear Colleague" letter to members of the minority party. Within party ranks, you are faced with the choice of asking strategic members for active support or sending out a description of the bill with an opportunity for members to sign up as supporters. While there is certainly strength in numbers, it can dilute the credit-claiming possibilities available to key players if you limit your search for sponsors; and in the perverse logic of politics, a long and strong list of cosponsors may be viewed as indicating weakness rather than strength: if you have the support of both the committee chair and party leadership, why do you need coprimes?

Moving a Bill

Former assemblyman Jerry Nadler (now a U.S. congressman) describes the Albany legislative process as "a big wind tunnel where you can see legislation go in at the front, but you sometimes don't see what happens to it inside that wind tunnel until it is too late. You just know that it is not coming out the other end. There are a lot of places inside that wind tunnel where your bill can stick and your job is to track its progress as closely as you can." Nadler tells of one piece of legislation that he was trying to pass on behalf of some statewide women's groups in the 1980s. State senator Mary Goodhue was the senate sponsor, and there was considerable concern over the bill's chances in the senate, where the issue was more controversial. The women's groups therefore concentrated their lobbying on Goodhue and her colleagues. They were so successful that Goodhue's strong support of what was really a Nadler bill persuaded the senate leadership to put the bill high on its "trade list" with the assembly at the end of session. Recognizing this concern, the assembly's top staff negotiators held the Goodhue bill hostage for a bill the assembly had on its trade list. This was a miscalculation. The senate would not trade for another assembly bill, and by the time assemblyman Nadler found out, it was too late to get the bill to the assembly floor in time to be passed that year. It passed the next session, but unexpected problems like that one can sometimes be fatal.

In examining legislation before the assembly, former chief counsel to the speaker, Ken Shapiro, liked to ask three basic questions: "Who is for it? Who is against it? How much does it cost?" The answers to these questions and assessments of their political weights can give a rough idea of a bill's chances. Even when support is strong, opposition weak, and resources abundant, however, there is no sure thing in politics. But the wind tunnel in Albany, as congressman Nadler now concedes, is far less mysterious and complex than in Congress. In Albany, success depends essentially on the member's ability to convince the party's leadership that the bill is worthwhile and, in turn, on the party leaders' ability to convince the governor and the leadership of the other house that the bill should go forward. Although there are in Albany, as in Washington, many spots in the legislative wind tunnel where a bill can mysteriously or perversely become stuck, the general rule is essentially the same: it takes only one negative decision to kill a bill; it takes many positive steps to make it into law.

Having drafted a bill and found whatever cosponsors seem useful, the member hopes that the leadership will accept the suggestion for committee referral. The bill must receive a sponsor's request for committee consideration (called a "99 request" in the assembly and a "form 63" in the senate). Since lobbyists and citizens have become more sophisticated in realizing that a bill that is not "99'd" is almost purely symbolic, most bills now are given that formal designation, even if the sponsor may privately let the committee staff know otherwise. Conversely, when a bill will not be passing the committee, a majority party sponsor will receive a phone call from the chair's office, asking that the bill be "held at sponsor's request." This saves the chair from having to give the committee a negative recommendation and saves the sponsor from the embarrassment of losing. Even when they have the votes to win, most sponsors withdraw such bills because they know it is essentially the committee chairs who determine whether bills will even be voted on and that inventive chairs can find other ways to kill bills further down the road.[13] In most U.S. legislatures, there are procedures for bypassing or, to use the technical term, "discharging a committee." Technically, it would be possible in New York for a majority of either house to force a bill out of any committee and bring it to a vote, but the process is so cumbersome that no one can recall its ever having happened. The exception, and it is a big exception, is the rules committee, which, in either house, can pull a bill from any committee to itself.

The most visible legislative proposals tend to be governor's program bills or those sponsored by the legislative leadership. Program bills usually are taken seriously, but are likely to pass only when they have leadership support. Generally, program bills from a Republican governor will not be taken up in the Democratic assembly until after they have passed the senate (and vice versa), when both houses are controlled by the same party there is no fixed rule, but the assembly tends to act first. A bill listing the speaker or senate majority leader as lead sponsor is generally considered a sure thing in chamber, but has no particular standing in the other body. "Departmental bills," though not of the same status as governor's program bills, also are given serious attention at the committee level. Indeed, departmental bills usually are carried by the chair of the committee of jurisdiction or someone whom the chair has designated for the honor. Such sponsorship does not mean that the committee chair necessarily supports the legislation. Sometimes a committee chair will sponsor the bill in order to control or even kill it. A bill sponsor cannot guarantee that a bill can pass, but generally *can* control its not passing and will be consulted about revisions. No bill moves unless the lead sponsor approves or unless the leadership folds it into negotiations on the budget. Sponsor control even applies to sending a bill to the governor after it passes both houses. The house that passes the bill first controls its submission to the governor, and the sponsor will play a key role in timing the process. Sometimes bills can be sent to the governor's desk and pulled back before the ten working days limit for the governor to veto. This also is part of bill negotiations, when the governor's office may need more time. Twice in the recent history of the legislature, bills that were passed by both houses never were officially submitted to the governor. Although there is no legal justification for such withholding—senate and assembly rules clearly mandate transmittal—it may be politically convenient to ignore the rules. It is unlikely that a lawsuit would be sufficiently timely to produce action or that the courts would not rule the issue essentially political and let the bill die.

Dual Committee Reference

There are three committees in each house that have "dual reference" power. These are the codes committee, ways and means in the assembly and finance in the senate, and the rules committee. The codes committee only can demand jurisdiction (called a flag for the mark that is put next to the bill) if the bill affects the criminal code. The ways and means and finance committees only can flag bills that have fiscal implications. In theory, the committees should consider only the bill's code or fiscal implications, not its merits. The reality may be that the sponsor will have to fight for the bill on the merits all over again in each committee as if they were committees of jurisdiction. The ways and means committee, in fact, is known as the Bermuda Triangle: bills go in there and are forever lost. What is particularly difficult about this committee is that it rarely schedules public debate. The committee staff can make a negative recommendation, the chair will report that recommendation, and the bill is dead.

Bills that are introduced early in the legislative session (most are introduced in

---

Box 7.1
The Rules Committees

Both houses have rules committees, but there are significant differences in how they work in each house and under different leaders. In the senate, the committee tends to hold regular public meetings. Often, in fact, lobbyists attend senate rules committee meetings in order to see what bills will be appearing on the senate calendar. The assembly rules committee is similarly composed largely of senior members and is only supposed to serve the largely routine function of routing and pacing the legislative flow of traffic. This limitation on the power of the assembly rules committee was a reform that the Democratic study group—a caucus of liberal junior members—negotiated in the mid-1970s to open the flow of legislation to the floor. Although the argument was made that these limitations did not challenge the power of the speaker, who already had the ability to influence what came out of the standing committees in the first place, few speakers were comfortable with the reform, and the assembly rules committee seldom met. "The rules committee," as one committee chair once put it, "meets in the speaker's hat." Generally the committee was a front for the speaker's staff deciding in what order bills will reach the floor during the end-of-session rush. This is partly true of the senate rules committee as well, though majority leaders have used the committee as a sort of party executive committee communicating between the party leadership and the other members of the party conference.

In a series of reforms adopted in 2003 and 2005, the assembly reinvigorated its rules committee and simultaneously limited its power. Assembly committees now have a much longer time in which to bring bills directly to the floor; only in the last few weeks of the session must they go through the rules committee. And though the committee still has the power to report a bill that another committee has tried to kill, the fact that rules committee actually meets regularly gives committee chairs a forum to make their case. Together with the party leaders, the rules committees are still very much in charge of whether and when the assembly and senate vote on a bill. What has changed, particularly in the assembly, is the tendency for these decisions actually to be made by the rules committee instead of by the speaker and the speaker's staff. The end-of-session lines of assembly bill sponsors that once formed outside the office of the speaker's council are now increasingly focused on the committee on rules.

---

the first few weeks of January) and are reported out of the standing committees reach the floor each week and are put on the legislative calendar that is published each Monday. Starting in mid-April, the number of bills reaching the floor increases to a point where the rules committees take jurisdiction. Thereafter, only bills that are reported by rules go to the floor. Although the rules committees of the assembly and senate differ in some respects (see Box 7.1) and are largely agents of the majority party leadership, the assembly in particular has opened a window of reform.

Thus the end-of-session flow of legislation, once regulated almost entirely by the speaker and senate majority leader, is beginning to open up. One sure sign that the legislature nearing adjournment used to be the line of sometimes quite senior members queued up outside the speaker's chief counsel's office, looking to get their bill either reported to the floor or put on the assembly trade list. Those lines are still there, but the rules committee now provides another road to the floor.

Getting to the Floor

When a bill is sent to the floor from a committee, it is given its first "reading" and printed on the senate or assembly calendar. The next day that the calendar is printed, the bill is on second reading. Not until it appears on the official "order of third report" can it come to a vote. The rules committee can make special exceptions, saving a day in the process, by reporting bills to the "order of special report." And the governor has the power to compress the process into a single day by issuing what is known as an "order of necessity." These fast-tracking devices are usually important only in the hectic days of putting the budget together or during the end-of-session rush. They are important in New York because of its tradition of not amending bills. Thus, if the assembly will agree to a senate bill only if it contains a clause not in the original senate bill, the only way to amend the senate bill is to report a new draft that would otherwise have to "age" three days before coming to a vote. Here again, the revitalized assembly rules committee, still speaker-dominated to be sure, is becoming a more important force.

Almost as quickly as bills move to the floor they can be moved back off, usually through a process known as starring. The sponsor of a bill may at any time request that a star be placed on the bill on the calendar. Legislative leaders used to have the power to star bills, but this power was relinquished by the assembly speaker in the Democratic study group reforms of the 1970s and by the senate majority leader in 2005. A star may be removed only by the sponsor or, in the senate, by the majority leader. In practice, of course, stars are almost always leadership devices, since it would be folly for an individual legislator to refuse to star a bill that the leadership opposes. As a general rule, stars are used to give party leaders and concerned lobbyists the bargaining time needed to work out deals with the governor and the other house of the legislature. Many, if not most stars are requested by bill sponsors, but the leadership's power to effectively keep bills off the floor is unique in the American states. Former senator Franz Leichter once described leadership stars as the "most absolute, undemocratic procedure that can possibly exist,"[14] which is one of the reasons they were abolished, but the reality is that with or without a star, control of the rules committee and the calendar gives the leaders of both houses a measure of agenda control found in no other American legislature. Thus, shortly after the senate reforms in 2005, the chair of the senate environmental conservation committee pushed a bill through to the floor before the new deadline requiring approval by the rules committee (which had killed a similar bill the year before).

Although the bill had been reported by an eleven-to-one majority in committee and reportedly had the support of more than three-quarters of the senate, the majority leader simply refused to put it on the "active" list, so the bill died.[15]

Studies of party influence in legislatures have tended to emphasize the agenda-setting powers of leaders who can directly "manipulat[e] the policy choices that are available for consideration" or indirectly induce other legislators to structure, bias, and block the consideration of issues.[16] Both directly and indirectly, formally and informally, the agenda-setting powers of New York's majority party leaders are extraordinary. As in all questions of party leadership, however, the powers of the assembly speaker and senate majority leader are powers of agency as well as command. Both directly and indirectly, leaders become leaders and remain leaders by gaining and maintaining the support of their respective party conferences. How far leaders respond indirectly to their conferences in exercising agenda control cannot be measured, but there is abundant evidence that the many hours each party spends in conference are in no small part devoted to such questions. A telling example can be found in two successive assembly considerations of the issue of capital punishment.

In 1995, George Pataki made Mario Cuomo's opposition to capital punishment a cornerstone of his campaign to unseat the governor. When the legislature convened in 1996, assembly speaker Sheldon Silver—himself a supporter of the death penalty—argued in the Democratic party conference that the party would suffer if it did not allow the issue to come to a vote on the floor. On a close, hotly contested vote, the conference agreed. A decade later, when the statute passed in 1996 was ruled unconstitutional by the court of appeals, Silver proposed passing a new bill correcting the flaws found by the court. This time the Democratic conference turned him down. Clearly the conference, not the speaker, was the agenda setter.

Debate

While there are interesting exceptions, committee meetings seldom produce surprise outcomes. According to the examination of major issues reported in 1997 through 2001 by the Brennan Center for Justice, 83 percent of the committee votes in the assembly were unanimous, as were 90 percent in the senate: "committee members overwhelmingly follow the lead of the committee chair in their votes, either literally by allowing the chair to vote their proxies, as routinely occurs in the senate, or by simply voting with the chair as a matter of course. Rank-and-file members do not have significant influence over the committee's ultimate consideration of a bill."[17] Actually, the proportion of bills producing split outcomes is remarkably high, especially in light of the fact that most proposed laws are either purely local (since any county or municipal tax increase must be approved by the legislature) or noncontroversial (such as a resolution saluting a New York sports team for winning a championship). While the usual protocol is for members who disagree with the chair to resolve the issue privately before the committee meets, the Brennan

Center's figures indicate that dissenting opinions quite frequently are voiced, even if they seldom change committee outcomes.

Full-scale debate is even less common on the assembly and senate floors than it is in committee. Fewer than 5 percent of the major bills considered by the Brennan Center were debated in either chamber. On session days, typically Monday, Tuesday, and Wednesday, the clerk will call the bills on third report in the order listed and votes will be taken without debate on those that are not controversial. A special consent calendar allows these routine matters—mostly dealing with local issues—to move quickly unless there is dissent. When all the noncontroversial bills are disposed of, consideration of more controversial bills begins. Although the majority party is always in firm control and almost never loses a vote, on rare occasions debate can be both vigorous and influential. Even the usually irrelevant minority party can be important if it uncovers substantive problems in a bill. Minority party arguments, moreover, may portend the kinds of problems a bill may encounter in the other house. On major bills, if significant arguments emerge, the leadership usually will recess to the party conference room for a candid, intraparty strategy session. If the really unexpected has happened, a bill at this point may be starred pending preparation of a new bill. Generally, however, mid-session party conferences are used to count heads, make sure there are enough votes to pass the bill, and discover how many members, if any, will be voting with the opposition.

Voting

Almost no decisions in the New York state legislature are made by voice vote or show of hands. Virtually every significant issue is decided by an electronically recorded roll call that becomes a matter of public record. There are three kinds of roll calls. Most common are the so-called fast roll calls, which were designed to expedite consideration of uncontroversial bills. In a fast roll call, the clerk calls the names of the first and last persons in the alphabetical list and the majority and minority leaders. Every member who has activated his or her electronic device is then recorded as having voted in the affirmative. Until 2005 in both houses, members were recorded as voting Yes whether they were actually present and voting or not. Those who wished to vote No had to push the No button and have their names specifically recorded. Fast roll calls on final passage were eliminated by the assembly in 2005, but are still common in the senate. Similar to fast roll calls are party votes. Here the party leaders agree to record all their respective members as voting in opposition to the other party: exceptions, as in fast roll calls, can be made, but unless a legislator specifically requests otherwise, all Republicans will be recorded as voting No, let us say, and all Democrats Yes. It is a rare day that individual members make such requests.

The third kind of roll call, slow roll calls, is the most fun to watch. Although everyone knows that the majority party is not going to lose—the leadership would not have allowed the bill to come to a vote if it had not counted a winning margin in advance—there are frequently unpredictable votes. In the ten to fifteen minutes that members have to push the buttons that will activate a green light for yes and a red for no, the board shows not only how each member is voting, but how long it takes them to make up their minds, or who, if anyone, changes his or her vote in light of how others are voting. Most interesting are those occasional votes in which the parties do not take positions.

As in Congress and in most states, a variety of organizations rate the members of the legislature on the basis of their roll call voting records. Thus the AFL-CIO evaluates members on their pro-labor records, the American Civil Liberties Union on their support for civil liberties, and the Farm Bureau on the percentage of agricultural issues on which individual legislators vote a pro-farm position. General "liberalism" scores are calculated by Americans for Democratic Action, with a "conservatism" index from CHANGE-NY serving as its mirror opposite. While the rating numbers generated by these groups provide a rough index of where individual members stand, the pervasive influence of the parties makes these ratings considerably less meaningful in New York than in most other states.

The End of Session

It is hard to describe exactly the end-of-session rush in the last few weeks of the legislative year. This crunch time has to be witnessed to be fully appreciated. Legislative sessions invariably end with a flurry of activity marked by two to three weeks of intensive work, usually capped by a weekend and an all-night session that can last well past dawn. In almost all legislatures, the flow of business follows the same pattern: early in the session there is a flood of initiation with dozens, even hundreds of new bills coming from the printer every day. This flood of proposals slows to a trickle as the session winds down, but the pace of enactment flows in the opposite direction. In the early months, while the leadership's attention is focused on the budget, committees are getting organized, and bills are being circulated for cosponsorship, almost nothing happens on the floor. A tourist, venturing into the senate or assembly chamber on a cold Tuesday in February, might see the legislature convene, spend an hour or so welcoming various visiting groups, engage in perfunctory debate on one or two bills (already defeated in the other house the year before), vote, and adjourn. That same tourist, arriving in the heat of late June, would see bills debated in a matter of minutes, ten or twenty roll calls an hour, and a legislature sometimes in session (or in party conference) for upward of twenty hours a day.

The 1999 session was somewhat atypical in that continuing arguments over the budget kept both bodies in session for a few extra weeks in July and August. But the rhythm of the session was typical. The senate passed 21 bills in January, 53 in February, 154 in March, and 135 in April—a total of 363 in the first four months. In June it passed 789, with almost 500 of these passing on June 14 through June 17, just before adjournment. The pattern in the assembly was much the same. In typical fashion, more than half the bills enacted in both houses passed in the last month, with 497 of the session's 1,580 bills passing one or both houses in the last four days alone. For the years 1997 to 2001, the Brennan Center found that approximately one bill in every four was passed in the final three days.[18]

A number of institutional reasons dictate this end-of-session rush. First, it naturally takes time for bills to work their way through the legislature, especially if they are compromise bills that require a lot of negotiation. Second, reluctant negotiators often need to make a tough decision about a bill that in theory could be negotiated forever in order to reach a final agreement that—without a deadline—they might never accept. Third, it is not uncommon, particularly in divided government, for one bill to be linked to another, related bill in such a way that, for example, senate acceptance of an assembly mass transit package becomes contingent upon assembly acceptance of a highway bill. The last reason is that many bills are linked politically in passage with other bills that may not be related in substance. One mid-Western party leader talked of "keeping as many House-filed [bills] in the bank as possible," and the former speaker of the Vermont house referred to "the normal hostage taking of bills," practices that seem to apply throughout the country.[19] All these bills will be done together. Unfortunately, that can make for sloppy drafting by exhausted staff members who have barely slept for the last week. The bills are then voted upon by equally exhausted lawmakers. At the end, this process takes on a life of its own, and nobody really controls the situation. Weary lawmakers still will be at their desks at five in the morning, waiting for revised bills to be delivered from the printer. The session continues until the bitter end because people are afraid that agreements will become unraveled if too much time lapses after agreement is reached. While the frantic pace at the end of a session sometimes allows really bad legislation to sneak through, what is more frequently the case is that a number of probably useful proposals never get passed.

Resolving Differences Between the Senate and Assembly

In order for a bill to be sent to the governor, it must be passed in identical form by both the senate and assembly. A bill that has passed one house is treated as a new bill in the other house and referred to the appropriate committee. If the committee chooses to send it to the floor unchanged, it is called a "unibill" and, if passed, can be referred directly to the governor. If, on the other hand, the committee chooses to pass its own bill—even if it differs in only the tiniest detail—it cannot become law without further action by the other house. On routine policy issues, when the assembly and senate pass different versions of the same essential bill, the committee chairs or their staffs will meet to see if a compromise can be reached. The assembly or senate may then agree to pass the other body's bill, or entirely new bills—embodying whatever compromises have been reached—may be passed in both houses. When relations between committee chairs are not cordial, lobbyists frequently act as go-betweens in these negotiations. On larger issues, and when negotiations fail, the bills are kicked up to the leadership. In some cases, where both sides generally want to act but have been unable to reach common ground on the details, high-ranking staff assistants attempt—in consultation with their respective committee chairs—to work out a deal. In many other cases, no action is taken because nobody really wants an agreement. The overwhelming majority of bills passed by both the assembly and senate are, in fact if not by design, one-house bills passed for ideological reasons or as bills to please individual members or lobbyists. In 2001, rather typically, 662 bills were passed by both houses and sent to the governor; 900 passed the senate but not the assembly, and 823 passed the assembly but not the senate.[20]

When one house or the other is serious about a bill rejected in the other body, the bill goes on a list of items—the trade list—to be negotiated by the party leaders either as part of the overall budget deal or during the end-of-session rush. For individual assembly and senate members, committee chairs in particular, and for lobbyists, a key test of their influence lies in their ability to get party leaders to put their bills on the trade list. This in itself is not easy, but it is still not enough. Even if the bill is passed by both houses, it must still go to the governor before it goes into the books. In the U.S. Congress and in all but two other state legislatures, differences between the two houses often are worked out in conference committees drawn from the appropriate standing committees of each house.[21] New York recently has begun to experiment with such committees, particularly, as covered in Chapter 8, in putting together the budget, but they have yet to become a consistently significant part of the legislative process in Albany. Whether the party leaders of either house ever would surrender their control over interhouse negotiations is problematic at best, particularly with both houses controlled by the same party.

The Governor Votes

The governor may sign a bill into law; if the governor fails to take action on a bill within ten days, it becomes law automatically. One peculiarity of New York politics, however, is the relatively high frequency of gubernatorial vetoes and the fact that these vetoes almost are never overridden. In analyzing the history of the veto, Zimmerman described the governor's veto power as "nearly absolute," and the term still applies.[22]

When a bill is sent to the governor, he or she has ten days in which to veto it or sign it, or thirty days after the legislature has adjourned. Technically, the governor also can "pocket veto" a bill by simply not acting on it after the legislature has adjourned. Customarily, New York governors have not used this device and in recent years could not have because the legislature has not formally adjourned. Stung by various governors' use of the period following adjournment to make unpopular interim appointments to the courts and various agencies, the senate and assembly have adopted the practice of recessing instead of adjourning when regular business is done. To meet the technical requirements of the constitution, a senator and an assemblyman from the Albany area actually go to the capital every weekday to convene a "session" that lasts just long enough for a quick prayer from the chaplain and a banging of the gavel. In order to give the governor time to consider the enormous flow of bills coming out of the end-of-session rush, the legislature has adopted the process of also using these mock sessions to spread the flow of bills to the governor. Thus a bill actually passed in June may not be formally "sent" to the governor until September, and it is only then that the ten-day clock begins to tick.

When a bill is sent to the governor, a "bill jacket" is created and the public invited to submit comments. Most affected interested groups and a surprisingly large number of ordinary citizens submit statements or letters that are then filed in the "jacket" folder and placed in a file available to the public for examination in the Capitol library. Less formally, the governor's counsel has the job of consulting with the top officials of those agencies most affected by a potential new law, and—if there are fiscal implications—with the budget office.

Most vetoes are not surprising; many are anticipated and even welcomed: "Sometimes, as Governor Rockefeller once explained, legislators went along with bills to please individual members as a courtesy on local matters only because they were confident there would be a gubernatorial veto. 'I'll be the guy who vetoes the bill,' the governor said. This is all part of the act."[23] Sometimes, indeed, legislators are surprised when the governor fails to veto a bill. This is apparently what happened in 1994 when Governor Cuomo, refusing to take the political heat from Staten Island, instead signed a bill he was "supposed" to veto giving the borough the right to secede from New York City. In 1995, knowing that a veto was not certain, the legislature itself refused to pass the bill.

Particularly through their line-by-line ability to veto increases in budget items, New York governors have made the veto power a significant source of political influence. They can block programs and expenditures that they do not like and also use the threat of a veto to secure support for things they want. Threats of vetoes are an extraordinarily useful tool in dealing with the speaker and majority leader during budget negotiations. Although there are methods by which the legislature can protect itself from certain kinds of budget vetoes, there is no doubt, as Rosenthal concludes, that the governor's veto is "a source of considerable power . . . [that] allows him or her to negotiate from a position of strength both with legislative leaders and with individual members."[24] The persistence of divided government made the veto a particularly potent gubernatorial weapon in New York if only because it put one house or the other in the position of embarrassing its party leader if it voted to override.

The Governor and the Legislative Process

Beyond the veto power, the governor is involved in the legislative process both informally in negotiating with party leaders and formally through budget and program bills, by the exercise of certain procedural powers, and through the issuance of executive orders that carry the force of law. The governor, as we have noted, cannot introduce a nonbudgetary bill without having a member of the legislature as its sponsor. The governor's role as the initiator of legislative issues has been limited in terms of the percentage of bills in the assembly and senate that can be traced to the second floor; but the governor's agenda-setting powers are enormous when defined in terms of the ability to move issues to active status. Bills that have been languishing in Albany for years—as one-house bills or going-nowhere-at-all bills—achieve new status when they are endorsed in the governor's State of the State address, introduced as program bills, or folded into the governor's budget. Except for their first terms, when there are campaign promises to fulfill, governors are seldom policy entrepreneurs. Whatever new directions they take are usually borrowed from someone else, but no other actor in the system can so quickly and surely make issues viable: when the governor gets serious about an issue, others get serious as well.

Once an issue is in the policy stream, the dynamic shifts again. In many ways, even with regard to program bills, the governor is just another lobbyist. Although governors frequently can call in the chips with their own party members, divided government requires negotiation. Thus, in the "normal" legislative process, the modern (post-Rockefeller) state legislature has played an increasingly important role, rising to an equal and sometimes preeminent position. But the legislature has never been able to assert its independence fully in crafting the budget; the more that the flow of budgetary politics overlays the stream of other business, the more the governor is again the dominant player. It is also significant, as we shall see with particular force in our discussion of the budget, that the governor gets to go last. Through regular and line-item vetoes, governors have the last say in the bargaining process. Although it can only be done at some risk to their long-term credibility, governors even may use their veto powers to void deals they had previously agreed to with legislative leaders.

Running on Two Tracks: The Budget and Other Business

The end-of-session rush was made considerably more difficult in the 1990s when the budget adoption was so late that it virtually became the end of the session. Traditionally, the year in Albany—or half year as it usually played out—was divided into three segments. The first period, extending roughly from the opening in the first week of January until the first of March, was devoted to organization, introduction, and preparation. Perhaps the most serious legislative business at this stage was at the staff level in the offices of the party leaders, ways and means, and finance, in preparation for negotiations over the budget. Legislators introduced bills, the governor introduced the budget, committees began to process bills, and party conferences increasingly focused on the budget. Relatively little of substance happened on the floor of either house.

In early to mid-March, the budget took over almost entirely. Typically, the legislative schedule shifted at this point into a higher gear. Members who had been arriving in Albany on Monday and heading home early on Wednesday afternoon now attended five-day sessions. Then, when the budget was passed, the pace receded for a few weeks before rebuilding to the end-of-session rush. The third phase of the process, historically extending from the budget deadline of April 1 through late May or early June, was the time for home rule bills, revisions in the criminal and civil codes, and most of the major (and minor) proposals for nonbudgetary changes in policy.

In 1988 the state's very poor fiscal situation exacerbated tensions between Governor Cuomo and the legislature, and the budget was not adopted until early May. In 1990 it was June. Indeed, between 1988 and 2002 the budgetary process was completed in April only three times. This means that the third stage of the "normal" process was compressed and, to an increasing degree, folded in with the budget. Since most important budget issues were negotiated by the previously described "three men in a room"—the governor, speaker, and senate majority leader—the last few weeks of the session took on an increasingly surreal quality. Prevented by the absence of a budget from moving on to other issues, yet largely peripheral to the main battles, legislators remained stuck in Albany, holding perfunctory sessions, waiting to be consulted and briefed by their leaders in party conferences, swapping rumors with lobbyists and with each other, and hoping for a breakthrough in the negotiations. The legislature's 1998 experiment with conference committees, appointed to work out differences between the houses, made the process more public and involved more members, but it is not clear whether the committees really made any difference, and the likelihood is that hard times—when resource scarcities make decisions more difficult—will take the process back to three men in a room.

With characteristic bluntness, former speaker Mel Miller says, "politics is the budget. Everything else is crap." Some issues do transcend Miller's epithet, but in both temporal and political terms, the budget has become the 500-pound gorilla of legislative politics, crowding or scaring almost everything else out of the arena. Meanwhile, it is worth noting that the process of policy-making neither begins nor ends with the legislature. Governors and bureaucrats make policy; so do the courts.

The Process of Administering and Executing the Laws

On the Thomas E. Dewey Thruway between New York and Albany, the posted speed limit varies between 55 and 65 miles per hour. That is the law. Or is it? The authors can attest from experience that you can go 65 in the 55-mile zones with no fear of being arrested. Generally you can get away with 67 or 68, but pass a radar gun at 70 and you will almost certainly see flashing lights in your rear-view mirror (yes, even if you have "Member of the Assembly" license plates). Since the 65-mile-an-hour limit is relatively new, the rules are less clear: the low 70s are acceptable, but over

75 puts you at risk. What is the real speed limit? Is it the 55 and 65 miles per hour enacted by the legislature, or is it the 67–68, 74–75 actually enforced?

The discretion of the state trooper in this case is matched by the discretion of the bureaucracy. While an occasional academic or political reformer rails against the evils of bureaucratic discretion,[25] most students of politics agree that a certain amount of flexibility is not only necessary but also desirable. The early twentieth-century ideal of dispassionate civil servants neutrally enforcing clearly defined laws has been dismissed as unrealistic. Few citizens would be happy with laws—like speed limits—that were too rigidly enforced, and in many technical areas the problems are simply too complex to be administered without flexibility. The legislature, for example, can set standards for road construction that specify in considerable detail the kinds of materials, thicknesses, gradients, and widths to be used in building new highways, but the particular mix of concrete to be poured in a particular location under varying weather conditions is best left to people more expert in road-building than most legislators. As the early civil service reformers used to argue, there is not a Republican or Democratic way to build a road. Where that road goes, however, is another question. While few citizens or their legislative representatives care whether a road is paved in asphalt or concrete, they do tend to care if it is routed through their homes or someone else's. If decisions such as these are to be made by bureaucrats, the administrative experts designing the highway should be subject to citizen control.

Just what does citizen control mean? In practice it means control exerted by those most closely affected by the policy, and this is where the problems begin. For many students of politics, the problem with citizen control is that the citizens in question are seldom a cross-section of the public. In this view, "what public bureaucrats mostly want to do is use the discretionary powers they confer on themselves to advance the interests of the very private actors—mostly the stockholders and managers of counterpart industries—who the bureaucrats originally were appointed to regulate."[26] In its extreme form, this view posits a set of "subgovernments" or "iron triangles" of specialized bureaucrats, interest groups, and the relevant subcommittees of the U.S. Congress operating with virtual independence from the president and Congress.

Empirical evidence supporting the subgovernment theory is spotty, and students of politics have begun to refer to "interest networks" and "advocacy coalitions" in order to account for the weaknesses of the iron triangles.[27] There remains a sense, however, that many parts of the bureaucracy are not fully accountable either to Congress or to the president. This is less true in New York, where the centralization of legislative and executive powers has seriously undermined the attempts of special interests to construct the kinds of issue networks that can lead to the development of iron triangles. In New York, the budget process gives both the governor and the legislative parties a strong weapon for micromanaging agency decisions. The weakness of the committee system in the legislature, moreover, by weakening a key leg in the structure of iron triangles, makes it more difficult to capture the lower levels of the administration.

This does not mean that the laws are administered without bias. Many environmentalists are convinced that the Department of Environmental Conservation, in its efforts to remove PCBs from the Hudson River, has been unusually lenient toward General Electric. The suspicion that major corporations and privileged individuals sometimes get special treatment is widespread. At the same time, many business leaders feel that government agencies are too meddlesome, too arbitrary in their decisions to make the economy work well. It is an article of faith among conservatives that through "rigid regulations that escalate the price of doing business, small firms are told directly and indirectly that they aren't welcome in New York State."[28] Larger firms sometimes argue that they are especially singled out by overzealous regulators, and there is often justification for this complaint. State law, for example, prohibits a form of deceptive advertising that features only the low-end price. If a week in Paris costs $999 to $1,999, the ad must include both prices in the same size type. With thousands of products advertised every day, the consumer affairs division of the Department of Law tends to enforce these regulations only on the largest offenders. Thus a small travel agency probably can get away with an ad that Liberty Travel cannot.

A certain amount of unevenness in the enforcement of the laws is inevitable. It would be prohibitively expensive and virtually impossible for the attorney general to monitor every travel advertisement in every newspaper and magazine. Similarly, there is no way that the state's Department of Environmental Conservation could monitor all disposals of hazardous waste. Its policy objective is thus "defined in terms of managing most of the waste, not most of the generators." The technical difficulties of its enforcement job are made manageable by the fact that "fewer than 150 companies produce nearly three-quarters of all the state's hazardous waste."[29] While the burden of law invariably falls more heavily on some shoulders than others, the state of New York has taken a number of historical steps to guard against favoritism and corruption in applying the laws. A few weeks after the federal government passed the Pendleton Act in 1883, New York governor Grover Cleveland signed a bill establishing a similar state civil service system that provided that all vacancies in the executive branch would be filled by those scoring highest on objective exams, that promotions would be based on merit, and that civil servants could neither be active in politics nor forced to contribute to campaigns. The state law also required local governments to implement comparable reforms.

As a result, "the New York State civil service system has a reputation as one of the best systems in the nation."[30] Since its establishment, charges of corruption, gross incompetence, and political bias seldom have been heard. One of the key goals of civil service reform was to limit the inclination of government officials to award contracts to other government officials on the basis of politics rather than merit, and in that respect it has been generally successful. Increasingly, moreover, more subtle forms of favoritism have been curtailed by requiring civil servants to implement the laws based on formal rules rather than considerations of the individual case.

Rule-Making

In early New York, and even today in some small towns, governments and citizens interacted face to face. Laws were administered by people who were known to their clients, and town officials exercised considerable discretion in deciding how the laws would apply. Increasingly, however, New York has become a society of formal rules. Indeed, this shift from interpersonal relations to interrelations based on laws is a hallmark of modernization, and it is also part of the democratic creed, which takes pride in providing what John Adams's original draft of the Massachusetts constitution proclaimed "a government of laws and not of men." If civil service reform was designed to take politics out of administration, rule-making is designed to wash out other forms of discrimination and thus neutralize the bureaucracy.

Administrative fairness comes at a price. The more elaborate and carefully designed the rules, the less flexibility bureaucrats are given, and the more likely it is that citizens will complain of bureaucratic insensitivity; and the clearer the rules, the more complicated they become. As Kaufman puts it:

> Were we a less differentiated society, the blizzard of official paper might be less severe and labyrinths of official processes less tortuous. Had we more trust in one another and our public officials and employees, we would not feel impelled to limit discretion by means of lengthy, minutely detailed directives and prescriptions or to subject public and private actions to check after check. If our policy were less democratic, imperfect though our democracy may be, the government would not respond as readily to the innumerable claims upon it for protection and assistance. Diversity, distrust, and democracy thus cause the profusion of constraints and the unwieldiness of the procedures that afflict us.[31]

What we sometimes rail against as red tape is, in other words, a check on arbitrary action, a means of ensuring objectivity and preventing corruption.

Given the complexity of the problems confronting the state, how can such objectivity be ensured? Surely we cannot expect a legislature composed largely of lawyers, teachers, and businesspeople to develop detailed rules governing all aspects of public policy. The senate and assembly can provide general guidelines for Medicare, but it would be absurd to expect them to set specific reimbursement limits for treating strep throats, removing tonsils, or putting casts on broken ankles. They can set general rules for highway safety, but have neither the time nor the training to decide at what point on Route 22 in Hoosick the speed limit should go from 55 to 45 (or should it be 30?). While it is inevitable that bureaucrats must be given some discretionary powers, there must be limits as well, limits that sustain the rule of law. One of the key arguments that Lowi and others have made against delegations of power is that they turn public policy into a series of private deals.[32] If administrators have too much flexibility, Lowi argues, citizens cannot know what rule they need to follow: is it safe to go 75 miles an hour in the 65-mile-per-hour zones? Is the speed limit a matter of fixed practice, which all drivers can understand, or is it the result of negotiations with a state trooper? The answer, increasingly, has been to delegate powers to the bureaucracy not in the form of individual discretion but through the administrative process of rule-making. According to Kerwin's definition, "Rules are products of the bureaucratic institutions to which we entrust the implementation, management, and administration of our law and public policy. . . . The rules issued by departments, agencies, or commissions are law; they carry the same weight as congressional legislation, presidential executive orders, and judicial decisions. . . . Rulemaking occurs when agencies use the legislative authority granted them by Congress."[33] Rule-making is a form of delegated power that stands between statutory law on one hand and bureaucratic discretion on the other.

Rule-making power generally is limited by the agency's defined role of authority in general and its specific statutory authority. The law that created, say, the Department of Agriculture and Markets lays out the broad areas of administrative authority that the agency can exercise. Various statutes—a law, for instance, to encourage organic farming—specifies the particular authority to be exercised. At both the national and state levels, a number of procedural safeguards also have been built into the process. The federal Administrative Procedures Act of 1946, which "was written by Congress to bring regularity and predictability to the decision-making processes of government agencies,"[34] has in general outline been copied by many states, including New York in 1975. Under the 1975 act, new rules may not go into effect within thirty days of publication, until the public has had an opportunity to comment. A 1978 act created the Administrative Regulations Review Commission (ARRC), composed of three members of each house of the legislature, to which all new rules must be submitted.

In practice, the rule-making process in New York typically begins with the statute itself and the guidelines it sets for the agency. Before the new regulations are filed with the secretary of state, they are cleared through the second floor, particularly if they have budgetary implications. A good lobbyist or well-connected legislator usually will have a pretty good idea of the general outlines of the new regs. While the governor's office often suggests modifications at this point, legislators and lobbyists usually will wait until the public comment period to make their case. If administrators and legislative committee chairs have good working relationships, preliminary conversations regarding the intent of the statute already may have taken place. In the formal commentary stage, interest groups, local governments, and individual legislators all will be heard from. In about one of every ten instances, the ARRC will contact the agency with objections to a proposed rule. Whether these suggestions come from the ARRC or from individual legislators, "agencies put a high priority on being responsive to legislators because they wish to foster and maintain positive relationships. When legislators express concern over a particular rule of regulation, agencies consider their comments seriously."[35] If an agency persists, there is always the possibility that the legislature will pass a new law, but the threat of legislation can achieve the same end. The Board of Regents, for example, has long tried to require all students to meet the same standards for achieving degrees, but the legislature has been considerably more sensitive to the special needs of students with disabilities. Thus, when the board attempted to set uniform rules and persisted throughout the review process, a bill was introduced in the legislature to change the statute on which the new regulations were based. The regents withdrew the rule.[36]

At both the federal and state levels, administrative procedure acts have made it difficult for bureaucrats to issue regulations that clearly subvert legislative intent, but some bending of the guidelines is not unusual and even may be encouraged. Those interest groups and legislators that are attentive at the rule-making stage are not always representative of those who were first involved in passing a bill. While all legislators, for example, participate in passing an insurance bill, and while a number of lobbyists may be involved in the legislative process surrounding it, the audience for the rule-making stage is likely to be composed largely of legislators on the insurance committees and lobbyists representing the industry. Rule-making thus meets only part of the objection that critics like Theodore Lowi bring to delegations of legislative power: it limits the discretionary powers of those enforcing the laws; but it does not eliminate—and may even promote—the fragmentation of the policy process into a series of deals negotiated by private interests. Rule-making, as Kerwin puts it,

> frees Congress to attend to many more problems than it would otherwise have time to deal with. It relieves Congress of the burden of maintaining and managing enormous staffs who possess the expertise essential to refining the operating standards and procedures for a myriad of programs. Finally, it is the best means yet found to break legislative deadlocks and to avoid difficult political decisions. On the other hand, as an indispensable surrogate to the legislative process, rule-making has a fundamental flaw that violates basic democratic principles. Those who write the law embodied in rules are not elected; they are accountable to the American people only through indirect and less-than-foolproof means.[37]

At both the state and national levels, there have been attempts to widen the access of a broader public to the rule-making process through the Internet. While these efforts facilitate access, they do not address the real barriers to citizen participation.

> Participating in a rulemaking requires, at a minimum, understanding that regulatory agencies make important decisions affecting citizens' interests, as well as knowing about specific agencies and the new rules they propose. Yet . . . the average citizen, who already shows declining involvement in politics, simply does not know a great deal about regulatory agencies or the policy issues underlying specific rulemakings. Indeed, it is almost a given that most citizens will not possess a good understanding of regulatory policy issues. If Congress delegates rulemaking authority at least partly because certain issues are so complex or technical that they require agency expertise, then the policy issues in rulemakings will tend systematically to be ones that are harder, rather than easier, for citizens to understand.[38]

Not surprisingly, business groups and other government agencies dominate rule-making participation; at the same time, "rules are a form of administrative action that is peculiarly susceptible to presidential [or, in New York, gubernatorial] scrutiny and influence."[39] In both the Clinton and Bush administrations, the White House was enormously active in setting the substance of administrative rules. In his first years in office, Governor George Pataki took an active role in attempting less to make new rules than to restrict the issuance of rules regulating business. His office of regulatory reform, headed by one of his closest advisers, proudly labeled itself the office of "bureaucracy busters" and required each agency's regulations to include a tilted cost-benefit analysis of the rule. In the short run, the office succeeded in essentially stopping the adoption of new regulations; as its original luster faded, however, it became simply another step in confounding and complicating the policy process. Today, though it seldom actively intervenes in the rule-making process, turning its attention largely to the job of facilitating economic development projects, the office continues to function as yet another layer of red tape.

Rule Enforcement

In most agencies, rule-making is separated from implementation. The legislature sets the speed limit, the DOT decides at what spot on the highway the speed limit will drop from 55 to 30, but it is the job of a state trooper or local police officer to decide whether going 63 or 70 in a 55-mile-per-hour zone is "speeding." Compounding the problem of rule enforcement in New York is its decentralized system of governance. More than most states, New York places the problem of implementation in the hands of local officials. Thus rule-making is separated from enforcement by being not only in a different office but at a different level as well. In the Medicaid program, for example, when the legislature (in 1991) enacted a mandatory program of managed care, it required each local service district to develop a specific plan for its patients. Each local plan is subject to state review and must conform to basic guidelines, but each plan is separate and distinct; there is, in other words, no state implementation of the rule.[40]

Similarly, the Board of Regents sets the basic standards of educational quality for the state, but actual implementation is in the hands of hundreds of elected and appointed school boards. Local control of education means that the board can mandate various standards of testing, teacher training, and class size, but will need to struggle constantly to see that these minimal levels are actually sustained. The Board of Regents, like most state agencies, spends a good deal of its efforts enforcing both statute laws and its own regulations on local districts. The comptroller's office is also heavily involved in the process of enforcing state rules on local governments. Finally, the courts play an important role in making sure that local governments meet state standards in enforcing the law.

"Contracting out" has not been as popular in New York as in other states, but a number of services are administered by private corporations and nonprofits. Whether it is a private carting firm that collects the trash in Buffalo or a church's drug treatment center, implementation is removed still another step from hierarchical control. There are strong arguments for privatization and local control, but the price of both is an elaborate structure of audit and control. The more policies are administered by persons who are not directly responsible to agency supervisors, the greater the need for monitoring their actions and ensuring equity. The resulting proportion of New York's civilian employees engaged in the job of managing, controlling, and auditing the others is extraordinarily high.

Corruption and Red Tape

In William Riordan's delightful evocation of Tammany Hall, the party boss, George Washington Plunkitt, carefully distinguishes between "honest" and "dishonest" graft. Taking a bribe, Plunkitt argued, would be dishonest, but seeing one's opportunities and taking them is quite another thing: "Suppos[e] it's a new bridge they're going to build. I get tipped off and I buy as much property as I can that has to be taken for the approaches. I sell at my own price later on and drop some more money in the bank. Wouldn't you? It's just like lookin' ahead in Wall Street or in the coffee or cotton market. It's honest graft and I'm lookin' for it every day of the year."[41]

Americans are more obsessed with official corruption than are the citizens of most other societies: the laws of both Albany and Washington are larded with checks on graft, whether "honest" or "dishonest" in Plunkitt's terms. As Plunkitt implies, the kinds of self-serving maneuvers that are applauded in the world of commerce are frowned upon in government.

There are, in essence, five techniques for limiting corruption: insulation, competitive bidding, audit, disclosure, and the limiting of discretion. The civil service was created, essentially, to insulate the bureaucracy from politics. Because they are not dependent upon politicians for their jobs, civil servants are in theory less likely to be pressured by certain individuals, interests, or communities in making decisions. And just to make sure that they are not getting delayed payoffs, government employees in New York are not allowed to work for private sector employees in their fields for two years after they leave the civil service. There is no doubt that civil service reforms largely freed the civil service from the most overt pressures of political favoritism, but just to make sure that individual bureaucrats do not cut deals of their own, a variety of auxiliary precautions have been built into the system. Competitive bidding generally requires all major purchases and service contracts to be advertised in advance and given to the low bidder. Thus, if an agency is buying new computers, it must solicit bids from at least three companies and buy from the one submitting the lowest bid. To provide a further check on possible corruption, a third set of controls—involving audits, disclosures, and other forms of investigation and exposure—also is required in many areas. Most large agencies have their own divisions of financial audit and control that, together with the office of the state comptroller, regularly audit the books. Government employees routinely are required to disclose aspects of their private lives: many agencies, for example, require periodic reports listing any sources of outside income; most require annual performance reviews; and some require periodic medical exams and drug tests. Special investigations of various agencies and individuals are not uncommon, and of course the press always is interested in stories involving official malfeasance. Even private firms and individuals who work for the state or local agencies are fair game for secret investigations of their finances and aspects of their private lives. In major cases, special prosecutors have been hired to investigate problems and bring offenders to trial (see Box 7.2). Finally, corruption can be controlled by limiting discretion, by erecting elaborate systems of rules and regulations that prescribe exactly how decisions must be handled.

While these checks undoubtedly have reduced the most blatant forms of corruption in state politics and sharply limited its appearance in local government, the pursuit of integrity comes at a price. While no one has systematically tallied the direct costs of testing civil servants, auditing agencies and contracts, investigating both public servants and suppliers, administering drug tests, processing the forms designed to limit conflicts of interest, and so on, there is no doubt that the direct costs of corruption control are substantial and growing. There are numerous indirect costs as well. If the copy machine breaks down in a government office, an administrator cannot simply go to the store and buy another one, as might be done in the private sector, nor call a temporary agency to replace a key worker who is ill. The requirements of competitive bidding and merit hiring that generally guide such acts in government often make it difficult to cope with emergencies of this kind. The number of steps that need to be taken before a purchase order can be processed is extraordinary: in the colleges of the City University of New York (CUNY), it can take months to replace the ink supply of a computer printer. And it takes so many weeks for most suppliers to be paid that many businesses simply refuse to take orders from branches of the CUNY system. In New York and probably in state and local governments more generally, "the public contracting system is in need of major surgery. It is mired in red tape and multiple levels of oversight."[42] The system of competitive bidding, auditing, and investigation requires those contracting with government agencies to jump through so many hoops that many refuse even to try. A cycle has been created in which the "perception that greedy, dishonest contractors are poised to exploit any opportunity to defraud the city has led to more monitoring, double-checks, stringent contract terms, slow payments, and lately the screening of contractors for integrity. In turn, this leads to increased cynicism among contractors who feel that they are being treated like quasi-criminals, and it provides them with a rationalization for further dubious practices. This, in turn, is likely to spawn more safeguards and greater suspicion."[43]

Civil servants are caught in the same trap. Knowing that they might not be able to replace a piece of equipment when it breaks down, they order a new one in ad-

Box 7.2
Special Prosecutors

Prosecuting corruption always has been good politics for ambitious district attorneys. Thomas Dewey was propelled into the governorship in the 1940s largely on the basis of his exposure of the connections between various Tammany leaders and the mob in New York City. Perhaps because of the Watergate investigation, which led to the resignation of President Richard Nixon in 1974, federal law enforcement agencies have become increasingly active in investigating and prosecuting corruption by state and local public officials, but there are circumstances under which even these overlapping layers of regular investigation and prosecution do not work.

In 1970, a series of articles in the *New York Times* uncovered pervasive patterns of bribery and extortion in the operations of the New York City Police Department. A commission to investigate allegations of corruption in the city, popularly known as the Knapp Commission, was appointed by the mayor. It found not only that the accusations were true, but also that in many cases known instances of corruption had not been prosecuted either by the police department's internal affairs divisions or by the city's district attorneys. Because the district attorneys were, as the commission put it, such "close allies" of the police department, only a special anticorruption prosecutor could be counted on to do the job. In authorizing the state attorney general to create the Office of the Special Prosecutor of Corruption, Governor Rockefeller similarly reasoned that "only an independent agency . . . can break through the natural resistance of government agencies to investigate themselves or their close allies, can overcome the force of inertia, and can finally deal a decisive blow to narcotics, crime and corruption in New York City."

The office of the special prosecutor continued to function until 1980, when Governor Cuomo concluded that it had done its job. Since then, numerous special prosecutors have, with varying degrees of success, investigated a wide variety of agencies and individuals, indeed becoming almost a constant force in government. While corruption has by no means been abolished, looming prosecutors have become almost a routine part of the public service. Calls for the appointment of a special prosecutor almost inevitably arise in cases where it is felt that local district attorneys are not doing their job.

Source: Frank Anechiarco and James B. Jacobs, *The Pursuit of Absolute Integrity: How Corruption Control Makes Government Ineffective* (Chicago: University of Chicago Press, 1996), Chapter 7.

vance. Unable to find a contractor willing to work under the conditions specified by law, they rewrite the request for proposals. Lacking authorization to buy a badly needed ink cartridge for the printer, they list it as stationery and conspire with a supplier to submit a phony bill. Auditors, in order to combat these evasions of the rules, tighten the rules still further. The cycle continues in no small part because no government agency wants to be caught in a conflict of interest. In the words of one former director of the federal budget office:

> The public servant soon learns that successes rarely rate a headline, but governmental blunders are front-page news. This recognition encourages the development of procedures designed less to achieve success than to avoid blunders. Let it be discovered that the Army is buying widgets from private suppliers while the Navy is disposing of excess widgets at a lower price; the reporter will win a Pulitzer prize and the Army and Navy will establish procedures for liaison, review, and clearance which will prevent a recurrence and also introduce new delays and higher costs into the process of buying or selling anything. It may cost a hundred times more to prevent the occurrence of occasional widget episodes, but no one will complain.[44]

In a similar manner, government rules designed to protect the environment, encourage minorities, decrease substance abuse, prevent injuries, and guarantee due process—all laudable goals—also serve to increase the cost of government, decrease its efficiency, and tie up the bureaucracy in more red tape. Citizens and politicians often complain about bureaucratic inefficiency, and bureaucrats, as a group, tend to be cautious; but much of what is called red tape is the product of very real, very important concerns about good government. As Kaufman puts it, "the more values the government tries to advance, the more red tape it inevitably generates."[45]

The Judicial Process

Structurally, as noted in Chapter 5, the court system in New York is as complicated as that of any two other states combined. Differences between New York City and the rest of the state, between county, municipal, and town courts, and between a bewildering complexity of specialized benches—such as surrogate's courts, family courts, traffic courts, trial courts, and the various courts of the appellate division—make it almost impossible to chart a typical case. Most legal issues in New York, nonetheless, tend to travel one of two well-worn paths. Civil cases, usually involving disputes between private parties, enter the process through civil courts of general jurisdiction and such specialized benches as housing, small claims, and family court. Criminal cases, in which the government is the prosecutor, enter through a trial court system with a separate set of rules and procedures. The systems merge as they move upward, culminating in a single state court of appeals.

In both civil and criminal courts, the rules of the game evolve out of a mix of the common law, statute law (which includes agency-drafted regulations), and the rather vague concept known as equity. New York's courts, like those of all but one other state,[46] have their roots in the common-law tradition of Great Britain and the principle of *stare decisis*, a Latin phrase that means "let the decision stand." There are still some legal rules in New York that can be traced to a decision reached centuries ago in an English court, but New York has long tended toward a more

Box 7.3
The Agony of Judicial Choice

Cases that actually come to trial are usually difficult ones: if they were not, they would probably have been resolved by plea bargains or agreements between the litigants. Most judges have had cases on which they would have liked to vote "yes and no" or "maybe" or perhaps "guilty but. . . ." Decisions are often second-guessed by the media in ways—frequently ill informed—that make judges look silly. And the losers in both civil and criminal cases sometimes hold the judge personally responsible: one town justice in the small town of Hillsdale told us she still got threatening, late-night phone calls from a woman she ruled against years ago in a domestic dispute.

Perhaps the worst nightmare of a judge is the possibility of making a judgment that will come back to haunt. Death penalty cases frequently involve that kind of risk; many judges prefer not to take them. But even a seemingly simple case can inspire regret. Years ago, an upstate family court judge made a routine decision in a custody case. A father who had won custody of his two children was having trouble caring for them and wanted to turn them over to the mother. The mother agreed and so did the judge. The mother had an extensive history of mental illness that was well known to the state office of mental health, but this information was not available to the judge. Six weeks after receiving custody, the woman drowned both children. That decision will haunt the judge for a long time.

And there are times too when the accumulation of seemingly routine cases "just grinds you down," as one Brooklyn civil court justice said after a day of credit card cases. "The people borrowed the money and the law is clear, but you just hate to order people to change their lifestyles because of a stupid mistake."

rigid system of legislated rules and executive decrees. Lacking access to the large case-law libraries needed to sustain a common-law system and confronted with cases unique to a new environment, New York and the other colonies began both to develop their own common-law tradition and to write their laws into statutory codes. Without access to printed records, "Case law—court decisions—did not easily pass from colony to colony. . . . To borrow statutes (even whole codes) was easier to do."[47] As early as 1664, the Duke's Laws—copied largely from existing codes adopted in Massachusetts and Virginia—were adopted as the prevailing rules in New York, Delaware, and Pennsylvania. Modified by state constitutions, legislative statutes, and the rulings of administrative agencies, this basic corpus of statutory law largely supplanted the British common-law tradition in governing the operations of the courts.[48]

Just as the U.S. Congress publishes federal laws in constantly revised series of volumes known as the *United States Code*, the collected statutes of New York State can be found in *McKinney's Consolidated Laws of New York* and *McKinney's*

Session Laws of New York, which provides annual updates. The many volumes of *McKinney's*—organized by topics such as "Real Property," "Assault," and "Evidence"—have become the guiding text for lawyers and judges in New York. Section 2, line 675 of the New York penal code, enacted in 1881, provided that "no act . . . shall be deemed criminal or punishable, except as prescribed or authorized by this Code, or by some statute of this state," language that would seemingly eliminate judge-made, precedent-based law. But statute law, like the common law, evolves through judicial interpretation: it is illegal under the code to tap your neighbor's phone wire, but does that make it illegal to listen in on your neighbor's cellular phone? The zoning laws permit a town to prohibit the construction of outbuildings. Does that mean that you cannot have a birdhouse on your property? Well, just how big a birdhouse are we talking about? *McKinney's* does not cover that question, but case law does. Civil law, even more than criminal, continues to give considerable latitude to judges in cases such as these.

From time to time judges are faced with cases they cannot decide fairly by application of any statute or precedent. Family courts in particular run into cases where the punishment of one party or the other would only make things worse (see Box 7.3). In such cases, judges sometimes apply their equity power, a right to decide according to principles of fairness. One judge's vision of fairness, of course, may not be another's, just as one's citing of precedent or the controlling statute may not agree with another's. It is in such cases that the appellate courts come into play, and their decisions in turn become part of the common-law tradition that will guide lawyers and judges in future cases.

Criminal Cases

There are, essentially, four ways that you can find yourself in court. The most pleasant way is to go as a tourist or student to get a sense of how the system works. Alternatively, you can go as a juror, and the chances are very good in New York that someday you will. Based on voter registration lists, utility billing records, and tax rolls, persons eligible for jury duty—and this includes almost all citizens—are chosen randomly by court clerks or jury commissioners to appear in the appropriate courthouse for anywhere from a few days to as long as it takes to conduct a trial. You also may find yourself in court either as the plaintiff or defendant in a civil suit. Finally, a far less pleasant way to get into court is to be arrested in a criminal case.

A criminal case usually begins with an arrest, at which time the accused must be informed of his or her basic rights. These include—as anyone who has ever watched a police show on television knows—the right to remain silent, to consult with a lawyer, and to have a lawyer provided if the accused person cannot afford one. The police cannot keep a person in custody without going before a judge to determine whether there is probable cause to believe that a crime has been committed. If the answer is no, the case is dismissed. If the answer is yes, the defendant will be indicted and scheduled to appear again. Most defendants will be released on bail, a deposit of money that must be forfeited if they fail to appear. First offenders with a stable home and job often will be released on their own recognizance—that is, a promise to show up at the appointed time. Repeat offenders with a high probability of leaving town may be given high bail or denied bail entirely.

At this point, responsibility for prosecution shifts from the police to the offices of the district attorney, who decides what charges to bring. The defendant is then brought back into court for arraignment and asked to plead either guilty, not guilty, or guilty by reason of insanity. An admission of guilt at this point is equal to conviction and constitutes a waiver of one's right to a trial. All that is left is for the judge to impose a sentence. Most criminal cases end at this point through a process known as plea bargaining, which allows the accused to avoid trial by pleading guilty to a lesser offense. Let us say that Defendant A has had a few too many at a wedding reception and is stopped by the police for driving while intoxicated (DWI). In New York, intoxication is defined largely by a blood test in which an alcohol level higher than .01 constitutes DWI and can result in a prison term, a fine, and the loss of one's driving license. Driving while ability impaired (DWAI)—showing a level between .005 and .01—is less serious, punishable by a fine and perhaps mandatory counseling. Unless A was in an accident or far above the .01 level, he will usually be allowed to "cop a plea." That is, his attorney will reach an agreement with the district attorney that her client will plead guilty to the offense of driving while impaired in exchange for dropping the DWI charge. If the judge agrees, a fine is paid, A avoids jail, the district attorney gets a conviction, and the state is saved the costs of a trial.

Although it saves time and money, plea bargaining is controversial. Conservatives often argue that it allows too many dangerous felons to avoid significant punishment. Civil libertarians argue that the real effect is often to inflate charges, to encourage district attorneys to seek stiffer penalties than the facts might justify. Ideology aside, plea bargaining has become an accustomed, almost essential part of the process. The statutes that provide uniformity and, in theory, equal justice cannot distinguish individual cases as the process of plea bargaining often does.

In many jurisdictions, small ones in particular, plea bargaining takes place between prosecutors, defense attorneys, and judges who have dealt with each other frequently in disposing of similar cases. A sort of common law of pleas develops in which the outcomes of similar cases in the past set the standards for what is happening now. In some jurisdictions, prosecutors, judges, and defense attorneys have been working with each other for so long that they seem more in cahoots than adversarial. One author goes so far as to describe the criminal court system as a bureaucracy and "the practice of law as a confidence game."[49] While this may be too strong a term to apply to most major cases, the day-to-day operations of most criminal courts are more bureaucratic than judicial. Traffic courts, which account for about half the cases brought in most jurisdictions, seldom do more than affirm the recommendations of the arresting officer, having earned the label "cafeteria courts" for their ability to process their patrons quickly to the cash register. Many trial courts operate in much the same way. It is their business, as Stumpf and Culver write, "to process large numbers of cases quickly and with an element of bureaucratic efficiency. . . . [M]uch of the work occurs in private—meetings between opposing counsel, conferences with the judges in chambers, and so on."[50] In civil court cases, a New York Bar Association study estimated that fewer than 4 percent of the poor in New York had adequate legal assistance; and although the Legal Aid Society and court-appointed attorneys provide a minimal level of representation in criminal cases; it is, in most cases, truly minimal. With fewer than 10 percent of New York's lawyers enrolled in pro bono programs and Legal Aid's caseloads often running to dozens of cases a day, most clients' days in court are begun and finished in a matter of minutes.[51]

If the defendant and prosecutor are unable to reach agreement on a plea bargain, or if the judge voids an agreement between the prosecution and the defense, or if defendant pleads not guilty, it is up to the judge—or, in the case of serious crimes, a grand jury—to decide whether to bring the case to trial. Assuming the case does go to trial—and relatively few are dismissed at this stage—it is now the responsibility of both sides, under our adversarial system of justice, to make their best case, advancing whatever evidence is in the best interests of their side. Both defense and prosecution can bring in expert witnesses, introduce physical evidence, and coerce testimony—through the issuance of subpoenas—to persons unwilling to come forth on their own. Because the state has the resources of the police on its side, the defense is given certain accommodating advantages: the state may not, for example, introduce a defendant's prior arrest records into evidence, compel the defendant to testify, or resort to evidence gained by illegal means (such as coerced confessions).

Every person charged with a felony in New York has the right to a trial by jury, though many defendants waive that right in favor of a trial before a judge, known as a bench trial. Jury trials begin with the selection of a jury of twelve citizens, with each attorney allowed to ask the judge to dismiss an unlimited number of jurors for cause—that is, because they are obviously prejudiced—and a limited number without specific reason. Each side then presents an outline of its case to the new jurors (or to the judge). Typically, the prosecution begins its case with testimony from the arresting and investigating police officers. As experienced witnesses, the police seldom surprise either the prosecution or the defense, and they are seldom tripped up on cross-examination. Yet this stage frequently involves an extended session of technical sparring as the prosecution tries to show both that the evidence is compelling and that it was properly obtained. If the defense can show, conversely, that the police ignored important procedural safeguards for the accused, it may lay the groundwork for a future appeal. When other witnesses take the stand, predictability declines. "Ordinary people," as Jacob observes, "feel great stress on the witness stand, may respond in quirky ways to cross examination, and may display mannerisms that belie their testimony."[52]

Highly publicized cases, especially those involving celebrities such as O.J. Simpson, Britney Spears, and Michael Jackson, leave many observers with serious doubts about the ability of juries to deal with emotionally volatile cases. The difficulty in making such judgments is that the public, relying on sometimes sensationalized media reports that are not subject to the legal rules of evidence, is not seeing the same case as the jury. The most thorough investigation of the issue compared more than 7,500 criminal and civil jury trials with the verdicts that the trial judges would have rendered: judge and jury agreed in three-quarters of the cases and disagreed in their reading of the evidence in some others, but in only 9 percent of the cases did the judges believe that the jury had substantially erred in its legal reasoning.[53] Also in contrast with public perceptions are the realities of civil court judgments. While public attention focuses on sensational cases in which people win millions of dollars for seemingly trivial injuries, plaintiffs were significantly more likely to win in bench as opposed to jury trials. And the median award in all cases in 2004 was only $28,000.[54] Perhaps reflecting this perspective, the proportion of jury trials has been declining slowly in criminal cases and has become far less frequent in civil cases.

Once the judge or jury has decided the question of guilt, the judge imposes sentence. In Jacob's study judges imposed prison sentences of more than one year in about 28 percent of the cases resulting in conviction and sentences of less than a year in another 28 percent. The remaining proportion of those convicted were sentenced to time served (because they could not raise bail), placed on probation, given suspended sentences, fined, or required to perform community service.[55] Quite clearly, however, the trend is toward both higher conviction rates and longer jail terms. Nationally, in 2004 state courts convicted more than 1 million defendants of felonies and sent 70 percent of them to jail; in New York, of the 145,721 defendants that came to trial, 97,925 (67.2 percent) were convicted, but less than half of them (48.7 percent) did time.[56] Typically, suspended sentences and probation are given to first offenders, while those who have been arrested before are likely to go to jail. Although the New York State legislature repeatedly refused to back Governor Pataki's "three strikes and you're out" bill, which proposed mandatory life sentences for third-time violent felons, repeat offenders tend to draw maximum sentences. A watered-down "three strikes" law, allowing judges to give longer sentences to repeat offenders, was ruled unconstitutional by a lower court in 2007 and is pending appeal. At the same time, sharply diminished crime rates throughout the state— and most dramatically in New York City—have reduced the number of prisoners in New York State from a peak of more than 100,000 in the 1990s to just under 90,000 in 2007. These prisoners are housed in seventy state correctional facilities, sixty county jails, sixteen New York City correctional facilities, 267 locally operated police department detention facilities, and four juvenile detention facilities operated by the Office of Children and Family Services[57] (see Box 7.4).

Box 7.4
Prisons and Politics

The United States, with about 5 percent of the world's population, houses nearly 25 percent of its prisoners. Because of declining crime rates, New York's inmate population is declining from a peak of more than 100,000 in 1999 to fewer than 90,000 today. Just over 63,000 of those inmates are housed in seventy state penitentiaries, forty-one of which were built in the last twenty-five years. Although almost two-thirds of these prisoners are from New York City, an estimated 91 percent are incarcerated upstate.[1] It is estimated that prison expenditures—including those by local governments—total nearly $5 billion a year.

The sad fact is that in many upstate communities prisons are the leading industries, providing relatively well-paying jobs for unskilled workers. In some rural counties, prisons provide as many as one-fifth of the jobs. Because the workforce remains constant while the inmate population declines, the annual cost per prisoner—already the highest in the nation—continues to rise, reaching nearly $48,000 per inmate in 2007.[2] Yet neither Governor Pataki nor Governor Spitzer was able to persuade the legislature to close a single jail.

While closing prisons would cost jobs, politics also plays a role in sustaining upstate prisons. Because the census bureau counts inmates by where they are incarcerated rather than where they are from, the population base for calculating legislative apportionment adds to the population of rural senate and assembly districts and subtracts from those in the city. Since prisoners cannot vote, it takes fewer actual voters to elect some upstate legislators than their urban counterparts.

1. *New York Times*, May 13, 2006.
2. "Agency Presentations," *New York State Executive Budget, 2007–2008* (Albany: Division of the Budget, 2008), p. 381.

Civil Cases

Civil cases arise from the failure of participants to resolve disputes. The plaintiffs in civil cases usually are asking the court to compel other parties to give them something to which they believe they are legally entitled, such as money, a divorce, bankruptcy, damages, custody of children, maintenance of an apartment, or an inheritance. Law schools tend to divide civil practice into four main areas: torts, which are disputes about alleged injuries; contracts, involving disagreements about the meaning of previous agreements; property; and domestic relations. In New York State, roughly 700,000 civil cases pending in a typical year are in family courts and involve such diverse issues as foster care, custody, adoption, chronic delinquency, and spousal abuse. More than one-quarter of the 900,000 other civil cases pending involve disputes between landlords and tenants, and about 10 percent involve small claims cases seeking judgments of less than $1,000.[58] Whatever the category, civil cases arise when people have grievances that they feel have been unjustly inflicted upon them by another party. Not all grievances become cases: if you fall down your own front steps, you may be injured, but unless the steps were improperly installed you have no one to blame but yourself. If you fall down the stairs of a hotel, however, you may have a case.

The United States generally is considered the most litigious society in the world, a reputation that is not entirely deserved. Although Japan has a dramatically lower rate of litigation than the United States, other countries—including Australia, Denmark, England, and Israel—are roughly comparable. Among the American states, New York is a leader. Most New Yorkers who fall down hotel stairs, in other words, do not blame themselves; they are more likely to call a lawyer. In tort cases such as this, lawyers usually work for contingency fees, payments contingent upon reaching a settlement with the hotel, in which case they may pocket up to one-third of the total award. In many civil actions, and for the hotel in cases such as these, the cost of hiring a lawyer provides a strong incentive to settle out of court.

A civil case typically goes through several phases. A case begins with a pleading in which a person files a complaint, explaining the basis of the suit, the law being invoked, and the damages or other relief being sought. If a defendant fails to reply, the court may order a default judgment in which the plaintiff automatically wins. In the discovery phase, each side is entitled—by subpoena if necessary—to all relevant information bearing on the case. Although such requests are generally quite limited, the discovery phase can be long, expensive, and embarrassing. Some clients are so reluctant to disclose certain facts that they settle rather than go to discovery. In a divorce case, for example, a philandering husband may agree to pay alimony rather than have his wife's attorneys interview every woman he knows.

During and following discovery, attorneys for both sides may file motions seeking further information, expanding the charges, or asking summary judgment. Frequently, a series of motions from both parties points the way toward resolution of a case. The general estimate is that about one-quarter of all civil cases are settled by the judge at this point in the process. Even when cases actually come to trial, it is not uncommon for the case to be settled in the judge's chambers before all the witnesses are heard. Many civil cases come to trial only because the parties have become so antagonistic that only a trial can force them to agreement. This is all too often true in divorce cases, in which it is sometimes said that the only winners are the lawyers. In the 1970s, New York modified its matrimonial laws to ease this process and consequently reduce the number of cases coming to actual trial. For many years the only grounds for divorce in New York had been adultery and extreme physical cruelty. Although many couples wanted divorces, few men or women were comfortable stipulating before a judge that they had cheated on or beaten their spouses. So-called no-fault divorce laws, in which couples simply may agree to separate, have both increased the actual number of divorces and decreased the proportion of such cases coming to trial.

Reducing the Caseload of the Courts

No-fault divorce laws show that there is a connection between statute law and the incidence of litigation. Despite various attempts to make it easier to settle disputes without going to court, however, litigation continues to rise. Between 1984 and 1990 the number of civil filings in New York increased by 73 percent, the largest increase in any of the states examined in one study.[59] A variety of reforms have been proposed to reduce the workload of the courts and bring greater logic to their organization. In the area of criminal justice, for example, the so-called Rockefeller drug laws—which mandate up to life imprisonment for dealers—put an enormous burden on the criminal justice system yet have not proven effective in controlling the drug trade. The creation of special drug courts, emphasizing treatment rather than punishment, has eased the burden somewhat, and although they are quite new in some parts of the state, they appear to be working well.

In the area of civil justice, Governor Pataki succeeded in making it more difficult for injured workers to sue large corporations, but other attempts to curb litigation in the area of liability law have proven unsuccessful. The Business Council has long argued that the state's liability codes allow plaintiffs too much latitude in the form of punitive damages and encourage litigation by allowing plaintiffs to go after the "deep pockets" in a case. The concept of punitive damages is intended to deter individuals and corporations from irresponsible behavior by allowing the victims of such behavior to sue not just for the cost of the actual injury they sustained, but also for added dollars designed to punish the company for its irresponsibility. Under the "deep pockets" rule, a plaintiff may sue many people—a car dealer, for example, and the mechanic who worked on the car and really caused the problem— and collect most of the money not from the person most responsible (the mechanic) but from the one best able to pay (the auto company).

A variety of other reform proposals have more or less possibility of being enacted. Tort law reform, many business interests charge, is blocked by the political power of the New York State Trial Lawyers Association. Drug law reform, many argue, is made politically impossible by the voters' simplistic equation of tougher laws with reduced crime. These "legal" issues, in other words, are intensely political. In a wonderfully refreshing book called *Why Courts Don't Work*, former justice Richard Neely of West Virginia's supreme court points out that some groups actually have an interest in maintaining legal inefficiencies and that many problems that are blamed on the courts result from citizens' political failure to decide what they really want the courts to do:

> For example, when courts work efficiently in civil litigation, the net result is that plaintiffs as a class prosper to the detriment of defendants as a class. Silly as it may sound, the world as a whole breaks down into groups like injured workers, who are usually plaintiffs in civil cases, and groups like insurance companies, which are usually defendants. In cases between working people on one hand and insurance companies, employers, or business people on the other, it is fair to say

that courts are in the business of redistributing the wealth. When the machinery breaks down, no wealth is redistributed; this is obviously an advantage to insurance, slum landlords, and fly-by-night businesses.[60]

The Appellate Courts

Losers in trial courts sometimes have the option of appeal. In order to achieve what judges call "standing" at the appellate level, the loser in a criminal or civil case must show that there has been some error of law or procedure in the precedent legal process. A good deal of the legal sparring during a trial has its origins in the attempts of one attorney or the other to score sufficient points to appeal the case. Fewer than 10 percent of state trial court cases are appealed, and most appeals are rejected, but most good lawyers are considering throughout the process what points they might later appeal. It is this long shadow of appellate proceedings, more even than actual cases heard and decided, that gives the appellate division its legal clout.

Through its interpretation of the rules, the appellate division is the real arbiter of what the laws mean. The seven-member court of appeals, standing at the top of the appellate division as New York's highest court, has the final word in this process unless there is conflict with a federal standard. There are whole categories of cases, particularly in the area of civil law, in which the rulings of the court of appeals are final. Generally, the court's rulings are grounded in interpretations of statutes, though the court does have the power of judicial review; that is, the power to rule a statute unconstitutional. It seldom does so. In fact, one study of the court's 1990 term found that constitutional issues were involved in only 20 percent of the cases decided.[61] Still less common are cases in which the constitutionality of a statute is challenged. From 1981 through 1985, for example, a total of just eighty cases were brought before the appeals court challenging the constitutionality of laws passed by the legislature. In only twenty was the law ruled unconstitutional.[62]

The appellate process begins with attorneys for the losers filing briefs explaining why their cases were improperly decided. Most of these motions are denied and the decisions of the trial courts stand. The number of cases reaching the court of appeals is very small, particularly in the area of criminal law. A few highly publicized cases have led some politicians to attempt to create an impression of the court as "soft on crime." In fact, the court in recent years has displayed a decided bent toward the prosecution. In its 1994–1995 term, for example, 3,036 defendants applied for hearings before the court of appeals; seventy-four received permission; and thirty-four—just over 1 percent—were granted new trials. In the same year, prosecutors were granted 11.7 percent of their motions for appeal.[63]

The court of appeals must hear cases in which the lower appellate division courts have disagreed or significantly modified the original opinion. While these cases often raise important issues, most judges and legal scholars probably would agree with Chief Judge Stanley Fuld, who wrote in 1967: "Innumerable appeals are brought to the Court as a matter of right, at the option of the litigants, not because they are of any moment or merit but merely because there has been some disagreement, no matter how trivial, either between the Appellate Division and the lower court, or within the Appellate Division itself, as to the proper final disposition of the case."[64]

Other cases are heard only by permission and tend to involve significant legal or constitutional issues. Unlike the U.S. Supreme Court, New York's court of appeals can issue advisory opinions and it need not have an actual "case or controversy" before it in order to hear a case. The court of appeals, moreover, has its appellate jurisdiction firmly established in the state constitution and the legislature cannot change it by ordinary law. Thus, although the court has exercised a degree of self-restraint in taking on the other branches of government, it is considerably less constrained in its formal jurisdiction than is the federal Supreme Court.

In the court of appeals, motions for appeal randomly are assigned to each of the seven judges for preliminary screening. After examining the papers filed by opposing attorneys and any friend-of-the-court briefs filed by other interested parties, the judge in question summarizes the case for his or her colleagues and makes a recommendation. By tradition, the court will grant a hearing if two judges agree that the case is one that should be reviewed.

New York's highest court is a highly collegial body. It meets each morning in the court's library to consider each justice's memorandums on assigned cases. These discussions are frank, learned, and sometimes heated: "almost all of the judges admit that they have felt one way about a case going into a conference but completely changed their minds before the conference was over."[65] After a short lunch, the court convenes in its chambers at two o'clock to hear oral arguments on cases already granted review. After another session in the library, the judges traditionally dine together in downtown Albany before going back to chambers to prepare the next morning's memorandums.

The public face of the court is tellingly revealed during oral argument. Attorneys are given fifteen minutes (half an hour in some cases) to defend their written briefs. For all but the most hardened veterans, it is an intimidating experience: the justices have done their homework and are quick to find and explore the weakest points. As the short period allocated to oral argument indicates, the bulk of the court's work in appellate cases consists of the careful reading and comparison of opposing written briefs, but most judges will concede that, occasionally, something said during oral argument has changed the direction of their thinking about a case.

After oral arguments, the judges retire to the conference room—sometimes called the "tea room"—where they draw from a deck of index cards containing the name of each case. Known as a "hot bench," because the judges do not know during oral argument who will be assigned which case, the drawing decides which justice will become the reporting judge on that case. In conference, discussion begins with the reporting judge who presents the case. The others comment in reverse seniority order and then, as a rule, a preliminary vote is taken. "Cases are primarily decided in conference, but the decisions are not finalized until draft opinions have circulated. Typically, if the reporting judge holds the majority, he or she will write for the court. Otherwise the junior judge in the majority will write the main opinion. If a dissent must be written, usually the first one to raise an objection—frequently a more junior jurist since the case is conferenced in reverse order of seniority—gets the chore."[66]

Although it is rare for judges to switch their votes on the basis of the written opinions, the case is not finally decided until both the majority and minority opinions have been studied by all the judges. In a long and firm tradition, the votes of the court in conference, the probable outcomes of cases being argued, and the nature of the arguments within the court have never been leaked. Not until the final vote is taken and opinions have been printed will the litigants or the public know who won or lost. A simple majority is all it takes to win, though four-to-three opinions are uncommon. What had been a largely consensual court has become more polarized in the twenty-first century. Where, for example, 91 percent of the cases decided in 1998 were by unanimous vote, the proportion was down to 84 percent in 2007.[67] By refusing to reappoint George Bundy Smith—perhaps the court's most liberal justice—in 2006, Governor George Pataki gave the court a more conservative bent. On issues involving criminal justice, for example, the four Pataki appointees voted in favor of the defendant an average of 23 percent of the time; judges Kaye and Smith (both Cuomo appointees) 51 percent; and Spitzer-appointed Theodore Jones 100 percent.[68] Governor Paterson's appointment of Jonathan Lippman as successor to Chief Judge Kaye (who reached the mandatory retirement age in 2008) is not likely to change this balance; barring early retirement, the Pataki appointees will constitute a majority of the court until 2015.

Some decisions of the state court of appeals, if they involve substantial federal questions, can be taken to the national level for further review. Most are not. It is also possible for the legislature and the governor to enact a law that effectively overrules a decision of the court. This is also a rare occurrence. And there are times when the decisions of the court are not fully enforced: when the police violate rules of procedure established for criminal cases, when the governor and legislature fail to provide sufficient funding to carry out a court order, or when lower courts gradually reinterpret the appeals court's ruling in applying it to new cases. The primary purpose of all the state courts remains the resolution of individual cases, but the courts are very much a part of the policy-making process in New York. As important as this role is, the courts in the American states will generally remain—as Alexander Hamilton described the Supreme Court of the United States—the "least dangerous branch," least dangerous, in large part, because they play at best a tangential role in directing the flow of economic resources.

8

Taxing, Spending, and Public Policy Priorities

Former New York City mayor Ed Koch once conceded that his eyes glazed over when he had to read a budget. Yet Koch undoubtedly recognized, as do most political leaders, that a budget "is a representation in monetary terms of governmental activity. . . . If one asks, 'Who gets what the government has to give?' then the answers for a moment in time will be recorded in the budget."[1]

The Budget as a Guide to Policy

In theory, a budget serves as a map of resource allocation. In fact, it is a map that few can follow and one that is frequently out of date before it is printed. Though it may fail to demonstrate what actually happens in terms of taxing and spending, it is a manifestly important statement of what the governor and the legislature want to happen in the coming year. Understanding state budgets is thus essential to understanding state government. There are, however, two particular reasons why budgets can be misleading and why politicians do not always know what they are doing when they create their budgets.

Predicting the Future

The first problem in budgeting is a problem of timing. New York State's fiscal year begins on April 1, so when the legislature passes a budget in, for instance, the spring of 2010, the money it allocates actually will be raised and spent over the *next* twelve months. The budget proposal that the governor submits in January is an attempt to predict what will happen four to sixteen months later, and when agencies submit their program requests to the governor's budget office, usually during the previous September, they are looking ahead an additional four months. The labor

261

department, for example, must try to predict in September 2009 how many people will apply for unemployment insurance in 2010–2011. The corrections department must try to predict how many prisoners will finish their terms and how many new convicts will arrive as much as a year and a half in the future.

In order to balance the budget, moreover, the governor's office must try to guess how much revenue the state will capture. It must predict the employment and inflation rates, the performance of the stock market, the amount of sales tax collected by retail stores, and so on. When the governor submits a budget to the legislature, these estimates will be among the first items of contention. The two houses of the legislature hire their own consultants to compare their projections with those of the governor and the comptroller, who generally produces still another set of revenue estimates.

Not surprisingly, these estimates of how much the government will take in and spend are seldom precise. There is no sure way to forecast how much snow will have to be cleared off the highways or what the unemployment rate will be next year, and the problem of prediction is compounded by its political loading. A politician who favors a tax cut or increase in spending has a short-term interest in overestimating revenues. Budgets passed in election years tend to be particularly optimistic. Politics aside, any attempt to estimate future economic activity, to predict the inflation rate in health care or the winter weather, is tricky at best. "By its nature," as one former budget director advised future governors, "budgeting is an error-prone activity. Those errors do not necessarily reflect a lack of technical capability or a failure of effort on the part of your budget staff. Forecasts are simply wrong, and from time to time your budget officer will bring you news of those errors."[2]

Interpreting the Numbers

The second important thing to understand about the budget of the state of New York is that it is too large and too complicated for a single individual—even the state's full-time budget director—really to understand. There are just too many units of government doing too many things. Budgets, generally, are high-level abstractions that sometimes relate only tenuously to programmatic realities. Here is an indicator from just one small part of state government, the political science department of the City College of the City University of New York (CUNY). What does it cost to offer roughly twenty-five courses in political science to approximately 550 students a semester? The most expensive item is the million or so dollars for the combined salaries and fringe benefits of thirteen full-time faculty members. Some faculty members, however, teach one or more of their courses at the graduate center, in the international relations program, in ethnic studies, or at the center for worker education. Others have college appointments as administrators. The department is compensated for some (but not all) of these faculty members' contributions to other programs with funds to hire part-time replacements. For needs like stationery, photocopying, telephones, and secretarial help, the department is given an annual allocation of money. For less direct services—such as those provided by campus security, college advisers, electricians, and librarians—the general college administration makes the allocations. In some systems of budgeting, the department would be charged its share for some of these college-wide services; in other systems they would go down as general overhead. There is no clearly right or wrong way to make these allocations, and City College does not really try. No one at the college can calculate accurately how much it costs to teach those twenty-five classes or how much is spent on political science education, as opposed to biology or history. Only in times of serious economic crisis is any serious attempt made to examine these overall allocations of resources. Most years, the college simply matches what the department did last year.

No one in the governor's office or the legislature has any idea how the department is spending its money. "Budget data," in this sense, "are like a fog bank. The current system gives one a feel for a tier of numbers, one or more times removed from the actuals."[3] What the city university system essentially does (reality is a bit more complex) is to allocate each college in the system a certain number of full-time faculty lines based on overall enrollments that, in budget jargon, are calculated as FTEs (an FTE is a full-time equivalent, meaning one student taking a full-time program of fifteen credits or five students taking three credits each). Every other budget line—from deans to desktops to part-time teachers—is some proportion of this number. The number itself does not indicate very much about how the college is educating its students or how much that process costs, but it serves as a crucial indicator of how the college stands in relation to other colleges in the State University of New York (SUNY) system. If FTE costs are higher at City College than at Queens or John Jay, the CUNY board of higher education is concerned. If FTE costs this year are significantly higher than last year, everyone is concerned. When the budget gets to Albany, figures from the CUNY system are compared with other FTE numbers in the SUNY system, and another round of judging begins.

Albany officials look at the colleges' enrollment, comparing the department of political science with, say, biology; comparing City College with other public colleges; comparing this year's costs with last year's. These comparisons provide a set of very rough indicators of how much is being spent to educate how many students. Beyond that, budget numbers indicate little. This is true not just for City College, but also for almost every bureau and commission in the state. Budgets show how many correction agents oversee how many inmates at the Greenhaven penitentiary, but not how many officers work in Cell Block E at midnight or how they interact with the prisoners. The number of patients treated in the emergency room of a hospital can be compared with the amount spent on doctors and nurses, but the result provides at best a rough estimate of how efficiently the hospital is run.

Given these conflicting perspectives, it is generally assumed that agencies will defend their programs and that budget people will challenge them. Bureaucrats are expected to believe that their programs are important. In most organizations, workers resent what they consider the insensitivity of budget people and use names like "number crunchers" to imply that they have little awareness of real-world problems.[4] Actual allocations of resources often emerge from a dynamic series of interactions between the numbers people and various agencies. At City College, to continue our example, the dean of social science will sometimes allow a small course to float if the chair of the department can make the case that the course is particularly important pedagogically or required for graduating seniors. The dean can allow such exemptions, but knows that she can get only so many of them past the provost, who knows in turn that he cannot allow more than a certain number of small classes to float without attracting the notice of the budget people at CUNY or in Albany, where a class with only nine students stands out like a sore thumb.

Tensions between agencies and budget officials grow as different agencies and programs are compared. When the dean of social science at City College makes her case to the provost, the provost is—implicitly at least—comparing the case for an under enrolled political science course with a comparable case being made by the dean of humanities for a philosophy course or for a course in the school of engineering—all in the context of overall FTE numbers. At the central office of the university, similar comparisons are made between City College and other CUNY colleges. And in Albany, the numbers from CUNY are matched with SUNY and, ultimately, with other agencies and programs in the budget. Most professors would bristle at the suggestion that they are competing with other departments or colleges, much less with the office of aging or the corrections department. Yet in a sense, every nickel spent by every agency is coming out of someone else's budget. The decision to float a small course or to put an extra guard in a prison is a decision with implications for others.

Strategic Budgeting

Individuals and families confront these same problems: money spent on movies cannot pay the rent. Corporations also must allocate resources and personnel. Governments differ from families in that many more people and problems are involved; they differ from corporations in that services are more difficult to compare. How does one decide how much collective welfare is gained by allocating money to prisons as opposed to colleges, health care as opposed to parks, or highways as opposed to subways? In families, resource allocations depend on the decisions of so small a number of people that they all know what they are getting. In the private sector, resource allocations are decided—in theory at least—by which divisions are most profitable. Government services, by their very nature, are neither simple nor measurable in strict economic terms. Brian Murtaugh, when he was chair of the alcohol and substance abuse committee in the New York assembly, could make a case that treatment was, in the long run, cheaper than incarceration for low-level drug-addicted dealers, but his case was soft by comparison with that of a corporate advocate showing that a company's product was more profitable than another division's.

Aaron Wildavsky's argument that all government budgeting is essentially incremental has dominated most studies of the process. Governments, he argues, are too large and complex to understand without simplifying shortcuts: "No human being," as a former chair of the house appropriations committee once put it, "regardless of his position and . . . capacity could possibly be completely familiar with all the items of appropriations contained in this defense bill." And even if one could really understand one agency's program,

> there remains the imposing problem of making comparisons among different programs that have different values for different people. This involves deciding such questions as how much highways are worth as compared to recreation facilities, national defense, schools, and so on down the range of government functions. No common denominator among these functions has been developed. No matter how hard they try, therefore, officials in places like the Bureau of the Budget discover that they cannot find any objective method of judging priorities among programs.

Budget officials, Wildavsky continues, make these complex calculations through a set of simplifying assumptions, the most important of which is "incrementalism":

> The beginning of wisdom about an agency budget is that it is almost never actively reviewed as a whole every year in the sense of reconsidering the value of all existing programs as compared to all possible alternatives. Instead, it is based on last year's budget with special attention given to a narrow range of increases or decreases. Thus the men who make the budget are concerned with relatively small increments to an existing base. Their attention is focused on a small number of items over which the budgetary battle is fought.[5]

In New York, as one assemblyman says, "we fight over maybe 2 to 3 percent of the budget. No matter how far apart the governor, the senate, and the assembly may seem, what is really quite remarkable is that we all take a base of about 100 billion for granted while we scream and shout about the other two."

Wildavsky's concept of incrementalism has been criticized for failing to encompass major upheavals such as that produced by the Proposition 13 tax-cutting initiative in California, the New York elections in 1994, or the economic collapses of 2001 and 2008. From the perspective of those who might be called "decrementalists," the "fundamental concepts of incremental budgeting are completely inverted by retrenchment. For example, although the incremental budgeting process is decentralized, decremental budgeting inherently requires centralization. Similarly, the substantive decisions of incremental budgeting are made in a fragmented manner, but decremental budgeting requires a comprehensive package."[6]

Such periods of retrenchment are not trivial, but they are episodic. Even when a governor with a new set of priorities comes into office, as did Pataki in 1995, the new administration is likely to focus major attention on at best four or five areas. Higher education took a very hard shot in Pataki's first budget, as did mental health, but subsequent changes in this areas were essentially incremental until 1999, when again a strong showing in the 1998 elections had strengthened his political position.

"Fair Share" and "Base"

Even when the process is not incremental, two of Wildavsky's analytic methods of dealing with complexity are likely to be used by most participants. These are what he calls an agency's "fair share" and "base." The base is "the general expectation among the participants that programs will be carried on at close to the going level of expenditures but it does not necessarily include all activities."[7] The budget of the city university, for example, may go up or down a few percentage points, but no college is likely to be closed, no major program terminated. The assumption is that the process of decision-making that led to the creation of a college or program in the first place took into account the major arguments for and against. If the arguments were good then, why bother reviewing them now? "No one was born yesterday; past experience with these programs is so great that total reconsideration would be superfluous unless there is a special demand in regard to a specific activity on the part of one or more strategically placed Congressmen, a new Administration, interest groups, or the agency itself."[8] Whatever the flaws of this approach, anyone who has seriously tried to put together a budget recognizes "that there has to some baseline; there is no way to budget without one. The issue is what baseline is to be used?"[9] Should it be last year's numbers? Or should they be adjusted for inflation? Most governments do adjust, using what is called a "current services estimate" that tries to predict what it would cost the agency to do last year's job at this year's costs; Governor Pataki tried more than once to fudge these numbers down for some programs.

"Fair share" is a more elusive concept. It means "not only the base an agency has established but also the expectation that it will receive some proportion of funds, if any, which are to be increased over or decreased below the base of various governmental agencies."[10] A new administration—like Governor Spitzer's in 2007—can change these calculations dramatically, and priorities may shift over time in such a way as to redefine the concept of fair shares. Over the past decade, for example, the state has gone from spending three times as much for higher education as for corrections, to budgets in which more money goes to prisons than to colleges, but even these changes, on a year-to-year basis, have been largely incremental. The magnitude of the cuts New York had to face in 2009, however, threw all these normal calculations out of whack: because certain programs simply cannot be cut below a certain level—those used to match federal grants, for example—others will have to do with far less than what might otherwise pass as their fair share.

Program advocates seek to protect their bases and maintain or expand their fair shares. A favorite agency device is to protect its revenue stream in the form of a "locked box," a tax or fee that can be used only for a specific purpose. (In New

York, for example, license fees for fishing must go into fishery management funds, Thruway tolls are controlled by the Thruway Authority, and so on). Different kinds of accounting procedures can be adjusted to alter perceptions of program effectiveness, and a variety of decision procedures can be used to circumvent budgetary guidelines. In the short run, agencies can tap into their capital funds, borrow against future revenues, or delay billings in order to meet current needs, but they can seldom get away with such evasions in the longer run.

The Budgetary Process

The Division of the Budget, or DOB, is at the center of the budgetary process. Its director and half a dozen top employees serve at the pleasure of the governor. Although its leadership became politicized under Governor Pataki, the working units of the division are composed largely of civil servants who take pride in their political neutrality. The DOB is organized by units to which various clusters of agencies are assigned. The health and social development unit, for example, is responsible for the departments of Social Services, Health, and Labor, the Division for Youth, the Office for the Aging, the Council on Children and Families, and the Division of Human Rights. Each of these units monitors its respective agencies for program evaluation and budget development. Their annual reviews of agency requests serve as a base for the process of developing the overall budget plan presented by the governor.

Preparing the Budget

Preparation of the executive budget typically begins in June, when each agency begins to compile its annual estimates for the following year. These requests are reviewed by budget analysts, who look for major changes, indications of padding, inaccuracies, and consistency with the programs of the governor. Meanwhile, the fiscal planning division of the DOB is beginning—in consultation with the governor—to develop estimates of revenues and overall levels of expenditure. When these numbers are fed back to the budget units, they are translated into preliminary projections for the next fiscal year's spending levels. Each budget division unit then sends its agencies budget guidelines in the form of a "call letter," calling upon them to submit budget and program proposals that conform with the projected fiscal estimates and the governor's program priorities.

Once each agency responds to the call letter and submits its plan to the DOB, budget examiners meet informally with the fiscal officers and top officials of each agency to hear requests for changes. Large departments and some with unique problems may be able to schedule formal hearings. At these hearings, "the commissioners make presentations to the Office . . . as well as the secretary and chair and staff personnel of the two legislative fiscal committees. Both major political parties are represented. During the past two decades these formal hearings have come to provide mainly an informal overview. One budget examiner described them as 'marketing sessions.'"[11]

What the commissioners are trying to market at these sessions is some notion either that their programs are being cut at the base and denied their fair shares or that some unique set of circumstances justifies special consideration. Whether this case is made in formal hearings or informal discussions with budget examiners, it is made in the context of the resources available in the governor's overall fiscal plan. In high revenue years, it may be possible to include new programs, providing a case can be made that they are needed, best handled in that particular department, realistic, and likely to achieve their stated goals. In bad times, it may be necessary to defend and compare existing programs. In 2008, for example, Governor Paterson asked the departments and agencies to prepare a "core mission budget" in which they rated their various programs as high, medium, or low in meeting their essential targets. More specifically, he asked them for specific cuts of 3.35 percent in March and another 10.15 percent in July in their 2008 budgets, as well as their scaled-down proposals for 2009.[12] These requests presaged a very difficult budget year for everyone.

When the budget examiners finish their program reviews (typically in late November), they present their recommendations to their unit heads in closed-door sessions that are, in many ways, at the heart of the budget preparation stage. Typically, the budget examiner's presentation is rooted in the baseline budgeting concept representing last year's services at next year's prices. For most agencies this is a fairly straightforward process. Salaries, for example, are adjusted upward (or down) to account for collective bargaining increases, retirements, and other changes in wages and personnel. Supply costs are adjusted for inflation, and so on. This process of projecting spending levels, known as annualization, is not always straightforward. If tougher sentencing laws, for example, make it likely that the prison population will increase, the spending baseline for the corrections department would seemingly be due for an increase, but the calculation of the size of that increase is much trickier than estimating the increase in the price of paperclips. In presenting the budget, moreover, a governor may have an interest in fudging baseline numbers in order to obscure painful cuts or make program comparisons difficult. In his 1999–2000 budget message, for example, Governor Pataki did not use baseline numbers in presenting his CUNY and SUNY proposals. By ignoring increased costs (including an already approved 4 percent salary increase), he could argue that what were really substantial net cuts was a budget "equal to the comparable 1998–99 academic year funding."[13]

While controversy abounds in areas such as this, the baseline concept has been widely accepted by budget-makers at the local, state, and national levels. It provides what most participants regard as a realistic picture of what each departmental program is most likely to cost in current dollars. As Forsythe says:

> From a broad political perspective, the idea of "current services" mirrors the last adopted budget and therefore uses the prior year's legislative agreement as

a starting point. From an agency manager's perspective, the upward adjustments made in the baseline budget mean that the agency at least starts even in its budget battles and does not have to fight for funds simply to pay for inflation or collective-bargaining adjustments, neither of which are under the agency manager's control. For the budget office, the baseline "exercise," as it is often called . . . provides a starting point for budget making that is more or less consistent from program to program and agency to agency.[14]

Once the examiner's reports and projections are completed, the process of comparing programs and adjusting them to the overall numbers begins at the higher levels of DOB and in the office of the governor. In December, as the outlines of the budget begin to emerge, a final round of communication with the agencies takes place. At this stage in Maryland, a state similar to New York in the extent to which party leaders dominate the legislature, "legislative leaders meet with the governor and express individual and collective priorities that run the gamut from local matters to executive departments and agencies to statewide policies. Governors usually try to accommodate these requests so the legislative leaders feel ownership and will push the budget through."[15] This seldom happens in New York. While committee chairs and legislative party leaders are sometimes consulted and informally advised of the budget outlook, the process of preparing the budget in New York is strictly in the provenance of the second floor. Indeed, the precise contours of the governor's budget are generally shrouded in considerable mystery until the day in mid-January when the governor officially delivers them to the legislature. A 2007 reform requiring the governor to submit preliminary estimates in December has only marginally changed this dynamic. With only the sketchiest projections available, Governor Paterson's attempt to get the legislature to anticipate future problems at a special November 2008 session was a failure. His mid-December projections, released a few weeks later, did allow local governments, interest groups, and legislative staff assistants to get a head start on their research, but had no impact on the formal legislative calendar.

As they prepare their budget messages for delivery in January, governors usually start with a fairly strong sense of their own priorities. New York's governor comes to the legislature in a remarkably strong strategic position. Among the states, few governors are better positioned to get what they want from the legislature. The governor's strength is rooted in part in the control over the executive branch and the consequent inability of most agencies to use subgovernment networks to end-run the governor. As one study of the process notes, "When the Governor's budget has been submitted to the Legislature, agencies are expected to fall in line and support the document. Even if some of their requests were slashed, appeals to the Legislature at this stage can be interpreted as treasonous. 'After all, we're all in the Executive Branch together,' stated one manager."[16]

Even in the absence of such togetherness, agency managers know that the governor is still likely to have the last word since the line-item veto applies to any increases the legislature may propose. At the same time, the path of least resistance suggests using baseline figures to keep things pretty much as they were the year before. And there are also important tactical considerations to take into account. A governor who wants, for example, to increase spending for a program that is not popular in one house of the legislature may propose drastic cuts in a more popular program, not out of genuine desire for the cuts, but in order to have something to trade. To read the governor's budget, then, as a statement of real priorities will not do. New York's constitution gives the governor thirty days to revise the original budget presentation (the 2007 reform act cuts this limit to twenty-one). Thus, by low-balling items popular with legislators, the governor enters the process with a large stack of bargaining chips. Almost all senators and assembly members, Republicans and Democrats, are strongly inclined, for example, to maintain school funding levels and those parts of the budget that support local governments. Almost invariably, governors submit budgets proposing low levels of expenditure in these areas. For the legislature to satisfy its local constituents and maintain state school aid levels, it must offer something that the governor wants, such as—in the case of Governor Pataki—tax cuts and increases in prison expenditures; for Spitzer and Paterson, smaller deficits.

Enacting the Budget

The budget presented by the governor to the legislature is referred to the fiscal committees, which quickly put their staffs to work on detailed analysis. The first items of legislative interest are the economic assumptions underlying the governor's overall numbers. Each house of the legislature has its own economic consultants who project the coming economic climate: how much the state can expect to collect in taxes, how much it will have to pay for necessary purchases. If it looks like a good year economically, there obviously will be more to spend. Because these projections are both difficult to make with any certainty and so important in setting overall taxing and spending levels, they often are controversial. Arguments over these numbers often have delayed the budgetary process for months as the legislature and governor seek common ground. One of the most important reforms adopted in 2007 required the comptroller to set these levels if the governor and both houses fail to agree by February 1. While the legislative leaders and the governor work out an agreement on these fiscal figures, formal legislative hearings are scheduled, giving interest groups an opportunity to be heard and agencies a last chance cautiously to appeal cuts. Meanwhile, party leaders, in consultation with the chairs of key committees and the staffs of the ways and means committee in the assembly and the finance committee in the senate, begin to prepare their own counters to the governor's budget. Some of the early maneuvering in the legislature, through press releases and informal negotiations, may produce relatively minor changes in the governor's revised budget. Until they are presented and until the fiscal committees complete their analyses, there is little significant movement toward compromise. In January and early February, the fiscal committees schedule a series of hearings on different parts of the budget. Although these hearings seldom develop any new insights or surprises, they are well attended by members, staff aides, and lobbyists who find in them what one staff aide describes as "both a useful review of the numbers and a series of insights into the political nuances. If you listen carefully," he continued, "to the kinds of questions asked and the ways in which people shade their answers, you can learn a lot about how strongly various people feel about different parts of the package."

Not until late February do the first real negotiations begin. These early sessions, typically, are rather large and formal, including both the majority and minority leaders of both houses, the governor, and numerous staff persons. As the process moves toward deadline, the number of participants decreases to the ultimate "three men in a room": the governor, the majority leader, and the speaker, plus a handful of top staff persons.

For many years, conventional wisdom held that "one and one makes three," meaning that if any two of the key negotiators cut a firm deal, the third would go along. The rule became less predictable as divided government became institutionalized; indeed, since the 1990s it sometimes has seemed advantageous to be that third one, particularly when issues are played out in the media. While Governor Pataki's fellow Republicans in the senate might have been expected to side with him, factors other than party allegiance, as Forsythe suggests, "can create a competitive relationship between a governor and a legislative leader. Deference to the chief executive is not necessarily a value that helps a leader win election in a legislature. Indeed, a newly elected legislative leader may find it necessary to do battle with a governor of the same party, as a demonstration of independence."[17]

Generalization in this area is difficult. Ken Shapiro, who served as chief counsel to three speakers, argues that although people "tend to remember the isolated instances" when the patterns were clear, in most sessions it would be impossible to "make determinations for the session and say 'This week we're going to be Warren Anderson's partner' or 'This year we're going to be Mario Cuomo's partner.' I think the issues and events during a given year determine who your partner will be."[18] Some patterns do persist. Both legislative parties, for example, try to protect their politically marginal members, who tend to come from the districts in the suburbs and small cities where school aid and general aid to localities are particularly important. Almost every year, and particularly in years when the cupboard is bare, therefore, legislative leaders tend to coalesce quickly in opposing cuts to these programs, but Shapiro's point that alliances are unpredictable and issue-specific is beyond refutation.

The 2003 budget fight is illustrative. Newly elected to his third term as governor, George Pataki confronted what was projected as a possible $11.5 billion shortfall in revenues. The governor's budget avoided tax increases through borrowing and large spending cuts, particularly in Medicaid and education.

Both legislative leaders, Democratic speaker Sheldon Silver and Republican senate majority leader Joe Bruno, on behalf of their caucuses, opposed a cut in local school aid, which would have resulted in a rise in local property taxes. The impact would have been too great on their constituencies. They chose instead to raise other taxes in order to support state services. Remarkably, the governor's cuts had the effect of uniting Bruno, a conservative upstate Republican, and Silver, a liberal New York City Democrat, as well as bringing together assembly Democrats and senate Republicans.[19]

Refusing to negotiate, the governor simply disappeared. But while Pataki was giving speeches around the state and nation, the two houses went to work and developed their own budget, passing it by more than the two-thirds vote required to overcome an expected veto. (The actual vote was along party lines, 102–45, in the assembly and a bipartisan 55–5 in the senate.) When Pataki returned to Albany, he vetoed, as expected, the tax increases and 119 separate spending items. The vote to override all the vetoes was swift and overwhelming in both houses, marking the first time in more than twenty years that a governor's veto was overridden. The "one and one makes three" rule prevailed in a remarkable turnaround from just five years before when the legislature had sustained every one of Pataki's record 1,300 vetoes.

Bargaining Postures

At the core of the speaker and majority leader's ability to negotiate with the governor is the question of trust. Their negotiating postures are firmly rooted in their ability to retain the trust of their respective party conferences. Whatever deals they negotiate with each other and with the governor must pass muster in their party conferences and ultimately in the legislature as a whole. From the very start of serious budget negotiations, talks among the three key actors frequently are punctuated with pauses during which the speaker and majority leader return to their party conferences for consultation and advice. The ability of legislative leaders to take a hard line in negotiations is a function of their ability to negotiate with solid party conferences behind them.

The Legislature and the Governor

Trust is also important in defining the relationships between party leaders and the governor. Until a final agreement is in place, there is a sense in which everything is always on the table. An agreement reached on the budget for, say, highway spending suddenly might come unglued when one of the key players compares it with a later agreement on something else. Most American legislatures decentralize these bargaining points. In Congress, for example, once the overall budget guidelines are set, substantive committees and appropriations subcommittees fill in most of the actual numbers and negotiate them with the other house. Despite New York's 1998 experiment with conference committees, and some later reforms that require them to meet, the bargaining process in Albany continues to focus on the "three men in a room." Although they are acting as agents of their party conferences and other forces, the fact that most deals must ultimately be cut this way significantly impacts the process and differentiates it from practice in other states.

With recent exceptions, preliminary negotiations are broken down into "tables," groups of staff people who focus on particular issues with representatives from each of the three negotiating groups. Certain tables almost always are kept open until the final days, each side holding open those issues that another cares about strongly. When the assembly, for example, cared a lot about welfare and the senate about elementary and secondary education, these tended to be the last tables to close. More recently, when prison cells were high-priority issues for the senate and Governor Pataki, and mental health for the assembly, these tables were kept open to give each side bargaining leverage. Although the budget is technically divided into separate chapters, and some tables conclude their work with little controversy, in practice the governor and both houses must agree to the budget as a total package. Even when a table is seemingly closed, the process, in the immortal words of Yogi Berra, "ain't over till it's over."

One of the interesting paradoxes of the budget process is the extent to which, as the key players move toward closure, the weak become strong. The rule of one plus one equaling three not only goes out the door at this point but also becomes inoperative. One top budget aide for Governor Cuomo suggests that some of Cuomo's most difficult negotiations with the state senate occurred in the years when he was closest to the assembly leadership. Acting on the widespread perception that the governor and speaker Saul Weprin were joined at the hip, the senate leadership made it increasingly expensive to "buy the final agreement"—that is, to find the funds to support the particular programs that the senate was pushing in order to reach a final deal. Many times, in the Cuomo years, the senate majority leader would come to a tentative agreement and then return to the next session and report that he could not sell it to his conference. Warren Anderson, according to Forsythe, "used to storm out of meetings every year" just as agreement seemed to be close. The walkout, for Anderson, "signaled the start of the final round of horse-trading, not a breakdown in talks."[20] In the Pataki years, assembly leader Sheldon Silver tried—with limited success—to play the same game with the governor and majority leader Bruno, but the rules of the contest have changed.

Throughout his twelve years in office, the player most likely to play the end-game role was Pataki. In legal terms, New York's governors—because they can still veto any items the legislature increases—are well positioned to take a tough negotiating stance. When relations between the governor and the legislative leaders are at their best, the process of bargaining is straightforward: the governor yields to the senate and assembly on some increases in education and aid to localities; the assembly and the governor give the senate more for highways; the governor and the senate force assembly acceptance of cuts in mental health in exchange for a few extra dollars in mass transit; and so on. But a governor serious about cutting funds that both houses of the legislature want—education is a good example—has enormous advantages.

As a governor plainly uncomfortable with the details of policy issues and the politics of negotiation, George Pataki encouraged alternatives to the traditional budgetary process. Some of these attempts—such as negotiating with legislative leaders in public sessions—were immediate failures, as they were to prove again in 2007 under Eliot Spitzer and in Paterson's fiscal crisis meetings in 2008. Others, particularly Pataki's heavy-handed use of his veto and resource allocation powers, are not new, but they carry political risks that suggest only sparing use. Combining these methods, however, with a willingness to simply walk away from the table, stay out of Albany, and leave the legislative leaders to stew, Pataki added a new wrinkle to the traditional process. Conventional wisdom had long suggested that it was the governor who had the most to lose from late budgets. By absenting himself, however, Governor Pataki managed to transfer the blame to the legislature. Indeed, the harder legislative leaders worked to reach a compromise that would bring the governor back to the table, the more the press and the public tended to focus on them rather than the absent governor as the source of the problem. Whether future governors will be able to play similar roles is not clear. Pataki nonetheless showed how the formal powers of the governor could be used to tilt the dynamic in his favor and away from a tripartite process of bargaining among equals. The most significant part of this change came through the governor's ability to make the budgetary process even more central to his policy agenda.

Greatly expanding on precedents set largely by Mario Cuomo, Pataki gradually began to add more and more programmatic language to his budget bills; that is, he increasingly specified not just how much would be spent on each budget item, but how it would be spent. Program language was used, for example, to change the kinds of medical procedures supported by Medicaid (a change normally covered in separate legislation) as well as the amount of dollar support the state would provide. "The conflict," as Rosenthal describes it, "came to a head in 2001, when assembly Democrats and senate Republicans joined forces against the Republican governor and passed a bare-bones budget that omitted executive language of purpose and asked that it be submitted as legislation. It was intended to force the governor to negotiate. Two weeks later Governor Pataki brought suit, charging that the legislature had 'unconstitutionally acted in a way that diminished the executive's power.'"[21]

In 2004 the governor's case and a countersuit led by the assembly speaker reached the state court of appeals, which decided decisively in favor of the governor. "The Legislature can cut down," the court held, "the Legislature can strike out, but they must approach it from the standpoint of a critic and not from the standpoint of a rival constructor."[22] So long as it was reasonably related to spending issues, the court said, the governor was free to put whatever language he wanted in the budget for the legislature to accept or reject but not change. Thus, when the governor coupled funding for the state library with a proposal to change its administrative structure, the legislature could vote to cut the library's funding or eliminate it entirely, but it could not restore its autonomy. If the governor proposed funding for a new prison in Syracuse, the legislature could decide whether to fund it or not, but could not move it to, say, Utica. Whether in response to these changes or because of forces internal to the legislature, a recent movement toward the establishment and use of conference committees also may have changed the dynamic.

Conference Committees

In New York, as we have noted, bills are not amended in the legislature. The usual way in which the two houses reconcile differences is by passing new bills. Unlike Congress or the legislatures in most states, the New York legislature has almost never used conference committees to negotiate differences between the houses. In 1995, a new joint rule was passed authorizing such interhouse committees, but although the bill increasing the state speed limit to sixty-five miles per hour was negotiated in a conference committee later that year, most legislation has continued to follow the traditional path. In 1998, in a dramatic departure from this tradition, the assembly and senate leaders appointed conference committees to negotiate the budget.

As many as nine subcommittees were appointed by party leaders to deal with particular chapters, such as taxes and economic development; transportation, the environment, and housing; public protection; and so on. Each subcommittee generally consisted of ten members, five each from the assembly and the senate, with four of the five appointed by the majority, one by the minority. A general budget conference committee met first to set spending targets for each subcommittee and later to approve the final packages. This committee included the top leaders of both houses, including the speaker, the majority and minority leaders, and the chairs of the finance committees.

The speaker and majority leader (in consultation with their respective party conferences) were clearly in control at almost every step in the conference proceedings. Especially in the early stages when basic resources were allocated—so much for education, public protection, human services, and so on—the majority party leaders were clearly in charge ("two men in a room," as one journalist quipped). One could argue, as some journalists have, that once these decisions were made, the work of the subcommittees was merely rearranging the deck chairs on a liner whose direction was already clear. At the other extreme were those who suggested that "the process puts to the lie the notion that . . . rank-and-file members were somehow incapable of participation."[23] At least for those on the committees, there was a strong sense of involvement, and it seems clear that within the overall fiscal context set by the leaders, details of the budget were worked out directly by the rank-and-file.

Seemingly the big loser in the reformed process was the governor, who not only was frozen out of negotiations over details but also forced—in final negotiations on the bottom line—to face a majority leader and speaker whose differences had already been negotiated. (The "one plus one equals three" rule was, in effect, institutionalized.) Governor Pataki, however, was able to use the new process to his advantage in 1998. He began by insisting that he would veto those parts of the legislative budget that raised total spending over the cap he had set. With that condition met, the governor and the legislative leaders called a press conference to announce the first nearly on time budget agreement in more than a decade. Unsuspectingly, the speaker and majority leader turned to other business and the legislature moved toward early adjournment. But the governor was not finished. In apparent violation of his agreement with the legislature, Pataki used his line-item veto on more than 1,300 budget items, many in the areas of education and aid to localities most sacred to legislators. With senate Republicans and Democrats in both houses outraged by the governor's seeming breach of faith, the stage seemed set for a rare legislative override of gubernatorial vetoes. Out of the west, however, came the ragtag cavalry of assembly Republicans—usually a cipher in the power game—with a quiet pledge to vote as a bloc to uphold every veto. The governor clearly won the battle. Whether he won the war is far less clear.

For the remainder of Pataki's years as governor, party leaders and their staff assistants asserted more control. In 1998 and to a lesser degree in 1999, there was a subtle but not insignificant shift in power to the more senior members serving on the conference committees and away from the central staff people who traditionally had bargained over the details left after the party leaders had reached their agreement on the overall numbers. This does not seem to have been the case in 2000. According to former majority leader Michael Bragman, "When one of the members of the General Conference Committee dared to suggest that they wanted to question one of the [staff] reports, a staff person, *a staff person*, dared to tell them that they could not do that."[24] In fact, for the remaining years of Pataki's governorship, conference committees met sporadically and only infrequently played a significant role. Both houses were simply too concerned about presenting a united front to the governor to risk spreading the action to more members.

Almost immediately after taking office in 2007, Eliot Spitzer reached an agreement with the legislature to reform the budgetary process by, among other things, requiring the conference committees to meet publicly. The working balance achieved between the three men in a room and the broadly representative conference committees produced both an on-time budget and what seems to have been a significantly more open, reformed process. But this was in a year when the state coffers were overflowing with new revenues. In the tighter fiscal environment of 2009 and 2010, there is little likelihood that these reforms will persist.

Keeping the Governor Honest

Normally, when the economy is good the process runs smoothly. This should have been the case in 1999 when a hyperactive stock market and a recovering economy began the fiscal year with a budget surplus of several billion dollars, but the 1997 and 1998 budgets had so backloaded tax cuts and spending increases into the

---

Box 8.1
Preparing for the Worst
(or At Least Making It Look As If You Are)

One way in which many families and governments avoid the risk of debt is by creating a contingency fund, otherwise known as saving for a rainy day. Thus the 2000–2001 budget adopted by the legislature in June 2000 provided for a seemingly prudent reserve of more than $4 billion set aside for unanticipated emergencies, downturns in the stock market, or faulty economic projections. As recalculated by the state comptroller, however, the real rainy day funds in the budget had a projected balance of only $550 million.

What the governor and the state legislature did in order to create a prettier picture was to place and sustain a number of programs in places where they were seemingly funded by sources outside the main budget. On closer scrutiny, however, these outside sources turned out to be the rainy day accounts. They also counted as "reserve" funds of more than $600 million allocated to increased salaries for state workers. Since the largest civil service union had already negotiated its contract, these numbers could easily have been folded into the budget. A parallel case would be a family who knew that its rent was going up by $100 a month, but instead of budgeting an extra $1,200 for twelve months of rent claimed to be "saving" that $1,200 for a rainy day!

The state's tax receipts were unusually strong in 1999. Even if they were to remain strong throughout the 2000–2001 fiscal year, tax cuts passed in 1998 that went into effect in 2001 made it more important than ever to have a strong reserve. Instead, the governor and the legislature chose, as many families do, to live for today and hope that tomorrow takes care of itself. As the comptroller pointed out, New York's actual "rainy day reserve represents a mere 1.5 percent of General Fund receipts; whereas, the national average for states is about 4 percent."[1] The comptroller's calculations, that this would leave the state with a projected shortfall of $3 billion in 2001–2002 and nearly $5 billion in 2002–2003 turned out to be just about on the mark.

1. H. Carl McCall, *2000–01 Budget Analysis: Review of the Enacted Budget* (Albany: Office of the State Comptroller, 2000).

---

future that most informed observers (comptroller H. Carl McCall in particular) were already warning of severe fiscal problems in 2000 and beyond (see Box 8.1). The governor's 1998 vetoes, moreover, had put a serious strain on his relations with the legislature. Unable to trust Pataki to keep his word, legislative leaders had been devising ways to force the governor to keep his part of the agreement when a final budget was passed.

The legislature usually takes some steps to, in effect, keep the governor honest. It can, as one former staff director of the ways and means committee put it, "set a series of time bombs" in the budget bills.[25] Typically the budget is put together in eight separate bills. Four of these are appropriations bills that deal largely with numbers, and four are "language" bills that detail how the dollar amounts in the appropriation bills actually will be spent. One way in which the legislature can time-bomb the governor is by passing two bills at a time, sending the governor the bills that include education, for example, ten legislative days before sending him the bill that includes corrections. In this way, the governor knows that the items he vetoes in the first bill may haunt him in trying to get what he wants in the second. The language bills also can be used to reduce the threat of vetoes, either by conflating budget items in such a way that the line-item veto does not work or by linking budget lines that the legislature wants to those on the governor's list of priorities.

Perhaps anticipating this kind of battle, Governor Pataki took the unprecedented step of submitting his 1999 budget in the form of one bill instead of the traditional eight. By folding all his "language" (which the legislature cannot change) into the budget and by sending everything in one package (which had to be passed or rejected all at once), the governor gave the legislature almost no negotiating power. His aides, speaking candidly but off the record, described "the packaging of the budget as a masterstroke that hobbles the Legislature and greatly increases the Governor's power."[26] Substantively, Pataki's budget did not include increased funds for reducing class sizes in grades one through three, funds he had specifically agreed to in a deal with the assembly to pass his 1997 plan for cutting school taxes. But Pataki had the legislature in the difficult position of having to take his budget essentially as submitted or craft a new one of its own. What enabled the legislature to reassert itself at this stage was the ability of the senate and assembly leaders to present a united front to the governor, insisting on their own priorities. This tactic worked, and the 2000 budget was submitted in a more traditional eleven chapters rather than one. The final agreement on an overall package—an agreement that included a pledge of limits on what kinds of vetoes the governor might exercise—was negotiated by the traditional triumvirate of the governor, speaker, and majority leader. The result was the longest budget standoff in the history of the state.

There is little doubt that the Pataki years saw an evolution toward more confrontational politics. Budgets, like other issues, were negotiated by press releases and oriented more toward symbols than substance, what a staff member once described as "the annual dance of the budget flamingoes . . . where the birds bow and then strut around flapping their wings" before getting down to serious negotiations.[27] And there were years under divided government when it was almost all flapping and strutting. With one-party control there may be less noise, but divisions between the governor and the two houses will not disappear. In his first budget fight, Governor Spitzer had as much trouble with assembly Democrats as he did with senate Republicans, just as Pataki had been unable to count on senate Republicans. The magnitude of the cuts proposed in Governor Paterson's 2009 and 2010 budgets all but guarantee sharp conflicts with both parties in both houses of the legislature. And the flamingoes continue to dance.

Administering the Budget

Once the budget has been approved, money must actually be allotted to each agency or local government. The legislature, when it passes the final draft of the budget, compiles its detailed summary of the agreements it has reached with the governor into a document known as *The Green Book*, which—although it does not have the legal status of the actual appropriations bills—is so much more user-friendly that most legislators and bureaucrats trying to figure out what the numbers mean use it instead. Within weeks of the budget agreement, each agency is required to submit a spending plan to the DOB that explains how it plans to operate within the budget and when it will need each allocation of funds. Before it can actually write any checks, an agency's spending plans must be approved by the DOB and cleared by the comptroller. While these clearances are normally routine, it is understood that as needs and circumstances change, adjustments must be made. When the highway department, for example, confronts a particularly stormy winter, the DOB usually will not challenge its need to exceed its budget authority for snow removal, though it may require it to find the money through savings in some other part of the departmental budget.

DOB approval of an agency's spending plans comes in the form of a certificate of approval confirming the availability of funds: without such a certificate, the comptroller may not issue any checks. In good times, an agency with a record of reliability and relatively predictable spending needs can get a certificate of approval for its entire budget. When funds are tight or when an agency lacks the confidence of the governor and the budget office, money may be allocated a quarter or even a month at a time.

Adding and Cutting Appropriated Funds

Theoretically, no agency can spend more or less than the amount of money budgeted for a specific function. Budget categories are usually broad enough to allow minor adjustments, and the rules are seldom so rigidly enforced that key programs are delayed or impaired. When an agency really faces a crisis, however, it must return to the legislature for what is called a deficiency appropriation. While the governor and the legislature will normally respond to such requests when essential, "they are not designed to provide another opportunity for the agencies to make a pitch for more money. One DOB examiner stated that, on occasion, agencies have come to the Division just a few months after the budget was passed, looking for substantial deficiency appropriations. 'There is a difference between a legitimate need for a deficiency appropriation, and a fundamental lack of respect for the laws, the Legislature, and the Governor.'"[28]

Agency funds, on the other hand, can be cut. Although the governor of New York is not authorized by the constitution to impound (or refuse to spend) appropriated funds, functional impoundments have become almost routine. They are restricted in three significant ways.

First, the governor may not touch the budgets of either the courts or the legislature. Second, debt payments and capital projects currently under construction cannot be stopped. Third, and most important, local assistance appropriations cannot be impounded or reduced. Once the state aid formulas for health care, schools, and general aid to localities have been signed into law, the state court of appeals has ruled, they cannot be changed.[29]

When projected revenues are coming up short, these restrictions put a heavy burden on state agencies. Because accounts that cannot be cut, aid to localities most importantly, constitute more than 60 percent of total state spending, the impact of even a small deficit on the remaining agencies can be quite significant. If state tax collections in November are running a billion dollars behind the amount projected in the budget, an across-the-board cut would reduce spending by less than 2 percent— *if* it was truly across the board. Most agencies can find ways to cut spending by 1 or 2 percent; but with so many budgets protected by law, the reality of a $1 billion cut for nonexempt agencies is cuts in the range of 5 percent or more. And since the fiscal year is half over and roughly half the originally planned dollars already have been spent, the impact in the last half of the year may be double that.

Funds that are withheld or impounded to meet a looming fiscal crisis seldom provoke great controversy unless there is a perception that the governor has unfairly concentrated on a few programs. In 1983–1984, when Governor Cuomo impounded funds that had specifically been added to his budget by the legislature, his move very nearly provoked a constitutional crisis. Although the governor had agreed to restore some of the funds his budget had cut from the offices of mental health and mental retardation and the state and city universities, he persisted in imposing staff cuts on these agencies in seeming defiance of his agreement with the legislature. The immediate crisis was resolved when Cuomo agreed to "very specific language requiring him to report on the deviations from the staffing levels that had been agreed to."[30] In subsequent budgets, the legislature bargained into its *Green Book* language that was very specific not just as to dollar amounts, but also as to minimum, maximum, and average staffing levels, and it added very specific reporting requirements to the appropriation language bills. Adding legislative language of this kind has become more difficult since *Silver v. Pataki*, but governors are nonetheless reluctant to risk antagonizing the legislature by stretching their impoundment powers. Although he did not get all the cuts he wanted, Governor Paterson solidified his standing with the legislature by calling in its leaders for consultations before ordering a series of midyear budget cuts in the fiscal crisis of 2008. His action was particularly appreciated by legislative leaders who had not generally received such consideration from Governor Pataki. Pataki had been unusually more willing than his predecessors to impound appropriated funds for programs that he simply did not like, but he paid for this willingness in the long run with a final few years in office in which he had virtually no credibility in either house of the legislature.

What does an administrator do when confronted with an impoundment order?

In 1995, when Governor Pataki announced that he was cutting the city university's budget for the spring semester, Chancellor Ann Reynolds acceded. Cries of outrage from some faculty, student groups, and legislators were of little avail as long as the chancellor herself was not prepared to spend the money. Although she was widely criticized for not taking a more aggressive stance, no administrator heading into a new budget year wants to begin by picking a public fight with the governor. One high official in the state insurance department told us that the only realistic option he would have in a similar circumstance was to "go to the second floor and beg."

Where the Money Comes From

Most of the time when journalists and politicians talk about "the budget," they are referring to the $120 billion or so included as "all funds" spending in the governor's budget. Of this amount, only about $85 billion is actually state money; the rest comes, essentially, from the federal government, and only about $55 billion is "general fund" spending.[31] It does not include funds borrowed for the capital projects of authorities and special programs nor the fees collected by independent authorities to support their operations. If the budget numbers were to include such sources of revenue as college tuition charges and license fees, the state actually raises quite a bit more than the budget reports. More importantly, New York, as we noted in Chapter 2, is unusually reliant on its localities—and on local taxes— to support major services. Thus, although its combined state and local tax burden amply justifies its reputation as a high-tax state, the state itself is below the national midpoint in taxes it directly imposes on its citizens. The formal state budget, to put it another way, is deceptively small and tells only a part of the story of how funds are raised and spent. The state and its local entities collected roughly $140 billion in 2006–2007. The state's share of this total amount, which is our focus for the next few pages, was—not including federal funds—a little more than half of the total.

State Taxes, Transfers, and Fees

In 2006–2007 the state took in roughly $60 billion in taxes, $21 billion in miscellaneous receipts, and $37 billion in federal grants. By far the most important source of tax revenue is the personal income tax, which generates more than half ($36.3 billion in 2006–2007) of all tax receipts. User taxes (mainly the sales tax) and fees (such as motor vehicle registration charges) are second in importance, generating $14 to $16 billion a year. Corporate taxes account for about $8.5 billion. As we have noted, however, these numbers tell only part of the story.

When we add in the capital budget, only part of which shows up in the budget adopted by the legislature, the $12 billion or so borrowed by various public authorities, other so-called off-budget accounts administered by state agencies, and the taxes and fees imposed by local governments, the most significant long-term trend in New York's pattern of raising revenue is a continuing decline in the proportion of dollars captured by taxes on individual and corporate income. The state income tax has been reduced at both ends to the point where it is virtually a flat tax. At the close of the Rockefeller era, New York had one of the country's most sharply progressive personal income tax systems, with the very poor paying nothing and the very rich paying as much as 15 percent on their highest earnings. Gradually the legislature worked with Governors Carey, Cuomo, and Pataki to cut the top rate and increase the low end at which people begin paying taxes. In 1998, the top rate was reduced to 6.85 percent, paid not just by millionaires but also on any income over $47,500 for a single person with no deductions. Under this system, state residents pay no taxes on their first $7,500. A single person earning $20,000 pays nothing on the first $7,500 and 4.3 percent on the balance. At $47,500, the first $7,500 is still exempt and every extra dollar earned is taxed at the maximum rate of 6.85 percent. From there up, taxes are no longer adjusted for income.

Despite cuts in corporate taxes and this new policy of taxing the rich at the same maximum rate as the middle class, the state was able in part to keep itself afloat through economic growth. In years when private sector income grew more rapidly than government spending, the state could afford tax cuts without significant cuts in services. Those years were few and far between through most of the Carey-Cuomo era. The Pataki administration benefited from an unusually long, strong period of sustained economic growth combined with record profits on Wall Street and a major decline in the number of people in need of social services. By cutting taxes still further and maintaining spending, however, it too was unable to effectively balance the budget. As in the Cuomo years, Pataki's administration essentially disguised and made up the shortfall by a variety of gimmicks and devolutions. Four were particularly important.

First, the state resorted to a variety of fiscal gimmicks that provided cosmetic rather than real solutions to the state's fiscal problems. The 2000–2001 budget adopted by the legislature in June 2000, as we have seen (see Box 8.1), seemingly included a reasonably prudent $4 billion in reserve and "rainy day funds" that turned out to be more fog than rain—actually only about $550 million, totaling just over 1 percent of total receipts. Second, New York continues to devolve an unusually high proportion of its tax burden to local governments. "The property tax is by far the largest tax imposed by local governments in New York State, representing 79 percent of all local taxes outside of New York City. Local property tax levies totaled $38 billion in 2005—reflecting an increase of more than $11 billion (42 percent) since 2000—and generating more revenue than even the State's $28 billion personal income tax."[32] New York City also raises more money from its own income, sales, and property taxes than it receives from the state. Third, the state has shifted the focus of its revenue collections from broad-based corporate and personal income taxes to a wide variety of more targeted taxes and fees, including the lottery (which nets about $1.6 billion a year). Governor Cuomo made up for some of the revenue lost in corporate and personal income tax cuts by sharply increasing so-called sin taxes on beer, liquor, cigarettes, and pari-mutuel betting. And Governor Pataki, at the same time that he was cutting the top end of the income tax rate schedule, sharply increased tuition at the state's public universities and the fees charged for the use of public facilities such as campgrounds. Local governments have followed much the same path. "In 1990, 22.5 percent of state general revenue from its own resources (not including federal aid) came from this source. For local governments, the percentage was 25.6."[33] The fourth way in which the state has made up for the revenues lost to tax cuts— particularly in bad years—has been by borrowing and by manipulating the accounts to make borrowing look as if it is something else.

Borrowing

When it resorted to borrowing to begin the Erie Canal in 1817, New York pioneered a new strategy of economic development that was soon imitated throughout the United States. A century later, Robert Moses expanded upon and refined this development strategy through the creation of a network of debt-funded public authorities. Local governments, with state encouragement, were soon to follow. Government borrowing generally takes three forms: long-term general obligation bonds, long-term revenue bonds, and short-term borrowing. Short-term borrowing is used largely to meet cash-flow problems and cover emergencies. The idea behind long-term debt is that some expenditures, particularly those for capital projects such as school buildings, highways, and fire trucks, need not be paid for all at once because they benefit future taxpayers as well as current ones.

General Obligation Bonds

Under the state constitution, long-term borrowing plans must be passed by the legislature and submitted to public referendums. If the electorate approves, the state—or one of its local governments—issues bonds, which it promises to pay off over a stipulated number of years. These bonds, called general obligation bonds, are backed by the "full faith and credit" of the state, which means, in essence, that the bondholders have first claim to the state's future revenues. Because of the security this commitment affords and because the interest earned on government bonds is tax-free, they can be sold at relatively low interest rates. Thus, by providing this safe investment, the state can borrow money at a lower rate than a corporation or private citizen would have to pay.

Bonds, like other investment tools, are sold in a competitive market. A bank or individual considering an investment in New York bonds will compare them with bonds from other state and local governments, corporations, and the federal government. Some of these investments are rated safer than others. Although it might seem unlikely that a state as wealthy as New York would not be able to pay its debts, defaults of this kind are not unheard of. In April 1975, for example, the city of New York ran out of money and no bank could be found to extend the loans that would allow it to pay its bills. This was, moreover, the third time in its history that the city had gone broke.[34] Many state and local governments—particularly during the Great Depression—have weathered similar crises. Obviously, investors seeking security are reluctant to loan money to cities or states with poor payment records. Governments with poor histories of debt management also can have problems with the voters. Although New York voters are generally supportive of government programs, since 1990 they have rejected four of the six bond issues put to them. The government, however, has found other ways of borrowing money.

Revenue Bonds

Unlike general obligation bonds, so-called revenue bonds are not backed by the full faith and credit of the state; instead, money from an identified revenue stream is pledged as a safeguard for investments. Bonds issued by the state dormitory authority are backed by the promise of future rentals to college students, state Thruway bonds by future tolls, and so on. Although neither the state itself nor its municipalities can issue revenue bonds without the approval of the electorate, public authorities need only the approval of the legislature to float new bonds. It is this ability to avoid the electorate and not add to general obligation debt that has led to the creation of so many public authorities in New York and other states.

Strictly speaking, funds borrowed through revenue bonds are supposed to be used to build facilities that will generate revenues. Some public authorities, however, have been allowed to bend the rules. City College's main classroom building, for example, was built by the state dormitory authority, though nobody has ever paid to sleep there. Increasingly, moreover, the state has allowed its public authorities to issue "moral obligation" bonds. Although there are limits on how much such paper can be issued, the line between revenue and general obligation bonds has been blurred beyond recognition. A relatively new device for avoiding the referendums required for general obligation bonds or the revenues backing revenue bonds is so-called lease-purchasing. The Albany South Mall and office buildings in Binghamton and Utica, for example, were built with local revenue bonds that were guaranteed by the promise of future rental of the facilities by the state. Years ago, one state agency "sold" the Attica prison to another agency, which paid for it with borrowed money and then leased it back.

The financial crisis faced by New York City in the 1970s was founded in a cumulative reliance on fiscal gimmicks such as these. Rather than raise taxes or cut services, the city continued to project unrealistic levels of economic growth. In good years, high tax collections and state and federal aid allowed the city to muddle through; in bad years, it resorted to borrowing so much that, in 1974, New York accounted for nearly 40 percent of all municipal debt in the United States![35] Some of these borrowed funds—such as the "transit fare stabilization fund"—did not even pretend to be for capital purposes. The governor and legislature authorized these gimmicks rather than face demands for more state money; eventually the city's short-term debt exceeded a full year's worth of revenues. The financial control mechanisms installed in bailing out New York City have banned some of these practices and strongly regulated others, but if the distinction between various kinds of debts was never precise, it is even murkier now.

Short-Term Borrowing and Fiscal Reality

As long as a government's credit is good, the advantages of long-term borrowing are clear. It both spreads payments over a long time span and generally comes at low interest rates. But there are times when more expensive forms of debt must be incurred. For many years New York State annually engaged in an expensive ritual known as spring borrowing. The problem was that even when the budget was in balance by the end of the year, the state usually had a stream of receipts at odds with the flow of disbursements. While most of the money disbursed to local governments and school districts went out in the first quarter (April through June), most taxes were collected in the fourth (January through March). For years the state paid literally hundreds of millions of dollars in interest on these loans, money that could have been spent on tax cuts or improved state services. The practice of spring borrowing has been replaced by changes in the flow of certain revenues and disbursements and by converting some forms of short-term debt into bonds. Nevertheless, both the state and its local governments must sometimes borrow to meet emergencies.

Short-turn borrowing always occurs when a downturn in the economy results in lower than expected revenues or when expenses are unusually high. But while such miscalculations may well occur from time to time, the frequency with which they have arisen in New York suggests that they are almost endemic to the budget-making process. Indeed, the governor and the legislature sometimes pass budgets that they know are unrealistic in the hope that they can make up the difference next year. As Raymond Keating says, this practice has been going on for a long time: "These shady debt practices . . . were perfected during Governor Rockefeller's tenure. Voter approval of long-term debt presented a serious drag on his plans for expanding state government, so Rockefeller stepped around the voters through the use of public authorities as well as debt arrangements with localities."[36]

As a result, New York's state debt has skyrocketed to an estimated $2,517 per person, fifth highest among the states and double the national average; this figure does not include local debt. More and more of this debt has come through back-door borrowing, borrowing that is not approved by the voters, which now makes up more than 90 percent of state-funded debt.[37] Not surprisingly, debt service is one of the fastest-growing categories in the state budget, projected by the comptroller to rise to more than $7.1 billion by 2010.

Periodically, governors and legislators express concern about the debt. But not until key business service organizations, like Moody's, rated New York's bonds among the lowest in the nation did Governor Pataki and the legislature begin serious discussions about using the surpluses generated in 1998–1999 and 1999–2000 to begin paying it off. While the legislature passed a debt retirement initiative proposed by the governor as part of his 1998–1999 budget, most of the payments it provided for were projected for future years and never actually put in place. In fact, the state actually contracted more debt in these two years than it paid off. Another serious initiative, in Governor Spitzer's first year, ran aground as the state's economy slipped in 2008. Borrowing by authorities and local governments, meanwhile, continues; it is difficult to contain as long as state aid lags behind needs. Focused on tax cuts and the maintenance of existing services despite a rate of economic growth that is too slow to pay for both at once, state and local politicians find that "circumvention is cheaper than change, even though its outcomes may well be far from ideal"[38] (see Box 8.2).

Who Pays?

In the normal order of things, economists rate the progressivity of a tax system according to the degree to which it taxes the rich at a higher rate than the poor. Sales and property taxes are considered regressive because they impose the same burden on everyone regardless of ability to pay; income taxes, because the rates typically rise with earnings, are progressive. In New York, ironically, conventional wisdom does not work very well. The very poor, those earning less than $15,000 to $20,000 a year, pay very little income tax. Middle-class families and individuals, on the other hand, pay income taxes at the same rates as those who are far more affluent. Because they are less likely to itemize deductions, in fact, middle-class families sometimes pay even higher effective rates than their wealthy neighbors. User fees, similarly, hit low- and middle-class families harder than the more affluent: in New York, a car owner pays the same fee to register a 1999 Chevrolet as a 2009 Rolls Royce; a millionaire pays the same fee for a fishing license as a pauper. The sales tax in New York, conversely, is not as regressive as it is in many other states because it excludes such items as food and medicine, which form a large share of a low-income family's budget.

Generally, the property tax is America's most hated tax: "Unlike other taxes, it usually has to be paid in one large, painfully visible lump sum. It doesn't go down when personal income and the ability to pay it go down. Its assessments are uneven: People who own similar properties may pay widely divergent taxes. And in many communities the weight of the tax is tilted to ease the burden of business so a heavier load falls on homeowners."[39] Because local governments rely on the property tax to fund so many key programs and because it forms the backbone of the state's system of local government finance, the property tax plays an unusually significant role in New York and, as we shall see, accounts for substantial inequities, especially in financing schools.

Gimmicks

"There are," Forsythe warns, "no simple definitions of 'budget success.' . . . A successful budget is one that delivers on a governor's programmatic objectives, and does so within financial constraints that help achieve or maintain structural budget

Box 8.2
Reading a Budget

Political science textbooks (like this one) try to make the case (as we do) that government budgets can explain what governments actually do. This is fine in theory, but not very helpful when one reads the actual documents or goes online to figure out whose money is being spent for what. As government becomes larger and more complex, budgets become more difficult to read. But complexity alone does not explain how extraordinarily opaque many budgets—including New York's—have become.

Those in power "sometimes prefer not to share accurate information with others." Indeed, *"bad* data is *good* for some participants in the process."[1] There is nothing new in this kind of deliberate obfuscation. It was said of one key congressman, "You can always tell how much money is involved by how hard it is to understand him."[2] And as far back as 1802, Thomas Jefferson warned his secretary of the treasury to beware of the numbers provided by his predecessor, Alexander Hamilton. Hamilton, Jefferson wrote, "in order to control the government, determined so to complicate it as that neither the President nor Congress should be able to understand it, or to control him. He succeeded in doing this, not only beyond their reach, but so that he at length could not unravel it himself. He gave to the debt, in the first instance, in funding it, the most artificial and mysterious form he could devise. He then mounded up his appropriations of a number of scraps and remnants, many of which were nothing at all . . . until the whole system was involved in impenetrable fog."[3]

It is worth peering into this fog, first through the governor's numbers and newspaper accounts. But the clearest analyses of particular parts of the budget are generally found in the reports of those most affected, such as the teachers' unions in the case of education or transportation companies in the case of transportation. Discounting for their biases, this is how most legislators pick their way through the budget. Even better are organizations set up specifically to explicate the budget. New York City and a number of states have citizens' budget committees to perform this role. In New York state, the union-backed Fiscal Policy Institute and the state Business Council do well from their particular perspectives. And the comptroller's annual reports, though they do not appear until after the budget is in effect, are usually quite a bit more readable.

1. Roy T. Meyers, *Strategic Budgeting* (Ann Arbor: University of Michigan Press, 1994), p. 19.
2. Ibid., 57.
3. Ibid., 209.

balance."[40] Throughout his intriguing memos to a hypothetical governor, Forsythe makes the sometimes explicit assumption that a key role of any governor is to keep a wild-spending legislature from giving away the store. It is true that legislators, without regard to party or ideology, are more generous with the taxpayers' money for certain kinds of spending programs. Because legislators' political risks are more localized, they tend to be more solicitous of local interests and thus are frequently at odds with governors in fighting reductions in school aid and general state aid to local governments. But for all their seeming frugality when it comes to such issues, all of New York's recent governors have promoted the construction of prisons, tax cuts, and economic development initiatives that often far outweigh all the spending increases proposed by the most spendthrift legislators.

How is it possible to cut taxes, increase school aid and transportation funding, build more prisons, and not make substantial cuts in vital areas such as health? The most desirable way is through the kind of economic growth that increases tax collections and lowers costs for social welfare programs—the rising tide that lifts all ships. Like the tide, however, such growth is something over which the state has little direct control. What the governor and legislative leaders can control are their perceptions and projections of economic growth. In bad times and especially in election years, all sides face a strong temptation to agree to raise their estimates in a triumph of hope over intelligence. If the budget ends up out of balance by a billion or so, they can worry about that next year.

Similar fudging can be achieved by introducing programs in stages, hoping that by the time the last payments are due there will have been enough economic growth to pay them. Governor Pataki's tax-cut plan, for example, was heavily backloaded, providing only $1.4 billion in cuts in its first year but rising to $11.3 billion in 2000–2001. Before the state changed its accounting rules in the 1980s, a favorite device for hiding deficits was to postpone expenditures—in effect, paying the bills late. If, for example, a payment to the civil service pension fund due in the last quarter of one fiscal year is not actually paid until the beginning of the next year, the money has apparently been "saved." (Do not try this at home.) Devices such as this, or the example given earlier of one state agency "selling" an asset to another and then leasing it back, are known as "one shots" since they only work once. Frequently deplored, they are just as frequently used to make budget agreements less painful. Longer-run solutions, such as "backdoor" borrowing (backdoor in the sense that it is neither approved by the voters nor dedicated to revenue-producing capital projects) or transferring the costs of state programs to local governments, are equally common. In the words of former state comptroller Ned Regan:

> The way Albany works is very clear: it's gain here, pain there. It's gain in Albany and pain in Yonkers or New York City. . . . It's gain here and the pain is fifteen years later when you're paying the debt service for all those borrowings made to balance the budget. It's always the same pattern, shift responsibility to another government, shift from the operating budgets to the capital budget. You shift the gain this year for the ribbon cutting ceremonies and the rebuilding effort and spread the pain out over time.[41]

New York is not unique in its resort to such gimmicks. There is, however, some consensus that the game is played more recklessly and persistently in New

York than in most other jurisdictions. One explanation, frequently offered, is that budget gimmicks are more common in New York because the state is so uncommonly generous in catering to special interests and the poor. Before we examine the overall dynamic of policy politics in New York, let us turn to the issue of how the state allocates its resources.

Where the Money Goes

It costs about $3 billion a year just to keep the government going. State courts alone account for more than $2 billion, the legislature for more than $200 million, and the offices associated with the governor a little over $125 million. It costs $430 million just to raise the taxes to pay for everything else. An additional $6 billion a year pays the interest on old debts, and another $5 billion pays the pensions of retired state employees. The state, in other words, spends more than $14 billion a year without educating a single child, repairing a road, or treating a gallon of sewage. Roughly one dollar in every seven of general fund disbursements supports the operations of past and present governments. Of the remaining six dollars, more than four are transferred to local governments. Only 19 percent of all general fund spending falls in the category of what are called "state operations."

If you strip the state budget to its naked essence, it amounts to this: pensions, debt services, and general government operations aside, about 30 percent of the state's money goes to health, 30 percent to education, and 40 percent to everything else. Much of this money is channeled through and frequently augmented by varying levels of local expenditure, but even at the local level, health and education constitute the big-ticket items on the government bill. Let us put this very explicitly: *if you really want to cut public spending in New York, you must cut funding for health or schools.*

Health

New York's public health care system is largely driven, as are those of most states, by the federal Medicaid program, but it is unique among state health care systems in both size and complexity. Long before the federal government became involved, New York government played a huge role in promoting the health of its citizens. While most states found Medicaid's cost-sharing requirements a drain on their treasuries, New York took the 1965 establishment of the federal program as an opportunity to use federal funds for services it already provided, augmenting and expanding existing state efforts.

Despite attempts to cut back, New York's system of health care delivery remains the largest, most closely regulated, and most complex in the United States. In 2006, the state maintained 203 hospitals with approximately 57,000 beds, and 638 nursing homes with just under 118,000 beds. Medicaid costs alone constituted $8.2 billion—or 18 percent—of the state's "all funds" budget. Although health systems throughout the state are administered by the state department of health, New York City's Health and Hospitals Corporation (HHC) actually has a larger payroll, and local governments throughout the state play an unusually large role both in managing and financing health policies. In few areas of public policy, and in few areas of the United States, is the term *marble-cake federalism* (see Chapter 2) a more appropriate descriptive term.

Medicare and Medicaid

Medicare and Medicaid were enacted in 1965 to provide public insurance to the elderly and low-income Americans, delivered through states. While many liberals had long been pushing for a program of national health along European lines, Medicare emerged as a compromise proposal focusing on the particularly acute needs of senior citizens. Almost as an afterthought, Medicaid was added on to help the non-elderly poor. Medicare, as an add-on to Social Security, is essentially a two-part program of health insurance and hospital insurance, paid for by federal taxes and individual payments. Except as to payment schedules and fees, the program has relatively little direct impact on state finances. Medicaid, conversely, because it is a program of matching funds, has a very substantial and direct impact on the state and its localities.

The line between Medicare and Medicaid is not as clear as it once seemed. Many elderly people require expensive, long-term care. Medicare does not cover all the attendant costs, forcing low-income retirees onto Medicaid as *dual eligibles*. A very substantial proportion of the funds spent on Medicaid go toward the long-term nursing home care of senior citizens who were not poor enough to qualify when they first became ill. Cumulatively, the numbers are staggering:

> In 2007, about 72 percent of New York State's 117,992 nursing home beds were paid for by Medicaid, with 13 percent by Medicare. New York has experienced a rapidly growing elderly population with more than a quarter of the state's population over sixty-five years of age. While those over sixty-five years of age comprise 11 percent of New York State's eligible Medicaid population, their care consumed 42 percent of New York's Medicaid budget in 2006. Thirty-seven percent of Medicaid went to pay for nursing home costs.[42]

Medicaid operates at the state level according to federal guidelines established by the Centers for Medicare and Medicaid. In New York, the federal government covers roughly half the overall costs and the state about one-third, with local governments (counties outside of New York City) responsible for the balance. Until recently, Medicaid funds were channeled through a broad array of local care providers including hospitals, clinics, nursing homes, physicians, dentists, and pharmacists. In this "fee for service" system, the provider billed the state according to a schedule of fees set by the state with federal approval. When the state attempted to save money by periodically cutting fees to lower levels, a growing number of private providers dropped out of the system, leaving much of it in the hands of government-run clinics and hospitals. Most of the private-practice doctors willing to accept the set rate of $11 per office visit were found in what became known as "Medicaid mills," privately run clinics in which the level of service was cursory at best. Medicaid mills could be highly profitable by processing patients very rapidly and by engaging in such practices as "ping-ponging" patients from one specialist to another.

Beginning in March 1997, the state received approval from the federal government to implement a statewide mandatory managed care program, essentially revamping health care delivery to Medicaid recipients. Although managed care is often criticized by both physicians and advocacy groups, it has proven enormously cost-effective in delivering at least minimal services to target populations. According to a report published by the New York City Department of Health, 2 million residents are enrolled in the New York Medicaid managed care program, of which 1.5 million reside in New York City.[43]

State Children's Health Insurance Program

In 1997, the largest expansion of health insurance since 1965 was passed and signed into law under President Bill Clinton. Augmenting Medicaid, the State Children's Health Insurance Program (SCHIP) provides coverage to uninsured low-income children who do not qualify for Medicaid. For the first time, working families above the official poverty level became eligible for government-supported health care. Partly funded by the states, SCHIP allows each state considerable latitude to decide eligibility levels and the kinds of services to be covered. Not surprisingly, New York opted in at a relatively generous level. In the sluggish economy of the Bush years, both Medicaid and SCHIP faced serious challenges. At the federal level, new guidelines reconfigured eligibility for the program and reduced the states' flexibility. These changes would have rather sharply reduced the number of children covered by SCHIP in New York. When Congress responded with a bill that would have given the more generous state plans increased funding, it was vetoed by the president, as was a later compromise bill. Eventually, the program was extended through March 2009, though without increased funding. This has left states like New York in the awkward position of trying to keep their more generous programs in place with decreased federal support.

The Politics of Health

Most Americans (53 percent)—and most New Yorkers (52 percent)—receive health coverage through their jobs. With its high poverty rate, New York is slightly above the national average in the percentage of those eligible for Medicaid (19 percent) and those with no health coverage at all (14 percent). Despite attempts by the state to increase Medicaid and SCHIP coverage to include the children of families above the poverty line, a substantial reduction in private coverage has resulted in a rapid increase in the ranks of the uninsured. The low-income working poor, recent immigrants in particular, are most disadvantaged, with 36 percent uninsured. New York City has a particularly large proportion of this population, with 28 percent uninsured as compared with 14 percent in the rest of the state.[44]

New York City's HHC is bigger by far than any other hospital system in the United States. While many hospital patients are privately insured or reimbursed through Medicaid, city hospitals serve enormous numbers of indigent, uninsured patients. This financial burden is compounded by the high incidence of tuberculosis and AIDS in New York City (in 2006, for example, 39 percent of all AIDS cases nationwide were in New York) and its high rates of homelessness, alcoholism, and drug abuse. To understand the dynamics of health care politics in New York, these differences between New York City and the rest of the state must be kept in mind.

Throughout the United States, the cost of providing health care has climbed at a rate far higher than inflation. Current estimates show that health spending constitutes 15.7 percent of the gross domestic product, the second-highest rate in the world. At all levels of government, cost containment has become crucial. By moving Medicaid patients into mandatory managed care programs, the state expects to realize significant savings through increased primary care use, lower emergency room use, and fewer inpatient days. Other attempts to cut spending on health care, however, have been strongly resisted by the legislature in general and the assembly's Democratic majority in particular. The legislature's general reluctance to cut the health care budget derives from three key political facts. First—and this applies to governors as well as legislators—health care is popular with voters, especially senior citizens and their children. Nursing home care in New York is expensive but it is also generally of higher quality than in other states. And the state's hospitals and doctors are among the finest in the world, with more prestigious teaching hospitals than anywhere else. Second, people do not like to see hospitals closed. Although many hospitals are inefficient or duplicate the services of nearby facilities, closing a hospital is a tough sell with voters. Third, the health care lobby is large and diversified. It spends a lot of money, employs some of Albany's most skillful legislative representatives, and cuts across the political spectrum. It includes both the Republican-leaning state medical society and two large labor unions representing hospital workers that have close ties to the Democrats. The lobby also includes several large insurance companies, the Greater New York Hospital Association, and the Healthcare Association of New York. Three of these organizations were among the top spenders listed in the lobbying commission's 2007 annual report.[45]

Democrats in the assembly are particularly protective of health care, partly because of these pressures, largely because they believe that the government should provide basic health care for all, and very significantly because even relatively small cuts in the state's health expenditures are magnified in the city. In the eleven hospitals and more than eighty community clinics operated by the city, most of the patients are poor and without private health insurance. The state adds a surcharge to all hospital care transactions to help finance a charity pool that reimburses both public and private hospitals for the cost of treating persons unable to pay their bills, but this fund typically covers less than half of the hospitals' actual costs.

For years hospitals absorbed the medically indigent by charging insured patients more. This practice, long attacked by the insurance industry, has become almost impossible under a managed care system of health. The problem for municipal hospitals is particularly acute. The more Medicare rules are tightened, the less revenue is received by the hospitals. In order to keep the city hospital system afloat, therefore, legislators from New York City must fight to keep Medicaid dollars flowing. Although the city puts up fifteen cents of every Medicaid dollar, it is the eighty-five cents in state and federal funds that keeps public hospitals running. Certain fixed costs must be paid whether hospital beds are empty or occupied. For public hospitals then, cuts in Medicaid, instead of saving the city money, may, paradoxically, force it to dig deeper into its own resources to keep marginal hospitals afloat. From a fiscal and political perspective, in other words, neither New York City nor its representatives in Albany can afford substantial cuts in state health funds.

Outside of the city, on the other hand, local governments must pay their largely private hospitals for every procedure, every patient. Their politicians, most vociferously Nassau County's Democratic county executive Thomas Suozzi, in what has been called a "county rebellion" have been lobbying for a cap on the local share of Medicare expenses. Jeffrey Kraus quotes state senator James Wright on what he calls "the dilemma of Medicaid reform": "There's not one area of Medicaid that is good. If you're going to reform it, [there's no reform] that doesn't have some political risk in terms of its impact on major employers, major service providers, major constituency groups. . . . That's just the reality of what we deal with. It's why you haven't seen major reform in 40 years."[46]

Education

New York State's public schools enroll nearly 2.8 million students at an average cost of more than $15,000 per student. As noted in Chapter 1, the state's students are highly diverse. A high percentage of New York's graduates are regularly among those writing advanced placement exams, winning prestigious prizes, and being commended by the National Merit Scholars Program. But while graduates of New York's public and private schools average considerably higher scores than the rest of the nation on college entry tests, New York ranked among the ten worst states in terms of estimated public high school graduation rates (see Box 8.3).

Funding the Public Schools

These extremes of excellence and failure are closely related to the extremes of poverty and wealth that characterize New York. Poor children and those from families

Box 8.3
Separate and Unequal
The Effects of Income Disparities on the Schools

The differences in per pupil expenditures described in the suit that the Campaign for Fiscal Equity filed against the state are not just numbers. They result in real differences that have been vividly described by education writer Jonathan Kozol, who has spent forty years comparing schools in inner cities and their more affluent suburbs. Despite increases in per pupil spending, Kozol notes, "the present New York City level is . . . almost exactly what Manhasset spent per pupil eighteen years ago." In the city, the median salary of schoolteachers in 2002–2003 was $53,000, as compared with $87,000 in Manhasset and $95,000 in Scarsdale. In one South Bronx school Kozol visited, "class size rose to thirty-four and more; four kindergarten classes and a sixth grade class were packed into a single room that had no windows. The air was stifling in many rooms and the children had no place for recess because there was no outdoor playground and no indoor gym." Libraries were virtually nonexistent in inner-city schools. Art and music programs had also for the most part disappeared. Kozol quotes the principal of an elementary school in the South Bronx: "When I began to teach in 1969, every school had a full-time licensed art and music teacher and librarian." During the subsequent decades, the principal recalled, "I saw all of that destroyed."

Most of the underfunded and poorly performing schools Kozol visited were essentially segregated. He describes schools in four cities, ironically named for Martin Luther King, that are almost entirely black and Hispanic: Boston (98 percent), Cleveland (97 percent), Philadelphia (98 percent), Los Angeles (99 percent). One school in New York referred to the "diversity" of its student body: of 2,800 children, it turned out, there was one Asian child and three whites. Kozol related this racial segregation to the schools' graduation rates:

In the 94 percent of districts in New York State where white children make up the majority, nearly 80 percent of students graduate from high school in four years. In the 6 percent of districts where black and Hispanic students make up the majority, only 40 percent do so. There are 120 high schools in New York, enrolling nearly 200,000 minority students, where less than 60 percent of entering ninth-graders even make it to twelfth grade.

Are these performance differences accounted for by money? Given the disadvantages that many inner-city children face—parents who are themselves poorly educated, the absence of preschool programs, cramped living quarters that make quiet study all but impossible—would spending more money on schools make any difference?

Some people who ask these questions, although they live in wealthy districts where the schools are funded at high levels, don't even send their children to
(continued)

Box 8.3 *(continued)*

these public schools but choose instead to send them to expensive private day schools. . . . Often a family has two teenage children in these schools at the same time, so they may be spending more than $60,000 on their children's education every year. Yet here I am one night, a guest within their home, and dinner has been served and we are having coffee now; and this entirely likable, and generally sensible, and beautifully refined and thoughtful person looks me in the eyes and asks me whether you can really buy your way to better education for the children of the poor.

Source: Jonathan Kozol, "Still Separate, Still Unequal: America's Educational Apartheid," *Harper's Magazine*, September 2005.

---

with substandard educations tend to do poorly in school. Higher-income families not only tend to provide home environments more conducive to learning, but they tend to live in communities where other families also value education. These differences are further exaggerated by a system of school financing that tends to provide good schools to the better-off students and very poor schools to the very poorest pupils.

Although most of the rules and regulations governing educational policy are state rules, local control of the schools is one of the most sacred cows of American federalism. Local school boards continue to play a minor role in setting policy, deciding, for example, whether to fund a football team or whether to require school uniforms, but their primary role is budgetary, and what local control really means is that each school district in the state is the ultimate arbiter of how much will be spent on education in each community.

New York's richest school district has a pupil-to-teacher ratio of four to one and spends more than $40,000 a year on each student. To compare these numbers with a school in New York City or in the northern Adirondacks, where per pupil expenditures may run as low as $7,000 per year, is to ignore too many complicating variables to be meaningful. The most widely accepted measure of equity in school funding compares the operating budgets of the schools in the top 10 percent in terms of per pupil expenditures with those in the bottom 10 percent. By this test, in 2005–2006 the districts in the highest percentile of expenditure per pupil spent 61 percent more than the districts at the lowest ($18,343 versus $11,371 per pupil).[47] Although state law is designed to give more help to students with the greatest needs, school districts in high-poverty areas often lack the resources to keep up. Inner-city districts do poorly, particularly in areas like Buffalo, where the tax base has been eroded both by suburbanization and a long period of economic recession, but poor rural areas are also at the low end of the expenditure scale.

These differences are due, in large part, to the fact that the lowest-wealth districts simply have less property to tax than their more affluent neighbors. Even if they tax property at a higher rate, they raise less money. "As a result of these major differences in local wealth, the highest wealth districts tax themselves far less heavily to raise these much greater revenues. While the lowest wealth districts tax at a rate of $13.93 per $1,000 of full value to generate $1,656 per pupil, the highest wealth districts tax at a rate of only $8.57 per $1,000 to generate $14,620 per pupil."[48] Even though the tax *rates* in more affluent communities are lower, however, the total tax bills many suburbanites get are very high. In a town like Rye, where the median value of a home exceeds $1 million, many homeowners pay more than $100,000 a year in local school taxes. The state provides some relief for homeowners through its State Tax Relief (STAR) program, adopted in 1997. Under the STAR program, all homeowners are exempt from taxes on the first $30,000 or more of their home's value, with the difference paid by the state. "Enhanced STAR," for low- and middle-income residents over age sixty-five, increases the exemption. At more than $4 billion a year, STAR has become one of the largest items in the state budget. Because it offers no help to renters and allocates larger dollar amounts to more affluent communities, STAR actually has served to increase the gap between rich and poor school districts, but its popularity—particularly in the vote-rich New York suburbs—is enormous.

The gap between rich and poor school districts has grown steadily. In 2000 New York ranked fifth among forty-nine states (Hawaii is excluded because it does not have separate school districts) on a scale measuring equity in per pupil funding. These differences are, by and large, less the product of deliberate policy than of two important demographic facts. First, income disparities in the state are not only growing at a dramatic rate but also becoming more geographically based, with wealthy communities and poor ones growing apart at an accelerating rate. Second, some districts with the fastest-growing student populations are in the poorest areas economically, and state aid formulas are slow to adjust to population growth. But although demographic variables are at the root of the equity problem, state policies supposedly designed to minimize the effects of these differences on the schools have not been doing the job. As in most areas of retrenchment, budget cuts have tended to have their most severe impact at the lower levels.

For years, New York courts refused to involve themselves in the issue, holding, as we have noted, that constitutional rules mandating equity were essentially guidelines to the legislature. In 2001, however, a trial court judge ruled in favor of a coalition of underfunded districts, the Campaign for Fiscal Equity, to the effect that, "in relation to students from New York City, the state's method of distributing education aid violated the mandate for a 'sound and basic education' included in Article XI of the state constitution as well as the rights of minority students as defined in Title VI of the 1964 Federal Civil Rights Act."[49] In 2003, the decision was affirmed by the state court of appeals.[50] As a remedy, the court ordered the state to determine

> the actual cost of a sound basic education and to reform the school finance system to ensure that every child receives the education to which they are entitled under

the state constitution. The court gave the State ample time, thirteen months, to enact the reforms. The July 2004 deadline came and went, however, without any action on the part of the State.

In March 2005, to fill in the political vacuum left by lawmakers, State Supreme Court Justice Leland DeGrasse ordered the State to ensure that students in the New York City public schools receive an additional $5.6 billion in operating aid (phased in over four years) and $9.2 billion in building aid.[51]

Governor Pataki filed a series of appeals to the ruling and, clearly using a strategy of delay, once again all but ignored the issue in his last budget message to the legislature.

A year later, fulfilling promises made during his campaign, Governor Spitzer met or exceeded nearly all of the court's guidelines in his first budget. Folding some thirty separate school aid programs into one basic package of "foundation" aid and eliminating regional share formulas, the 2007–2008 budget gave an immediate increase of $1.1 billion, with increases over the next three years bringing the total to $5.5 billion in new funds for the neediest. In order to buy the agreement of the legislature, the governor was forced to include an extra package of aid for Long Island in the bill, a reminder of the political forces that for so long have blocked attempts to reform the school aid formula; still, a breakthrough seemed to have been made.

The Politics of Education

New York State's system of school funding gives each school district a per-pupil allocation from the state. In order to equalize opportunity, this basic allocation is adjusted to give more state aid to districts with fewer resources, measured largely by property values. The premise here is that the poorer the district, the less able it is to raise money from local property taxes, the more state aid it will get. As summarized by the education department, "districts vary dramatically in their wealth per pupil," so the state aid they get "is wealth equalizing. Low-wealth districts receive almost six times more aid per pupil than the highest wealth districts ($7,462 versus $1,282)."[52] In reality, the system of school funding is more complex.

The problem begins with the process of putting the budget together. Except in the rare case of an election year in which the state is awash with money (as in 1996), governors almost invariably propose cuts in baseline funds for education. They do so knowing that there has not been a governor's education budget in recent history that the legislature did not augment. By underestimating their school budgets, governors are able to offer a "balanced" budget overall that also includes room for later bargaining. Because legislators—suburban legislators in particular—fight hard for their education dollars, when it comes time to cut money from, say, parks, the governor can say, "Look, I've given you this money for schools; now help me balance the budget." In the final analysis, no one can accuse the governor of hurting schoolchildren, who get their money; park supporters and others whose funds are cut blame the legislature for cutting the governor's original numbers; and the state gets pretty much the kind of balanced budget that the governor originally wanted.

Problem two for the poorer school districts derives from the way in which the legislature goes about restoring these gubernatorial "cuts." Within days of the governor's budget presentation, the state education department fleshes out the raw numbers with computer printouts describing precisely how the numbers will impact every school district not among the Big Five (the five largest cities in the state: Buffalo, New York City, Rochester, Syracuse, and Yonkers). Local newspapers in every corner of the state report exactly how much each community will lose, speculating about which school programs will have to be cut and how much the property tax will have to be increased. Every legislator from outside the Big Five districts, knowing exactly what each of the school districts in that constituency will get from the state if the governor's budget goes through unchanged, is likely to be inundated with letters and phone calls from unhappy voters in the towns threatened by cuts. To isolate themselves from such pressures, rural and suburban legislators have built a variety of protections into the aid formula. The most important of these are the so-called save-harmless formulas that make sure that no district loses state money while others gain. By constructing this kind of floor under the amount of aid that goes to the wealthier districts, the legislature typically leaves little money for the upgrading of schools in the poorer districts, or those with rapid growth. An informal system of "shares," moreover, has effectively guaranteed that Long Island will always receive at least 13 percent of any increases in educational spending, while New York City will get no more than 38 percent.

Why do the representatives of the poorer districts put up with this system? Why don't the Republicans representing poor rural districts team up with Big Five Democrats to equalize educational opportunities for their constituents? There are, of course, political problems in forging such an alliance, and it is also true that poor people are both less likely to vote and less likely to be attentive to school budget issues than those from more affluent areas. More importantly, schools are just not the dominating issue in rural and urban districts that they are in the suburbs. The reality of the assembly's Democratic conference on school funding issues is that the tail often wags the dog. The core of the party is liberal, largely urban, and increasingly black and Hispanic. About half of the 100-plus Democrats in the assembly are from New York City. Another fifteen, typically, are from the four other big cities. Most of these big-city Democrats have little trouble beating their Republican opponents in the general election. Altogether these urban Democrats dominate the Democratic conference by a margin of more than two-to-one. But with 60 to 65 seats, they are nowhere near controlling a majority of the 150 seats in the lower house as a whole. Their continuing ability to elect a speaker, to dominate committees, politics, and policy, depends on their continuing ability to elect Democrats from outside the cities, particularly in the suburbs.

How does a suburban Democrat get reelected? Certainly not by cutting school aid. So if party leaders want to save the seats of marginal members, they must give Democrats from affluent communities the ability to go back to their districts with the good news of a save-harmless deal on the school budget. City Democrats go along because they understand that if they lose their party majority in the assembly, they will lose their influence in education, mass transit, housing, health, and other areas. They also know that nobody back home has those nasty printouts: if urban schools deteriorate, they can blame the mayor—"We gave him the money; he just didn't spend it on schools."

Meanwhile, the senate reveals a similar, though slightly subtler political dynamic. Here the marginal seats also are largely suburban. Democrats can consolidate their control of the senate only by winning seats in the suburbs, particularly in the areas surrounding New York City. Large numbers of people living in the bedroom communities of Long Island, and Westchester and Rockland counties chose to move there and put up with long commutes in no small part because of the high reputation of the schools. Driven by the concerns of state senators representing these areas, the Republican conference has almost always been friendly to increased spending for schools in general, to save-harmless formulas in particular, and to their increasingly marginal Long Island members specifically. The 1988 overthrow of majority leader Warren Anderson, as we have seen, originated largely in his failure to understand the importance of the school issue to the suburban Long Island members of the Republican conference.

One final wrinkle in the process also contributes to the underfunding of poor schools. In the Big Five districts, per-pupil aid does not go directly to local school boards. Instead, each city gets a lump-sum payment into its general account. When municipal finances are shaky, it is possible for city governments to divert increases in school aid to other uses. From time to time the legislature has tried to block these diversions through so-called maintenance-of-effort laws that require the Big Five to use increased education funds on education. In 1996, however, when both houses of the legislature passed a maintenance-of-effort bill, it was held on the majority leader's desk instead of being sent to the governor, an extraordinary procedure that kept the bill from becoming law. While there was some speculation that New York City mayor Rudolph Giuliani, faced with serious budget shortfalls, had gotten to his fellow Republicans, it seems equally likely that Democrats on the New York City council had worked through the assembly speaker to have the bill put aside so that they could divert part of the increased aid to a threatened summer youth program. Maintenance-of-effort thus may have lost in 1996 not because New York City Democrats do not care about schools, but because they have so many other good programs to fund that education just becomes part of the mix. In New York City and in many poor rural districts upstate, members must concern themselves with a variety of noneducational programs for Medicaid, public health, and public housing that are of little concern to higher-income districts. In this respect, members from rural areas and small towns upstate resemble urban Democrats rather than their suburban colleagues. Faced with poverty-related issues and burdened too with enormous road maintenance bills and the unique concerns of agriculture, they do not have the luxury of fixating on the issue of school funding. Education groups, such as the United Federation of Teachers and the school boards association, are, as indicated elsewhere in this volume, high on the list of well-financed and effective lobbies. As such, they make an important contribution to this political dynamic. While they all support high levels of spending on schools, none of them have any abiding interest in issues of equity since their members come from both rich and poor districts.

All these factors combined to make Governor Spitzer's 2007 budget changes seem all the more remarkable. To go back to the theories of budgeting discussed at the beginning of this chapter, the victory of the Campaign for Fiscal Equity defies the rules of incrementalism laid out by Wildavsky. And in contrast with the decrementalists—who argue that such concepts as "base" and "fair share" get thrown out the window when the winds of change blow against government spending—these reforms required a commitment to both *expanding* and reallocating educational resources. Some social scientists have used the term *punctuated equilibriums* to describe this process. It seems plausible that the forces producing change and stability "are at work simultaneously in American politics, and that they tend to produce long periods of relative stability or incrementalism interrupted by short bursts of dramatic change."[53]

CUNY, SUNY, and Other Claimants

Neither education nor health care becomes cheaper over time. New technologies in both fields and the labor-intensive nature of the delivery systems militate against cost-cutting. No one wants to have hospitals with bigger caseloads and ancient X-ray machines or schools with larger class sizes and no computers. The strong desire of state legislators to sustain these programs puts intense pressure on other parts of the budget when times are difficult. Because school funds and health funds, which jointly absorb nearly three-fifths of the state's operating budget, are virtually untouchable, there is little room left to maneuver in other areas. Only the most essential and/or politically powerful programs can avoid taking the brunt of whatever cuts hard times, tax decreases, or other political dynamics dictate.

The city and state university systems have become increasingly vulnerable to cuts. Unlike elementary and secondary school taxes, which show up directly on annual property tax bills, the costs of college education are borne more directly by the state. Because tuition costs at these public universities are still a bargain by comparison with costs at most private colleges, parents are unlikely to be too upset by modest increases in tuition and fees. College students, moreover, do not vote in large numbers, and neither they nor the faculties are strongly represented in Albany. Most importantly, perhaps, New York does not really have a tradition of public higher education. Although the City College of New York (CUNY) was established in 1848 as the first public, free-tuition institution of higher learning in the country, New York State did not create land-grant state colleges and—a handful of teacher's colleges excepted—did not get into the business of higher education until after World War II. All this was to change when Nelson Rockefeller effectively "created" the SUNY and CUNY systems in 1959,[54] but public education in New York—particularly when compared with systems in other states—continues to play the role of ugly stepchild to the private colleges.

Because the legislature has so much trouble cutting health and education spending, programs such as higher education take unusually hard hits when times are bad. Even if revenues are off by as little as 1 or 2 percent, fixed cost programs such as debt service and politically safe programs such as elementary and secondary education force legislators to look for extra large savings from other areas. Thus funds for colleges, mental health agencies, parks, arts programs, and programs for the poor and the disabled tend to fluctuate dramatically from one year to the next, lurching, as it were, from crisis to crisis. The exceptions to this rule are those programs that either perform highly popular functions in the context of the times or are politically connected to the politically powerful. Perhaps the best example of the former type, in recent years, has been correctional institutions, which—fueled by tough anticrime measures and the "war" on drugs—were a growth industry for many years and have managed to resist significant cuts even as crime rates have fallen.

Some other programs have survived in hard times and grown in good times because they are either the favorites of powerful interests or favorably situated politically to maximize their basic clout. The state's transportation budget in many ways epitomizes the importance of politics in program preservation. Voters in New York City, where fewer than half the adults even have licenses to drive, have little interest in highways or commuter rail lines. Rural voters depend on their cars, trucks, and the highway systems as part of their everyday lives. Suburbanites worry about commuter lines and to a lesser degree about highways and other forms of mass transit. These transportation concerns set the stage for complementary logrolling: senate Republicans write their own ticket with regard to highways in exchange for assembly Democrats enjoying the same privilege with regard to mass transit; suburban legislators in both parties broker the deal and cut their own share for commuter lines. The result, in other words, is a compromise achieved not by splitting the difference but by letting each side write its own ticket. Once they agree on how much to allocate to each function, city residents decide how mass transit money will be spent, rural and suburban interests allocate highway funds, and suburbanites allocate funds for commuter lines.

Less fluidly, the assembly and senate bargain urban housing and social welfare programs for upstate agricultural issues, and so on. Although logrolling allows the legislature to avoid protracted fights over many of these issues, these programs are not as firmly entrenched as health and education issues to survive the ups and downs of the economy or the will of a governor determined to change spending priorities. Unlike schools and most health programs, then, transportation and other issues are not highly predictable.

The Ongoing Woes of Local Government

The so-called devolution revolution, as noted in Chapter 2, may or may not have returned control over many programs to local governments, but it has transferred the burden of paying for many services from both the federal and state levels to localities. General fund aid to localities in New York, which doubled every ten years from 1960 to 1990, began to level off as the millennium approached. As both state and federal funds declined as a share of local expenditures, the fiscal health of most municipalities—a measure of the balance between a community's effective expenditure needs and its revenue-raising capacity—declined significantly. One study of big-city politics between 1982 and 1988 placed both Buffalo and New York City in the top quartile of cities whose fiscal health had declined.[55] New York City's financial picture improved dramatically during the boom years of the stock market, took an enormous hit with 9/11, improved dramatically as the market rose again, and crashed just as quickly with the 2008 downturn. Other local governments—in the large urban areas particularly—have been neither as volatile nor as well endowed.

Cities, some analysts have charged, have tried to do too much. By attempting to sustain major social problems and cater to the demands of countless special interests, their reach has increasingly exceeded their grasp. Problems rooted in bad policies, this argument continues, have been compounded in cities like Buffalo and New York by problems rooted in bloated bureaucracies and government inefficiency. As agriculture continues to decline, small towns and cities outside New York City's suburban fringe also are falling on hard times. Upstate New York as a whole simply did not participate in the economic boom of the 1990s that eased the financial woes of New York City and its surrounding metropolitan area. New York City climbed out of the disaster it faced in the 1970s largely through the cash windfall that filled the city's coffers by virtue of the sustained bull market on Wall Street. Absent economic growth in this sector, the city economy has essentially been in decline for two decades, and despite expanding tax revenues, the city still has difficulty balancing its budget. Absent Wall Street, many upstate cities have been mired in a twenty-five-year slump. Thanks to the sustained nature of this recession, for many communities borrowing is no longer an option, the tax base is already severely stretched, and basic city services are already underfunded. Almost one-quarter of the 2005 budget of the city of Syracuse—to use an extreme but increasingly typical case—was used to pay for interest on past debts. Troy has only recently emerged from a three-year period when it was, in effect, operating under the bankruptcy direction of the state comptroller's office. Overall, the debts of local governments (not counting New York City) have risen even faster than the state's, to $32.8 billion in 2005 from $16.9 in 1995. As with the state, not all of these funds have been invested in capital projects, and the state comptroller estimates that the carrying charges will total nearly $4 billion a year.[56]

Big-City Governments, Politics, and Fiscal Constraints

The declining ability of local governments to maintain fiscal soundness has been—to revert to the models introduced earlier in this chapter—both incremental and episodic. Mayors, and local governments generally, have a significant impact on expenditures but very little control over income. Intergovernmental aid, or money that comes to New York City directly from the state or federal government, has declined significantly from the halcyon days of the 1970s. A process of slow erosion in the long run was punctuated by dramatic cutbacks during the early Reagan years in Washington and in 1994–1995, when New York's local governments confronted both a newly elected governor, Pataki, and a Republican Congress in Washington bent on reducing the size of government. In the 1970s, federal programs such as general revenue-sharing simply gave federal funds to local governments; the state aid to localities program was a major budget item. Today, however, virtually all the state and federal funds that are transferred to local governments are earmarked for such purposes as Medicaid, transportation, housing, or education. One tabulation, by the state comptroller, after excluding aid for these specific functions, put the proportion of the state's budget allocated to "support for local governments" at a measly 3.2 percent.[57]

The Big Five cities in New York have, in theory at least, more flexibility in allocating resources than do the state's other localities. The mayors and councils of Buffalo, New York, Rochester, Syracuse, and Yonkers have fewer obvious rivals for power in setting their budgets. School aid, in particular, flows into their general budgets instead of to the independent school boards that control school budgets in the rest of the state. New York City, moreover, shares neither functions nor funds with county governments.[58] However, the plethora of independent authorities that blankets the state looms even larger in urban areas, particularly in New York City. Agencies such as the Metropolitan Transit Authority, the Port Authority of New York and New Jersey, and the City University of New York are largely independent of local political control.

Politically too, the fiscal constraints on local governments loom large. In most towns and cities, major chunks of the budget are virtually untouchable. The amount that local governments spend on health, social welfare, and, to a lesser degree, education and transportation "is formula based; that is, a predetermined formula or set of variables is used to calculate the amount of aid the city receives."[59] These numbers are basically out of the control of local governments—worse, they tend to go up in years when revenues are going down. (When the economy is bad, tax revenues decrease at the same time that more people fall below the poverty line, making them eligible for safety net programs.) Many other services that are technically subject to budget controls are virtually uncontrollable in the real world. It is politically very difficult, for example, to make serious cuts in expenditures for law enforcement, to close a firehouse, or to cut the budget for snow removal. Even more than at the state level, therefore, political actors in local politics are often

Table 8.1

Changing Sources of New York City Revenue, 1980 and 2008
(in millions of dollars and as a percentage of total revenues)

Revenue source	1980	2008
Property tax	3,196 (24 percent)	13,204 (21 percent)
Income tax	879 (7 percent)	9,764 (16 percent)
Other taxes	2,884 (22 percent)	15,632 (25 percent)
Fees and miscellaneous	964 (7 percent)	6,475 (10 percent)
State and federal grants	5,269 (40 percent)	17,367 (28 percent)
Total	13,192	62,430

Source: New York City Independent Budget Office, *City Revenue and Spending Since 1980* (New York: Independent Budget Office, 2008), Table 1.

faced with the prospect of making enormous cuts in programs with weak political constituencies and/or low public priority. Little wonder that local governments are even more inclined than the state to resort to fiscal gimmicks and borrowing, particularly when nonincremental cuts in state or federal aid hit home.

As can be seen in Table 8.1, New York City, like the state, taps its revenue from a variety of streams. It has been able to offset sharp declines in state and federal aid through enhanced income, sales, and other taxes and a growing variety of miscellaneous charges and fees. It is the only city in the state that levies its own income tax. Other local governments in New York rely far more heavily on the property tax, with local school districts almost entirely dependent on it for local source revenues. Very affluent communities, with rising property values, have been able to reduce their tax rates without cutting services, but many upstate towns and cities are caught in a downward spiral of decreasing values and increasing rates. Buffalo's decline was precipitous: "Revenues from property taxes fell nearly $19 million between 1994 and 2004. Dividing the budget pie became a nightmare, with 70 percent of the city's treasury going to pay for police, fire, and fringe benefits such as health insurance."[60] With virtually nothing left for parks, recreation, libraries, and the other amenities of urban life, the city became a less attractive place to live and the decline in property values deepened.

Despite the constraints within which local governing officials operate, some mayors have been able to change the direction of spending in significant ways. City-funded spending in New York City, for example, increased by an average of 7.4 percent per year between 1982 and 1990, by 4.7 percent between 1991 and 1995, but only by a projected 2.1 percent between 1996 and 2000. From 2000 to 2008, however, it rose again by an average of nearly 8 percent a year.[61] Where Mayor Giuliani cut the rate of growth in spending, Mayor Michael Bloomberg increased it to rates not seen since the mayoralty of Ed Koch. Under Bloomberg, there also has been an unusually significant shifting of priorities from social services and education to public safety. In his drive to reduce taxes, cut spending, and shift government priorities, the mayor has had a lot of help from changes in state and federal policies as well as the windfall from Wall Street. Welfare reform and a variety of cost-cutting mandates relating to both Medicare and Medicaid have saved New York City literally billions of dollars.

It would be misleading to suggest that municipal governments lack the power or will to effect substantial changes in policy. Between March 1995 and March 1998, to use figures provided in the mayor's fiscal year 2000 executive budget, the welfare caseload in New York City declined by 40 percent, a rate far in excess of the national average. The booming city economy contributed to some of this decline, and Mayor Giuliani achieved further savings by persuading the city council to pass local laws strongly enforcing the new federal guidelines. He also was helped by state implementation laws that, for example, made it virtually impossible for welfare recipients to attend four-year colleges. Giuliani also used his executive powers to cut the welfare rolls by ordering his social services administrators to slow the processing of applications, force recipients to meet the absolute letter of the law, deny benefits to those who failed to complete increasingly complex application forms accurately, and refuse emergency assistance to most applicants. These changes were challenged in court and by the federal government and many were ruled illegal. Moreover, by seeking refuge in shelters for the homeless, in hospitals, and even in jail, many of the city's most needy residents wound up costing the city in other parts of its budget. There is little doubt, however, that in the short run at least the mayor substantially reduced the social services budget and the public assistance caseload. If the state constitution, as we argued in Chapter 5, sharply limits the powers of local governments, strong political leaders, as Giuliani showed, can overcome these limitations.

New York City and Rochester: A Tale of Two Cities

As important as what students of urban politics call "the permanent government" is in constraining urban policy options, Giuliani's first six years as mayor serve as a reminder of the potential powers that are inherent in the office of mayor. Despite revisions in the city charter that gave the city council significantly more power, the council's overwhelmingly Democratic majority by and large accepted the mayor's restructuring of fiscal priorities; Giuliani was able to promise tax cuts totaling nearly 3 percent of total revenues by the year 2000. His administrative orders making it difficult even for the most needy to qualify for welfare illustrate the important part that controlling the bureaucracy plays in setting policy priorities.

One way of demonstrating both the potential and limitations of politics in urban policy is by comparing the budgetary priorities of two diverse cities: New York and Rochester. Rochester has far fewer extremes of wealth and poverty than New York, is a far smaller (some would say "more manageable") city, and shares taxing and governing authority with surrounding Monroe County. Although it is another world entirely from New York City in the way it raises money and spends it, in the final analysis the two cities' bottom lines are quite similar.

Rochester gets almost 40 percent of its revenue from taxes on real property, New York City a little more than half that proportion, or 21 percent. New York City, at the same time, has an income tax, which Rochester does not, and that tax accounts for roughly one-eighth of the city's budget. Another eighth of New York City's budget comes from federal grants, compared with only 2 percent for Rochester. Most of this money, however, is for Medicare and Medicaid, which in Rochester is paid for by the county: 19 percent of county revenues are from the federal grants. Rochester relies far more heavily than New York on the sales tax (27 percent as opposed to 9 percent) and receives an extra rebate on Monroe County's share of sales tax receipts, but New York City more than makes up for this difference through an astonishingly high array of miscellaneous taxes and fees, ranging from a stock transfer tax to taxes on hotel rooms and flights from the city's airports, and fees for everything from vendor's licenses to building permits. Almost 30 percent of New York City's revenues come from such taxes and fees as opposed to only 16 percent of Rochester's. The most important difference, a legacy perhaps of New York City's more liberal political past, is the 10 percent of its revenues it raises through taxes on banks and corporations, taxes that are relatively trivial in Rochester and Monroe County and that have declined in New York City as well.

In terms of expenditures, the most striking differences between New York City and Rochester occur in the area of elementary and secondary education. Until the 2007–2008 budget began to implement a fiscal equity program for New York City, the city of Rochester often spent as much as 20 percent more per pupil than did New York City, although Rochester has far less wealth to tax. The differences between Rochester and its surrounding suburbs, moreover, are not nearly so striking as in the New York City metropolitan area. Thus the poorest school district in Monroe County, Honeoye Falls/Lima, spent $13,895 per student in 2006–2007, while the wealthiest district, in suburban Wheatland, spent $20,424. Per-pupil spending in Rochester was $16,940. In the counties adjoining New York City, only two school districts spend less per student than the city average, but suburban districts in communities like Quogue ($31,263) and Pocantico Hills ($30,006) spend nearly twice as much.[62]

New York City's schools have been shortchanged in part, as we have noted, by state aid formulas that do not provide the equalization funds promised in the basic aid law. Unlike Rochester, moreover, which gets help from its surrounding suburbs through Monroe County, New York City is on its own. Except for a relatively small income tax on commuters (which the legislature and governor voted to abolish in 1999) and the nickels and dimes they contribute in taxes on lunches and theater tickets, New York's suburban neighbors contribute nothing to the city's budget. The city also has more competing demands on its resources. In 1975, New York City's short-term debt (not capital debt, which is still larger) had risen to equal a full year's tax revenue, and the predicted shortfall for 1976 was almost 17 percent of total spending. By creating the municipal assistance program, the state helped New York City convert much of this burden into longer-term obligations that it is still paying off. After 9/11, another round of debt creation was added, and the city has found ways of tapping still other borrowing sources so diverse that no one seems sure just how much the city owes. In the city's recent budgets, an average of more than $4 billion a year has been allocated to formal debt service, but the real number is almost certainly higher. Even in the prosperous 1990s, the city continued to spend more than it took in, adding to its future debt. Rochester and Monroe County, though they never fell to the depths of New York City in 1975 and have balanced their most recent budgets, must still allocate nearly 6 percent of their combined budgets to debt service.

Along with debt service, New York City's budget can be explained essentially in terms of three large operating budget categories: education (25 percent), health and social services (26 percent), and police, fire, corrections, and sanitation (14 percent). These are also the primary spending categories in Rochester and Monroe County, though the proportion allocated to education is considerably higher and the allocations to the uniformed services lower. In both New York City and Rochester, the bottom line is roughly the same: beyond debt service, schools, social services, and protection—functions mandated either by the state or political necessity—less than one-quarter of the municipal budget goes for everything else.

Government at the Grassroots

The residents of New York's small cities and towns often pay taxes to so many different jurisdictions that generalization is virtually impossible. In essence, the local school tax bill is the high-ticket item, the county bill—which covers Medicare—is second, and a variety of local services third. Mayors, county and town supervisors, and other local officials operate in a world of strong constraints. State mandates, funded, unfunded, and partially funded, determine where most of their tax dollars will go. History, geography, and demographics also impose significant constraints. Even if he wanted to, Mayor Bloomberg could not abolish the city tax on corporations without the unlikely consent of the state legislature. Today's mayors in New York, Syracuse, and Troy must pay off the debts incurred by previous administrations. Neither Rochester nor Monroe County can realistically avoid paying more per capita for snow removal than cities in the southern part of the state. New York City has more citizens of school age and more below the poverty line than most other municipalities: its budgets for schools, Medicaid, and Medicare invariably reflect that reality.

Elected officials are able to order some priorities at the local level. For ordinary citizens it makes a difference where they live and who their public officials are. Monroe County and the city of Rochester have made a financial commitment to public education that manifests itself in better schools than those in New York

City or the other Big Five cities. If you move from New York to one of its more affluent suburbs, you will trade a small income tax and a lot of nuisance taxes on such things as parking for a much higher property tax. You almost certainly will have better funded (and probably better) schools. In the grand scheme of things, however, your quality of life in New York is set more by what happens in Albany than in New York's city hall, in Monroe County, the city of Rochester, or the East Greenbush town hall. One of the continuing ironies of New York politics is that most of its citizens know and care a great deal about their local governments, which affect them less than the state system to which they pay little heed.

Conclusion: New York's Changing Fiscal Priorities

New York remains in many ways one of the most progressive of the states in the ways in which it raises and spends money. By exempting food, for example, its sales tax is less of a burden on the poor and middle class than it is in most other states. New York City and Yonkers, by keeping property taxes low on one- and two-family homes and by imposing rent controls on many large apartment buildings, help make housing affordable for millions of people in one of the world's most expensive real estate markets. By relying heavily on income taxes to raise revenues for the state and its largest city, New York—in theory at least—retains one of the nation's more progressive tax systems.

In its spending priorities, New York has a long tradition of providing for the unfortunate, with many of its social welfare programs serving as prototypes for other states. It maintains some of the most generous Medicare and Medicaid programs in the country. Its public park system is among the most extensive in the nation, as is its system of mass transportation (particularly in the New York metropolitan area). In countless small ways as well, New York continues to develop innovative and progressive social policies, pioneering in equal rights laws, in regulating and improving the environment, in treating people with AIDs, and in providing homemaker and other in-house services to senior citizens.

Clearly, however, the focus has been shifting, overtly in the Pataki administration, more quietly but no less decisively during the Carey and Cuomo years. The fiscal crisis of the 1970s, which first erupted in New York City's brush with bankruptcy and spread to state agencies, such as the dormitory authority, that were overburdened with debt, forced Governor Carey and the legislature to tighten up both its own borrowing and spending policies and those of local governments and state authorities. As part of the price of this overhaul, Carey began a policy of cutting taxes and expenditures that has continued to this day. On the tax side of the ledger, the most significant cuts have been from the higher brackets, giving all but the very poorest citizens what amounts to a flat tax in which the working poor, the middle class, and the very rich all pay essentially the same rate. Corporate taxes also have been cut substantially. The state has saved money by effectively ending general aid to localities and by cutting back on its share of targeted local aid accounts, thus forcing local governments outside of New York City to rely more on regressive property taxes. In the city and in other local jurisdictions, governments have tried to capture lost revenues by turning increasingly to fees for everything from garbage disposal and water and sewer hook-ups to library cards and tire disposal. Most of these fees, together with higher tuition costs at CUNY and SUNY and sharply increased taxes on cigarettes, beer, and gambling, also have had regressive impacts. The 2008 downturn in the economy—particularly in state revenue losses from Wall Street—put increasing pressure on the state to increase these fees and nuisance taxes.

In terms of spending, local governments have been increasingly squeezed by cutbacks in federal and state funding for education and, more recently, health care. The economic boom of the 1990s helped both the state and its municipalities avert the kinds of fiscal crises that hit in the 1970s, but also it served to obscure some very deep structural problems lurking in the budgets of the state and many local entities. Further borrowing as a means of rebuilding the state's crumbling infrastructure is an increasingly less viable action; although the state can maintain most social services in good years, its ability to sustain programs for the poor when revenues are short, or to expand them when the coffers are full, is practically nonexistent. With many citizens living longer, moreover, Medicaid will continue to swallow up whatever discretionary funds might be left in a good year's budget. Thus, although New Yorkers may still be less inclined than the citizens of some other states to let the poor fend for themselves, the prospects for redistributive policies are not good. Even if the will were there to equalize educational opportunities, to bring the state and city university systems back to the level of other states, to broaden the economic safety net for the poor, or to rebuild decaying highways and rail systems, the effort would require tax increases and financial reforms that few have been willing to espouse.

9

New Directions for New York

New York is not an easy state to govern. Because the gap between rich and poor is so large, because the tensions between New York City and the rest of the state are so persistent, because of its amazing ethnic diversity, it is difficult for its governing elites to find common ground. The earlier chapters of this book have shown, we hope, that in many ways the system works. Strong governors and strong parties in the legislature have historically been able to negotiate agreements that kept the state running and sometimes made it a model of political reform. Even in the days of machine politics, New York did a creditable job of assimilating and educating millions of immigrants and building a solid infrastructure of transportation, water and sewage facilities, parks, and colleges.

The past few decades, however, have not been particularly good ones for the Empire State. It has been more than thirty years since Governor Hugh Carey solemnly told the people of New York that their days of wine and roses were over, that the new watchwords of politics in the state would be fiscal caution and restraint. A case can be made that New Yorkers have had neither the wine and roses nor the restraint.

Taxes, Fees, and Debt: The Real Costs of Government

Mario Cuomo cut taxes. George Pataki cut taxes even more. Yet the overall state and local tax burden has remained stubbornly unchanged. Combined state and local taxes in 1982 cost the state's citizens 11.8 percent of their income; in 2008 the rate was 11.7.[1] The Cuomo and Pataki tax cuts were almost entirely at the very lowest and upper brackets of the income tax, but the revenue shortfalls were filled in from other sources. What actually happened is that taxes were not so much cut as shifted from the very poorest and wealthiest New Yorkers to everyone else. When Carey was governor, for example, the top tax rate on income was 12 percent; now it is less than 7. But the tax on gasoline went from eight cents a gallon to 31.9 cents in 2008.

The tax on beer has gone from five cents a gallon to eleven; on cigarettes from fifteen cents a pack to $1.50. Increasingly, moreover, the state has put a separate price tag on services that once were free and increased the everyday costs of basic services. So-called taxes by another name (T-BANs) are littered throughout the budgets of the state and its localities. Snowmobiles, not regulated in 1982, now require a $100 registration fee; boat registrations and camping fees have doubled. It costs $135 to be registered as a nurse; $650 a year to operate a commercial vessel on the Erie Canal. Tuition at the state and city universities has gone from $950 a year to $4,500 at the City University of New York (CUNY) and $5,525 at the State University of New York (SUNY). It costs $2.50 to dispose of an old tire, $45 for a death certificate (but only $30 to prove you were born). Airline tickets include take-off and landing fees. For 2009, Governor Paterson asked the legislature to add naturally sweetened soft drinks, saltwater fishing permits, satellite television, and some eighty-four other T-BANs to the list. Only some of these fees are found in state and local budgets as "taxes," but the best estimates we could find (see Chapter 8) put the total of these fees as constituting as much as 25 percent of the real costs of government.

The state also has gone on a borrowing spree, much of it hidden in the accounts of local governments and public authorities. President Harry S. Truman had a sign on his desk that said, "The buck stops here." In New York, the buck has yet to stop: not since the restructuring of New York City's debt in 1975 has anyone stepped up to say the buck stops here. Passing the buck takes two forms, analogous to the lateral and the forward pass in football. In the lateral, one group of politicians simply passes the costs of vital programs sideways to others, from the federal government to the states, from states to localities, or from state agencies to off-budget authorities. In the forward pass, costs of current programs are passed to succeeding generations, largely in the form of bonds, but more subtly through tax cuts and spending programs that phase in over a period of time and usually place the bulk of the fiscal burden in the year immediately following the next election.

How do politicians cut taxes, increase spending, and still balance the budget? One way, as Governor Pataki and the legislature demonstrated in 1998, was to throw a forward pass and hope that if they looked good enough throwing it no one would notice whether it got caught. In crafting the budget that election year, the governor and the legislature made a deal: in exchange for billions of dollars in tax cuts pushed largely by the governor, assembly Democrats received a commitment to cut class sizes in the first three grades of school and to fund a statewide system of prekindergarten instruction. The beauty of this wonderful deal was that it did not cost the taxpayers a penny (at least not in 1998–1999). The governor, his budget "balanced," could boast of the billions in dollars in income tax savings soon to be realized. His office sent out official notices advising homeowners how to register for the property tax savings they would realize under the new State Tax Relief (STAR) program. Democrats, meanwhile, a balanced budget behind them, could trumpet the soon to be realized improvements in education and the tax cuts as well.

The governor's 1999 effort to welsh on his part of this deal by leaving the education funds out of the budget put the Democrats in a bad position since it would have been extremely difficult for them to retaliate by rescinding the tax cuts already officially promised to voters. But that is beside the point here. The primary concern is the glib willingness of both parties to claim political credit for economic commitments they both knew they could not meet. Despite the continuing strength of the economy, the most optimistic estimates of the budget gap in 2001, if the tax cuts and educational spending plans both were to take effect, ran from $4 billion to $6 billion, and both the governor and legislative leaders had these figures in hand.

Add to this shortfall the amount borrowed that same year—with voter approval—under the environmental bond act, the amounts borrowed through revenue bonds, authority bonds, local bonds, and so on, and the truth emerges: a government funding its present operations and cutting taxes for this generation in order to present the bill to its successors. As we noted in Chapter 8, the comptroller has estimated that because of years and years of deals such as these, in 2010 the state will be paying more than $7 billion a year in interest costs alone. Even Eliot Spitzer, though his 2007–2008 budget was unusually transparent, backloaded much of his plan to meet the requirements of the Campaign for Fiscal Equity suit increasing state support for city schools in 2009 and 2010. Most of the increases in funding for the state's poorest schools were scheduled for future payment even though the governor's own budget figures projected deficits for both years. In football jargon, this is known as a Hail Mary pass: throw it as far as you can and pray for a miracle.

The Bureaucracy Problem

In their creative schemes to hide the real costs of government, governors and legislators have created a rich array of new institutions to confuse and complicate the administrative process. Almost every new fee requires new clerks to collect them. Every college in the state and city university system has an office to collect tuition and one to disburse the Tuition Assistance Program grants that allow needy students to pay it. Both CUNY and SUNY have central staff people whose job it is to monitor these offices, and the state comptroller has accountants to audit them. It costs the State Thruway Authority $200,000 a year to collect less than $600,000 in tolls. On top of the state's Empire Development Corporation, almost every county and large city in the state has an authority trying to lure new businesses to the area. Instead of adding new programs to old agencies, the state has increasingly created new corporations and authorities, each with its own staff and management. Among them are the following:

- the Albany Convention Center Authority: three employees, one director making over $100,000 a year
- the Empire State Development Authority: 419 employees, 103 executives making more than $100,000 each

- the Thoroughbred Breeding Development Corporation: ten employees, two making more than $100,000
- the Industrial Exhibit Authority: 188 employees
- the Olympic Regional Development Authority: 948 employees, two at more than $100,000
- the Port of Oswego Authority: twelve employees, one at $100,000

Most of these authorities are well run and perform important functions. Some, such as the proposed Albany Convention Center, were created to highlight the singular importance of a particular project. In a few cases, the motive may have been to provide patronage jobs for political friends of the governor or key legislators. In too many cases, however, as we argued in Chapter 8, they were created to allow them to borrow money off the books, as it were, or in order to avoid public scrutiny, voter approval, or debt limit laws. Because the regular bureaucracies' rules are so complex, some were created quite specifically to avoid the normal rules. And avoid them they have: in 2003 the Long Island Power Authority, for example, paid its interim chief financial officer more than four times the salary of the highest-paid administrator in the governor's cabinet. The head of the New York Racing Authority spent more on entertainment than the governor earned. The head of the Canal Corporation, who did not have to comply with the advertising or competitive bidding rules that apply to regular departments and agencies, sold exclusive rights to development along the Erie Canal for $30,000 to a major campaign contributor. And the Metropolitan Transit Authority was found to have cooked its books to misstate the need for a fare hike.[2]

Sometimes it seems as if the state chooses the most complicated and expensive way possible to perform rather simple tasks. Instead of providing local property tax relief by simply raising the amount of state aid, the STAR program created thousands of new bureaucratic jobs for local officials who process the application forms, for state number crunchers who devise the rebate formulas, and for bursars who send out the checks. New York, quite simply, has too many public officials, patronage employees, and civil servants, not so much in Albany as throughout the state, in an indefensible mess of overlapping local governments, special districts, and public authorities. In 1995, the Brookings Institute published a book by Paul Light called *Thickening Government* in which he described what he called the "thickening" of the federal bureaucracy: "New agencies and units widened the government's base, while new management layers increased its height. Together these two tightly related events pushed the hierarchy upward and outward, expanding the president's scope beyond any hint of scientific control."[3]

Although government organizations are not immortal, either in New York or in Washington, they can live far beyond the life spans of many organisms. Instead of coming under the general jurisdiction of the state highway department, for example, most of the state's major highway bridges are controlled by separate boards and authorities. Although the bonds that were originally used to create these authorities

314 NEW YORK POLITICS

have long been paid off, the organizations that run them continue to function. In the governor's office in Albany are three separate agencies dealing with general economic development, working with a rich variety of county, regional, and municipal development agencies performing many of the same functions. At the local level, a snarl of overlapping towns, villages, counties, authorities, and special districts diffuse accountability and frustrate cost-saving efforts.

Checks on Checks

As in Light's study of the federal bureaucracy, the thickening of government in New York takes a variety of forms. At the highest levels of the state, the total number of senior executives and gubernatorial appointees continues to grow in a pattern that Light describes as "vertical" thickening. As in Washington, there appears to be considerable growth in the number of layers of management found in most executive departments, although an explosion of titles makes it difficult to profile the hierarchy accurately. As of 2006, for example, the insurance department boasted at least sixteen senior management levels below the commissioner:

- one superintendent
- one first deputy superintendent
- one senior deputy superintendent
- four deputy superintendents
- one special deputy superintendent
- one assistant deputy superintendent
- one legislative counsel
- four chiefs
- two co-chiefs
- three assistant chiefs
- two deputy chiefs
- one director
- one deputy assistant director
- one supervising examiner
- one principal examiner
- one senior examiner

These twenty-six high-ranking administrators supervised a department with a budget line of $2 million and fewer than a thousand employees.[4]

As in Light's study, "it is important to note that these . . . layers do not stack neatly one on top of the other to compose a unified chain of command."[5] Nor does the hierarchy of one department reveal much about another. In the department of insurance, for example, the offices of the first deputy superintendent and general counsel are combined, though there is a special counsel as well. There also are a number of titles reflecting the special mission of the agency, such as "supervising attorney" and "assistant chief examiner," that one does not find in other departments. While it is, again, difficult to discern exactly how many senior levels there are in the superintendent's office and how many head field offices, the ratio of supervisors to employees—one for every thirty-five—is high but not unusual.

"Horizontal" thickening, to again borrow Light's terminology, involves the proliferation of government agencies. The state constitution, as we saw in Chapter 5, limits New York to twenty executive departments, but a quick perusal of the state *Red Book* shows some fifty-five offices in the executive branch that report directly to the second floor and thus have at least quasi-departmental status. Outside of, but clearly overlapping at least in part with, the Department of Health, for example, the state has an office for the blind; an office for the aging; a developmental disabilities planning council; a department of mental hygiene (which also includes an office of mental retardation and developmental disabilities); a commission on quality care and advocacy for persons with disabilities; an office of national and community service assisting individuals (which is part of the office of children and family services); and a stem cell innovation and fund corporation (which includes the commissioner of health even though it is not in the health department).

President Franklin Roosevelt liked to create administrative overlap on the premise that competing agencies would keep him informed of each others' failings.[6] But Roosevelt's Washington of the 1930s was nowhere near as complicated, redundant, and large as today's bureaucracy in Albany, where all too often one hand does not know what the other is doing. Every year, City College submits a wish list of capital improvement projects to the state. A few years ago, the college sought funds to renovate the interior and fix the leaky roof of a badly deteriorating building. The proposal had to be split and sent to two different offices, which approved the interior renovations but put off the roof job. By the time the roof work was finally approved, some four years later, the completed renovations of the interior had been literally washed away.

A third form of thickening occurs both within agencies and around them. Within the major executive departments, there has been a proliferation of monitoring and control offices with such titles as auditor and inspector general; of outreach agencies including divisions of public affairs, communications, and legislative affairs; and internal support divisions for such tasks as data management, planning, and information systems. Light quotes from a study group headed by Vice President Al Gore: "Counting all personal, budget, procurement, accounting, auditing and headquarters staff, plus supervisory personnel in field offices, there are roughly 700,000 federal employees whose job it is to manage, control, check up on or audit others. *This is one third of all federal civilian employees.*"[7]

New York State takes these controls to an extreme. As the only state that requires a local contribution to Medicaid, for example, every such transaction in New York must be processed and audited three times instead of twice.

Too Many Governments

Still another aspect of the thickening of government is vividly evident at the local level where the inefficiencies of small units are compounded by a crazy-quilt pattern of overlapping jurisdictions and authority. A small but telling example comes from the rural community of Copake, where the popularity of taking an evening walk has grown to the point where the town board was thinking it might be a good idea to install streetlights and walkways along the most popular trail. There are already three existing streetlights on the route, installed more than fifty years ago to help dairy farmers load their morning milk for predawn pickups. The lights were installed by a local lighting authority controlled by the town's dairy farmers. The farmers created the original authority that floated the bonds to pay for the lights, which only the farmers needed. It would hardly make sense for the town to ignore the existing lights, which the lighting authority still owns, but to hook into the existing system would cause an accounting nightmare, and it would make little sense to put in all new wires and poles alongside the old. To abolish the lighting authority, on the other hand, would require both a costly public vote and approval by the state legislature. The lighting plan has been put on a back shelf.

Counting entities such as the lighting district, the number of "governments" in New York is enormous. The commission on local government efficiency and competitiveness estimates that

> there are some 4,720 local government entities, that is, independently managed organizations that can make decisions affecting local taxes either directly or indirectly. This is, we should note, higher than the 4,200 figure we have been using since the inception of the Commission—our research has identified additional districts and entities that meet the definition above. Moreover, we must confess that the tally remains uncertain with regard to special purpose local governments and other entities—there are simply too many.[8]

Nor do many of the boundaries of these districts, or the rules governing them—often dating back to horse-and-buggy days—make sense today. A town with a population of 755,000, for example, cannot have a municipal fire department, while one with 500 can. Special district expenses are far from incidental, representing an estimated 70 percent of town property taxes in Nassau County[9]; and most special districts, like the lighting district in Copake, are prohibitively difficult to abolish.

> Over the years, as needs have changed, our solution to this outdated structure has been to add to it frequently with additional governmental units, special districts, local public authorities, and other entities. Only rarely have we simplified this system. The net result is a complex amalgamation of governmental entities which can obscure responsibility, reduce accountability and raise equity concerns for basic public services split between many entities and elected officials.[10]

Municipalities, particularly small towns and villages, frequently duplicate services or provide services that could be performed far more efficiently at the county or state level. Vital statistics in New York are kept in some 6,400 registration districts—nearly one-quarter of those in the entire United States. Every county in the state now has a 911 emergency phone center, but in most counties local governments retain their own systems, causing an overlap that sometimes confuses emergency responders and certainly costs money. Onondaga County reportedly saved $681,000 a year when it went to a single 911 center in 1992,[11] but few other counties have followed its example. New York's system of assessing property values and collecting property taxes is also among the most fragmented in the country.

> New York currently has 1,128 individual assessing units, 981 city and town assessing units, two county assessing units, and 145 villages which assess property for village tax purposes (a duplicative function in that the towns in which these villages are located assess the same parcels). There are 1,376 assessor positions, including approximately 150 three-person boards of assessors. Only three states—Wisconsin, North Dakota, and Michigan—have more assessing jurisdictions than New York.[12]

Court consolidation and a restructuring and reform of the town justice system are also long overdue,[13] and substantial savings also could be realized by encouraging counties to share prisons. The fact that most towns are almost irrationally wedded to having their own justices, assessors, and other officers makes reform in this area difficult, but state law also serves as a significant barrier. The efficiency and competitiveness commission, for example,

> found great inconsistencies in how municipalities may be consolidated, merged, or dissolved. Archaic sections of law exist which described processes that are unclear and seldom—if ever—applied, such as town dissolution (since 1900, only two towns have dissolved—Cold Spring in Cattaraugus County and West Turin in Lewis County) or village-to-village consolidation (used only once, in 1975 when Pelham and North Pelham consolidated). Some consolidations require citizen petitions, some not, and for others it is unclear. The form the petitions must take, and the number of signatures they must contain, also can be unclear. We think the statutes should be simplified and provisions made part of a single merger statute.[14]

The Politics of Reform

The bureaucratic redundancies, overlapping local governments, and increasing layers of auditors and supervisors come at a price. In 1955, 91 percent of the professionals in the public schools were teachers; in 1975 they were 87 percent and in 2005, 83 percent. In the state university, less than two-thirds of full-time professionals are faculty members, which means that more money goes for less teaching. The growing costs of education in New York are directly related to the proliferation of deans, directors, counselors, principals, assistant principals, auditors, and superintendents, a pattern that is repeated throughout the bureaucracy. In addition to regular audits by the comptroller, most agencies have internal audits and budget reviews; their employees are required to provide information on their outside income and have annual performance reviews; to inform the affirmative action office every year if they are still white, black, male, or female; to be trained in sensitivity, tested for drugs, and report all contacts with the public. In some agencies, as many as six in ten employees are devising, reading, evaluating, and filing these reports or, in other words, watching the four in ten who actually do the work. The checks and counterchecks in purchasing are so cumbersome that most economical contractors simply refuse to bid on state jobs.[15]

In a sense, complexity and redundancy are the price of diversity. The idea that somewhere someone may be getting away with something has—as we showed in Chapter 7—created a huge apparatus of corruption-control mechanisms that enormously inflates the cost of governing. Yet all the rules and regulations that make New York an expensive state to govern are there for what some people think are good reasons. Whether significant savings can be achieved by streamlining the bureaucracy is not as clear as it seems on the surface. Civil servants in New York are not paid enough to make a huge difference in the overall budget. But if the notion that major savings could be achieved by simplifying the government is simplistic, it does not mean that it is not worth the effort for other reasons. One of the worst problems with complex institutions is a tendency to become rule-bound. As the chain of command becomes more difficult to trace, more monitoring agencies and rules are developed to guard against empire building, delinquency, and deviance. Because it is not always clear, in other words, who reports to whom, compliance is increasingly secured by rules that limit individual discretion and by monitoring agencies (like auditors, inspectors general, personnel directors, and internal affairs units) that enforce these rules and require piles of reports. The attempts by New York's mayor Ed Koch to clean up the contracting process described in Box 9.1 are unfortunately typical. The institutions created to deal with a particular crisis outlive the event, adding still more layers of processing to an already cumbersome system. Not only is the government incapable of acting, but it inspires a great deal of mistrust in citizens who literally do not know whom they have to see in order to get something done.

The Eroding Base of Citizen Support

The most fundamental premise of a democratic polity is that the citizens have the power to "throw the rascals out." Citizens may not know if the candidate they are voting for will do any better, but the retrospective ability to fire the official whose performance they do not like is fundamental. A public that does not know whom to blame is denied this basic right. By confusing lines of responsibility, New York confuses its voters and muddies its politics.

Box 9.1
Political Damage Control and Its Unintended Consequences

In 1986, the borough president of Queens, Donald Mannes, committed suicide in the midst of a bizarre chain of events that ultimately revealed an extensive network of political corruption in New York City's process of awarding municipal contracts. Mayor Koch responded, as politicians often do in such cases, by centralizing control over the process in his office. Every appointment to a city board or commission, every contract obligating the city to pay more than $10,000, had to be screened through the mayor's office. Predictably, the new machinery, in Charles Orlebeke words, "had the effect of slowing decisions to a crawl. The system choked up; actions were delayed; very little was getting done":

> Eventually, Koch's safeguards were to suffer the fate of all such attempts to centralize a multitude of discrete decisions. As any Management 101 text will explain, the volume of pending actions sooner or later overwhelms the capacity of the central command point to respond. To avoid a near-paralysis in the flow of decisions, there are not many options. One is to turn the control point into a rubber stamp. . . . The other . . . is to redelegate most decision-making authority back to the operating agencies.

In other words, another layer is added to the process of decision-making with very little effect on how decisions are actually made, except that of further confusing the process. "In post scandal politics," Orlebeke concludes, "the inexorable logic of decentralized management eventually overcomes the initial centralizing reflex. But the transition process can take quite a long time and is likely to be bumpy." Eventually, participants in the process learn to adjust: agencies become accustomed to submitting their appointments and contracts to the central offices; the central offices develop routines for processing them; it takes a few more weeks (or months) to fill a vacancy or sign a contract. The scandal that led to the creation of the new review offices is long forgotten, but the new layer of bureaucracy lingers on. Through years of scandals, both the city and state (not to mention the federal government) have enormous, often duplicative networks of corruption control agencies that spend most of their time shuffling papers to deal with scandals that are long in the past.

Source: Charles J. Orlebeke, *New Life at Ground Zero: New York, Home Ownership, and the Future of American Cities* (Albany: Rockefeller Institute Press, 1997), pp. 123–124.

We have no empirical evidence that New York's abysmally low rates of voter turnout are connected with citizen confusion or disgust. As we saw in Chapter 3, the state features a variety of demographic variables, including large numbers of immigrants and persons of low income and education, that are correlated with nonvoting. New York's arcane election laws and gerrymanders that reduce competition are also important factors. But even when these variables are taken into account, voter turnout rates in New York are strikingly low: in races for governor between 1989 and 1994, for example, only five states had rates lower than New York's rate of 33.4 percent.[16] In 2008, with 55.4 percent of those eligible casting votes for president, New York's turnout remained forty-fifth in the nation; and, as we have noted, turnout in primaries—often the only elections that really count—is even lower.

There is, as we have noted, a circular relationship between turnout and public policy: the young and the poor whose nonvoting is based in part on their perception that politics is irrelevant to their lives are ignored by politicians in search of votes, thereby fulfilling the expectations of those who feel ignored. The gap between rich and poor in New York is thus both economic and political and widening along both dimensions. Theorists since Aristotle and modern empirical studies as well have traced a strong connection between the existence of a viable middle class and the persistence of stable democracy. To this extent, New York is a troubled state and getting worse.

Gradually, as we saw in Chapter 3, the state has eased its registration rules and modernized its election machinery so today few serious legal barriers to voting exist. But there are three crucial ways in which the state's politicians continue to discourage participation. First, the legislature's bipartisan gerrymandering draws most district lines in such a way as to minimize party competition, making elections less interesting to voters. Why vote when the outcome is a foregone conclusion? Second, voting is depressed by repetition: most New Yorkers were called upon to vote at least four times in 2008—in the presidential primaries in February, in local school board elections in the summer, in the legislative primaries in September, and in the November general election. Finally, still another layer of elections for minor offices are frequently added at other times when most voters hardly notice: "The Nassau County Executive's Office conducted a study of election dates for the sanitary, water, and library districts operating within Nassau County. It revealed that there is, on average, one special district election every 10.9 business days. There are twenty-four different special district election dates. Not a single special district election is held on the date of the general election in the fall when voter turnout is typically highest."[17] Not surprisingly, voter turnout rates in these special district elections seldom exceed 10 percent. Besides the extra expenses of these multiple elections, the problem of "voter fatigue" is very real. Although this system no doubt protects incumbents (who, with their families, are often about the only people who vote), there is no sound basis in a rational polity for continuing it.

The "Dysfunctional Legislature"

In a study published in 2004, the Brennan Center of New York University Law School concluded that the New York state legislature was essentially "dysfunctional." The study, along with a follow-up issued in 2006, provided a close analysis of the legislative process that we found enormously useful in updating our materials for this book. However, for all its careful scholarship, the report as a whole is reminiscent of an old word game called "leaving out the *e*," in which players compete to see how clever a sentence they can construct without using the letter *e*. The *e* in the Brennan report is the governor, who goes virtually unmentioned in the catalogue of dysfunction.

From the state's phony sale of Attica prison to itself, to the array of nuisance taxes and T-BANs proposed by Governor Paterson in 2009, virtually all the money-raising gimmicks have come not from the legislature, but from the second floor. Most of the reform proposals that the Brennan Center and other reform groups have recommended with regard to the legislature could be applied with equal or more compelling force to the chief executive. These critics have rightly complained about the legislature's frequent failures to make major decisions in public, but they fail to note how disgracefully opaque the governors' budgets have become, with real spending hidden behind thick layers of obfuscation. The legislature itself is more victim than perpetrator of these hidden ball tricks, and, indeed, it is to the legislature's final numbers rather than the governor's that most insiders turn when they want to find out what the budget numbers actually mean; and they do so at a relatively modest cost (see Box 9.2).

Reform groups regularly target the relationships between lobbyists and legislators. As noted in Chapter 4, we have yet to encounter any legislators who would change their vote in exchange for a seventy-five-dollar dinner (or, as one assemblyman put it, "the legislator who sells his vote for a steak is not likely to be a person of great influence"). We are a little skeptical whether a reform that went into effect in 2009 preventing former legislative staff members from working as lobbyists will have much real impact. Whether legislators should be allowed to collect fees for speaking before advocacy groups probably is not going to matter as much as some reformers believe.[18] What is striking is how few of these reform proposals have been put forth vis-à-vis the executive branch. It might be appropriate to prohibit the chief of staff of the assembly transportation committee from taking a job with a company seeking highway contracts. But if the legislative staff person is barred from that job, what about the person in the highway department who has been working in the division that awards the contracts? Few governors were as successful in raising campaign funds, rewarding contributors, and increasing their own income through speaking fees as Governor George Pataki, whom even one of his earliest supporters accused of fostering a "culture of corruption."[19] If legislators are denied honorariums, why should governors be exempt?

More and more legislators, as we have shown, consider public service a full-time job. Yet some—most notably speaker Sheldon Silver and former majority leader Joseph Bruno—continued to have part-time jobs representing undisclosed clients. Few other states, even those with avowedly part-time legislatures, permit this. Similarly, Pataki's wife was on the payroll of various wealthy individuals (most consistently the cosmetic heir Ron Lauder) for tens of thousands a year in "consult-

Box 9.2
The Costs of Governing
The Legislature and the Office of the Governor

In the widespread media acceptance of the term *dysfunctional* to describe the state legislature, an equally dysfunctional executive branch has escaped scrutiny. The New York legislature is generally ranked as one of the most "professional-ized" in the United States, meaning—among other things—that it is expensive to run. The 2007–2008 state budget included $219 million for the senate and assembly, a total exceeded only by the legislature of California. While this amount is often cited as evidence of excess, the $131 million allocated to the governor's executive chamber and division of the budget is seldom questioned.

At just over $1 million per member, the legislature gets quite a bit out of its staff: it sustains 212 district offices serving communities throughout the state, provides each member with at least one professional assistant in Albany, and hires budget analysts, policy experts serving each of the sixty-nine specialized committees of the senate and assembly, and a variety of clerks, janitors, electricians, and security guards who keep the Capitol running. Partly because legislators are reluctant to pay their staff people more than they make themselves, salaries are relatively low: only forty-one of the senate's 1,465 employees, for example, made more than $100,000 in 2008. In the governor's office, more than one-third (sixty-seven) of the 195 people working in the executive chamber made more than $100,000, as did sixty of the 377 employees in the budget division.

Source: Empire Center for New York State Policy, www.seethroughny.net/payrolls.

ing fees." It is one of the most remarkable facts of political life in New York that seventy-five-dollar dinners and gifts have received more attention than these kinds of emoluments. Despite some important reforms in campaign finance, particularly those improving reporting requirements, the system in New York remains badly flawed, but the problem transcends the legislature. The cocktail parties most legislators host (for $200 and up) during the session, which do give some lobbyists access to key members, deserve the attention that reformers have given them, but the far more serious problem is the continuing ability of very large contributors to hide their "donations" in a variety of off-the-books, unreported accounts.

On the Decline of Representative Democracy

A competitive party system can function as a democratizing force. Greedy for votes, competitive parties reach out to all comers, offering programs designed for mass appeal and proving—through effective governance—that they can deliver. Electoral competition, because it is a process of mobilizing large numbers of people, has, in theory at least, the capacity to marginalize the role of special interests by forcing politicians to focus on large blocs of the public. In the responsible parties model, "popular control over government . . . can best be established by the popular choice between and control over alternate responsible political parties; for only such parties can provide the coherent, unified set of rulers who will assume collective responsibility to the people for the manner in which government is carried on."[20]

An alternative model of representation stresses the dynamic role of interest groups engaged in a pluralistic battle for political influence in which politicians are forced to balance and weigh the competing claims of a rich variety of self-interested champions of particular causes.

In New York, the trappings of party responsibility remain carefully draped on the body politic, but they serve only to hide a system that is failing as an effective vehicle of either representation or governance. Similarly, the pressure system pulsates with vigor, yet its representative nature is questionable in both scope and quality. Too few groups have any say in Albany, and those that have do not always represent the long-term best interests of their members.

The Miasma of Responsible Parties

Parties in New York are not lacking in cohesion. The old days when the county leaders called the shots for their delegations in Albany or when the governor owned one house and had a lease on the other are over. The legislature is ruled, as the responsible party model suggests, by cohesive parties that, when they achieve internal consensus, can present their programs effectively. The minority in each house essentially plays the role of a critic who hopes that exposing the flaws in the majority's programs will force reconsideration and that posing overall alternatives to the majority party agenda will allow the minority to defeat its opponents in the next election. The financing of competitive campaigns and even the nominating process in the case of open legislative seats have become increasingly centralized.

For three reasons, however, the strong party system has not worked either to define real alternatives for the voters or to encourage responsible governance. The first of these problems, endemic to American politics in the past few decades, may indeed be exacerbated by strong parties:

> Politicians have become increasingly sophisticated in their ability to anticipate how the news media will report their words and deeds, and how the public will respond to these reports. They have developed increasingly effective strategies for managing or circumventing the news, shaping the images, and channeling public perceptions. . . . The result is a democracy of the uninformed, one that is ever more vulnerable to the wispiest breezes of public expediency.[21]

Individual politicians who are more interested in making news than in making policy are tolerable to a point. Playing what often is called the outsider role, these politicians can revise the political agenda, bring new questions to the public's attention, or question the prevailing orthodoxy. But when party leaders use their weekly public opinion polls to play on the latest popular events, they are neither innovating nor questioning. By trying to one-up each other in exploiting the latest fads, they tend, in divided government, to lock themselves into positions that make compromise virtually impossible. Passing press releases and one-house bills is not the same as passing laws, though there are times when contemporary leaders seem more interested in seeing their work in the evening news than in *McKinney's*. The quickly forgotten flap over the so-called troopergate scandal that tied Albany in knots during Eliot Spitzer's brief tenure as governor had no substantive bearing on any of the issues confronting the state, yet it divided the governor from the senate majority and virtually drove real issues off the agenda. It was a classic, but unfortunately not unusual, example of what Giovanni Sartori calls "video" politics, which "under the guise of visibility . . . is a display of petty appearances that leaves the issues in greater darkness than ever."[22]

A second problem with party government, as it works in New York, is that it keeps much of the process hidden from public view. We do not believe that sunshine laws need apply to all political meetings: sometimes meaningful compromise can be achieved best behind closed doors, especially when the result of deliberations is more important for the public to know than who traded what for what. The free-swinging give-and-take of the party conferences often works to keep the leaders in touch with the rank-and-file only when it is carried out in private. Increasingly in New York, however, it is not just the public that is kept out of the meeting rooms, but major players as well. Governors who seldom consult their commissioners, party leaders who bypass committee chairs in drafting new policies, are both wasting talent and stifling the deliberative process.

Finally, New York's disciplined parties are not responsible in providing the public with a coherent set of alternatives. Instead of a Republican and a Democratic Party, each with a defined set of policy goals, there are three Republican parties and three Democratic parties that only coincidentally read from the same page. Advocates for responsible parties have cited the role that party discipline can—and, in their mind, should—play in overcoming the deadlock and inertia that often characterize politics in a system of separated powers. A popular governor, in theory, should be able to sweep fellow party members into the legislature, where they can put the party's campaign platform into policy. Three decades of partisan reapportionment, the rise of campaign finance committees controlled by the legislative parties, and the generous staff and mailing allowances that make most incumbents unbeatable have combined to increase rather than minimize the gaps between the gubernatorial, senatorial, and assembly parties. Party cohesion in a legislature that was permanently divided between the two parties was a recipe, in the media age, for deadlock and demagoguery rather than responsibility. How the situation will play out now in a state dominated in all three branches by the Democratic Party is yet to be seen. The great challenge for the Democrats as the dominant party will be attaining and sustaining a degree of cohesion that can allow the three legs of the party—assembly, senate, and governor—to work together yet apart. Responsible parties, so accustomed to using each other as foils, will find it difficult to act as a responsible governing coalition, particularly when a slumping economy requires them to cut back rather than merely divide the goodies.

Perverted Pluralism

When party systems are weak, there is a tendency for interest groups to be strong, providing, in effect, a supplementary system of representation known as pluralism. Strong interest groups coexist with strong parties in New York, often working in partnerships, particularly in the area of campaign finance. As in national politics and in the other state capitals, pluralism in New York is not representative of a broad spectrum of the state's population: the universe of organized interests underrepresents the poor and such broadly diverse groups as consumers. Although unions are bigger and more organized in New York than in most states, the business community, as we saw in Chapter 4, is the voice that speaks loudest in terms of money and effective representation in Albany.

What most distinguishes the pressure system in New York is the nature and extent of the accommodation it has achieved with the entrenched party system. In Chapter 4, we described many groups in New York as powertropic, tilting in the direction of those best able to serve their short-term interests as plants turn toward the sun. Divided government makes it easy for those groups whose goal is the preservation of the status quo cheaply to defend their core interests. Since a bill can be blocked in either house of the legislature, groups strongly identified with the Democratic Party count on the Democratic assembly to protect their interests. Republican groups long counted on the senate in the same way. The net result for the people of New York is that it has been extraordinarily difficult to get anything done that affects the well being of an entrenched group. Examples abound on both sides of the aisle. Some seemingly simple environmental measures have been blocked because they would be expensive to a corporation or industry with strong ties to senate Republicans. On the other side, the state's Wick's law—which requires most construction projects to be broken down into jobs for small contractors—is opposed by almost everyone. Yet the assembly fails to repeal the law largely, it seems safe to guess, because of the strong ties between the building trades unions and the Democratic Party.

A number of groups, just to be safe, play both sides of the aisle. This is particularly true of groups like the teachers' and public employees' unions that may need both houses of the legislature to fend off budgetary attacks from the governor. Although the Public Employee's Federation, the United Federation of Teachers, and the Civil Service Association typically take stands on a variety of legislative issues and tend—on most of these issues—to side with the Democrats, most of their real efforts are directed toward organization maintenance and the narrow interests of their members. The work of interest groups would become more transparent and perhaps more broadly focused if party leaders in both houses delegated more control over the details of legislation to the relevant committees. Open hearings on important bills and actual mark-up sessions in which both majority and minority party members could debate the merits of legislation would at once utilize the talents of rank-and-file members, improve the quality of many bills, and force lobbyists to present their wares in a challenging public forum. The growing use of parliamentary committees in Canada, Great Britain, and other countries shows that they are not incompatible with party government.

The bottom line, quite simply, is that the political system in New York frustrates change. A limited suffrage, an inattentive electorate, and an ossified party and pressure system combine to make sure that this year's policies will look pretty much like last year's. Even the seeming mandate that George Pataki brought to the governorship in 1994 resulted, in the long run, in nothing much new. His conservatism, like Mario Cuomo's liberalism, proved to be more poetry than prose. And the key lesson from Eliot Spitzer's brief term as governor was just how difficult it was to push his agenda of reform. As we write, Governor Paterson has shown little interest in reviving it.

With the Democrats now in nominal control of all three lawmaking institutions, however, the dynamic is likely to shift, though perhaps less dramatically than one might expect. If, as we expect, the Democrats are able to maintain control of the state senate and consolidate their hold on both houses through control of the redistricting process in 2010, party competition statewide will occur largely at the gubernatorial level, where real discussions of real reform might take place. They may also take place, less visibly form a public perspective, within the three branches—assembly, senate, and gubernatorial—of the Democratic Party. Within days of David Paterson's swearing in as governor, there was speculation in Albany as to who in the party would challenge him in the 2010 primary. The trick for the "three men in a room" will be not merely scoring debating points in the media, but rather developing a cohesive governing majority that unites a diverse party behind programmatic change.

The Potential for Change

One of the enduring ironies of American politics, one that continues to keep democracy alive despite evidence to the contrary, is that many of its seemingly most unchangeable realities are not that unchangeable at all. A strong, programmatic governor could do much to trim and reorganize the state bureaucracy. The patchwork of local governments will prove more resilient, but perhaps a serious, strong, and independent commission could make a cogent enough case to the legislature to at least begin a move toward consolidation. A regional effort of this kind has enjoyed some success in identifying possible reforms in the Albany area, but its limited ability to inspire real change also shows how deeply entrenched many local forces are.

The chance for New York to get a grip on state and local debt offers a stronger prospect. Liberals got the message a long time ago about social programs that cost money. Although the state has many pressing needs in areas, such as health and education, that scream for attention and have strong public support, few politicians in New York or anywhere else want to campaign as big spenders. And the public, it seems, has begun to see through the "tax cut" scam that closes the library on Tuesdays, increases school class sizes, raises college tuition, and saves eighty-seven cents a week on the average taxpayer's paycheck while costing twice that amount on other taxes and fees. The defeat of the 1998 school bond issue and the narrow victory of an environmental bond act the year before demonstrate considerable concern for the overall issue of public debt. If another wake-up call was needed, the 1999 downgrading of the bonds of Nassau County—one of the wealthiest counties in the country—may have been it.

There is an obvious need for campaign finance reform, recognized by every recent governor, by both houses of the legislature, and by virtually every newspaper in the state. As in Washington, however, rhetoric and reality seldom meet on this issue. Most reform proposals are politically loaded, with some having strong partisan implications, others impacting incumbents as opposed to challengers, and so on. The last time the legislature was able to agree on a significant package of reform, it was vetoed by Governor Cuomo, whose own fund-raising efforts would, to be candid, have been limited by the law more than those of most legislators. But by picking on a few pieces of a complex bill, the governor made the legislature look like it was passing a self-serving piece of garbage in the name of reform. Editorial opinion throughout the state, echoing the governor's rhetoric, proved highly embarrassing to speaker Mel Miller and majority leader Ralph Marino, who—whatever the faults of the bill—felt they had made a sincere effort at real change. Subsequent party leaders (and governors as well) have been extremely reluctant to fall into the same trap, resorting instead to a stream of one-house bills and press releases that, in the name of reform, are really party-serving attacks on the core financial constituencies of their opponents. The 1999 session was typical: the assembly passed a bill that would have reformed the system largely by closing loopholes that particularly advantage corporations and wealthy individuals, key groups for Republicans; the senate favored proposals aimed largely at limiting the financial contributions of labor unions, which give most to Democrats. The governor weighed in with a slightly more balanced proposal, but did not offer it until almost the last day of the legislative session, when he could be fairly certain it would go nowhere.

The fight for campaign finance reform is not really a fight over policy issues at all. Few politicians already in office, having done rather nicely by the existing rules, are sincerely enthusiastic about changing those rules, especially in ways that might weaken advantages for incumbents. The various proposals floated in recent years have been glorified press releases, designed to embarrass other parties rather than serve as blueprints for law.

A public fed too many such hollow press releases will become increasingly cynical about politics and politicians. There was a refreshing sort of honesty in Mario Cuomo's admission that the aspirational "poetry" of his State of the State addresses to the legislature was not to be confused with the more realistic "prose" of his budgets. There also was something horribly cynical about thus teasing the public with a vision of policies he had no intention of implementing. George Pataki seriously pushed a promised program of anticrime legislation, tax cuts, and substantial cuts in state spending on education and social services in 1995. Pursuing what was widely perceived as a conservative mandate when he first took office, Pataki marshaled the conservative wing of his party in the state senate and rolled over the frightened assembly Democrats to get much of what he wanted. In the classic tradition of the responsible parties model, the voters were given a clear choice. Within two years, however, whatever had been clear in the governor's stands on issues had become murky at best. Pataki seemed disinterested in governing, and neither the assembly Democrats nor the senate Republicans tried to stake out distinctive policy agendas. Even with the reform-minded Eliot Spitzer in office, victories in Albany were measured more in column inches and sound bites rather than chapter codes of law. The opportunity given to David Paterson, first when he fell into the governorship, second when his party gained control of both houses of the legislature, lost much of its luster when the bottom fell out of the economy.

Government by press release is bad government. It will end, in the final analysis, only when attentive publics in the state focus more on substance than rhetoric, when politicians are rewarded for what they do rather than what they say, when the press begins to pay serious attention to what happens in Albany, when the rank-and-file of the labor movement and other associations insist on real representation, and when average citizens begin to realize how important the government in Albany is to their lives.

Appendix A

A Citizen's Guide to the 2009–2010 New York State Legislature

The State Assembly

Member	District	Town or Borough	Party	2008 General election (%)	District phone no.	Albany ext.
Peter J. Abbate, Jr.	49	Brooklyn	D	72	718-232-9565	3053
Marc A. Alessi	1	Wading River	D	60	631-929-5540	5294
Thomas Alfano	21	Franklin Square	R	62	516-437-5577	4627
George A. Amedore, Jr.	105	Amsterdam	R	62	518-843-0227	5197
Carmen E. Arroyo	84	Bronx	D	97	718-292-2901	5402
Jeffrion L. Aubry	35	Corona	D	100	718-457-3615	4561
James Baccalles	136	Bath	R	100	607-776-9691	5791
Gregory R. Ball	99	Brewster	R	58	845-279-5301	5783
William A. Barclay	124	Fulton	R	68	315-598-5185	5841
Robert D. Barra	14	Lynbrook	R	57	516-561-8216	4656
Inez D. Barron	40	Brooklyn	D	97	718-257-7824	5912
Michael R. Benedetto	82	Bronx	D	83	718-320-2220	5296
Michael A. Benjamin	79	Bronx	D	99	718-589-6324	5272
Jonathan L. Bing	73	Manhattan	D	74	212-605-0937	4794
William F. Boyland, Jr.	55	Brooklyn	D	98	718-498-8681	4466

(continued)

329

The State Assembly

Member	District	Town or Borough	Party	2008 General election (%)	District phone no.	Albany ext.
Philip M. Boyle	8	Bay Shore	R	57	631-647-9400	4611
Adam T. Bradley	89	North Castle	D	100	914-686-7335	5397
James F. Brennan	44	Brooklyn	D	84	718-788-7221	5377
Richard L.Brodsky	92	Elmsford	D	100	914-345-0432	5753
Alec Brook-Krasny	46	Brooklyn	D	70	718-266-0267	4811
Daniel J. Burling	147	Warsaw	R	72	585-786-0180	5314
Marc W. Butler	117	Johnstown	R	71	518-762-6486	5393
Keven A. Cahill	101	Kingston	D	68	845-338-9610	4436
Nancy Calhoun	96	New Windsor	R	53	845-567-3141	5441
Karim Camara	43	Brooklyn	D	93	718-756-1776	5262
Ronald Canestrari	106	Albany	D	100	518-455-4474	4474
Ann-Margaret Carrozza	26	Bayside	D	73	718-357-3588	5425
Nelson L. Castro	86	Bronx	D	95	718-933-6909	5511
Joan K. Christensen	119	Syracuse	D	69	315-449-9536	5383
Barbara M. Clark	33	Queens Village	D	100	718-479-2333	4711
William Colton	47	Brooklyn	D	73	718-236-1598	5828
James D. Conte	10	Huntington Station	R	58	631-271-8025	5732
Vivian E. Cook	32	Jamaica	D	100	718-322-3975	4203
Jane L. Corwin	142	Elmira	R	89	716-675-7170	4601
Clifford Crouch	107	Binghamton	R	100	607-648-6060	5741
Michael J. Cusick	63	Staten Island	D	65	718-370-1384	5526
Steven Cymbrowitz	45	Brooklyn	D	100	718-743-4078	5214
Francine DelMonte	138	Niagara Falls	D	62	716-282-6062	5284
Michael G. DenDekker	34	Jackson Heights	D	100	718-457-0384	4545
RoAnn M. Destito	116	Utica	D	68	315-732-1055	5454
Ruben Diaz, Jr.	85	Bronx	D	96	718-893-0202	5514
Jeffrey Dinowitz	81	Bronx	D	96	718-796-5345	5965
Janet L. Duprey	114	Plattsburgh	R	100	518-562-1986	5943
Patricia Eddington	3	Medford	D	65	631-207-0073	4901
Steve Englebright	4	East Setauket	D	66	631-751-3094	4804

Name	District	Location	Party	%	Phone	Room
Joseph A. Errigo	130	Henrietta	R	100	585-334-5210	5662
Adriano Espaillat	72	Manhattan	D	94	212-554-2278	5807
Herman D. Farrell, Jr.	71	Manhattan	D	93	212-234-1430	5491
Ginny Fields	5	Bayport	D	64	631-589-8685	5937
Gary D. Finch	123	Auburn	R	65	315-255-3045	5878
Michael J. Fitzpatrick	7	Smithtown	R	62	631-724-2929	5021
Dennis H. Gabryszak	143	Cheektowaga	D	69	716-686-0080	5921
Sandra A. Galef	90	Ossining	D	69	914-941-1111	5348
David F. Gantt	133	Rochester	D	100	585-454-3670	5606
Michael N. Gianaris	36	Astoria	D	100	718-545-3889	5014
Joseph M. Giglio	149	Olean	R	72	716-373-7103	5241
Deborah Glick	66	Manhattan	D	100	212-674-5153	4841
Timothy P. Gordon	108	Castleton-on-Hudson	D	60	518-479-0542	5777
Richard N. Gottfried	75	Manhattan	D	86	212-807-7900	4941
Aurelia Greene	77	Bronx	D	96	718-538-2000	5671
Aileen M. Gunther	98	Monticello	D	100	845-794-5807	5355
Stephen M. Hawley	139	Albion	R	100	585-589-5780	5811
James P. Hayes	148	Amherst	R	62	716-634-1895	4618
Carl Heastie	83	Bronx	D	98	718-654-6539	4800
Andrew D. Hevesi	28	Forest Hills	D	73	718-263-5595	4926
Dov Hikind	48	Brooklyn	D	94	718-853-9616	5721
Earlene Hooper	18	Hempstead	D	87	516-489-6610	5861
Sam Hoyt	144	Buffalo	D	71	716-885-9630	4886
D. Janele Hyer-Spencer	60	Brooklyn/Staten Island	D	55	718-492-2462	5716
Rhoda S. Jacobs	42	Brooklyn	D	94	718-434-0446	5385
Ellen C. Jaffee	95	Pearl River	D	100	845-6244601	5118
Hakeem S. Jeffries	57	Brooklyn	D	98	718-596-0100	5325
Susan V. John	131	Rochester	D	67	585-244-5255	4527
Tony Jordan	112	Fort Edward	R	57	518-747-7098	5404
Brian P. Kavanagh	74	Manhattan	D	85	212-959-9696	5506
Micah Kellner	65	Manhattan	D	76	212-860-4906	5676
Brian M. Kolb	129	Geneva	R	66	315-781-2030	5772

(continued)

The State Assembly

Member	District	Town or Borough	Party	2008 General election (%)	District phone no.	Albany ext.
David Koon	135	Fairport	D	60	585-223-9130	5784
Rory I. Lancman	25	Fresh Meadows	D	100	718-820-0241	5172
George S. Latimer	91	Mamaroneck	D	71	914-777-3832	4897
Charles D. Lavine	13	Glen Cove	D	65	516-676-0050	5456
Joseph R. Lentol	50	Brooklyn	D	90	718-383-7474	4477
Barbara S. Lifton	125	Ithaca	D	100	607-277-8030	5444
Peter D. Lopez	127	Schoharie	R	100	518-295-7250	5363
Vito J. Lopez	53	Brooklyn	D	94	718-963-7029	5537
Donna A. Lupardo	126	Binghamton	D	100	607-723-9047	5431
William Magee	111	Oneida	D	100	315-361-4125	4807
William B. Magnarelli	120	Syracuse	D	66	315-428-9651	4826
Alan N. Maisel	59	Brooklyn	D	95	718-968-2770	5211
Margaret M. Markey	30	Maspeth	D	67	718-651-3185	4755
Nettie Mayersohn	27	Flushing	D	100	718-969-1508	4404
David J. McDonough	19	Bellmore	R	62	516-409-2070	6633
John J. McEneny	104	Albany	D	79	518-455-4178	4178
Thomas McKevitt	19	Garden City	R	58	516-739-5119	5341
Grace Meng	22	Flushing	D	88	718-939-0185	5411
Joel M. Miller	102	Poughkeepsie	R	53	845-463-1635	5725
Joan L. Millman	52	Brooklyn	D	92	718-246-4889	5426
Marcus J. Molinaro	103	Red Hook	R	61	845-758-9790	5177
Joseph D. Morelle	132	Rochester	D	100	585-467-0410	5373
Catherine T. Nolan	37	Sunnyside	D	100	718-784-3194	4851
Robert Oaks	128	Lyons	R	100	315-946-5166	5655
Daniel O'Donnell	69	Manhattan	D	100	212-866-3970	5603
Tom O'Mara	137	Elmira	R	100	607-732-3500	4538
Felix Ortiz	51	Brooklyn	D	87	718-492-6334	3821
William L. Parment	150	Jamestown	D	100	716-664-7773	4511
Amy Paulin	88	Scarsdale	D	69	914-723-1115	5585
Crystal D. Peoples	141	Buffalo	D	100	716-897-9714	5005

Name	District	City	Party	%	Phone	
Jose R. Peralta	38	Jackson Heights	D	100	718-458-5367	4567
N. Nick Perry	58	Brooklyn	D	100	718-385-3336	4166
Audrey I. Pheffer	23	Ozone Park	D	67	718-641-8755	4292
Adam Clayton Powell, IV	68	Manhattan	D	92	212-828-3953	4781
J. Gary Pretlow	87	Yonkers	D	94	914-375-0456	5291
Jack Quinn	146	Blasdell	R	73	716-826-1878	4462
Ann G. Rabbitt	97	Goshen	R	62	845-291-3631	5991
Andrew P. Raia	9	Northport	R	63	631-261-4151	5952
Philip R. Ramos	6	Brentwood	D	100	631-435-3214	5185
Bill Reilich	134	Rochester	R	64	585-225-4190	4664
Robert P. Reilly	109	Clifton Park	D	64	518-371-0568	5931
Jose Rivera	78	Bronx	D	90	718-933-2204	5414
Naomi Rivera	80	Bronx	D	91	718-409-0109	5844
Peter M. Rivera	76	Bronx	D	92	718-931-2620	5102
Annette Robinson	56	Brooklyn	D	99	718-399-7630	5474
Linda B. Rosenthal	67	Manhattan	D	84	212-873-6368	5802
Addie Russell	118	Watertown	D	59	315-786-0284	5545
Joseph Saladino	12	Massapequa	R	68	516-844-0635	5305
Teresa R. Sayward	113	Elizabethtown	R	100	518-873-3803	5565
William Scarborough	29	Jamaica	D	100	718-723-5412	4451
Michelle Schimel	16	Great Neck	D	63	516-482-6966	5192
Robin Schimminger	140	Kenmore	D	91	716-873-2540	4767
Mark J.F. Schroeder	145	Buffalo	D	75	716-826-0152	4691
Dierdre K. Scozzafava	122	Gouverneur	R	100	315-287-2384	5797
Anthony S. Seminerio	38	Richmond Hill	D	100	718-847-0770	4621
Sheldon Silver	64	Manhattan	D	79	212-312-1420	3791
Frank K. Skartados	100	Newburgh	D	51	845-562-0888	5762
Michael J. Spano	93	Yonkers	D	74	914-779-8805	3662
Albert A. Stirpe, Jr.	121	Cicero	D	59	315-452-1115	4505
Robert K. Sweeney	11	Lindenhurst	D	64	631-957-2087	5787
James N. Tedisco	110	Schenectady	R	100	518-370-2812	3751
Fred W. Thiele, Jr.	2	Bridgehampton	R	62	631-537-2583	5997

(continued)

The State Assembly

Member	District	Town or Borough	Party	2008 General election (%)	District phone no.	Albany ext.
Matthew J. Titone	61	Staten Island	D	73	718-442-9932	4677
Michele R. Titus	31	Far Rockaway	D	100	718-327-1845	5668
Louis R. Tobacco	62	Staten Island	R	72	718-967-5194	4495
Darryl C. Towns	54	Brooklyn	D	95	718-235-5627	5821
David R. Townsend, Jr.	115	Sylvan Beach	R	88	315-762-4383	5334
Rob Walker	15	Hicksville	R	60	516-937-3571	4684
Helene E. Weinstein	41	Brooklyn	D	84	718-648-4700	5462
Harvey Weisenberg	20	Long Beach	D	67	516-431-0500	3028
Mark Weprin	24	Little Neck	D	100	718-428-7900	5806
Keith L.T. Wright	70	Manhattan	D	97	212-866-5809	4793
Kenneth Zebrowski	94	New City	D	100	845-634-9791	5735

Each member also maintains a website which may be accessed through www.assembly.state.ny.us.

The e-mail address of a member is typically his or her last name and first initial, as in AbbateP@assembly.state.ny.us. The exceptions are Earlene Hooper and Daniel Burling, who do not list e-mail addresses, and the following: AllessM, BarclaW, BenedeM, BenjamM, BradleA, BrodskR, CalhouN, CanestR, CymbroS, DelMonF, DestitR, DinowiJ, EdingP, EngleS, EspaiIA, FarelH, GianarM, GottfrR, GuntheA, LatimeG, MagnarW, MayersN, McDonoD, McEnenJ, McKeviT, MorellJ, ParmenW, PeopleC, PeraltJ, PheffeA, PretloJ, RabbitA, ReilicW, RosentL, SaladiJ, SaywarT, ScarboW, SchimmR, SchroeM, ScozzaD, SenineA, Speaker (for Sheldon Silver), Sweeney, TediscJ, TownseD, WeinstH, and WeisenH.

The State Senate

Member	District	Town or Borough	Party	2008 General election (%)	District phone no.	Albany ext.
Eric L. Adams	20	Brooklyn	D	93	718-284-4700	2431
Joseph P. Addabbo	15	Queens	D	63	718-738-1111	2322
James S. Alesi	55	Fairport	R	60	585-223-1800	2015
Daniel J. Aubertine	48	Watertown	D	53	315-782-3418	2761
John J. Bonacic	42	Middletown	R	100	845-344-3311	3181
Neil D. Breslin	46	Albany	D	90	518-455-2225	2225
John A. DeFrancisco	50	Syracuse	R	69	315-428-7632	3511
Ruben Diaz, Sr.	32	Bronx	D	98	718-991-3161	2511
Martin Malave-Dilan	17	Brooklyn	D	92	718-573-1726	2177
Thomas K. Duane	29	Manhattan	D	86	212-633-8052	2451
Pedro Espada, Jr.	33	Bronx	D	97	not listed	3395
Hugh T. Farley	44	Amsterdam	R	68	518-843-2188	2181
John J. Flanagan	2	Smithtown	R	66	631-361-2154	2071
Brian X. Foley	3	Hauppauge	D	59	631-360-3356	2303
Charles J. Fuschillo, Jr.	8	Massapequa	R	61	516-882-0630	3341
Martin J. Golden	22	Brooklyn	R	100	718-238-6044	2730
Joseph A. Griffo	47	Utica	R	88	315-793-9072	3334
Kemp Hannon	6	Garden City	R	51	516-739-1700	2200
Ruth Hassell-Thompson	36	Bronx	D	97	718-547-8854	2061
Shirley L. Huntley	10	Jamaica	D	100	718-322-2537	3531
Craig M. Johnson	7	Garden City	D	57	516-746-5923	2622
Owen H. Johnson	4	Babylon	R	60	631-669-9200	3411
Jeffrey D. Klein	34	Bronx	D	73	718-822-2049	3595
Liz Kreuger	26	Manhattan	D	75	212-490-9355	2297
Carl Kruger	27	Brooklyn	D	93	718-743-8610	2460
Andrew J. Lanza	24	Staten Island	R	70	718-984-4073	3215
William J. Larkin, Jr.	39	New Windsor	R	61	845-567-1270	2770
Kenneth P. LaValle	1	Selden	R	100	631-696-6900	3121
Vincent L. Leibel, III	40	Brewster	R	100	845-279-3773	3111

(continued)

The State Senate

Member	District	Town or Borough	Party	2008 General election (%)	District phone no.	Albany ext.
Thomas W. Libous	52	Binghamton	R	100	607-773-8771	2677
Elizabeth O.C. Little	45	Glens Falls	R	100	518-743-0968	2811
Carl L. Marcellino	5	Oyster Bay	R	61	516-922-1811	2390
George D. Maziarz	62	Whetfield	R	68	716-731-8740	2024
Roy McDonald	43	Albany	R	60	518-455-2381	2381
Hiram Monserrate	13	East Elmhurst	D	100	212-788-6862	2529
Velmanette Montgomery	18	Brooklyn	D	96	718-643-6140	3451
Thomas P. Morahan	38	Nanuet	R	63	845-425-1818	3261
Michael F. Nozzolio	54	Seneca Falls	R	71	315-568-9816	2366
George Onorato	12	Long Island City	D	81	718-545-9706	3486
Suzi Oppenheimer	37	Port Chester	D	68	914-934-5250	2031
Frank Padavan	11	Queens	R	50	718-343-0255	3381
Kevin S. Parker	21	Brooklyn	D	90	718-629-6401	2580
Bill Perkins	30	Manhattan	D	100	212-222-7315	2441
Michael H. Ranzenhofer	61	Amherst	R	53	not listed	3161
Joseph E. Robach	56	Rochester	R	52	585-225-3650	2909
Stephen M. Saland	41	Poughkeepsie	R	58	845-463-0840	2411
John L. Sampson	19	Brooklyn	D	95	718-649-7653	2788
Diane J. Savino	23	Staten Island	D	79	718-727-9406	2437
Eric T. Schneiderman	31	Manhattan	D	90	212-928-5578	2041
Jose M. Serano	28	Manhattan	D	93	212-828-5829	2795
James L. Seward	51	Oneonta	R	63	607-432-5524	3131
Dean G. Skelos	9	Rockville Center	R	65	516-766-8383	3171
Malcolm A. Smith	14	St. Albans	D	100	718-528-4290	2701
Daniel Squadron	25	Manhattan	D	87	212-298-5565	2625
William T. Stachowski	58	Buffalo	D	53	716-826-3344	2426
Toby Ann Stavisky	16	Flushing	D	69	718-445-0004	3461
Andrea Stewart-Cousins	35	Yonkers	D	62	914-771-4190	2585

Antoine M. Thompson	60	Buffalo	D	100	716-854-8705	3371
David J. Valesky	49	Syracuse	D	64	315-478-8745	2838
George H. Winner, Jr.	53	Elmira	R	58	607-732-2765	2091
Catherine M. Young	78	Olean	R	78	716-372-4901	3563

All members of the state senate have websites which may be accessed through www.senate.state.ny.us.

Generally, a senator's e-mail address is his or her last name @senate.state.ny.us (e.g., addabbo@senate.state.ny.us). The exceptions are: eadams, aubertin, jdefranc, bfoley, fuschill, hassellt, shuntley, ojohnson, jdklein, lkreuger, senator [libous], marcelli, monserra, montgome, oppenhei, ranz, schneide, masmith, stachow, scousins, athompso, and cyoung.

Appendix B
Maps

Map B.1 **New York State Senate Districts**

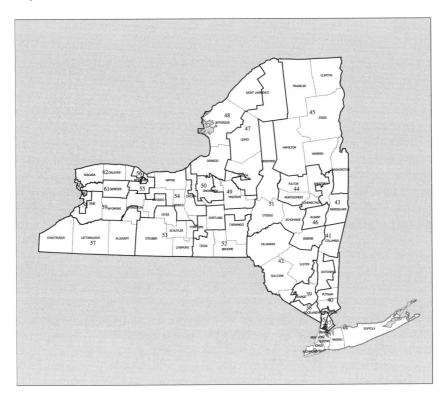

Source for all maps: New York State Legislative Task Force on Demographic Research and Reapportionment, www.latfor.state.ny.us.

339

340

Map B.2 **City of New York Senate Districts**

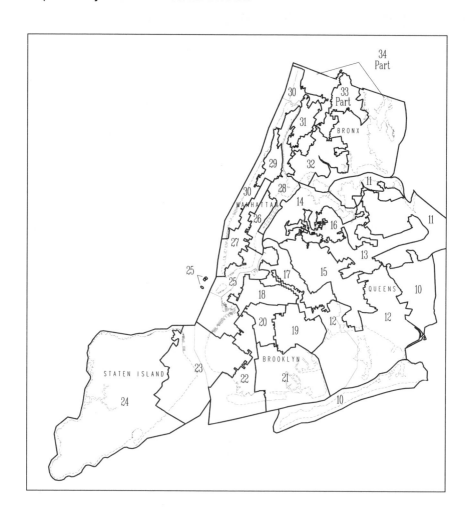

Map B.3   **Long Island Senate Districts**

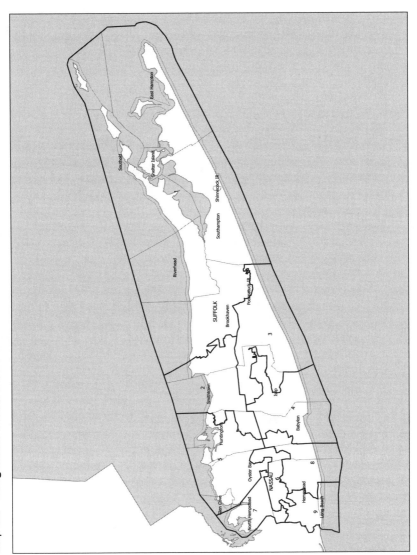

342

Map B.4 New York State Assembly Districts

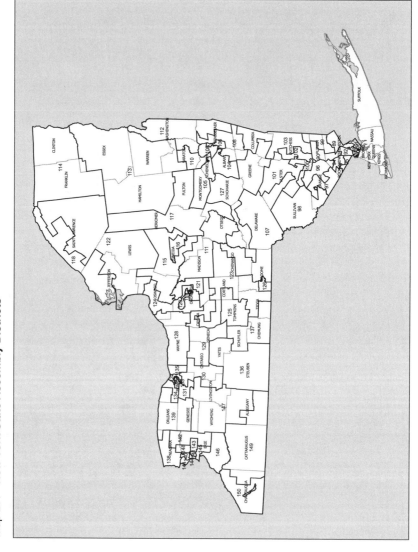

343

Map B.5 City of New York Assembly Districts

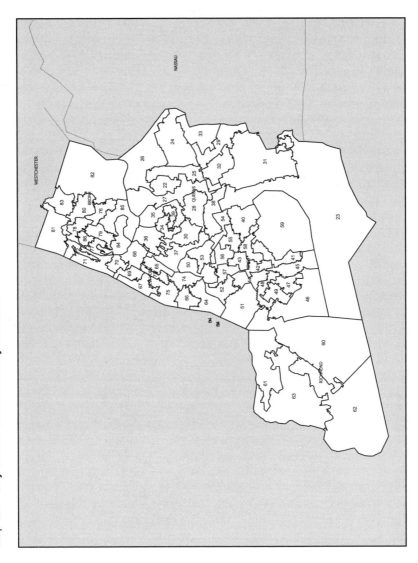

344

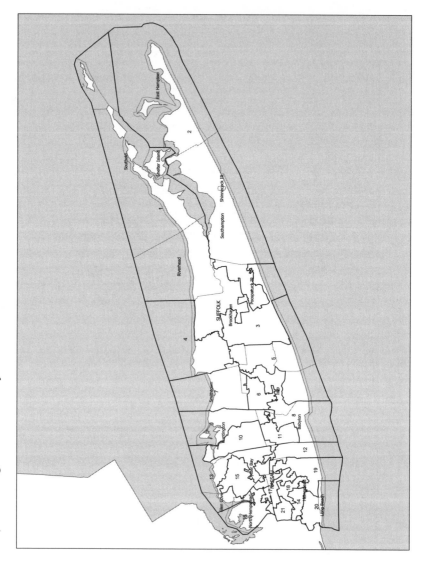

Map B.6 Long Island Assembly Districts

Notes

Notes to Chapter 1

1. Mark Twain, *Life on the Mississippi* (London: Chatto and Windus, 1883), p. 9.

2. William Cronin, *Changes in the Land: Indians, Colonists, and the Ecology of New England* (New York: Hill and Wang, 1983), p. 12.

3. Russell Shorto, *The Island at the Center of the World* (New York: Doubleday, 2004), p. 304.

4. Milton M. Klein, "New York in the American Colonies: A New Look," reprinted in *The Politics of Diversity* by Milton M. Klein (Port Washington, NY: Kennikat Press, 1974), p. 189.

5. Joyce D. Goodfriend, *Before the Melting Pot: Society and Culture in Colonial New York City, 1664–1730* (Princeton, NJ: Princeton University Press, 1992), p. 41. Although it focuses largely on Southeast Asia, an excellent history of the Dutch role in colonial history is George Masselman, *The Cradle of Colonialism* (New Haven: Yale University Press, 1963).

6. David M. Ellis, James A. Frost, Harold C. Syrett, and Harry T. Carman, *A Short History of New York State* (Ithaca, NY: Cornell University Press, 1957), p. 118.

7. Ibid., p. 163.

8. Ibid., p. 264.

9. Ibid., p. 281.

10. Chris McNickle, *To Be Mayor of New York: Ethnic Politics in the City* (New York: Columbia University Press, 1993), p. 5.

11. Ellis et al., *Short History*, p. 472.

12. David M. Ellis, *New York: State and City* (Ithaca, NY: Cornell University Press, 1979), p. 140.

13. Ibid., p. 134.

14. Ellis et al., *Short History*, p. 403.

15. John Hull Mollenkopf, *A Phoenix in the Ashes: The Rise and Fall of the Koch Coalition in New York City Politics* (Princeton, NJ: Princeton University Press, 1992), p. 47.

16. Herbert London and Edwin S. Rubenstein, *From the Empire State to the Vampire State* (Lanham, MD: University Press of America, 1994), p. ix.

17. R. Scott Fosler, William Alonso, Jack A. Meyer, and Rosemary Kern, *Demographic Change and the American Future* (Pittsburgh: University of Pittsburgh Press, 1990), p. 24. Unless specifically noted, the population statistics presented in this section are taken from various years and publications of the United States Bureau of the Census.

18. Nathan Glazer, "The New New Yorkers," in *New York Unbound: The City and the Politics of the Future*, ed. Peter D. Salins (New York: Basil Blackwell, 1988), p. 65.

19. David Halle, "Introduction: The New York and Los Angeles Schools," in *New York and Los Angeles*, ed. David Halle (Chicago: University of Chicago Press, 2003), p. 27.

20. Ellen Percy Kraly and Ines Miyares, "Immigration to New York: Policy, Population and Patterns," in *New Immigrants in New York*, ed. Nancy Foner (New York: Columbia University Press, 2001), p. 63.

21. The national studies of income are derived largely from studies by the Congressional Budget Office, Citizens for Tax Justice, and the Bureau of the Census. Figures for New York were compiled by the Center on Budget and Policy Priorities, *Pulling Apart: A State-by-State Analysis of Income Trends* (Washington, DC: Economic Policy Institute, 2006).

22. On the local level, the Census Bureau's online sources are not easy to access, and fewer and fewer libraries stock print records. For New York, a very useful print source is *Profiles of New York State: History, Statistics, Demographics, 2005–2006* (Millerton, NY: Grey House Publications, 2006).

23. Glazer, "The New New Yorkers," pp. 68–69.

24. Andres Torres, *Between Melting Pot and Mosaic: African Americans and Puerto Ricans in the New York Political Economy* (Philadelphia: Temple University Press, 1995), p. 87.

25. William L. Riordan, *Plunkitt of Tammany Hall* (New York: Alfred A. Knopf, 1948), p. 86.

26. John Rennie Short, *Liquid City: Megalopolis and the Contemporary Northeast* (Washington, DC: Resources for the Future, 2007), p. 27.

27. Rolf Pendall, *Upstate New York's Population Plateau: The Third Slowest Growing "State"* (Washington, DC: Center on Urban and Metropolitan Policy, Brookings Institute, 2003).

28. Ibid., p. 17.

29. Andrew A. Beveridge and Susan Weber, "Race and Class in Developing New York and Los Angeles Metropolises," in Halle, *New York and Los Angeles*, p. 63.

30. David Halle, Robert Gedeon, and Andrew A. Beveridge, "Residential Separation and Segregation, Racial and Latino Identity, and the Racial Composition of Each City," in Halle, p. 166.

31. Robert F. Pecorella, "The Two New Yorks in the Twenty-First Century," in *Governing New York State*, 5th ed., ed. Robert F. Pecorella and Jeffrey M. Stonecash (Albany: State University of New York Press, 2006), p. 8.

32. Daniel J. Elazar, *American Federalism: A View From the States*, 3rd ed. (New York: Harper and Row, 1984). See also Ira Sharkansky, "The Utility of Elazar's Political Culture: A Research Note," in *The American Cultural Matrix*, ed. Daniel J. Elazar and Joseph Zikund II (New York: Thomas Y. Crowell, 1975), pp. 262–284; and Jody L. Fitzpatrick and Rodney E. Hero, "Political Culture and Political Characteristics of the American States: A Consideration of Some Old and New Questions," *Western Political Quarterly* 41 (June 1988): 145–153. A University of Nebraska Press series of books planned to cover all fifty states uses the Elazar construct as its principal organizing theme, but the New York volume, edited by Sarah Liebschutz, does not emphasize the concept.

33. Mollenkopf, *Phoenix*, p. 77.

34. These quotes are taken from *The Federalist*, Number 10, originally published under the pen name of Publius in the November 23, 1787 issue of the *New York Packet*. Available in numerous reprints, the essays in *The Federalist Papers* are traditionally cited by the numbers used in the span of eighty-five essays penned by James Madison, Alexander Hamilton, and John Jay in support of the proposed Constitution of the United States.

35. Ibid.

36. Ibid.

37. Robert A. Dahl, *Who Governs? Democracy and Power in an American City* (New Haven: Yale University Press, 1961), p. 12.

38. Gerald Benjamin and Robert T. Nakamura, *The Modern New York State Legislature: Redressing the Balance* (Albany: Rockefeller Institute, 1991), p. xviii.

39. *The Federalist*, Number 51.

40. Rockefeller Institute, *New York State Statistical Yearbook* (Albany: Rockefeller Institute, 2007), Table F-1.

41. Charles J. Orlebeke, *New Life at Ground Zero: New York, Home Ownership and the Future of American Cities* (Albany: Rockefeller Institute, 1997), p. 4.

42. Robert S. Erikson, Gerald C. Wright, and John P. McIver, *Statehouse Democracy: Public Opinion and Policy in the American States* (New York: Cambridge University Press, 1993).

43. Quoted in Gerald Benjamin and Robert C. Lawton, "New York's Governorship: Back to the Future?" in *Governing New York State*, 4th ed., ed. Jeffrey M. Stonecash (Albany: State University of New York Press, 2001), p. 125.

44. Jay Gallagher, "Spitzer Reaps the Whirlwind," *Rochester Democrat and Chronicle. com*, November 18, 2007.

45. Austin Ranney, *Curing the Mischiefs of Faction: Party Reform in America* (Berkeley: University of California Press, 1975), pp. 24–25.

46. Oliver E. Allen, *The Tiger: The Rise and Fall of Tammany Hall* (Redding, MA: Addison-Wesley, 1993), pp. 51–52.

47. Alan Tully, *Forming American Politics: Ideals, Interests, and Institutions in Colonial New York and Pennsylvania* (Baltimore: Johns Hopkins University Press, 1994), p. 430.

Notes to Chapter 2

1. Morton Grodzins, "Centralization and Decentralization in the American Federal System," in *A Nation of States*, ed. Robert A. Goldwin (Chicago: Rand-McNally, 1963), pp. 3–4.

2. James Madison, *The Federalist*, Number 39.

3. Three times during the congressional consideration of the Bill of Rights advocates of state power tried to add the word *expressly* to the sentence referring to powers delegated to the national government. Three times they lost. Although this would seem to indicate an expansive view of federal powers, some advocates of states' rights—including, most notably, former Chief Justice William Rehnquist—continue to construe the text as if federal powers were limited to those "expressly" delegated.

4. *McCulloch v. Maryland*, 4 Wheaton 316 (1819) 322.

5. *Gibbons v. Ogden*, 9 Wheaton 1 (1824) 3.

6. New York, which was then richly endowed with private colleges, chose to give its grant to Cornell University instead of establishing its own public university system.

7. David B. Walker, "The Evolving Federal Role in Program Administration," in *Managing Public Programs: Balancing Politics, Administration, and Needs*, ed. Robert E. Cleary, Nicholas Henry, and associates (San Francisco: Jossey-Bass, 1989), p. 39.

8. Richard Snelling, as quoted in Russell L. Hanson, in *Politics in the American States*, 6th ed., ed. Virginia Gray and Herbert Jacob (Washington, DC: CQ Press, 1996), p. 45.

9. Lawrence D. Brown, "The Politics of Devolution in Nixon's New Federalism," in *The Changing Politics of Federal Grants*, ed. Lawrence D. Brown, James W. Fossett, and Kenneth T. Paler (Washington, DC: Brookings Institute, 1984).

10. Richard P. Nathan, "The 'Devolution Revolution': An Overview," in *Rockefeller Institute Bulletin*, ed. Michael Malbin (Albany: Rockefeller Institute, 1996), p. 11.

11. Quoted in Theodore J. Lowi, "Ronald Reagan—Revolutionary?" in *The Reagan Presidency and the Governing of America*, ed. Lester M. Salamon and Michael S. Lund (Washington, DC: Urban Institute Press, 1984), p. 96.

12. Quoted in Nathan, "'Devolution Revolution'," p. 29.

13. Chris Edwards, "FREDralism," TCSdaily.com, September 13, 2007.

14. Chris Edwards, "Federal Aid to the States: Historical Cause of Government Growth and Bureaucracy," *Policy Analysis*, May 22, 2007, p. 1.

15. J. Edwin Benton, "George W. Bush's Federal Aid Legacy," *Publius: The Journal of Federalism* 37 (Summer 2007): 384.

16. Daniel Patrick Moynihan, "Introduction," in *The Federal Budget and the States: Fiscal Year 1999*, ed. Herman B. Leonard and Jay H. Walder (Cambridge, MA: Kennedy School of Government, 2000), p. 10. The time series figures compiled during Senator Moynihan's tenure are difficult to replicate. Even simpler measures are difficult to extend over time as the Census Bureau has changed its standards of measurement. More importantly, when the Bush administration cut back its state aid budget it also stopped publishing the detailed state-by-state program numbers traditionally provided in a section known as *Budget Information for the States*. Publication has not been resumed.

17. Donald J. Boyd, "Political Conflict and Intergovernmental Fiscal Relations," in *Governing New York State*, 3rd ed., ed. Robert Pecorella and Jeffrey M. Stonecash (Albany: State University of New York Press, 1994), p. 58.

18. Rochelle L. Stanfield, "Playing Computer Politics with Local Aid Formulas," in *American Intergovernmental Relations*, ed. Laurence J. O'Toole (Washington, DC: CQ Press, 1985), p. 172.

19. Paul Posner, "The Politics of Coercive Federalism in the Bush Era," *Publius: The Journal of Federalism* 37 (Summer 2007): 404.

20. Martha Dethrick, "Preserving Federalism: Congress, the States, and the Supreme Court," *Brookings Review* 4 (November 1986): 36.

21. Advisory Commission on Intergovernmental Relations, *Significant Features of Fiscal Federalism* (Washington, DC: Advisory Commission on Intergovernmental Relations, 1994).

22. Joseph F. Zimmerman, "Financing National Policy Through Mandates," *National Civic Review* (Summer–Fall 1992): 368.

23. Ibid.

24. Timothy J. Conlan, James Riggle, and Donna E. Schwartz, "Deregulating Federalism? The Politics of Mandate Reform in the 104th Congress," *Publius: The Journal of Federalism* 25 (Summer 1995): 27.

25. Timothy J. Conlan and David R. Bream, "Federal Mandates: The Record of Reform and Future Prospects," *Intergovernmental Perspective* 18 (March 1992): 7.

26. Congressional Budget Office, *Cost Estimate*, July 11, 2006.

27. Posner, "Politics of Coercive Federalism," p. 403.

28. Catherine M. Sharkey, "Preemption by Preamble: Federal Agencies and the Federalization of Tort Law," *DePaul Law Review* 56 (2007): 1–62.

29. Posner, "Politics of Coercive Federalism," p. 408.

30. Warren Moscow, *Politics in the Empire State* (New York: Alfred A. Knopf, 1948), p. 218.

31. Joseph F. Zimmerman, *The Government and Politics of New York State* (New York: New York University Press, 1981), p. 331.

32. Tax Policy Center, www.taxpolicycenter.org/TaxFacts/Tfdb.

33. *City of Clinton v. Cedar Rapids and Missouri Railroad Company*, 24 Iowa 455 (1868), 471.

34. *Curtis v. Eide*, 244 NYS, 2nd (1963), 330.

35. Management Resources Project, *Governing the Empire State: An Insider's Guide* (Albany: Rockefeller Institute, 1988), p. 194.

36. This quote and the surrounding discussion of mandate types is taken from Management Resources Project, *Governing the Empire State*, pp. 192–193.

37. Fiscal Policy Institute, www.fiscalpolicy.org/2006FPIBudgetBriefing.pdf.

38. Boyd, "Political Conflict," p. 42.

39. Fiscal Policy Institute, "Budget Briefing 2006."

40. Boyd, "Political Conflict," p. 42.

41. Frank B. Moore, "Early History of Town Government in New York State," introduction to Book 61, *Town Law*, of *McKinney's Consolidated Laws of New York Annotated* (St. Paul, MN: West Publishing, 1965), p. vii.

42. Ibid.

43. Empire State New York State Data, www.empire.state.ny.us/nysdc/census2000, p. 194.

44. Keith M. Henderson, "Other Governments: The Public Authorities," in *Governing New York State*, 3rd ed., ed. Jeffrey Stonecash, John Kenneth White, and Peter W. Colby (Albany: State University of New York Press, 1994), p. 212.

45. New York Department of State, *Local Government Handbook*, 5th ed. (Albany: Department of State, 2000), p. 161.

46. Henderson, "Other Governments," p. 220.

47. C. Herman Pritchett, *The Federal System in Constitutional Law* (Englewood Cliffs, NJ: Prentice-Hall, 1978), p. 298.

48. Simon Lazurus, "More Polarizing than Rehnquist," *American Prospect* 18 (May 2007): 26.

49. This quotation was taken from Scalia's majority opinion in the 2006 case of *Gonzalez v. Raich* as cited in Lazurus, "More Polarizing than Rehnquist," p. 24.

50. Pritchett, *Federal System*, p. 299.

51. G. Allen Tarr and Mary Cornelia Aldis Porter, *State Supreme Courts in State and Nation* (New Haven: Yale University Press, 1988), p. 8.

52. Daniel C. Kramer and Robert Riga, "The New York Court of Appeals and the U.S. Supreme Court, 1970–76," in eds. G. Alan Tarr and Mary Cornelis Aldis Porter, *State Supreme Courts: Policy Makers in the American Federal System* (Westport, CT: Greenwood Press, 1982), p. 196.

53. Herbert Jacob, *Law and Politics in the United States*, 2nd ed. (New York: Harper and Collins, 1995), p. 272.

54. Ibid.

55. Harry P. Stumpf and John H. Culver, *The Politics of State Courts* (New York: Longmans, 1992), p. 3.

56. Ibid., pp. 23–24.

57. James Willard Hurst, *The Growth of American Law: The Lawmakers* (Boston: Little, Brown, 1950), pp. 85–197; Harry P. Stumpf, *American Judicial Politics* (New York: Harcourt, Brace, Jovanovich, 1988), p. 74.

58. Tarr and Porter, *State Supreme Courts*, p. 28.

59. Harold J. Spaeth, *Supreme Court Policy Making* (San Francisco: W.H. Freeman, 1979), pp. 6–7.

60. 4 Dallas (1789), 1.

61. Jameson W. Doig, *Empire on the Hudson: Entrepreneurial Vision and Political Power at the Port of New York Authority* (New York: Columbia University Press, 2002).

62. Lawrence M. Friedman, *A History of American Law*, 2nd ed. (New York: Simon & Schuster, 1985), pp. 661–662.

63. *Garcia v. San Antonio Metropolitan Transit Authority*, 490 U.S. 552 (1985).

64. Grodzins, "Centralization and Decentralization," p. 9.

Notes to Chapter 3

1. Unless otherwise noted, all election numbers reported here are taken from the excellent, user-friendly website of the New York State Board of Elections, www.elections. state.ny.us.

2. As quoted by Robert J. Spitzer, "Third Parties in New York State," in *Governing New York State*, 5th ed., ed. Robert F. Pecorella and Jeffrey M. Stonecash (Albany: State University of New York Press, 2006), p. 86.

3. Chris McNickle, *To Be Mayor of New York: Ethnic Politics in the City* (New York: Columbia University Press, 1993), p. 196.

4. Michael Barone and Grant Ujifusa, *The Almanac of American Politics 1994* (Washington, DC: National Journal, 1993), p. 862.

5. Chao-Chi Shan, "The Decline of Electoral Competition in New York State Senate Elections," unpublished doctoral dissertation, Syracuse University, 1991, as cited in Spitzer, "Third Parties," (2006), p. 108.

6. Howard A. Scarrow, *Parties, Elections, and Representation in New York State* (New York: New York University Press, 1983), p. 25.

7. Ibid., p. 26.

8. Nebraska's unicameral legislature was not included in the rankings. Alan Rosenthal, *The Decline of Representative Democracy* (Washington, DC: CQ Press, 1998), pp. 73–74.

9. Jeffrey M. Stonecash, "Political Parties and Partisan Conflict," in *Governing New York State*, 3rd ed., ed. Jeffrey M. Stonecash, John Kenneth White, and Peter W. Colby (Albany: State University of New York Press, 1994), pp. 83–84.

10. Jeffrey M. Stonecash and Amy Widestrom, "Political Parties and Elections," in *Governing New York State*, 5th ed. (see note 2), p. 60.

11. Scott Thomas, "The Tale of Two States," *Empire State Report*, January 1983, p. 34.

12. Ibid., p. 37.

13. Warren Moscow, *Politics in the Empire State* (New York: Alfred A. Knopf, 1948), p. 41.

14. Robert W. Speel, *Changing Patterns of Voting in the Northern United States: Electoral Realignment, 1952–1996* (University Park: Pennsylvania State University Press, 1998), pp. 136–137.

15. Stonecash, "Political Parties and Partisan Conflict," p. 96.

16. Robert K. Merton, *Social Theory and Social Structure* (Glencoe, IL: Free Press, 1957), p. 71, uses the term "latent" functions to distinguish the machine's societal impact from its "manifest" function of winning elections.

17. Frank S. Robinson, *Machine Politics: A Study of Albany's O'Connells* (New Brunswick, NJ: Transaction Books, 1977).

18. For a good description of the Schenectady County organization and the reform coalition that challenged it, see James A. Reidel, "Boss and Faction," *Annals of the American Academy of Political and Social Science* 353 (1964): 14–26.

19. Daniel Patrick Moynihan, "When the Irish Ran New York," in *The City Boss in America*, ed. Alexander B. Callow Jr. (New York: Oxford University Press, 1976), pp. 120–121.

20. Robert Pecorella, *Community Power in a Post-Reform City: Politics in New York City* (Armonk, NY: M.E. Sharpe, 1994), p. 35.

21. Rachel Sady, *District Leaders: A Political Ethnography* (Boulder, CO: Westview Press, 1990), p. 130.

22. Michael P. McDonald, "The Myth of the Vanishing Voter," *American Political Science Review* 95 (December 2002): 963–974. McDonald also notes that voter turnout has been rising since the low points of the 1970s, though this is less true in New York than in other states.

23. Bruce F. Berg, *New York City Politics: Governing Gotham* (New Brunswick, NJ: Rutgers University Press, 2007), p. 150.

24. This synthesis is implicit in Francis Fox Piven and Richard Cloward, *Why Americans Don't Vote* (New York: Pantheon Books, 1988), and spelled out in their remarks in a symposium in the June 1990 issue of *PS: Political Science and Politics.*

25. Ron Hayduk, *Gatekeepers to the Franchise: Shaping Election Administration in New York* (DeKalb: Northern Illinois University Press, 2005).

26. Voter Assistance Commission, City of New York, *1994 Annual Report* (New York: Voter Assistance Commission, 1994), p. 44.

27. *Diaz v. Silver*, 932 F. Supp. 462 (E.D. N.Y. 1996), 221.

28. Voter Assistance Commission, *1994 Annual Report*, p. 69.

29. Fairvote2020.org.

30. Moscow, *Politics in the Empire State*, p. 167. It is worth noting that since the method of selecting delegates to future constitutional conventions was to be by election from these same upstate-biased senate districts, the possibilities of change by that route were also very limited.

31. 369 U.S. 186 (1962).

32. 328 U.S. 549 (1946), 565–566.

33. *Reynolds v. Sims*, 377 U.S. 533 (1964), 568.

34. Joseph F. Zimmerman, *The Government and Politics of New York State* (New York: New York University Press, 1981), pp. 118–119.

35. Peter A.A. Berle, *Does the Citizen Stand a Chance? Politics of a State Legislature: New York* (Woodbury, NY: Barron's Educational Series, 1974), pp. 9–10.

36. *Miller v. Johnson,* 515 U.S. 900 (1995), 910.

37. *Diaz v. Silver*, p. 79.

38. Ibid., p. 33.

39. Ibid., p. 66.

40. Interview with John F. Haggerty, in Gerald Benjamin and Robert T. Nakamura, *The Modern New York State Legislature: Redressing the Balance* (Albany: Rockefeller Institute, 1991), p. 290.

41. For a classic discussion of critical elections, see Walter Dean Burnham, *Critical Elections and the Mainsprings of American Electoral Politics* (New York: W.W. Norton, 1970).

42. Moscow, *Politics in the Empire State*, p. 87.

43. Stonecash, "Political Parties and Partisan Conflict," p. 87.

44. David R. Mayhew, *Divided Government* (New York: Macmillan, 1992), p. 24.

45. Bob Gruwitt, "Joseph L. Bruno: Nobody's Puppet," in *State Government: CQ's Guide to Current Issues and Activities 1995–96*, ed. Thad L. Beyle (Washington, DC: CQ Press, 1995), p. 117.

46. Jeffrey M. Stonecash, "The Legislature: The Emergence of an Equal Branch," in *Governing New York State*, 3rd ed. (see note 9), pp. 154–155.

47. Stonecash and Widestrom, "Political Parties and Elections," p. 62.

48. John Hull Mollenkopf, *A Phoenix in the Ashes: The Rise and Fall of the Koch Coalition in New York City Politics* (Princeton, NJ: Princeton University Press, 1994), p. 88.

49. Richard C. Wade, "The Withering Away of the Party System," in *Urban Politics New York Style*, ed. Jewell Bellush and Dick Netzer (Armonk, NY: M.E. Sharpe, 1990), p. 282.

50. Mollenkopf, *Phoenix*, p. 128.

51. Wade, "Withering Away," p. 283.

52. Mollenkopf, *Phoenix*, p. 170.

53. Ibid., p. 181.

54. Ibid, p 199.

55. Ibid., p. 214.

56. Asher Arian et al., *Changing New York City Politics* (New York: Routledge, 1991), p. 199.

57. Berg, *New York City Politics,* pp. 163–164.

58. Cornelius P. Cotter, James L. Gibson, John F. Bibby, and Robert J. Huckshorn, *Party Organizations in American Politics* (Pittsburgh: University of Pittsburgh Press, 1989), p. 28.

59. Raymond Wolfinger, "Why Political Machines Have Not Withered Away and Other Revisionist Thoughts," *Journal of Politics* 34 (May 1972): 365–398.

60. Mollenkopf, *Phoenix,* pp. 77–78.

Notes to Chapter 4

1. Clarence N. Stone, *Regime Politics: Governing Atlanta, 1946–1988* (Lawrence: University Press of Kansas, 1989), p. 219.

2. Robert F. Pecorella, *Community Power in a Post-Reform City: Politics in New York City* (Armonk, NY: M.E. Sharpe, 1994), pp. 14–15.

3. Wallace B. Sayre and Herbert Kaufman, *Governing New York City* (New York: Russell Sage Foundation, 1960). On the rise of the "new machines," see Theodore J. Lowi, "Machine Politics: Old and New," *Public Interest* 9 (Fall 1967): 83–92.

4. Paul Peterson, *City Limits* (Chicago: University of Chicago Press, 1981), p. 209.

5. John Hull Mollenkopf, *A Phoenix in the Ashes: The Rise and Fall of the Koch Coalition in New York City Politics* (Princeton, NJ: Princeton University Press, 1992), p. 200.

6. Hank V. Savitch and Paul Kantor, *Cities in the International Marketplace: The Political Economy of Urban Development in North America and Western Europe* (Princeton, NJ: Princeton University Press, 2002).

7. E.E. Schattschneider, *The Semisovereign People: A Realist's View of Democracy in America* (New York: Holt, Rinehart and Winston, 1960), p. 40.

8. David C. Nice, *Federalism: The Politics of Intergovernmental Relations* (New York: St. Martin's Press, 1987), pp. 29–30.

9. Elizabeth Drew, "Charlie," in *Interest Group Politics*, ed. Allen J. Cigler and Burdett A. Loomis (Washington, DC: CQ Press, 1983), p. 230. Originally published in *The New Yorker*, January 9, 1978.

10. Clem Miller, *Member of the House*, ed. John W. Baker (New York: Charles Scribner's Sons, 1962), pp. 137–140.

11. Jennifer Wolak, Adam J. Newmark, Todd McNoldy, David Lowery, and Virginia Gray, "Much of Politics Is Still Local: Multi-State Lobbying in State Interest Communities," *Legislative Studies Quarterly* 27 (November 2002): 540–541.

12. Nice, *Federalism*, p. 31.

13. Robert B. Ward, *New York State Government*, 2nd ed. (Albany: Rockefeller Institute Press, 2006), p. 571, counts seventy-eight government corporations and municipalities registered in 2005.

14. Seymour P. Lachman, *Three Men in a Room: The Inside Story of Power and Betrayal in an American Statehouse* (New York: New Press, 2006), p. 100, citing data from the Center for Public Integrity in Washington.

15. Clive S. Thomas and Ronald J. Hrebanar, "Interest Groups in the States," in *Politics in the American States: A Comparative Analysis*, 6th ed., ed. Virginia Gray and Herbert Jacob (Washington, DC: CQ Press, 1996), p. 149.

16. Schattschneider, *Semisovereign People*, p. 35.

17. Roberto Michels, *Political Parties* (New York: Dover Books, 1959).

18. Theodore J. Lowi, *The Politics of Disorder* (New York: Basic Books, 1971), p. 31.

19. From numerous private conversations between Edward Schneier and the late Professor Wildavskyl.

20. An excellent summary and analysis of the literature comparing the American states in this regard can be found in Sarah M. Morehouse, "Interest Groups, Parties and Policies in the American States," paper delivered at the annual meeting of the American Political Science Association, Washington, DC, August 28–31, 1997.

21. David L. Cingranelli, "New York: Powerful Groups and Powerful Parties," in *Interest Group Politics in the Northeastern States*, ed. Ronald J. Hrebenar and Clive S. Thomas (State College: Pennsylvania State University Press, 1993), p. 276.

22. Clive C. Thomas, "The Changing Nature of Interest-Group Activity in the Northeast," in *Interest Group Politics in the Northeastern States* (see note 19), pp. 383–384.

23. Virginia Gray and David Lowery, "Reflections on the Study of Interest Groups in the States," in *Representing Interests and Interest Group Representation*, ed. William Crotty, Mildred A. Schwartz, and John C. Green (Lanham, MD: University Press of America, 1994), pp. 57–66.

24. John W. Kingdon, *Agendas, Alternatives, and Public Policies*, 2nd ed. (New York: Harper Collins, 1995), p. 150.

25. *New York Times,* August 21, 2008.

26. Cingranelli, "New York," p. 271.

27. The study is the fourth in a series, all of which are available from Pew at www.campaigndisclosure.org.

28. Frank J. Sorauf, "Political Action Committees," in *Campaign Finance Reform: A Sourcebook*, ed. Anthony Corrado, Thomas E. Mann, Daniel R. Ortiz, Trevor Potter, and Frank J. Sorauf (Washington, DC: Brookings Institute, 1997), p. 124.

29. Alan Rosenthal, *The Decline of Representative Democracy: Process, Participation, and Power in State Legislatures* (Washington, DC: CQ Press, 1998), p. 223.

30. Richard L. Hall and Frank W. Wayman, "Buying Time: Moneyed Interests and the Mobilization of Bias in Congressional Committees," *American Political Science Review* 84 (September 1990): 797–820.

31. Editorial, *New York Times*, October 13, 2003, p. A16.

32. Warren Anderson in Gerald Benjamin and Robert T. Nakamura, eds., *The Modern New York State Legislature: Redressing the Balance* (Albany: Rockefeller Institute, 1991), p. 64.

33. Benjamin and Nakamura, *Modern New York State Legislature* (see note 29), p. 42.

34. Jeffrey M. Stonecash, "Working at the Margins: Campaign Finance and Party Strategy in New York Assembly Elections," *Legislative Studies Quarterly* 13 (November 1988): 485.

35. Ibid., p. 490.

36. Daniel M. Shea, *Transforming Democracy: Legislative Campaign Committees and Political Parties* (Albany: State University of New York Press, 1995), p. 167.

37. Ibid., p. 170.

38. As quoted in Kevin Sack, "The Great Incumbency Machine," *New York Times Magazine*, September 27, 1992, p. 60.

39. www.nynpa.com/ContentManager/index; www.nynewspapers.com.

40. *New York Times*, October 8, 2008.

41. David Morgan, *The Capitol Press Corps: Newsmen and the Governor of New York State* (Westport, CT: Greenwood Press, 1978), p. 112, asked a sample of Albany correspondents whether "political news from the State level suffers by contrast with the frequency and immediacy of local and/or Washington news"; 78.3 percent answered yes.

42. Martin Linsky, "Legislatures and the Press: The Problems of Image and Attitude," *State Government* 59 (Spring 1986): 159.

43. Morgan, *Capitol Press Corps*, p. 21.

44. Linsky, "Legislatures and the Press," p. 158.

45. Morgan, *Capitol Press Corps*, p. 39.

46. Grant Reeher, *First Person Political: Legislative Life and the Meaning of Public Service* (New York: New York University Press, 2006), pp. 16–17.

47. Morgan, *Capitol Press Corps*, p. 106.

48. Ibid.

49. Jeffrey Stonecash, "Critics of Legislature Are Failing to See Democracy," Syracuse *Gazette*, October 9, 1994.

50. Technorati is a search engine that organizes and indexes blogs while also performing meta-analysis.

51. Laura McKenna and Antoinette Pole, "What Do Bloggers Do: An Average Day on an Average Political Blog," *Public Choice*, October 2007.

Notes to Chapter 5

1. *Wein v. State*, 383 NYS 2nd 225 (1976), p. 228.

2. Richard Briffault, "State Constitutions in the Federal System," in *The New York State Constitution: A Briefing Book*, ed. Gerald Benjamin (Albany: Rockefeller Institute, 1994), p. 11.

3. Ibid., p. 12. For comparisons with other states, particularly in recent years, see G. Alan Tarr, *State Constitutions for the Twenty-first Century: The Politics of State Constitutional Reform* (Albany: State University of New York Press, 2006).

4. Peter J. Galie, *Ordered Liberty: A Constitutional History of New York* (New York: Fordham University Press, 1996), p. 24.

5. Ibid., p. 36.

6. Ibid., p. 89.

7. Ibid., p. 112.

8. Vernon O'Rourke and Douglas Campbell, *Constitution-Making in a Democracy: Theory and Practice in New York State* (Baltimore: Johns Hopkins University Press, 1943).

9. Unless otherwise noted, the figures cited here are taken from the very useful tables compiled in the annual Council of State Governments, *The Book of the States* (Lexington, KY: Council of the States, 2008).

10. Thad L. Beyle, "Enhancing Executive Leadership in the States," *State and Local Government Review* 27 (1995): 18–25.

11. As calculated in Kevin B. Smith, Alan Greenblatt, and John Buntin, *Governing States and Localities* (Washington, DC: CQ Press, 2005), p. 231. For a full discussion of the measures used, see Thad Beyle, "Governors: The Middlemen and Women in Our Political System," in *Politics in the American States: A Comparative Analysis*, ed. Virginia Gray and Herbert Jacob (Washington, DC: CQ Press, 1996), p. 237.

12. *Pataki v. New York State Assembly* and *Silver v. Pataki*, 791 N.Y.S. 2nd 458, 4 N.Y. 3rd 75.

13. Council of State Governments, *Book of the States*, p. 68.

14. Joseph F. Zimmerman, *The Government and Politics of New York State* (New York: New York University Press, 1981), p. 188.

15. Alan Rosenthal, *Heavy Lifting: The Job of the American Legislature* (Washington, DC: CQ Press, 2004), p. 177.

16. Beyle, "Governors," p. 228.

17. Quoted in Gerald Benjamin and Robert C. Lawton, "The Governorship in an Era of Limits," in *Governing New York State*, 3rd ed., ed. Jeffrey M. Stonecash, John Kenneth White, and Peter W. Colby (Albany: State University of New York Press, 1994), p. 134.

18. George Weeks, "A Statehouse Hall of Fame," *State Government* (Fall 1982), as cited in Benjamin and Lawton, "Governorship," p. 134 (see note 17).

19. Louis Galambos, *The New American State: Bureaucracies and Policies Since World War II* (Baltimore: Johns Hopkins University Press, 1987), p. 2.

20. Management Resources Project, *Governing the Empire State* (Albany: Rockefeller Institute, 1988), p. 18. This otherwise dry guide to state government has an especially sensitive and still cogent analysis of the governor's office that we draw upon here.

21. Quoted in Management Resources Project, *Governing the Empire State*, p. 22.

22. Ibid., p. 27.

23. Keith M. Henderson, "Other Governments: The Public Authorities," in *Governing New York State*, 3rd ed. (see note 17), p. 220.

24. Benjamin and Lawton, "Governorship," p. 141.

25. Ibid.

26. James Bryce, *The American Commonwealth*, vol. 1 (New York: Macmillan, 1906), p. 539.

27. Nelson W. Polsby, "The Institutionalization of the U. S. House of Representatives," *American Political Science Review* 62 (March 1968): 144–168.

28. Ibid., p. 145.

29. Jeffrey M. Stonecash, "The Legislature: The Emergence of an Equal Branch," in *Governing New York State*, 3rd ed., p. 153.

30. Robert B. Ward, *New York State Government*, 2nd ed. (Albany: Rockefeller Institute, 2006), p. 129.

31. Stonecash, "Legislature," p. 155.

32. Gerald Benjamin and Robert T. Nakamura, *The Modern New York State Legislature: Redressing the Balance* (Albany: Rockefeller Institute, 1991), p. xxiv.

33. Stanley Fink, as quoted in Benjamin and Nakamura, *Modern New York State Legislature*, p. 117.

34. Stonecash, "Legislature," pp. 156, 158.

35. Quoted in Leonard Ruchelman, *Political Careers: Recruitment through the Legislature* (Rutherford, NJ: Fairleigh Dickinson University Press, 1970), p. 153.

36. Stonecash, "Legislature," p. 159.

37. Ibid., p. 158.

38. Zimmerman, *Government and Politics*, p. 132.

39. Kremer interview in Benjamin and Nakamura, *Modern New York State Legislature*, p. 157.

40. Malcolm E. Jewell and Marcia Lynn Whicker, *Legislative Leadership in the American States* (Ann Arbor: University of Michigan Press, 1994), Chapter 1.

41. Alan Rosenthal, "The Legislative Institution: In Transition and at Risk," in *The State of the States*, 2nd ed., ed. Carl Van Horn (Washington, DC: CQ Press, 1993), pp. 136–137.

42. Jewell and Whicker, *Legislative Leadership*, p. 8.

43. As quoted in Benjamin and Nakamura, *Modern New York State Legislature*, p. 70.

44. This quote is taken from a series of remarkably candid interviews that Senator Ralph Marino granted us in 1999 and 2000. Marino, it turns out, was right: despite increasingly close margins in the senate, the minority Democrats never successfully invoked the 60 percent rule.

45. Galie, *Ordered Liberty*, p. 156.

46. Nancy Burns, *The Formation of American Local Governments* (New York: Oxford University Press, 1994), p. 53.

47. Ibid., p. 6.

48. John Caher, "Court Marks 150 Years," Albany *Times Union*, September 8, 1997.

49. David B. Rottman, William E. Raftery, and Amy E. Smith, *Judicial Compensation in New York: A National Perspective* (Washington, DC: National Center for State Courts, 2007).

50. Chief Judge Charles D. Breitel as quoted in Special Commission on the Future of New York State Courts, *A Court System for the Future: The Promise of Court Restructuring in New York State* (New York: Special Commission on the Future of New York State Courts, 2006), p. 8.

51. Editorial, "Reforming the Courts," *New York Times*, January 14, 2007.

52. Brian J. Nickerson and Thomas W. Church, "New York's Courts," in *Governing New York State*, 5th ed., ed. Robert F. Pecorella and Jeffrey M. Stonecash (Albany: State University of New York Press, 2006), p. 199.

53. *People ex. rel. Arcara v. Cloud Books*, 68 NY 2nd 553 (1986), p. 558.

54. Peter J. Galie, *The New York State Constitution: A Reference Guide* (Westport, CT: Greenwood Press, 1990), p. 57.

55. Burton Agata, "Criminal Justice," in Benjamin, *New York State Constitution* (see note 2), p. 63.

56. Ibid., p. 64.

57. Gerald Benjamin and Melissa Cusa, "Amending the New York State Constitution Through the Legislature," in Benjamin, *New York State Constitution* (see note 2), pp. 63–64.

58. Edward V. Schneier and Bertram Gross, *Congress Today* (New York: St. Martin's, 1993), pp. 485–487.

59. Richard Briffault, "State Constitutions in the Federal System," in Benjamin, *New York State Constitution* (see note 2), p. 4.

Notes to Chapter 6

1. Interview with Stanley Fink in Gerald Benjamin and Robert T. Nakamura, *The Modern New York State Legislature: Redressing the Balance* (Albany: Rockefeller Institute, 1991), p. 117.

2. Karl Kurz, "Tennessee and New York Senates Have Most Stable Leadership," July 10, 2008, www.ncsl/the_thicket/leadership.

3. Tom Loftus, *The Art of Legislative Politics* (Washington, DC: CQ Press, 1994), p. 52.

4. Malcolm E. Jewell and Marcia Lynn Whicker, *Legislative Leadership in the American States* (Ann Arbor: University of Michigan Press, 1996), p. 63.

5. Ibid., p. 70.

6. Loftus, *Art of Legislative Politics*, p. 52.

7. Interview with Stanley Fink, p. 119.

8. Alan G. Hevesi, *Legislative Politics in New York State: A Comparative Analysis* (New York: Praeger, 1975), p. 60.

9. Alan Rosenthal, *Heavy Lifting: The Job of the American Legislature* (Washington, DC: CQ Press, 2004), p. 225.

10. Hevesi, *Legislative Politics*, p. 60.

11. Ralph Wright, *All Politics Is Personal* (Manchester, VT: Marshall Jones, 1996), pp. 24–25.

12. Shaun Bowler, David M. Farrell, and Richard S. Katz, "Party Cohesion, Party Discipline, and Parliaments," in *Party Discipline and Parliamentary Government*, ed. Shaun Bowler, David M. Farrell, and Richard S. Katz (Columbus: Ohio State University Press, 1999), p. 15.

13. Alan Rosenthal, *The Decline of Representative Democracy* (Washington, DC: CQ Press, 1998), p. 258.

14. These numbers are set in the bills that the legislature passes every year (see, for example, S. 6801B and A. 9801B in 2008). They have been essentially unchanged since 2005. The actual dollar amounts specified in the 2005 law can be tricky to locate, but are available through the assembly information office.

15. Editorial, *Newsday*, October 28, 2002.

16. Cited in Rosenthal, *Decline of Representative Democracy*, p. 275.

17. Alan Rosenthal, *Engines of Democracy: Politics and Policymaking in State Legislatures* (Washington, DC: CQ Press, 2009), p. 256.

18. Jeffrey M. Stonecash, "The Legislature: The Emergence of an Equal Branch," in *Governing New York State*, 3rd ed., ed. Jeffrey M. Stonecash, John Kenneth White, and Peter W. Colby (Albany: State University of New York Press, 1994), p. 150.

19. Michael Bragman, New York State Assembly *Record of Proceedings*, May 22, 2000, p. 31.

20. Jewell and Whicker, *Legislative Leadership*, p. 125.

21. Ibid., p. 129.

22. Ibid., p. 127.

23. Seymour Lachman, *Three Men in a Room: The Inside Story of Power and Betrayal in an American Statehouse* (New York: New Press, 2006), p. 107.

24. Jewell and Whicker, *Legislative Leadership*, pp. 130–135.

25. Rosenthal, *Decline of Representative Democracy*, p. 137.

26. Wayne L. Francis and James W. Riddlesperger, "U.S. State Legislative Committees: Structure, Procedural Efficiency, and Party Control," *Legislative Studies Quarterly* 7 (November 1982): 457.

27. Nancy Martorano, "Balancing Power: Committee System Autonomy and Legislative Organization," *Legislative Studies Quarterly* 31 (May 2006): 205–234. Figures for individual states provided in Martorano's 2001 survey may be found in Karl Kurz, "How Autonomous Are Our Legislative Committees," www.ncsl/the_thicket, accessed October 8, 2007. The New York assembly in these rankings was in the middle group, the senate among the lowest fifteen.

28. Rosenthal, *Decline of Representative Democracy*, p. 141.

29. For patterns in other states, a comprehensive survey of the literature can be found in Keith R. Hamm and Ronald D. Hedlund, "Committees in State Legislatures: Structure, Procedural Efficiency, and Party Control," in *Encyclopedia of the American Legislative System*, ed. Joel H. Silbey (New York: Scribner's, 1994), p. 693.

30. John J. Pitney Jr., "Leaders and Rulers in the New York State Senate," *Legislative Studies Quarterly* 7 (November 1982): 496.

31. Frank Mauro in Benjamin and Nakamura, *Modern New York State Legislature* (see note 1), p. 331.

32. Ibid., p. 229.

33. Richard E. Neustadt, *Presidential Power: The Politics of Leadership* (New York: Wiley, 1960), pp. 1, 58.

34. Thad Beyle, "Governors: The Middlemen and Women in Our Political System," in *Politics in the American States: A Comparative Analysis*, ed. Virginia Gray and Herbert Jacob (Washington, DC: CQ Press, 1996), p. 222.

35. Alan Schick, "The Budget Bureau That Was: Thoughts on the Rise, Decline and Future of a Presidential Agency," *Law and Contemporary Problems* 55 (Summer 1970): 22.

36. Martha Wagner Weinberg, *Managing the State* (Cambridge, MA: MIT Press, 1977), p. 210.

37. Daniel C. Kramer, *The Days of Wine and Roses Are Over: Governor Hugh Carey and New York State* (Lanham, MD: University Press of America, 1997), p. 323.

38. George J. Martin, *Squandered Opportunities: New York's Pataki Years* (South Bend, IN: St. Augustine's Press, 2006), p. 220.

39. Neustadt, *Presidential Power*, p. 58.

40. Norman M. Adler in Benjamin and Nakamura, *Modern New York State Legislature* (see note 1), p. 479.

41. Quoted in Hy Rosen and Peter Slocum, *From Rocky to Pataki: Character and Caricatures in New York Politics* (Syracuse, NY: Syracuse University Press, 1998), p. 168.

42. *Silver v. Pataki*, 824 N.E. 893 (2004).

43. John T. Buckley, "The Governor From Figurehead to Prime Minister: A Historical Study of the New York Constitution and the Shift of Basic Power to the Chief Executive," *Albany Law Review* 68 (Fall 2005): 904.

44. Rosenthal, *Decline of Representative Democracy*, p. 295.

45. Nelson W. Polsby, *Political Innovation in America: The Politics of Policy Initiation* (New Haven: Yale University Press, 1984), p. 3.

46. Nicholas Confessore, "Paterson Moves to Help Democrats in State Senate," *New York Times*, October 5, 2008.

47. Kevin Sack, "The Great Incumbency Machine," *New York Times Magazine*, September 27, 1992, p. 49.

48. "Foye's E.S.D.C. Targets Empire Zones," *New York Observer*, July 19, 2007.

49. James Fine, "Praxair Receives ESD Assist in Jamestown," *Business First of Buffalo*, October 28, 2008.

50. Herbert Jacob, "Courts: The Least Visible Branch," in *Politics in the American States: A Comparative Analysis*, 6th ed., ed. Virginia Gray and Herbert Jacob (Washington, DC: CQ Press, 1996), p. 253.

51. M.L. Henry Jr., *Characteristics of Elected versus Merit-Selected New York City Judges, 1977–92* (New York: Fund for Modern Courts, 1992), pp. 1–2.

52. Testimony of Marc H. Alcott, president of the New York State Bar Association, before the Senate Judiciary Committee, Albany, January 8, 2007, p. 1.

53. As cited in Lawrence M. Friedman, *A History of American Law*, 2nd ed. (New York: Simon & Schuster, 1985), p. 573.

54. Ibid., p. 576.

55. Ibid., p. 574.

56. *McKinney's* has been published annually since 1943 by West Publishing Company of Minneapolis, MN.

57. William Lasser, *The Limits of Judicial Power: The Supreme Court in American Politics* (Chapel Hill: University of North Carolina Press, 1988), p. 263.

58. The history of the Campaign for Fiscal Equity's twenty-year road to success in the court of appeals in 2003 together with four frustrating years of its failure to have the court decision enforced is found on its website at www.cfequity.org/ns.nys.htm.

59. *United States v. Richardson*, 418 U.S. (1974), 166, 192.

60. Quoted in John M. Caher, *King of the Mountain: The Rise, Fall, and Redemption of Chief Judge Sol Wachtler* (Amherst, NY: Prometheus Books, 1988), p. 164.

61. G. Alan Tarr, *Judicial Process and Judicial Policymaking* (St. Paul, MN: West Publishing, 1994), p. 316.

62. Caher, *King of the Mountain*, pp. 115, 117.

Notes to Chapter 7

1. Management Resources Project, *Governing the Empire State: An Insider's Guide* (Albany: Rockefeller Institute of Government, 1988), p. 118.

2. These figures are compiled each year and published in the annual summary volume of the bill-drafting commission's *Legislative Digest.*

3. James David Barber, *The Lawmakers: Recruitment and Adaptation to Legislative Life* (New Haven: Yale University Press, 1965).

4. These figures were compiled in 1986 by Professor Jeffrey Stonecash and published in the annual handbook of the Assembly Internship Committee.

5. Frank E. Horack Jr., "The Common Law of Legislation," *Iowa Law Review* 23 (1937): 42.

6. Figures on the sources of legislation and much of the argument that follows are taken from a random sample of a hundred bills studied by Schneier and his students in the

Assembly Internship Program in 1985–1986 and reported in a paper called "On the Origins of Legislative Issues," delivered at the 1988 annual meeting of the Southwestern Political Science Association in San Antonio, Texas.

7. James Anderson, *Public Policy Making* (New York: Holt, Rinehart, and Winston, 1982), p. 37.

8. George C. Edwards III, *At the Margins: Presidential Leadership of Congress* (New Haven: Yale University Press, 1989), p. 223.

9. On this point, see especially Nelson W. Polsby, *Political Innovation in America: The Politics of Policy Initiation* (New Haven: Yale University Press, 1984).

10. Harry Jones, "Some Reflections on a Draftsman's Time Sheet," reprinted in *Legislation: Cases and Materials*, ed. Frank C. Newman and Stanley S. Surrey (Englewood Cliffs, NJ: Prentice-Hall, 1965), p. 535.

11. Edward V. Schneier and Bertram Gross, *Legislative Strategy: Shaping Public Policy* (New York: St. Martin's Press, 1993), p. 18. The quotation is from Aaron Wildavsky, *The Politics of the Budgetary Process* (Boston: Little, Brown, 1974), p. 22.

12. Robert A. Caro, *The Power Broker: Robert Moses and the Fall of New York* (New York: Random House, 1974), p. 174.

13. Murtaugh, knowing that he had the votes to win in the higher education committee, once refused a request from the committee chair Ed Sullivan to hold a bill. The bill passed over Sullivan's objections, but although Sullivan never mentioned it again, the bill somehow died in the rules committee.

14. As quoted in John J. Jitney Jr., "Leaders and Rules in the New York State Senate," *Legislative Studies Quarterly* 7 (November 1982): 491, 494.

15. Lawrence Norden, David E. Pozen, and Bethany L. Foster, *Unfinished Business: New York State Legislative Reform, 2006 Update* (New York: Brennan Center for Justice at NYU School of Law, 2006), p. 18.

16. For a first-rate summary and analysis of the literature, see Steven S. Smith, *Party Influence in the Congress* (New York: Cambridge University Press, 2007).

17. Jeremy M. Creeland and Laura M. Moulton, *The New York State Legislative Process: An Evaluation and Blueprint for Reform* (New York: Brennan Center for Justice at NYU School of Law, 2004), p. 19.

18. Ibid., p. 34.

19. Alan Rosenthal, *Heavy Lifting: The Job of the American Legislature* (Washington, DC: CQ Press, 2004), p. 153.

20. *New York Times*, June 21, 2001.

21. Nebraska, because it has a unicameral legislature, does not have conference committees, nor does Delaware, which relies on joint committees instead. See Creeland and Moulton, *New York State Legislative Process* (see note 18), pp. 35–36.

22. Joseph F. Zimmerman, *The Government and Politics of New York State* (New York: New York University Press, 1981), p. 203.

23. Gerald Benjamin, "The Governorship," in *New York State Today*, ed. Peter Colby (Albany: State University of New York Press, 1981), p. 203.

24. Alan Rosenthal, *The Decline of Representative Democracy: Process, Participation, and Power in State Legislatures* (Washington, DC: CQ Press, 1998), p. 297.

25. See, for example, David Schoenbrod, *Power Without Responsibility: How Congress Abuses the People Through Delegation* (New Haven: Yale University Press, 1993).

26. James L. Perry, *Facing the Bureaucracy: Living and Dying in a Public Agency* (San Francisco: Jossey-Bass, 1993), p. 33.

27. For a short history of studies in this area, see chapter 2 of B. Dan Wood and Richard V. Waterman, *Bureaucratic Dynamics: The Role of Bureaucracy in a Democracy* (Boulder, CO: Westview Press, 1994).

28. Herbert London and Edward S. Rubenstein, *From the Empire State to the Vampire*

State: New York in a Downward Transition (Lanham, MD: University Press of America, 1994), p. 343.

29. Robert Pecorella, "Federal Mandates, State Policy Coalitions, and Waste Management in New York State," in *Governing New York State*, 3rd ed., ed. Jeffrey Stonecash, John Kenneth White, and Peter W. Colby (Albany: State University of New York Press, 1994), p. 343.

30. Zimmerman, *Government and Politics*, p. 251.

31. Herbert Kaufman, *Red Tape: Its Origins, Uses, and Abuses* (Washington, DC: Brookings Institute, 1977), pp. 58–59.

32. Theodore J. Lowi, *The End of Liberalism*, 2nd ed. (New York: W.W. Norton, 1979).

33. Cornelius M. Kerwin, *Rulemaking: How Government Agencies Write Law and Make Policy*, 3rd ed. (Washington, DC: CQ Press, 2003), pp. 3–4.

34. Ibid., p. 3. On state administrative practices, see Arthur Bonfield, *State Administrative Rulemaking* (Boston: Little, Brown, 1986).

35. Management Resources Project, *Governing the Empire State*, p. 166.

36. Ibid., p. 167.

37. Kerwin, *Rulemaking*, p. 161.

38. Cary Coglianese, "Citizen Participation in Rulemaking: Past, Present, and Future," *Duke Law Journal* 55 (2006): 3.

39. Kerwin, *Rulemaking*, pp. 183, 463.

40. Alice Sardell, "Health Policy in New York State: Health Care Needs and System Reform," in *Governing New York State*, 3rd ed. (see note 30), p. 308.

41. William Riordan, *Plunkitt of Tammany Hall* (New York: Dutton, 1963), p. 23.

42. Frank Anechiarco and James B. Jacobs, *The Pursuit of Absolute Integrity: How Corruption Control Makes Government Ineffective* (Chicago: University of Chicago Press, 1996), p. 200.

44. Ibid., p. 135.

44. Kermit Gordon, as quoted in Kaufman, *Red Tape*, p. 14.

45. Kaufman, *Red Tape*, p. 60.

46. The exception is Louisiana, whose roots are essentially in the Napoleonic Code.

47. Lawrence M. Friedman, *History of American Law*, 2nd ed. (New York: Simon & Schuster, 1985), p. 92.

48. Similar borrowing took place across the United States as resource-poor territorial legislatures sought to establish their legal systems prior to statehood. For a fascinating survey of these early legislatures, see Peverill Squire, "Historical Evolution of Legislatures in the United States," *Annual Review of Political Science* 9 (June 2006).

49. Abraham S. Blumberg, *Criminal Justice* (Chicago: Quadrangle Books, 1969), p. 110.

50. Harry P. Stumpf and John H. Culver, *The Politics of State Courts* (New York: Longman, 1992), pp. 22–23.

51. Ibid., pp. 77–78.

52. Herbert Jacob, *Law and Politics in the United States*, 2nd ed. (New York: Harper and Collins, 1965), p. 171.

53. Harry Kalven Jr. and Hans Zeisel, *The American Jury* (Boston: Little, Brown, 1966), p. 21.

54. Bureau of Justice Statistics, *Civil Justice Survey of State Courts, 2004* (Washington, DC: United States Department of Justice, 2005).

55. Jacob, *Law and Politics*, pp. 172–173.

56. Bureau of Justice Statistics, *Civil Justice Survey*; Nelson A. Rockefeller Institute of Government, *2006 New York State Statistical Yearbook* (Albany: Rockefeller Institute of Government, 2006), p. 332.

57. "Agency Presentations," *New York State Executive Budget, 2007–08* (Albany: Division of the Budget, 2008), p. 359.

58. Rockefeller Institute, *2006 Statistical Yearbook*, p. 323.

59. G. Allen Tarr, *Judicial Process and Judicial Policymaking* (St. Paul, MN: West Publishing, 1994), p. 253.

60. Richard Neely, *Why Courts Don't Work* (New York: McGraw-Hill, 1983), p. 10.

61. James A. Gardner, "The Failed Discourse on State Constitutionalism," *Michigan Law Review* 90 (February 1992): 270.

62. From an unpublished paper by Craig Emmert cited in Henry R. Glick, "Policy Making and State Supreme Courts," in *The American Courts: A Critical Assessment*, ed. John B. Gates and Charles A. Johnson (Washington, DC: CQ Press, 1991), pp. 87–88.

63. Dorothy J. Samuels, "Mistaken Identity: Bum Rap Against New York Court," *New York Times*, March 18, 1996.

64. Quoted in Zimmerman, *Government and Politics*, p. 277.

65. John M. Caher, *King of the Mountain: The Rise, Fall, and Redemption of Chief Judge Sol Wachtler* (Amherst, NY: Prometheus Books, 1988), p. 154.

66. Ibid., p. 157.

67. These figures are from the court's annual reports.

68. Vincent M. Bonventre, "Court of Appeals of New York State, the Election Process," Social Science Research Network, October 2007, www.ssrn.com/abstract=1142703.

Notes to Chapter 8

1. Aaron Wildavsky, *The Politics of the Budgetary Process*, 4th ed. (Boston: Little, Brown, 1984), p. 4.

2. Dall W. Forsythe, *Memos to the Governor: An Introduction to State Budgeting*, 2nd ed. (Washington, DC: Georgetown University Press, 2004), pp. 6–7.

3. A long-time budget technician quoted in Roy T. Meyers, *Strategic Budgeting* (Ann Arbor: University of Michigan Press, 1994), p. 19.

4. The idea that all bureaucrats seek to maximize their own budgets has been challenged on both theoretical and empirical grounds. One recent study of senior executives in Washington found, for example, that they were actually less likely than the general public to favor higher spending. See Julie Dolan, "The Budget-Minimizing Bureaucrat? Empirical Evidence from the Senior Executive Service," *Public Administration Review* 62 (2002): 42–61. At the same time, it is rare for any agency to request significant cuts in its own budget without prior prodding from the budget office.

5. Wildavsky, *Politics of the Budgetary Process*, p. 10.

6. Robert D Behn, as quoted in Meyers, *Strategic Budgeting*, p. 11.

7. Wildavsky, *Politics of the Budgetary Process*, p. 17.

8. Ibid., p. 15.

9. Irene S. Rubin, *The Politics of Public Budgeting: Getting and Spending, Borrowing and Balancing*, 5th ed. (Washington, DC: CQ Press, 2006), p. 80.

10. Wildavsky, *Politics of the Budgetary Process*, p. 17.

11. Management Resources Project, *Governing the Empire State: An Insider's Guide* (Albany: Rockefeller Institute of Government, 1988), p. 39.

12. The DOB has a user-friendly website that provides quarterly updates of its economic forecasts and useful summaries of overall revenue and spending. These figures are taken from www.budget.state.ny.us.

13. *1999–2000 New York State Executive Budget* (Albany: Division of the Budget, 1999), Appendix I, p. 13.

14. Forsythe, *Memos to the Governor*, pp. 28–29.

15. Alan Rosenthal, *The Decline of Representative Democracy: Process, Participation, and Power in State Legislatures* (Washington, DC: CQ Press, 1998), p. 309.

16. Management Resources Project, *Governing the Empire State*, p. 59.

17. Forsythe, *Memos to the Governor*, p. 49.

18. Interview with Kenneth Shapiro in Gerald Benjamin and Robert T. Nakamura, *The Modern New York State Legislature: Redressing the Balance* (Albany: Rockefeller Institute, 1991), p. 221.

19. Alan Rosenthal, *Heavy Lifting: The Job of the American Legislature* (Washington, DC: CQ Press, 2004), p. 206.

20. Forsythe, *Memos to the Governor*, p. 72.

21. Alan Rosenthal, *Engines of Democracy: Politics and Policymaking in State Legislatures* (Washington, DC: CQ Press, 2009), p. 269.

22. *Silver v. Pataki* and *Pataki v. New York State Assembly*, 824 N.E. 893, 898 (2004).

23. Assembly minority leader John Faso as quoted in the Albany *Times Union*, April 20, 1998.

24. New York State Assembly, *Record of Proceedings*, May 22, 2000, p. 29.

25. Interview with Frank Mauro in Benjamin and Nakamura, *Modern New York State Legislature*, p. 340.

26. *New York Times*, February 8, 1999.

27. As quoted in Rosenthal, *Decline of Representative Democracy*, p. 307.

28. Management Resources Project, *Governing the Empire State*, p. 51.

29. *County of Oneida v. Berle*, 398 NY Supp. 2nd (1980), 600.

30. Mauro in Benjamin and Nakamura, *Modern New York State Legislature*, p. 332.

31. Unless otherwise noted, most of the numbers used here come from those reported for 2006–2007 in Governor Spitzer's *2007–2008 Executive Budget*.

32. Office of the Comptroller, *Property Taxes in New York State* (Albany: Office of the Comptroller, 2006), p. 2.

33. Ibid., p. 4.

34. The cycles of financial collapse and their political repercussions in New York City are richly detailed in Robert F. Pecorella, *Community Power in a Post-Reform City: Politics in New York City* (Armonk, NY: M.E. Sharpe, 1994), Chapter 2.

35. Dick Netzer, "The Economy and the Governing of the City," in *Urban Politics New York Style* ed., Jewell Bellush and Dick Netzer (Armonk, NY: M.E. Sharpe, 1990), p. 46.

36. Raymond J. Keating, *New York by the Numbers* (Lanham, MD: Madison Books, 1997), p. 17.

37. Office of the Comptroller, *Comprehensive Annual Financial Report for Fiscal Year Ended March 31, 2008* (Albany: Office of the Comptroller, 2008).

38. Alberta M. Sbragia, *Debt Wish: Entrepreneurial Cities, U.S. Federalism, and Economic Development* (Pittsburgh: University of Pittsburgh Press, 1996), pp. 214–215.

39. Penelope Lemov, "Taxes: The Struggle for Balance," *Governing* (August 1994): 32.

40. Forsythe, *Memos to the Governor*, p. 2.

41. Edward Regan, as quoted in an interview in Herbert London and Edwin S. Rubenstein, *From the Empire State to the Vampire State: New York in a Downward Transition* (Lanham, MD: University Press of America, 1994), p. 207.

42 Kaiser Family Foundation, www.statehealthfacts.org/profileind.jsp?ind=178&cat=4&rgn=34.

43. New York City Department of Health and Mental Hygiene, *New York City Medicaid Managed Care Update, Winter 2007* (New York: Department of Health and Mental Hygiene, 2007), p. 1.

44. The Commonweatlh Fund, www.commonwealthfund.org/usr_doc/ sandman_nyc-factsheet_369.

45. New York State Commission on Public Integrity, *2007 Annual Report* (Albany: Commission on Public Integrity, 2008), Appendix C.

46. Jeffrey Kraus, "Health Care in the Empire State" in *Governing New York State*, 5th ed., ed. Robert F. Pecorella and Jeffrey M. Stonecash (Albany: State University of New York Press, 2006), p. 346.

47. State Education Department, *Analysis of School Finances in New York State School Districts 2004–05* (Albany: State Education Department, 2007), p. 17. The per pupil costs cited here are for basic instructional costs and not for capital costs, which can vary markedly from one year to another, or the costs of transportation. Generally speaking, capital spending gaps between poor and wealthy districts are even larger than differences in operating costs.

48. Ibid.

49. Robert F. Pecorella, "The Politics of State Education Aid," in *Governing New York State*, 5th ed. (see note 46), p. 281.

50. *CFE v. State of New York*, 100 NY 2nd 893 (2003).

51. Campaign for Fiscal Equity, *CFE's Analysis of Governor Pataki's 2006–2007 Executive Education Budget: Governor's Continuing Contempt of Court Trumps Needs of State* (New York: Campaign for Fiscal Equity, 2006), p. 1, www.cfequity.com.

52. Ibid., p. 15.

53. Frank R. Baumgartner and Bryan D. Jones, *Agendas and Instability in American Politics* (Chicago: University of Chicago Press, 1993), p. 10.

54. Robert H. Connery and Gerald Benjamin, *Rockefeller of New York: Executive Power in the Statehouse* (Ithaca, NY: Cornell University Press, 1979), p. 298.

55. Helen F. Ladd, "Big City Finances," in *Big City Politics, Governance and Fiscal Constraints*, ed. George E. Patterson (Washington, DC: Urban Institute Press, 1994), p. 249.

56. Division of Local Government and School Accountability, *Layers of Debt: Trends and Implications for New York's Local Governments* (Albany: Office of the Comptroller, 2007).

57. Ibid.

58. The presidents of New York City's five boroughs, which are, in a sense, counties by another name, do have small budgets of their own, but they constitute an essentially trivial proportion of the overall city budget. Boroughs do not have anything near the scope of authority enjoyed by county governments in the rest of the state, which, in rural areas in particular, often provide basic police, sanitation, and health services.

59. Bruce F. Berg, *New York City Politics: Governing Gotham* (New Brunswick, NJ: Rutgers University Press, 2007), p. 39.

60. Diana Dillaway, *Power Failure: Politics, Patronage, and the Economic Future of Buffalo, New York* (Amherst, NY: Prometheus Books, 2006), p. 208.

61. New York City Independent Budget Office, *City Revenue and Spending Since 1980* (New York: Independent Budget Office, 2008), Table 1.

62. State Education Department, *Analysis of School Finances*, p. 313.

Notes to Chapter 9

1. Easy-to-access figures comparing the taxes and tax rates of the fifty states can be found on the website of the Tax Foundation, www.taxfoundation.org.

2. Blair Horner, *Reform New York: 10 Steps on the Path to Change Albany* (Albany: New York Public Interest Research Group, 2004), pp. 15–16.

3. Paul C. Light, *Thickening Government: Federal Hierarchy and the Diffusion of Accountability* (Washington, DC: Brookings Institute, 1995), p. 1.

4. Mary Ann Ryan-Germani, ed., *The New York Red Book, 2005–2006*, 98th ed. (Albany: New York Legal Publishing, 2005). The payroll listings of the department (which can be

found at www.seethoughny.net/payrolls) show quite a few more "special assistants" and so on in the higher (over $150,000) pay billets.

5. Light, *Thickening Government*, p. 7.

6. The classic description of how President Roosevelt pitted one agency against another is found in Richard E. Neustadt, *Presidential Power* (New York: Wiley, 1976), Chapter 2.

7. Light, *Thickening Government*, p. 63.

8. New York State Commission on Local Government Efficiency and Competitiveness, *21st Century Local Government* (Albany: Commission on Local Government Efficiency and Effectiveness, 2007), p. 10.

9. Ibid., p. 45.

10. Ibid., p. 21.

11. Ibid., p. 11.

12. Ibid., p. 17.

13. New York Unified Court System, *Action Plan for the Justice Courts* (Albany: New York Unified Court System, 2006).

14. Commission on Local Government Efficiency, *21st Century Local Government*, p. 26.

15. In 2008 the senior author of this book, Edward Schneier, rented his Albany apartment to an intern working with a project funded by the Research Foundation of the State University. The lease was signed in December; I got my first check in May. The incident reminded me of my days as a department chair at City College when the discount stationery stores refused to take orders from the College because we were such notorious late payers and we had to pay nearly twice the going cost for such basics as paper.

16. John F. Bibby and Thomas M. Holbrook, "Parties and Elections," in *Politics in the American States*, 6th ed., ed. Virginia Gray and Herbert Jacob (Washington, DC: CQ Press, 1996), p. 110.

17. Commission on Local Government, *21st Century Local Government*, p. 42.

18. All these reforms are supported by a coalition of reform groups, as summarized in Horner, *Reform New York*.

19. George J. Marlin, *Squandered Opportunities: New York's Pataki Years* (South Bend, IN: St. Augustine's Press, 2006), p. 183.

20. Austin Ranney, *The Doctrine of Responsible Party Government* (Urbana: University of Illinois Press, 1962), p. 12.

21. Jarol B. Mannheim, *All of the People, All of the Time* (Armonk, NY: M.E. Sharpe, 1992), pp. 4–5.

22. Giovanni Sartori, *Comparative Constitutional Engineering: An Inquiry into Structures, Incentives and Outcomes*, 2nd ed. (New York: New York University Press, 1997), p. 134.

Index

About the Authors

Edward V. Schneier is Professor Emeritus of political science at the City College of New York and the graduate center of the City University of New York (CUNY). Before his retirement in 2003 he also taught at Colgate, Columbia, Johns Hopkins, and Princeton universities; was a research fellow at the Brookings Institution; and worked as legislative assistant to U.S. Senator Birch Bayh. Dr. Schneier served as a Fulbright fellow in Iceland in 1989 and Indonesia in 2001, and has twice been awarded research grants from the National Endowment for the Humanities. From 1985 to 1987 he served as professor-in-residence for the Internship Committee of the New York State Assembly, and he has worked as a registered lobbyist in Albany. He has long been active in New York politics, running for Congress in 1976, serving as president of the Downtown Independent Democrats, and as a long-time member of the Columbia County Democratic Committee. He is president of the board of trustees of the Roeliff Jansen Community Library and a trustee of Columbia-Greene Community College. His publications include *Party and Constituency* (1969); *Vote Power* (1974); *Legislative Strategy* (1993); and *Crafting Constitutional Democracy* (2006).

John Brian Murtaugh recently retired from the office of court administration in the united court system of New York state, but continues to teach courses in New York politics and government as an adjunct professor of political science in the City University. He has had extensive experience in New York politics, having been the legislative aide to a New York City Council member and Democratic District Leader from the 72nd Assembly District of Manhattan in the 1970s, and in the New York State Assembly from 1981 through 1996. During his eight terms in the legislature, Murtaugh chaired the Assembly Standing Committee on Alcohol and Substance Abuse for eight years from 1988 through 1996, and sponsored over 100 laws in housing, health care, mental health, and alcoholism and substance abuse. He also served as chair of the Democratic Study Group and chair of the Speaker's Office on State-Federal Relations.

Antoinette Pole is Assistant Professor of Political Science and Law at Montclair State University, Montclair, New Jersey. After receiving her PhD in Political Science from CUNY Graduate School and University Center, she was Post-Doctoral Research Fellow at the Taubman Center for Public Policy at Brown University during 2005–2007. In 1991 she worked in the New York State Assembly for Assemblyman Frederick D. Schimdt (38th AD). Her areas of expertise include state politics, and information technology and politics. She has writen a book on political blogs titled *Blogging the Political: Politics and Participation in a Networked Society*. She has published in a variety of journals, including *Public Choice, International Journal of Technology, Knowledge and Society, State and Local Government Review, and Spectrum: the Journal of State Government*. She has been interviewed for her cutting-edge work on political blogging by the *Chicago Tribune, Philadelphia Tribune, Boston Globe, Rhode Island Monthly Magazine, Unity News, WBRU* (radio), *Silvio Canto Talk* (Web-based radio), and *Carpe Diem* (a local television show airing throughout New Jersey).